no ¶   no paragraph

p   error in punctuation (pp. 369–380)

paral   faulty parallelism (pp. 170–174, 360–361)

pas   unnecessary or ineffective passive construction (pp. 188–190)

prom   paragraph is faulty—try the promise pattern (pp. 91–99)

pron   error with pronoun (pp. 342–343)

pv   check point of view (pp. 133–134)

ref   vague pronoun reference (p. 342)

rep   unnecessary repetition

ro   run-on sentence (p. 368)

sb   check the sentence base rule (pp. 168–169)

sp   spelling error

split   split construction (pp. 356–357)

ss   check sentence structure (pp. 184–191)

sub   faulty subordination (pp. 175–176, 361–363)

t   error in verb tense (pp. 343–345)

th   clarify the thesis (pp. 24–26)

tr   effective transition needed (pp. 110–111)

un   unity—check for unnecessary shifts in wording, tone, or attitude

vb   error with verb (pp. 343–346)

wdy   wordy

wr   write out—do not abbreviate or use numbers (pp. 381, 383–384)

ws   check your writer's stance (pp. 3–12)

X   obvious error

∧   insertion (pp. 354–355)

?   I don't understand

Additional Symbols

Strategies of Rhetoric with Handbook

Third Edition

Strategies of Rhetoric with Handbook

Third Edition

A. M. Tibbetts
Charlene Tibbetts
University of Illinois at Urbana-Champaign

Scott, Foresman and Company
Glenview, Illinois
Dallas, Tex.
Oakland, N.J.
Palo Alto, Calif.
Tucker, Ga.
London, England

Library of Congress Cataloging in Publication Data

Tibbetts, A. M.
    Strategies of rhetoric with handbook.

    Includes index.
    1. English language—Rhetoric. 2. English language—Grammar—1950—
I. Tibbetts, Charlene, joint author.   II. Title.
PE1408.T49 1979   808'.042   78-13769
ISBN 0-673-15178-6

Acknowledgments

Judd Alexander. Excerpt from "Truth and Consequences," from *Vital Speeches of the Day* (July 1972). Copyright © 1972 by The City News Publishing Company. Reprinted by permission of The City News Publishing Company.

Nelson Algren. Excerpt from "Down with Cops," from *The Saturday Evening Post* (October 1965). Reprinted by permission of Candida Donadio & Associates, Inc. Copyright © 1965 by Nelson Algren.

Excerpt from "Ants." *Réalités* magazine (September 1952); reprinted by permission.

"Asking for It." Reprinted courtesy of the *Chicago Tribune*.

Isaac Babel. "My First Goose" reprinted by permission of S. G. Phillips, Inc. from *The Collected Stories of Isaac Babel*. Copyright © 1955 by S. G. Phillips, Inc.

Bruno Bettelheim. Excerpt from "The Roots of Radicalism," originally appeared in *Playboy* magazine; copyright © 1971 by Bruno Bettelheim. Reprinted by permission of the author.

Charles Blair. Excerpt from "Those Slam-Bang Smokies Streams," from *Wilderness Camping* (1976). Copyright © 1976 by Wilderness Camping. Reprinted by permission of Wilderness Camping.

Daniel J. Boorstin. Excerpt from "Too Much, Too Soon," from *TV Guide* (December 1972). Copyright © 1972 by Daniel J. Boorstin. Reprinted by permission of the author.

Urie Bronfenbrenner. Excerpts from "The Disturbing Changes in the American Family," from *Search*, Vol. 2 (Fall 1976). Copyright © 1976 by *Search* magazine. Reprinted by permission of *Search* magazine.

Ajay Budrys. Excerpt from "The Self-Reliant Bicycle Camper," from *Better Camping and Hiking* (May 1974). Copyright © 1974 by Ajay Budrys. Reprinted by permission of the author.

(Acknowledgments continued on p. 417)

Preface

Sometimes we think that this book had a will of its own. The idea for it began as a package of mimeographed handouts we put together to supplement the many rhetoric texts and handbooks we have used through the years. As we taught the handouts, discussed them with other instructors and with students, we added more materials. The First Edition of *Strategies of Rhetoric* came from those discussions and materials. The Revised Edition added many ideas offered by instructors of composition across the country. Now the Third Edition—both this text with a full Handbook and its alternate volume with a brief Handbook—is even more indebted to their ideas and suggestions. The title, *Strategies of Rhetoric with Handbook*, is significant: with the addition of a full Handbook, the text continues the growth and the responsiveness to the needs of users that marked its beginnings.

The changes we have made in the Third Edition reflect the problems and interests of those users, students and instructors alike. First, we have added more explanatory material and details. Where before there was one example of a compositional device, now there are often two or more. In the first chapter, we have sharpened the idea of the *writer's stance*, that all-important starting point for any writer. We have added new techniques (and examples) to the discussion of thesis development in Chapter 2, and to the material on the strategies of organization in Chapter 4.

Similarly, Chapter 5, which discusses paragraph organization, has been refined. Here we have more fully explained the *promise pattern*, which forms the controlling structure of so many effective paragraphs written today. We have completely rewritten the two chapters on the sentence. Chapter 8 has a great deal of new material and many new examples that clearly explain the *sentence base rule*, a device that has proved highly effective in helping students write better sentences. Chapter 9 goes one step further by showing students how they can analyze their sentences for errors and how they can correct them.

At the request of many users, we have expanded considerably Chapter 12, "The Research Paper," to include more material on library work and reference sources, advice on quoting and paraphrasing, and more examples of footnote and bibliography forms. In addition, we have provided a new sample research paper—on the changing role of the American family. In Chapter 13, "Writing for the Business World," we have included a section on the *negative message*, a type of communication that is widely used in business and government. This unusually thorough chapter will be of interest to the student who finds that the flood of letters and memos in the world decreaseth not.

Most important, we have added, for the first time, a full Handbook that answers a multitude of student questions on grammar, sentence structure, punctuation, and mechanics. In order to make the Handbook as useful as possible, we have included many exercises, an alphabetized glossary of grammatical terms, and a key to the Handbook inside the back cover. *Strategies of Rhetoric with Handbook* provides an alternate choice to the briefer edition for instructors who wish more in-depth coverage of writing problems.

Both versions of the Third Edition, like their predecessors, owe much to many people—so many that we are sorry we cannot list all their names. Certain people, however, have given us particularly helpful advice and ideas: Aspasia Anastos, Mt. Wachusett Community College; Kirby L. Duncan, Stephen F. Austin State University; Arra Garab, Northern Illinois University; Mary Hoag, University of Illinois; William Landau, Los Angeles Pierce College; James A. Parrish, University of South Florida; Tori Haring Smith, University of Illinois.

For assistance in finding and using student exercises and themes, we are grateful to Peter Clarke, Karen Haselden, Kevin Eddleman, Jeanette Goines, Alice and John Tibbetts, and Kathy Weinstein.

Once again, we pay tribute to our editor, Stan Stoga, whose skill and patience have greatly enriched the book.

And, finally, we thank the thousands of students who have taught us over the years; much of their work—from single sentences to full themes—has found its way again into these pages.

A. M. Tibbetts
Charlene Tibbetts

Urbana, Illinois

Overview

Solving Early Problems

1 The Writer's Stance

2 Forming a Thesis

3 How to Make a Helpful Outline

4 Developing Themes: Seven Strategies

Writing Better Themes

5 Organizing Clear Paragraphs and Themes

6 Improving Theme Content

7 Succeeding with Words

8 Shaping Better Sentences (I): Effective Structure

9 Shaping Better Sentences (II): Revising and Editing

Handling Special Assignments

10 Writing a Persuasive Argument

11 The Research Paper

12 The Literary Paper

13 Writing for the Business World

Handbook

GA Grammatical Analysis

G Forms of Grammar

S Sentence Structure

P Punctuation

M Mechanics

DY Using the Dictionary

PP Polishing and Proofreading

GL Glossary

Contents

I Solving Early Problems

1 The Writer's Stance 3

Writer's Stance—A Definition 4
Applying the Principles of Stance 5
You and the Writer's Stance 6
  The Role 6
  The Thesis 7
  The Reader 8
  Stance: Limitations and Possibilities 9
  Example of a Completed Stance 10
Creating "Distance" 10
Stance and the "Strategies" of Rhetoric 12
Practice 13

2 Forming a Thesis 18

The Assignment and the Thesis 20
  A Thesis Notebook 21
  The Thesis As Answer to a Question 23
Improving Your Thesis 24
Practices 18, 26

3 How to Make a Helpful Outline 28

Types of Outlines 28
The Form of Outlines 30
Four Typical Questions About Outlines 31
How a Thesis Suggests an Outline 34
How to Check an Outline 34
Some Final Comments on Outlining 35
Practice 36

4 Developing Themes: Seven Strategies 38

Strategy 1 Personal Experience 40
Strategy 2 Definition 45
    Techniques of Defining 47
    Avoid Errors in Defining 49
    Some Final Suggestions for Defining 50
Strategy 3 Cause and Effect 53
    Recognizing the Signs of Causation 54
    Suggestions for Writing Causation Themes 56
Strategy 4 Process 61
    What Is Process? 61
    Suggestions for Writing Process Themes 63
Strategy 5 Analogy 67
    Literal and Figurative Analogies 67
    Suggestions for Writing Analogies 68
Strategy 6 Classification 73
    The "Ruling Principle" in Classification 74
    Suggestions for Writing a Classification Paper 77
Strategy 7 Comparison-Contrast 80
    Planning the Comparison-Contrast Theme 80
    Organizing Comparison-Contrast Themes 82
Practices 42, 45, 51, 55, 59, 62, 64, 70, 76, 78, 81, 86

II Writing Better Themes

5 Organizing Clear Paragraphs and Themes 91

The Promise Pattern 91
Writing Successful Paragraphs 96
Non-promise Paragraphs 101
    Suspense Paragraphs 101
    Transitional Paragraphs 102
How to Arrange Your Ideas 103
    Start with a Simple or Familiar Idea 104
    Use a Graded Order of Ideas 105
Introductions and Conclusions 107
Transitions 110
Organizing by "Creative Repetition" 111
Practices 94, 100, 103, 107, 113

6 Improving Theme Content 116

Be Factual 117
    General and Particular Facts 119
    Loose Generalizations 123
    How to Qualify a Generalization 124

Make Your Writing Informative and Lively 126

Use Description and Narrative 131
    Description 131
    Narrative 135
    Dialogue in Description and Narrative 136

Practices 116, 121, 125, 129, 137

7 Succeeding with Words 140

Accurate Words 140

Suitable Words 142

Effective Words 143
    Be Specific 143
    Watch Your Connotations 146
    Use Figures of Speech Carefully 149
    Use Standard English 153
    Be Idiomatic 155

Ineffective Words 157
    Types of Ineffective Wording 157
    Avoid Jargon and Shoptalk 159

Practices 142, 145, 148, 151, 153, 156, 159, 160

**8 Shaping Better Sentences (I):
    Effective Structure 163**

The Typical Sentence 163

Sentence Bases 164

Free Units in the Sentence 165

Sentence Signals 167

The Sentence Base Rule 168

Parallelism 170
    Using Parallelism 171
    Avoid Faulty Parallelism 173

Subordination 175

Variations on the Typical Sentence 177
    Try Different Beginnings 178
    Employ Inversion 178
    Try a Periodic Sentence 179
    Use Qualifying and Balancing Devices 179
    Let Meaning Determine Your Structure 180

Practices 169, 172, 174, 176, 181

9   Shaping Better Sentences (II):
    Revising and Editing 184
    Suggestions for Revising and Editing 184
    A Final Note on Editing 191
    Practice 191

III   Handling Special Assignments

10   Writing a Persuasive Argument 195
    Use a Human Approach 198
    Ethical Proof 198
    The "You-Attitude" 200
    Give Solid Evidence 202
    Factual Evidence 202
    Authoritative Evidence 203
    Use Good Logic 206
    Induction and Deduction: A Definition 207
    Using Induction and Deduction 208
    Avoid Fallacies 211
    Recognizing and Correcting Fallacies 211
    Use a Clear Argumentative Organization 218
    Theses of Fact and of Action 218
    Organization of Fact Arguments 219
    Organization of Action Arguments 221
    Organization of Refutation Arguments 223
    Practices 196, 201, 202, 205, 210, 216, 225

11   The Research Paper 229
    Step 1: Choose Your Subject 229
    Reference Books 230
    The Card Catalog 232
    Periodical Indexes 233
    Step 2: Make Your Working Bibliography 236
    Step 3: Read, Take Notes, Evaluate the Evidence, Create a
    Stance, and Look for a Thesis 237
    The Form of Notes 237
    Taking Notes 238
    Accurate Paraphrasing 238
    Proper Techniques for Quoting 240
    Plagiarism 241
    Thesis and Stance 242

Step 4: Make an Outline 243
Step 5: Write the Paper 243
Footnote and Bibliography Forms 244
Footnote Forms 244
Footnotes As They Might Appear in a Paper 247
The Bibliography 248
Checklist for the First Draft 251
Sample Research Paper 252
A List of Reference Works 268
General Reference Works 268
Special Reference Works 269
Practices 233, 235, 241, 250, 266

12 The Literary Paper 274
What Is a Literary Paper? 274
Reading and Understanding the Literary Work 278
Brief Glossary of Literary Terms 278
The Narrative Work 280
The Non-narrative Work 282
Questions to Ask About a Work 284
Writing the Literary Paper 286
The Assignment 287
Knowing the Work 288
The Writer's Stance 289
What to Avoid in Writing the Literary Paper 289
Practices 274, 290

13 Writing for the Business World 301
Business Writing: Five Emphases 301
Using Illustrations 304
The Letter 310
Form of the Letter 310
Psychology of the Letter 310
Two Sample Letters 312
The Job Application Letter 316
The Data Sheet 316
The Application Letter 318
The Memo 321
Form of the Memo 322
Two Sample Memos 322
Negative Messages 325
Reports 328
Practices 308, 315, 320, 323, 326

Handbook

GA   Grammatical Analysis   331

GA 1   Learn the Parts of Speech   331
GA 2   Learn to Identify Clauses   334
GA 3   Learn to Identify Phrases   338
Practices   334, 336, 337, 339

G   Forms of Grammar   341

G 1   Possessive with Gerund   341
G 2   Vague or Ambiguous Pronoun Reference   342
G 3   Wrong Form of Pronoun   342
G 4   Appropriate Verb Tense   343
G 5   Faulty Principal Part of the Verb   345
G 6   Proper Use of the Subjunctive   345
G 7   Piling Up Verbs   346
G 8   Confusion of Adjectives and Adverbs   346
G 9   Degrees of Comparison for Adjectives and
        Adverbs   347
G 10   Misuse of Noun As Adjective   348
G 11   Faulty Verb Agreement   349
G 12   Faulty Pronoun Agreement   351
G 13   The Generic Pronoun   352
Practices   341, 343, 344, 345, 346, 348, 350, 352

S   Sentence Structure   353

S 1   Unnecessary Shifts   353
S 2   Omissions and Incomplete Constructions   354
S 3   Faulty Comparison   355
S 4   Split or "Separated" Constructions   356
S 5   Misplaced Modifiers   358
S 6   Squinting Modifiers   358
S 7   Dangling Modifiers   359
S 8   Faulty Parallelism   360
S 9   Proper Subordination   361
S 10   Faulty Subordination   362
S 11   Faulty Coordination   363
S 12   Faulty Complements   364

S 13   Sentence Fragments 366

S 14   Comma Splices 367

S 15   Fused Sentences 367

S 16   Run-on Sentences 368

Practices 354, 355, 356, 357, 358, 359, 360, 361, 362, 363, 364, 365, 366, 368

P Punctuation 369

P 1   Use a Period When . . . 369

P 2   Use a Question Mark When . . . 369

P 3   Use an Exclamation Mark When . . . 370

P 4   Use a Comma When . . . 370

P 5   Use a Semicolon When . . . 371

P 6   Use a Colon When . . . 372

P 7   Use Parentheses When . . . 373

P 8   Use a Dash When . . . 373

P 9   Use an Apostrophe When . . . 374

P 10   Use a Hyphen When . . . 374

P 11   Use Quotation Marks When . . . 375

P 12   Use Italics When . . . 376

Rhetoric of Punctuation

Practices 376, 380

M Mechanics 381

M 1   Abbreviations 381

M 2   Capitalization 381

M 3   Manuscript Form 382

M 4   Numbers 383

M 5   Syllabication 384

DY Using the Dictionary 385

Practice 387

PP Polishing and Proofreading 389

GL Glossary 391

Index 419

Solving Early Problems

1 The Writer's Stance

First, a small confession. Our ideas about the art and craft of writing are a little different from those of some textbook authors. We haven't always been teachers, and from time to time have had to make a living as professional writers and editors of nonfiction. The modern professional may work for a large oil company, "translating" the jargon of scientists; for a publishing concern, editing hundreds of pages a month; for himself as a free-lance author, writing articles and books for money. Whatever he does, he soon learns—as we did—that there are certain iron laws in the field of written communication.

Let's mention three important ones. First, the writer must be read. It will do him no good to produce wonderful prose (wonderful to him) if nobody wants to read it. Second, he must always be aware of those readers: real people out there somewhere, who are more or less like him. They can be tired, hungry, eager, illogical, intelligent, foolish, happy, indulgent, loving—just as he is from time to time. Finally, although readers read for all kinds of reasons—curiosity, duty, a need for diversion and so on—they require that the writer make a point. If the main idea or point of a communication is vague, ambiguous, or (worst of all) missing, the professional is in trouble. His family may not eat very well that month.

The writing situation is fundamentally no different with you, the student nonprofessional. If you bend or break one of these iron laws, you will discover certain consequences: in college, low grades on themes and papers; and in the outside world, where you will find yourself more quickly than you think, employers who complain that your letters, reports, and memos are not doing the job.

Digression: college students still occasionally remark to us that they don't need to improve their writing—their high-school training, they tell us, is sufficient. Try telling this to a college sophomore after he asked a professor to discuss an assigned paper topic and the professor said: "I'm not doing your thinking and writing for you—you've had freshman English." Or tell it to the graduating senior who sat uncomfortably in the office of a vice-president of an accounting firm while that gentleman said over the phone to an English instructor: "Yes, I know he got a B in composition—what I need to know is, can he *write?* We can hire any number of straight-A accountants; but we don't hire anybody unless he can write reports for our clients." Or tell it to the graduate in psychology who landed a good job with a large grocery chain and found herself writing up to thirty-five letters a day to customers. The clear fact is that America runs on writing as never before. The worlds of business, government, and education would stop turning without effective written communication.

Our small confession, then, leads to a couple of premises about writing we want to share with you. One is that in this book we deal mainly with the practical side of writing, tending to ignore theory unless it will work for you during the course and — more important — after you complete it. The other is that we will emphasize in most chapters the triple problem that all writers of nonfiction, regardless of age and training, must face: how to present themselves in their writing, how to appeal to their reader, and how to make their point clear.

Writer's Stance — A Definition

Writer's stance involves three major elements in a piece of writing:

1. Your *role* as a writer.

2. Your *thesis* — your point in writing. The thesis is a paper's main idea, usually stated in one complete sentence. It is discussed more fully in Chapter 2.

3. Your prospective *reader*.

To understand how you find a suitable stance for a theme, consider the case of a real student writer with a real — and interesting — idea for a paper: that cab driving is an unglamorous job. Here is one of the student's paragraphs in his first draft:

> Traffic can destroy patience faster than threading heavy thread through a needle. City driving sneaks up on your nerves. It doesn't blast you; it just gnaws at your stomach. Cars are death traps. It takes so little to be behind a wheel — almost anyone can get a license. And there's not much money in it. Driving all day I saw them all, wild drivers, incompetent drivers, angry drivers. I made mistakes too and put lives in jeopardy; I came to respect the power of the automobile.

When he talked to his instructor, the student said that he did not feel comfortable with what he had written. Something, he wasn't sure what, had gone wrong; he was stuck and could not continue with any confidence.

The problem was that he had not yet found an appropriate stance for the theme. What was he trying to say about cab driving? His paragraph made three or four points without developing any one of them adequately. Who would care to read these rambling remarks? To improve his work, he needed to take every element of his stance into consideration — in short, as Wayne Booth puts it — to define "his audience, his argument, and his own proper tone of voice."

Applying the Principles of Stance

Our student decided to clarify his stance:

Role: I am a student working part-time as a driver for a local cab company. I am 18 years old.

Thesis: Driving a cab part-time is a poor way for a college student to make money.

Reader: The "general reader."

About the general reader we will have more to say later. Our student began to rewrite his paper, getting this result for two paragraphs:

On an average twelve-hour workday on Saturday or Sunday, I make fifteen to twenty dollars after paying for half of the gas I use — a company requirement. I start at six o'clock in the morning, and finish at seven in the evening. But since the supper hour is the busiest time of the day, I often have to stay an hour late. The cabs eat gas like luxury cars. Twenty-five percent of my profits are lost in paying for gas. In the winter, between calls, I either turn off the engine or burn up all my profits. Cold, cold.

I receive tips from perhaps one-fifth of the fares. If a person gives me a quarter he smiles benevolently as if he has finally proved to himself that he really has a philanthropic heart. "Well, how much do you get as a tip?" some will ask. Or: "What's the right amount to tip?" A common comment, after a toothy smile: "Well, you got me here safely, didn't you? I think you deserve a tip." An extra dime falls into my hand, and after my word of thanks, I hear a chuckle or two, and a pleasant, "You're welcome, you're quite welcome."

Not perfect, but a better job than before — more interesting, readable, and informative. We know who the writer is, why he wishes to communicate to us, what the point of his communication is.

As a part of a new assignment, our student tried shifting his stance:

Your cabs are in terrible condition; some are actually unsafe. The horn did not work on mine all last weekend. The brakes on No. 37 are so badly worn that they will not respond without pumping. Since most of us have to drive fast to get from one place to another to pick up a new fare, we are endangering our lives and other people's — just to do our jobs.

The writer's role here stays the same, but he has changed his thesis and his reader, who is now the owner of the cab company.

You and the Writer's Stance

A successful piece of writing is written by somebody, to somebody, and for a purpose. When you plan your writing, employ the principle of stance as follows:

Consider each of your themes as a little exercise in convincing a reader. This advice applies not only to themes but to almost any piece of writing you will do in or out of college. A term paper, a letter to a creditor, an analysis or review of a new movie, an auditor's report, a procedure for mixing cement — all of these are written to convince a reader of something. The more artfully you create your stance, the more convincing and successful your written communications will be.

In order to make your themes convincing and easier to write, specify each part of your stance (role, thesis, reader) before you start writing.

THE ROLE

You do not use a role to cover up your true self or to give a false impression to a reader. Nor do you use it to play out a fictional part, as you might if you were acting on stage or in a film. Your role as a writer is a legitimate part of you and your existence. Who are you? What do you know? What do you do? How many roles do you adopt as a matter of course in your daily life?

Our part-time cabdriver could easily adopt certain roles. At one time or another he has been:

— a small businessman (was once in charge of ten paper routes)
— a hobbyist (rock music)
— a musician (clarinet)
— a hitchhiker (about 4,000 miles around the United States)
— a boy friend

- a hospital patient (a broken arm, a broken leg, and one severe continuing allergy)
- an agnostic
- a prospective English major
- a mainly skeptical observer of politics
- an amateur golfer

Here are some roles another student found she could adopt:

- a backpacker
- a car owner
- a consumer
- a taxpayer (five cents on every dollar)
- a lab technician (part-time)
- a daughter
- a sister
- a U.S. citizen
- a college student
- a rugby player
- an environmentalist
- a Catholic
- a member of an antiabortion group, "Right to Life"

To keep these lists from getting too long, we have omitted those roles that might overlap for our two people. For instance, both could adopt the role of backpacker because both have been "on the trail."

THE THESIS

The thesis, discussed at length in the next chapter, is partly dependent on your role and reader. If you change either of these two, as did the part-time cabdriver, your thesis will probably also change.

The student whose possible roles were just listed wanted to write a paper on backpacking in Europe. But she had difficulty narrowing and unifying her thesis. What were her choices? She could discuss the language problems she encountered, the difficulties of travel for someone without much money, the sights to see, or the problem of communicating with parents and friends thousands of miles away. In addition, she noted that her thesis would be dependent on what she knew about her subject. For example, she remarked that, besides English, she "knew only a little French." Given this fact, it is doubtful that a thesis of hers could easily deal with the Italian language, classical French literature, or modern Greek grammar. But with the knowledge about Europe gained in her travels, she might construct a number of interesting theses such as these (for the purposes of illustration, we will ignore here the issues of role and reader):

- The average Englishman seems friendlier to the backpacker than the average German.
- If you want to stay healthy in Europe, stick to simple foods and carry plenty of stomach medicine.
- For an American traveling in Europe, French is the most useful foreign language to know.
- Although France has the reputation of being anti-American, France seems more Americanized than England, Germany, Greece, Italy, or Spain.
- The American Youth Hostel Association needs tighter control from its top administration.
- The beauty of Greece is undeniable; but its beauty is unvarying and after a while, rather boring.

But she kept coming back to one idea that she considered important. Too many young Americans, like herself, went off merrily to Europe without being properly prepared for what they were to encounter. Her thesis suggested itself. Why not try to warn travelers about three or four problems they might encounter, and how they could go about solving them? See p. 10 for the final version of her thesis.

THE READER

You seldom, if ever, write anything that is directed to all types of readers. Most pieces of writing are directed to a special reader or group of readers. This textbook is directed to one group of readers; an article in *TV Guide* is directed to another; and a set of directions on repairing a motorboat engine to yet another. While these groups of readers may overlap somewhat, they usually do have certain characteristics you should be aware of.

Sometimes you will write for the *general reader*, a term which covers a class of people who vary somewhat in age, occupation, and interests. But you should always specify and describe even your general readership because it will usually have certain characteristics that set it off from the "whole world" of readers. A letter written to your local newspaper on air pollution should not be directed to all readers of the paper because all of them are not equally interested in the subject, affected by the problem, or (perhaps most important) able to do something about it.

To take another example, a critical paper on a novel should not be written for "everybody" but only for those interested in serious fiction generally and in your novel specifically — usually someone, by the way, who has read the novel. If your group of readers has not read it, then that fact affects your thesis and your theme, which in this instance is likely to take the form of a review ("For the following reasons, this book is good. Read it.").

"General readers," we may conclude, tend to have something in common. This may be an interest, however varied, in the problem of pollution or in a new book that has just appeared on the bestseller lists. A good way of appealing to your reader is to find this commonality.

Many students believe that their readership consists of one person, the instructor. In one sense, this is true. But in a more important sense, he or she is your *teacher-editor*, a trained professional who stands between you and your intended readers, pointing out where you have gone wrong in your essay, what you have done well, *how you can make your work more convincing*. This is the sort of thing that our own editor has done for us on this book. A part of this section was written at his suggestion that we needed to explain more fully the problems of thinking about the general reader.

STANCE: LIMITATIONS AND POSSIBILITIES

Of course, you are limited to some extent by the roles and readers that, in a practical way, are available to you. If the student whose roles are listed on page 7 were given the topic "Defend or Attack Legalized Abortion," she would probably be limited in her choice of a role because she is Catholic and also a member of an antiabortion group, "Right to Life." As to what this specific limitation might amount to, she would have to decide for herself. But there is a positive side to her situation: her religious philosophy may suggest a large number of interesting roles or theses. Each of you has your own limitations and possibilities. They are governed by age, philosophy, political and religious beliefs (or lack of them), experience, knowledge of the subject, and so on. On most topics, even when limitations exist, there will be several roles open to you.

For most topics, you may also have several possible "readerships." On the abortion topic, your readership might be one or more of these:

— legislators considering an abortion bill
— married women with young children
— pregnant unmarried women
— parents of young people
— religious leaders of a particular faith
— other college students of your "type"
— parents too poor to get private medical attention
— any persons interested in the topic

— any persons uninterested in the topic (a challenge to the writer!)
— a writer who has written an argument for or against legalized abortion
— a mother on welfare

EXAMPLE OF A COMPLETED STANCE

The student mentioned earlier decided that her decisions about role and thesis seemed to suggest a certain group of readers—those young American backpackers with little money who intended to see Europe but who wouldn't always know what to expect. Now her completed stance looked like this:

My Role: I am a young American who traveled through Europe this summer. I would like to show how other backpackers can do the same thing, but do it more easily than I did.

My Thesis: In order to make traveling easier and more pleasant in Europe, buy three informative books, learn about Youth Hostels, and be prepared for the "male problem."

My Reader: Young Americans, both men and women, who might want to travel as I did. My theme will be slanted somewhat to women, but men should definitely be interested too.

Creating "Distance"

Consider these two statements:

I am a new member of the Independent Students' Association, and I am rather disturbed to find that, as Director of Security, you will not allow us to have security guards at our rock concerts.

The Director of Security stated today that he will not allow the Independent Students' Association to employ security guards at their rock concerts.

The first sentence employs the first-person *I* and, in addition, addresses the reader as *you*. The second sentence avoids both the first and second person, employing a neutral attitude toward the material. Yet these sentences differ in more than just their pronouns and attitude. In the first, the writer shrinks the *distance* between himself and his subject, and between himself and his reader. He might be in the room talking to the Director. Perhaps he is making an appeal to him for a change in policy. In the second, our writer has expanded the distances between himself, reader, and subject. Clearly he is directing his statement to a general readership. This technique "cools" the rhetoric, making it seem more objective and impartial. Indeed, in the second sentence alone, we don't know whether the writer is involved in the controversy about guards at all. When the student who wrote the paper about driving a cab spoke directly to the owner of the cab company and took a more personal and direct attitude by asking for a change, he shortened the *distance* between himself and his reader.

Your decisions about *distance* are made along with those about writer's stance. Besides knowing that you must take both stance and distance into account, and that they are clearly interdependent, you must decide how to relate them. Addressing a particular reader or readership—for example, the Circulation Librarian *or* those students who use the library a great deal—also influences your stance. This is not bad; it is just something you must be fully aware of and try to control.

In many writing courses, you will be asked to write papers for the general reader as a way of disciplining yourself to be objective and impartial, to look at evidence from a neutral viewpoint. Perhaps you will be asked to avoid the first person and to concentrate on the ideas of others. There is no problem with such requests; you simply adjust both stance and distance to fit the assignment.

You can also adjust distance to fit your own purposes. How close, or far away, for example, do you wish to be from your reader and subject? Here is how one writer answered that question. He decided to maintain a discreet distance from his subject and audience.

> [1]This morning one of the open boxcars carries several men. They are railroad tramps. Nobody in authority knows they are there. In this giant caravan, they are as weightless as flies.
>
> [2]Ever since the great expansion of the railroads in the 19th century, these travelers—hoboes, tramps, migrants, sightseers—have fastened on for free rides. They are part of the spirit of the trains, like the cars and the track, which often they helped lay. Glimpsed, over the years, as the trains passed through towns, these anonymous, dirt-stained figures have acquired a halo of fame. Yet few people have ever known who they were. Few know now that their history goes back 100 years or forward to today. In regions of the West, during warm weather, as many as three out of four freight trains have tramps aboard. And as a tramp said recently, "Hell, as long as there's freight trains, wine and blood banks, we'll always be around." (There are some hospitals, research institutions and private blood banks across the country that pay donors an average of $15 for a pint of blood. Certain diseases, such as hepatitis, permanently disqualify donors.)—Roger Warner, "Riding Freights"

Writing for the general reader, Warner himself does not appear anywhere in the description, nor does his reader; there is no *I* or *you*. This consistently maintained distance lends a pleasant sense of neutrality to the exposition.

What happens if we use a different approach to a part of this material?

> Just as I swung aboard the boxcar, a strong hand came out of nowhere and lifted me to safety. I was tired and stumbling, and might not have made it without help. Panting on the floor of the car, I looked up into a lined old face and inhaled the fumes of 99-cents-a-bottle muscatel. Do you know what I thought of first? *This old guy is going to knock me on my head and take my last ten dollars. First time I ever ride a freight train, I'm going to get beat up.* But it did not happen. Instead I got a free meal — bad food, but appreciated — and a lecture on the sociology of tramps.

The wording in this passage is more colloquial and informal. Just as important, the stance has been changed, and the writer's narrowing of distance helps bring the reader into the scene. This narrowed distance between writer, reader, and subject makes the whole affair more personal.

We are not implying that the second piece of writing is inferior to the first; they simply try to do different things.

Stance and the "Strategies" of Rhetoric

Rhetoric is one of the oldest academic subjects in the Western world, having begun in ancient Greece long before the birth of Christ. The main issues in rhetoric, often called written composition in modern colleges and universities, have not really changed in over two thousand years. And the principle underlying the subject over this long period of time has remained basically unchanged also. Both in the past and the present, the study of rhetoric has been mainly concerned with "the convincing presentation of truth."

Creating a good writer's stance, along with what we have called a suitable distance, is fundamental to successful rhetoric. In order to write convincingly, you need to define your *role* and *reader* accurately and to make a truthful point *(thesis)*. But there are no set ways of doing these things. If there were, they would have been found hundreds of years ago, and this book would not be necessary. Instead of set ways for attaining success in rhetoric, there are what we call "strategies" — various methods and techniques for choosing words, constructing sentences, making logical connections, organizing paragraphs, avoiding errors in grammar.

Rhetoric deals with the art of making proper choices among these available strategies of writing. The writer's stance is fundamental to choice and strategy because a poorly chosen stance affects every aspect of writing, from word choice to sentences to organization. Stance even affects grammatical choice. We can't stop now to explain all this—if we did, this first chapter would run several hundred pages. The rest of the book will provide detail and explanation.

PRACTICE

More exercises are provided here than at the end of most chapters.

1. Read this brief student essay, and then prepare the questions after it for class discussion.

> [1]The critic Arthur Koestler has stated that creatures in science fiction are "too alien to be true" and that each should be given what our instructor has called a "human reference point." But is this true? If the writer is good at presenting the story in a logical, scientific, and yet enjoyable manner, then the reader should be open-minded enough to accept any form of alien life.
>
> [2]One of the most popular episodes of the *Star Trek* television series featured the Medusan—a mass of twinkling lights that formed images too horrible for the human eye to behold. The Medusan, even with no human features whatever, was believable because of the overall plausibility of the story. The writers exploited the Medusan's highly unusual appearance and repulsiveness in such a way that the unlikeliness of its existence was forgotten.
>
> [3]Another example of bizarre alien life, again from *Star Trek*, is the Horta. Many scientists believe that the only possible form of life is based on carbon, a substance all plants and animals on earth contain. However, the writers and "creators" of the Horta formulated the theory of silicon-based life. As living rock, the Horta drew its life from silicon. Impossible? Perhaps, but the show presented the Horta in a manner which made human standards of life unimportant. What *was* important was the fact that the lives of the *Enterprise* crew were endangered. Because the Horta was presented so convincingly, viewers could readily accept the existence of a very alien alien.
>
> [4]If one is to agree with critics and demand "human reference points" for all science-fiction aliens, then part of the challenge for the author and all the excitement for the reader would be lost. Human reference points are not important; an imaginative story that is "true" for the human characters *is*.

Note: Some of the following questions deal with ideas about writing that we have not covered yet. Try them anyway—discussing them may give you some fresh ideas about composition.

a. Explain in detail the stance in this essay. What is the writer's thesis? Where is it placed? Why is this placement important? What is his role? What sort of reader does he have in mind? How much distance has the writer placed between himself and his reader, himself and his subject? Why has he chosen such distance?

b. Why does he use the quotation from Arthur Koestler? In what way does it help him organize his writing?

c. How does the writer employ the word *alien*? Explain.

d. The paper is shorter than many pieces of student writing. Do you believe that its brevity makes the communication less convincing? Explain.

e. Like many pieces of nonfiction writing, this is an argument. What has this fact to do with the success of the paper on aliens in science fiction? With the general idea of stance and distance?

f. If you were to write a paper agreeing with Koestler, would you adopt the same stance or a different one? Explain.

2. One of us received this letter, quoted in its entirety. After you have read it, comment on its effectiveness.

Dear Professor Tibbetts:

This letter is to inform you of the death of Mr. _____, who is currently enrolled in your English 302, Sec. B. The student's registration will be officially cancelled by the appropriate college office in the near future.

Sincerely,

_____, Associate Dean

3. Read this extract from a student's research paper. Describe and justify the student's use of distance.

[1]Most authorities agree that *handedness* is the tendency to use a certain hand to perform most tasks. Modern authorities agree that handedness is related neurologically to the brain. One popular theory is that of "cerebral dominance," which means that one side of the brain dominates the other, this dominance being translated into the preference of one hand over the other.

[2]The researcher encounters difficulty finding good authorities on the subject of handedness. First, the subject itself has no common name. One may have to look in his sources under *left-handedness, right-handedness, laterality,* and *handedness* before he can find information. Many good reference works (for example, the *Collier's Encyclopedia*) have no material on the subject. Those authorites which are available fall roughly into two groups: (1) the medical and (2) the psychological and educa-

tional. Since these two groups of authorities often do not agree with each other, one must decide whether to use certain information or to throw it out as being unscientific or unreasonable. In the latter category may be put the theory of Professor _____ in Educational Psychology 280. He told his class that handedness was the result of accident, depending upon which hand a child used in his crib or ate with. If the professor were correct, the laws of probability should require that about half of the population be right-handed and half be left-handed.

4. You recall the backpacker, and the problems she had planning her stance. Here are two paragraphs from her finished paper. Given her stance, described on page 10, explain in detail how her writing — words, sentences, choice of details, etc. — fits the stance she created. How does she use distance?

> [1]If you women are planning to spend any time at all in Italy, Greece, or Spain, you should be forewarned about the male population. (This section should be read by you men too because you will undoubtedly be approached by an American girl looking for someone to protect her or just to sit with her until her harassers leave.) The first thing you have to realize when traveling in these countries is that a local woman does not ordinarily walk out on the street without a sister or an older woman with her. So when you go out on the street alone you are automatically taken to be a tourist — and available.
>
> [2]Also, the men have some kind of Early Detection device for American girls. It doesn't matter what you look like or what you are wearing. In Italy particularly you will be leered at, jeered at, whispered to, pinched, and generally driven crazy by the men. Don't think you can go unnoticed; the mere fact that you are an American on the street draws attention to you. Being with a man helps sometimes, but not always. My girl friend and I were with eight British and American boys in Rome, and it made absolutely no difference. You can be wearing a potato sack and the men will still bother you — I wouldn't recommend wearing a dress or shorts and halter tops anywhere. Wearing jeans instead will save you a lot of trouble. All of this may sound exaggerated to you, but it isn't. And it's better to expect the worst. If you are bothered less than you expected to be, it's better than entering a country like Italy unprepared for the hassles.

5. The remarks below are taken from an address delivered by George Plimpton at the Harvard spring commencement of 1977. Plimpton is probably best known for his book *Paper Lion*. His speech was quickly reprinted in several places, most notably the *New York Times*. Why so much interest in the piece as both speech and essay? Give specific reasons.

> [1]I have been led to understand that tomorrow you are going to graduate. Well, my strong recommendation is that you don't go. Stop! Go on back to your rooms. Unpack! There's not much out here. . . .

2The point is we don't want you out here very much. We on the outside see graduation as a terrible event — the opening of an enormous dovecote from which spring into the air tens of thousands of graduates. What is particularly disturbing is that you all come out at the same time — June — hordes, with your dark graduation cloaks darkening the earth. Why is it that you can't be squeezed out one at a time, like peach pits, so that the society can absorb you without feeling suffocated?

3My own profession is being swamped with writers coming out of college, despite the condition out here that no one reads. Indeed, my friend Kurt Vonnegut was saying the other day that the only solution to the moribund state of publishing would be to require of all those on welfare that before receiving their welfare checks, they must hand in a book report. . . .

4If your parents insist you pack up and come home, there are always measures. If you're a chemistry major, tell them that you've become very attached to something in a vat of formaldehyde. If you're in pre-law, tell them that you're thinking of bringing home a tort. Your parents will probably have forgotten what a tort is, if they ever knew, and it *sounds* unpleasant — something that your Mom wouldn't want to have stepping suddenly out of a hall closet. Surely, there is hardly an academic field of one's choice which does not have a nightmare possibility with which to force one's parents to pony up enough to allow nearly a decade of contemplation in one's room.

5You'll remember the King in Alice in Wonderland. When asked: "Where shall I begin?" the King says, "Begin at the beginning, and go on until you come to the end; then stop." What I am suggesting is that you stop at the beginning, stop at your commencement. It's not very interesting to stop at the end — I mean *everyone* does that. So stop now. Tell them you won't go. Go back to your rooms. Unpack!

6. Write two versions of the same essay. For your major you are required to take a course for which you believe there is no practical use.

   a. Write an essay directed to the dean of your college, explaining why you and your fellow majors should not be required to take the course. Be cool and objective.

   b. Write to other students in your major field. Try to get them to support you in your efforts to have the requirement abolished. In this version, your stance and approach to the subject will be more personal, and you may narrow the distance between you and your reader.

7. There is a bill before the state legislature that will impose a severe punishment for hitchhiking in your state. (We will assume that the laws now covering hitchhiking are often not enforced and the punishments, if any, are mild.) Consider these roles, along with the suggested readers. You are:

a. A state trooper writing to your state representative.
b. A student living 50 miles from campus; you are writing to your campus newspaper.
c. A trucker writing to the Opinion column of your union's monthly magazine.
d. A woman student writing to your worried mother who lives in another state.

Write a paragraph for each of these four situations, filling out your stance with a clear thesis. Let your paragraph be the *introduction* to your letter or article. Consider how rhetorical distance may vary for each situation.

Given the general problem, what other stances are citizens in your state likely to take?

8. Describe the good qualities — or shortcomings — of a particular institution or organization you are familiar with. Examples: a high school, a church, an athletic team, a company that employs young people. Write for the general reader and use an appropriate distance.

9. Here is an exotic writing assignment, one which you should not consider unless your instructor — in his unwisdom — insists.

You are a "Sand Dolphin," a species of intelligent beings (as yet unknown to people) that live mainly in the South Seas. One day you discover a well-preserved 1974 Volkswagen "Bug" lying in ten feet of water. Of course, you don't know it's a VW. One door is open and swinging slightly in the current. Nothing on the VW is obviously broken. (Where did it come from? You don't know, and neither do we. Perhaps it fell off a ship transporting it.)

The Sand Dolphins have a highly developed culture, complete with an elaborate communication system. It is your responsibility to report the objects you have found to the Ministry for USO's (Unidentified Sunken Objects).

The members of the Ministry — like you — look, feel, and (most important) *think* like sea creatures. For instance, their idea of measurement is based upon the dimensions and physiology of a fish. They would never describe any object as being so many "feet" long.

Taking a Sand Dolphin's stance, write a report to the ministry describing *in detail* the object you have found. You may use or ignore the fact that dolphins are mammals.

Forming a Thesis

After you have worked for a while with the idea of the writer's stance and practiced creating your own stances, you will probably discover that only the thesis gives you any continuing trouble. So let's consider a few practical strategies for arriving at a thesis and making it more useful in planning your themes.

Every written communication must make a point. A letter to your newspaper, a note to the postman, an article on Democrats in the state legislature, a memo to your boss at work, a textbook on the American colonial period, one of your themes—each makes a point about something. The sharper the point, the more successful the communication. In written form, your theme's point is its thesis—the main idea stated in one specific sentence. The thesis that you use to guide your early planning does not always appear word for word in the theme itself. Sometimes, in order to fit a thesis into the flow of your writing, you may have to reword it slightly or take two or three sentences to state it. But for the purposes of planning, practice putting each thesis in a single sentence.

Why is a thesis useful? First, it helps you respond to the theme assignment and shape your ideas before you write. Second, the thesis helps you organize your material as you write; it keeps you from wandering away from your topic. Third, after you have completed your theme, you can use your thesis to judge whether you have done what you set out to do. Fourth, in conferences both you and your instructor will refer to your thesis when you discuss your theme's effectiveness—for example, its organization and the relevance of supporting material.

PRACTICE

1. Read the following theme for class discussion. The student stopped writing toward the end of paragraph 4. Can you guess why? What seems to be the thesis of her essay? Can you give her any advice for rewriting the theme and improving it? Center your comments on the problem of the theme's point.

   ¹I first got interested in horses when our family went to my uncle's farm and he let me ride an old plow horse. He was an old horse and was

never used for anything, and he would not go faster than a walk. But I was fascinated by his personality, if that is what you want to call it. He seemed very wise and responsive, as if he were listening to you talk to him. I used to ride him two or three times a day and talk to him and he would act as if he understood me.

²That same year I started taking riding lessons at a stable near home (there is only one in the area). Since we are not particularly well off, I had to work for my lessons. Every Saturday, I would ride my bike — along with several girl friends — to the stable and work out the horses, clean the stall, and do general handyman work. For this I would get a half-hour's lesson which consisted mainly of yells and shouts of "Donna, GET YOUR FEET TURNED IN!!!" and "You got TERRIBLE hands, Donna!"

³My grandmother in Nebraska heard about my working in the stable and wrote me a worried letter saying that the stables were no place for a girl and that I should stay away from them except when taking lessons. She apparently remembers the stable life from her girlhood in Texas, which was probably very different from today's.

⁴I got to ride in a few shows, and won a ribbon or two, and then I was really hooked. I wanted my own horse, but we could not afford one. The situation got worse at the stables — the instructor yelling at me and telling lies about me to my mother, who insisted that I keep riding no matter what. I wanted to ride but I hated the instructor, and my mother kept getting in the situation, until finally I didn't know what to do. So I quit for a while . . . . [end of draft] *OFF the main subject of being interested in horses*

2. Read the following two paragraphs and prepare to discuss them in class. Considering the two paragraphs as a brief essay, do you think that Plumb has a clear thesis? If you believe that he has, state it. Does Plumb tend to organize his ideas, in relation to his thesis, in any particular way? Explain, giving examples.

¹How much privacy have great men ever enjoyed? How far has it been possible to separate their public and private lives? Throughout recorded history and discernibly beyond there have been persons and families of distinction who have been known by name and fame and special status to all members of their communities. High priests, kings, Caesars, popes, emperors — all have belonged to the world in a very special sense. The kings of France dressed and undressed in public, were ceremonially fed before their court; they had an audience for their wedding night, and their wives labored in rooms crowded with nobility. Although it is true that the royal bed was railed off, the rest of the chamber would be thronged with courtiers, listening to the queen's groans, peering and peeping, joking and talking bawdily.

²For royalty death was no easier than birth. The courtiers of Carlos II of Spain stood about as the doctors tried the warm entrails of a pigeon on his belly His priests, putting more faith in San Isidro, brought his mummified remains to the bedside. Their prayers and the hushed gossip of the grandees were drowned by the chants of rival priests, who carried round

the room the corpse of San Diego of Alcalá sitting in its urn. It was not much better for Queen Caroline of England rolling in agony in her own putrefaction, whilst her husband, distracted with grief, upbraided her for looking like a dying cow. The grossly fat prime minister knelt by her side and could not get up. The Archbishop of Canterbury mumbled his prayers. The queen, still in possession of her wits, sent for the lord chancellor to make absolutely certain that Frederick, Prince of Wales, would not inherit one iota of her possessions. As she said on this deathbed, she wished him in the bottommost pit of hell. And there in the corner was little Lord Hervey, rouged, powdered, flamboyantly epicene, taking it all down and doubtless inventing what he could not quite hear. He knew he was present at a moment of history, that posterity would be wide-eyed and open-mouthed for every gory detail of the queen's death. To be royal was to live even the most intimate moments of one's life before the hostile, loving, or indifferent eyes of one's court. — J. H. Plumb, "The Private Grief of Public Figures"

The Assignment and the Thesis

You write because you need to, whether the "need" is imposed from within or without. Ordinarily, in your composition class, you write in response to an instructor's assignment. So let's now turn to the problem of the typical writing assignment and consider how it can lead to a thesis.

There are, roughly, three kinds of assignments. Here are examples, ranging from the general to the specific:

1. A brief general request for written work:

"Write a theme for next Friday."

2. A request for a type of theme or for a particular theme topic:

a. "Write a theme convincing someone to take up your hobby."
b. "Write a theme explaining a cause or effect."
c. "In your theme, discuss the characterization of Willy Loman in *Death of a Salesman*."

3. A more specific request that tends to control your response as you write:

a. "Write a paper that supports an idea that some people ordinarily do not agree with, for example, that organized athletic programs do not foster team spirit or group loyalty in the players; that strongly religious persons can be evil; that going to college may be a serious mistake for certain young people."

b. "If you were to call for a change in any university (or college) policy or practice, what would that change be? Write a letter to someone in authority outlining the policy or practice and stating your reasons for suggesting the change."

c. "Some persons believe that Willy Loman is not a tragic character. Define the term *tragic character,* and argue that Willy either is or is not tragic. (You may take the position that he is partially tragic.)"

While assignments **1** and **2** give you more freedom than **3** does, they may be harder to prepare. You have to specify most of the elements of the topic yourself, and you may spend as much time finding and limiting a topic as you spend actually writing the theme. But instructors continue to use assignments like **1** and **2** because with them you can choose your own material and create your own stance. You can write themes that you might not otherwise get a chance to write with the more limited assignments.

A THESIS NOTEBOOK

In order to show how you can take a topic and mold it into a suitable thesis, let's see how one student responded to an assignment. Here are some thoughts and impressions she recorded in a notebook during the third week of the term. After her instructor spent two class periods discussing theses, she gave assignment **3a** above.

1. I was standing at my dorm window when I heard a sharp blast on a car horn. This blast was followed by a howl of locked brakes, a yell from somebody, and then the familiar crashing sound of metal meeting metal. By the time I got my eyes focused on the street, the accident was over. The two cars were there all right, locked together, one of them at right angles to the other.

2. I shall spare the reader the rest of this scene, including my dashing downstairs, gawking at the wreck, and so on. By the time I climbed back upstairs, an hour was lost, but I did have one thing, though—a glimmer of an idea for a subject.

3. Auto accidents are something I know about. For two years I worked as an assistant to the ambulance drivers for the Pemberton Funeral Home on weekends and during the summer. As a part of the ambulance team, I saw thirty or forty accidents, a few of them fatal.

4. So here was my general subject, auto accidents. But I had learned the hard way that much bad writing came from not knowing a subject well enough or from not narrowing it sufficiently to make a particular point. If I prepared a vaguely written paper, I might as well not bother to hand it in.

5. Further thought was required. I mulled over possible theses: "Auto accidents should be prevented"? Objection: of course, they should be prevented; who would argue they shouldn't be? Another possibility: "There are fewer auto accidents in Tennessee than in Illinois." But I don't really know very much about auto accidents in Tennessee, even though I was born there.

6. Trouble. More thought. I remembered my instructor's advice, took out a piece of scratch paper, and put down whatever came into my head in a list:
autos
accidents
injury
mothers
fathers
worry for them because they're hurt
auto accidents expensive
new engine — cost?
burial?
casket?
relatives worried
cost — expensive!
cost of blood — how much?
cost of surgery?
doctors' fees
nurses
ambulance costs
ambulance driving

7. I looked over the list and was struck by the number of items that had to do with the financial cost of accidents. It suddenly occurred to me that if the persons in the accidents paid it out, somebody earned it — doctors, nurses, hospitals, morticians, garages, and mechanics. There was my subject. Everybody was always talking about the cost of accidents but never about the profit in them. There was good money in accidents; I had made good money as a part of the ambulance team. Here was a thesis: *Contrary to what many people think, there is a lot of money to be made from automobile accidents.*

8. The next step was to determine the range of my authority on the subject. From experience, I knew the costs and also the money to be made from ambulance calls, and I knew from being around the Pemberton Funeral Home how much caskets and funerals cost. Other fees — those charged by garages and hospitals — I was less familiar with and would have to check on. I started on an outline of the theme that night.

9. The next morning, I called two local hospitals and two garages and obtained a page of typical charges for typical injuries and damages, from broken legs to smashed fenders. This took me only half an hour and was the extent of my research. I could now speak with

reasonable authority on the subject. Or could I? While reading my thesis over to myself, certain questions arose: "A lot of money to be made from auto accidents. Where? New York State? San Francisco? Am I implying that auto accidents 'cost' the same everywhere? What's my authority for this?"

10. To establish and limit the range of my authority on the subject, I added four words to the thesis: *Contrary to what many people think, there is a lot of money to be made from auto accidents in the Urbana area.* The theme I wrote turned out to be easy to write mainly because I felt comfortable with the subject and had a lot of available material, most of it taken from memory.

Another example of thesis development may be useful here. The assignment is: "Write a theme convincing someone to take up your hobby." In checking the assignment, you find that the key words are *convincing*, *take up*, and *hobby*, which help in clarifying your subject. You settle quickly on a writer's *role* (that of a young person who needs to earn money for school expenses) and on a *reader* (a similar type of person, particularly one who can work with his hands).

Now you start specifying a point:

1. *My hobby* . . . used to be sports, but a compound fracture took care of that . . . spend more time "clocking" now than in any other leisure-time activity . . . .

2. *Hobby is repairing clocks* . . . odd hobby for a kid . . . took it up by accident . . . money in it . . . tell why money in clock repair . . . .

3. *Good money in repairing clocks* . . . but it's interesting too . . . almost everyone is fascinated by an old clock . . . that's all I work on . . . remember I have to *convince* someone to take up my hobby. . . .

4. *Thesis:* If you want an interesting and profitable hobby, take up clock repair.

Since the thesis is clear, narrowed, and specific, it should be a good one to use when organizing and writing the theme.

THE THESIS AS ANSWER TO A QUESTION

Finding a workable thesis often seems to involve "thinking out loud," picking your way through ideas as they occur to you, selecting and discarding as you go along. Look for key words in an assignment and underline them. If other key words occur to you, put them down on scratch paper before they get away. As you think out loud, ask yourself the questions in the following list. (The word *something* stands for your subject or an important idea about it.)

— What was the effect of *something*? Its cause?
— Can I break *something* down or analyze its main parts in order to understand it better?

- Can I compare *something* to another thing?
- Can I define *something*?
- Is *something* typical for some persons and not for others?
- Is *something* good or bad, or partly good and partly bad?
- Who knows about *something*? Who would I see or read to find out?
- What class or category of ideas or objects is *something* in?
- What are the facts about *something*? What things aren't known?
- Can I tell a story about *something*?
- Does *something* do any job that is necessary for a group, large or small?
- How is *something* made or created? Destroyed?
- How can one do or perform *something*?
- Can I recommend *something* to other people? Not recommend?
- Should I suggest changes in *something*?

Note: We discuss the development of answers to many of these questions in Chapter 4.

Here are two examples of how a thesis can be an answer to a question:

> *Question:* How can one do *something*?
>
> *Thesis:* Anyone can put up a standard house wall if he buys good-quality straight studs, can use a level accurately, and makes all measurements carefully.

> *Question:* What is a *sonnet*?
>
> *Thesis:* A sonnet is a poem of fourteen lines, written in one of several set forms that follows a particular rhyme scheme.

The theme written from the last thesis would explain and exemplify the forms and rhyme schemes, and give examples of typical sonnets.

Improving Your Thesis

As you work on your thesis, consider these suggestions for making it useful and effective:

1. Make Your Thesis Authoritative.

In other words, "write about what you know" — one of the soundest pieces of advice on student writing. Even though you may not picture yourself as such, you are an authority on a variety of subjects. So write about them: your family; your friends; your hometown; the politicians, doctors, mechanics, plumbers, carpenters, or lawyers you know; the crabgrass in your front lawn; your parents' divorce; your stereo set; your friend's broken arm; your first vote; your failure to pass trigonometry; your A in Spanish.

But do not try to write about the United Nations, poverty in America, racial problems in our cities, Lincoln's first administration, the creation of the American Constitution, the writings of Norman Mailer, the movies of Humphrey Bogart, *unless* (1) in the past you have done considerable research on one of these subjects, and have made yourself a sort of amateur "authority" in the field; or (2) you are willing to commit yourself to hours of research in the library or elsewhere to make yourself reasonably authoritative on the subject.

This advice is necessarily somewhat general. Check with your instructor when you have doubts about your subject and your "authority."

2. *Narrow Your Thesis.*

Because most themes are relatively short, you can't adequately support a very broad thesis in 500 words or so. Narrow your thesis to fit your theme length:

> *Poor:* People in my hometown are selfish. *(Topic is too broad.)*
> *Improved:* Some of the neighbors on our block will not give to charity or the United Fund because they are selfish.

> *Poor:* CB radios are a popular form of mass communication.
> *Improved:* Among my friends, CB's are so popular that they have replaced the telephone as the chief method of talking with one another.

3. *Unify Your Thesis.*

In your theme, discuss one thing, or group of things.

> *Poor:* Cheating in my high school was widespread, and it didn't work very well. *(Two subjects)*
> *Improved:* No matter what methods they tried, students who cheated in my high school usually did not improve their grade averages.

> *Poor:* Motorcycles are fun, providing fast, inexpensive, and dangerous transportation.
> *Improved:* Motorcycles provide inexpensive but dangerous transportation.

The last poor thesis would require the writer to juggle four somewhat illogically associated points about motorcycles. The improved thesis reduces these to two easily associated points by saying, in effect: the machine may not cost much but it can kill you.

4. *Specify Your Thesis.*

As you have probably guessed by now, the whole business of improving a thesis is a continuous process. When you make your thesis authoritative, and when you narrow and unify it, you are simply sharpening your theme's point. And the best single way to make that point even sharper is to avoid general words and to use specific ones instead.

Poor: Sororities are getting better.
Improved: Because they offer better housing, better food, and better facilities for study than the dorms offer, sororities at this college are getting more pledges.

Poor: Children watch television all the time.
Improved: My little brother and his friends plan all their other activities — playing ball, eating, even sleeping — so that they don't miss their favorite shows.

PRACTICE

1. You can learn much about writing useful theses by imitating those used in successful themes. Here are six such theses with certain key words and phrases in italics. Imitate them using your own ideas and material. For example, an imitation of **a** might be: "Unlike my sister, who went out for the swimming team because she thought swimming was glamorous, I tried out only because I badly needed the exercise." Are any particular writers' stances suggested by the theses?

    a. *Unlike* my uncle, *who was* a compulsive *alcoholic*, my father *drank* too much simply because he *liked* the *comradeship* of other drinkers.
    b. *Racial problems* in Penant High School *existed* for two years *before busing started*.
    c. For good *apples* in September, *spray* the *trees* with dormant oil just before the *buds* open in the spring.
    d. We *lost* eight basketball *games* that year because we didn't *practice* our basic *plays* enough.
    e. To get a natural color on fresh hardwood, use *first* a light *stain* and *then* a quick-drying standard *varnish*.
    f. Since the independents did not *campaign* in all campus areas, *they failed* to reach many students and *lost* the *election*.

2. Discuss and evaluate each of the following poor theses. How can they be improved?

    a. Traffic destroys superhighways.
    b. Biking and hitchhiking through Maine are safe.
    c. The Berlin Wall is necessary to the Soviet Union.
    d. Adopting the metric system is a mistake.
    e. Working and eating in a pizza parlor is boring, hard work, and gives me indigestion, plus the boss is a jerk.
    f. The earth is getting hotter.

g. Intercollegiate sports cost the university too much money.
h. Nuclear-power plants should be shut down.
i. Welfare takes too much of the tax dollar.

3. Here are some typical assignments you may encounter early in the term. For each assignment, (a) underline the important words or phrases; (b) write a narrowed, unified, and specific thesis.

   a. Tell your reader about the most important event in your life. Do not merely relate the event; describe it and explain in detail why you believe it is "important." (Do you need to define *important?*)
   b. In the past two or three years, several things probably have happened in your hometown, or area where you have been living, that you do not approve of. Write a theme explaining one of these events—a decision by an authority, a change in local government, etc. State specifically why you do not approve. Hint: Don't spend so much time in description that you are unable to be specific concerning your disapproval.
   c. Write a theme about a clash of personalities that you have experienced or closely observed. What effect on friends or relations did this clash have? Explain by giving details and examples.
   d. Write a theme about a person—you or someone you know—who has been successful or unsuccessful doing something. Describe the person's success, or lack of it, and explain in detail why he was (or was not) successful.

4. Write two specific theses that answer questions like those on pp. 23–24. You may make up your own questions.

5. For *two* of the following topics, develop a thesis that will form the basis of a 500-word essay. Be sure that your thesis is reasonably authoritative, narrowed, unified, and specific.

   a. seat belts in cars
   b. fishing
   c. intramural sports programs
   d. house plants
   e. movies
   f. hobbies
   g. cooking
   h. reading

3 How to Make a Helpful Outline

If you make a good outline before you write, you will improve the quality of your completed theme a great deal. An outline is no more than a series of ideas—in skeleton form—that shows you what direction your thoughts on a topic are taking:

Thesis:
Introduction to topic
Supporting point one
Supporting point two
Supporting point three
Etc.
Conclusion to topic

An inspection of your outline can suggest:

1. *Whether your material supports your thesis.* Do the supporting points tell your reader what the thesis promises that you will tell him?

2. *Whether the supporting points specify enough.* Are they so general that your theme written from the outline might be vague and unconvincing?

3. *Whether your supporting points are in the proper order.* If point two, for instance, is the most dramatic or important, should it be made the last point, coming just before the conclusion?

Let's take a detour for a minute on two important subjects—the *types* and the *forms* of typical outlines.

Types of Outlines

There are four main types of outlines: the *topic*, the *sentence*, the *mixed*, and the *paragraph*.

The *topic outline* uses phrases or single words in the headings, as in the following example. (In all the outlines in the chapter, we are not including the introduction and the conclusion, which we assume are added to the finished theme.)

Thesis: Major-league baseball is too slow.
  I. Pitcher's delay
      A. Use of rosin bag
      B. Adjusting uniform
      C. Pitcher-catcher delay
 II. Hitter's delay
      A. Before hitting
      B. Between pitches
      C. Fouling off
III. Delay between innings
      A. Fielders' warm-up
      B. Umpire's delay

In the *sentence outline*, you expand each part into a full sentence. Here, you can see every idea in its complete form:

Thesis: Major-league baseball is too slow.
  I. The pitcher fiddles around too long between pitches.
      A. He picks up the rosin bag (whether he needs it or not) and tosses it down.
      B. He adjusts his uniform—pulls on his cap, straightens his shirt, etc.
      C. He peers down at the catcher for what seems like five minutes, and then brushes off the sign.
 II. The hitter has his own methods of slowing up the game.
      A. Before hitting, he wanders around helplessly as if hunting for the batter's box.
      B. Between pitches, he steps out of the box, picks at his uniform, knocks his cleats with his bat.
      C. He may foul off five or six pitches before either striking out, hitting, or walking.
III. Other men waste time between innings.
      A. The fielders have to throw the ball around.
      B. The umpire struts up and down, stuffs or unstuffs his pockets, brushes away imaginary dust from the plate.

The sentence outline is specific but sometimes bulky and hard to comprehend at a glance. The topic outline is easier to work with and has the virtue of brevity. Most textbooks warn against mixing these types, but many students have found that one type of *mixed outline* is often useful. This type allows you to put your main ideas in complete-sentence form and your subordinate ideas in topic form. Such an arrangement gives you a relatively specific check on the structure of your theme, from the first main idea to the last:

Thesis: Major-league baseball is too slow.
  I. The pitcher fiddles around too long between pitches.
      A. Use of rosin bag
      B. Adjusting uniform
      C. Pitcher-catcher delay

II. The hitter has his own methods of slowing up the game.
  A. Before hitting
  B. Between pitches
  C. Fouling off
III. Other men waste time between innings.
  A. Fielders' warm-up
  B. Umpire's delay

Finally, in the *paragraph outline*, you list the topic ideas of each main paragraph in order:

I. (paragraph) The pitcher fiddles around too long between pitches.
II. (paragraph) The hitter has his own methods of slowing up the game.
III. (paragraph) Other men waste time between innings.

The Form of Outlines

Use an accepted form in the outline. It is customary to employ numerals and letters in this order, according to the rank of ideas or to the *levels of subordination:*

I. First level (main heading)
  A. Second level
    1. Third level
    2. Third level
      a. Fourth level
      b. Fourth level
  B. Second level
II. First level (main heading)

Headings on the same level of subordination should be roughly parallel—that is, equal in importance and grammatical form. The following example violates this principle in three ways:

I. Between pitches
  A. Fouling off
  B. The hitter has his own methods of slowing up the game.
II. There is too much time wasted between innings.

A and B are improperly subordinated to Part I. A and B are not parallel in importance or grammar. Part II is put in sentence form, which violates the form established in Part I. (The rule is this: When for the first time you use a particular form for a heading—a full sentence, a phrase, a single word, for example—use *the same form in subsequent entries for that level of heading.*)

Avoid single headings like II-A below.

   I. Pitcher's delay
      A. Use of rosin bag
      B. Adjusting uniform
      C. Pitcher-catcher delay
  II. Hitter's delay
      A. Before hitting
 III. Delay between innings
      A. Fielders' warm-up
      B. Umpire's delay

When you break a heading into subordinate headings, you must get at least two of these lower-level headings. Often when a single heading hangs out in space, you will find that it really belongs with the previous major heading.

Four Typical Questions About Outlines

1. *What type of outline should I use?*

The answer to this depends on many factors—the length of your paper and the complexity of your material, to name only two. When preparing to write a long paper which presents a lot of material and complex issues, you might like to make a complete sentence outline that maps out every detail of your argument and its evidence. If you are going to do a short, relatively uncomplicated paper, perhaps a brief topic outline would be sufficient.

Not the least important factor in your choice of outline is your own preference. What type of outline do you feel most comfortable with? For most assignments, which type seems to work best for you?

2. *How specific should an outline be?*

Specific enough to do the job. It should suggest what your paper is going to do—what its thesis is and what its main supporting points are. It should also supply some examples of evidence or detail that you will use in developing your ideas. But the outline is, as we said earlier, just a skeleton; and it can suggest only the bare bones of your completed theme.

If you have any doubts about a particular outline, show it to your instructor.

3. *What can I do if I start an outline, get a point or two down, and then can't continue?*

When this happens, you may be trying to build a house before acquiring concrete, bricks, lumber, and shingles. Before you can build a theme, you need materials for it—a number of main and subordinate points written down so that you can consider and arrange them easily.

First, let's assume that you have at least a working thesis, and you have some ideas to put into the theme. Get some 3-×-5 or 4-×-6 file cards, or small pieces of stiff paper cut to size. Next, write down your thesis on a sheet of paper and place it where you can see it. Start writing your ideas down on your cards, one idea to a card. Note that —one idea to a card; preferably, one complete sentence to a card. The point is to separate your ideas so that you can later classify and organize them.

For a working thesis, let's use: *Moving furniture as a summer job requires stamina.* (You may change it later, but this is a start.) As each idea pops into your head, write it down on a separate card.

1. A mover's workday can vary from 10 to 18 hours.
2. A mover has to work in temperatures that vary greatly.
3. Some days it is 95 degrees with 95% humidity.
4. Going in and out of air conditioning is hard on the body.
5. Moving furniture demands speed because movers must keep a schedule.
6. A mover is expected to lift at least 100 pounds alone.
7. When customers live in second- or third-floor apartments, moving furniture is difficult.
8. Sometimes a crew moves 2 or 3 households in a day.
9. Apartment buildings often have narrow stairs and landings.
10. Heavy furniture and appliances sometimes must be lifted over the head to get upstairs or downstairs.
11. Some furniture has sharp edges which cut into the hands.
12. Moving furniture, particularly on stairways, demands agility and strength.
13. A mover must hold onto the furniture to prevent accidents.
14. The boss-driver, not the furniture mover, sets the pace.
15. The mover has to please the driver, customer, and management.
16. Masculinity is the code of furniture movers.
17. Moving furniture in the summer requires stamina to work long hours in hot weather.

In this jumble of cards, look for major ideas that would support and develop your thesis. As you look through your cards, you notice that they fall into three categories:

I. Moving furniture in the summer requires stamina to work long hours in hot weather.
II. Moving furniture, particularly on stairways, demands agility and strength.

III. Moving furniture demands speed because movers must keep a schedule.

Notice that your original thesis said that moving furniture requires stamina. After classifying your evidence, you discover that you have added agility and speed to your list of requirements. So you see that you should change your thesis to *Moving furniture, as a summer job, requires stamina, agility, strength, and speed.*

Classify your cards under these headings. Numbers 11, 15, and 16 don't seem to fit anywhere, so put them aside (but don't throw them away!). Arrange the cards in each stack so they appear in a reasonable order. Write an outline from this revised sequence (note the subordination of items in I-B and II-B):

I. Moving furniture in the summer requires stamina to work long hours in hot weather.
   A. A mover's workday can vary from 10 to 18 hours.
   B. A mover has to work in temperatures that vary greatly.
      1. Some days it is 95 degrees with 95% humidity.
      2. Going in and out of air conditioning is hard on the body.
II. Moving furniture, particularly on stairways, requires agility and strength.
   A. A mover is expected to lift at least 100 pounds alone.
   B. When customers live in second- or third-floor apartments, moving furniture is difficult.
      1. Apartment buildings often have narrow stairs and landings.
      2. Heavy furniture and appliances sometimes must be lifted over the head to get upstairs or downstairs.
   C. A mover must hold onto the furniture to prevent accidents.
III. Moving furniture demands speed because movers must keep a schedule.
   A. The boss-driver, not the mover, sets the pace.
   B. Sometimes a crew moves 2 or 3 households in a day.

There you have a standard sentence outline, and you are ready to write your theme.

4. *I know I shouldn't do it, but I always make an outline after I write the paper. How can I train myself to make one before writing?*

An outline is supposed to show you where you are going before and as you write. Outlining after the fact at least shows you where you have been; you can always rewrite a theme if such "outlining" reveals flaws of logic or arrangement. But you should discipline yourself to outline before you write—it will save you the time and trouble of writing unnecessary drafts. Consider your outline as a figurative road map—refer to it before you start on your trip so that you won't end up at the seashore when you wanted to go to the mountains.

How a Thesis Suggests an Outline

The phrasing of the thesis often suggests a pattern in the outline. A typical thesis:

          I   III

As a result of *student visitation*, my *life in the dormitory* is much different

          II

from *my life at home.*

In creating your stance, you direct your ideas to someone who is not directly familiar with visitation rules. After considering the phrasing of the thesis, construct an outline like this:

I. Definition of *student visitation*
II. Description of home life
III. Description of dorm life

To gain emphasis and drama, you decide to describe dorm life after home life.

Here is another example:

Thesis: The Mexican-American Council has said that *students should*

             I   II

avoid using their primary language or *dialect* in writing in order

         IV   III

to *concentrate on learning* so-called *standard English.*

I. Brief description of "primary language"
II. Brief description of problems of "dialect"
III. Definition of *standard English*
IV. Value of standard English to students

How to Check an Outline

Before you move on to the main business of writing your theme, check over your outline to see where it is taking you.

1. See that all the *parts* of the outline are there—thesis, main headings, and subordinate headings.

2. Use the proper outline *form* (see pp. 30–31). Make particularly sure that your headings are reasonably parallel. There are minor exceptions to this rule. Sometimes you can't quite get your headings parallel; the idiom of the language won't allow it. But you should get as close to complete parallelism as you can.

3. Make your outline reasonably *specific*, particularly in your thesis and the main headings (I, II, III, etc.).

4. Check the outline for *logic*. Do all the parts fit together? Does every supporting point firmly fit your thesis? If necessary, try the subject-predicate test.* To make the test, write the major parts of your outline in full-sentence form, using clear subject-predicate patterns:

> I. MY CAR MECHANIC *was very thorough.*
>   A. HE *checked the distributor twice.*
>   B. HE *cleaned the carburetor, even though it did not appear to need cleaning.*
> II. But THE MANAGER *did not appreciate the mechanic's work.*
>   A. THE MANAGER *said that the mechanic spent too much time on routine jobs.*
>   B. HE *refused to give the mechanic overtime to complete important repairs.*

If your outline is logical, and all its parts fit together, you can draw connecting arrows (as shown above) from SUBJECT to SUBJECT and from *predicate* to *predicate*.

5. Check the outline for the proper order—that is, for a sensible sequence or organization of ideas. Check each level separately—first I, II, III, etc.; and then A, B, C, etc.; and so on. Except for the general rule that important ideas are often placed last, there is no special rule about order. The arrangement of your points should make sense and not be incongruous. The order of points below, for example, would not be very sensible:

> I. The manager did not appreciate the mechanic's work.
> II. The mechanic was very thorough.

This order would force you to describe the manager's attitude toward the mechanic's work before you had described that work. It's hard to write a paper backwards.

Some Final Comments on Outlining

An outline is a plan. Don't consider it as a fixed structure that you must follow blindly. Nor is outlining a fixed step in a rigid system of planning. (Many students tell us they believe they must find a subject, create a thesis, make an outline, write a paper from that outline—and never deviate from these steps.)

Generally speaking, successful writers—whether amateurs or professionals—simply do not work this way. They may go through all

*This test was suggested to us in 1954 by the staff of the Writing Lab of the University of Iowa.

the steps; but they may also work forward and backward through the process, refining, changing, switching main ideas or moving them about, inserting and deleting details. A writer may often consider, or actually follow, all the steps in the theme-writing process. But he does not allow the process to overrule his good judgment concerning any part of the final theme.

For instance, if you can't make your outline fit your thesis exactly, it may be wise not to force a perfect fit. Theses and outlines are tools for shaping materials, and sometimes materials refuse to be perfectly shaped. If you think it is necessary, try changing the thesis to fit the outline or changing both to fit each other. But don't change them so much that you distort the truths in your subject.

Sometimes, you may have trouble following the outline as you write the theme. This may mean that the outline is poorly made—inspect it for logic and order. But this may also mean that a "logic of writing" is (legitimately) taking over. A piece of writing often seems to develop an order and a coherence all its own that are determined partly by the subject and partly by the way you choose to organize it. If you like the way your theme is going, and its new direction appears to be appealing and honest, consider changing the outline to fit fresh developments. Outlines are helpful and good, but they are not written on tablets of stone.

PRACTICE

1. From two themes, we borrowed the outlines and scrambled their main and subordinate points. Also, we took their theses and combined them into the list of points. After writing each item on a single note card, rearrange each list into a logical outline. Put the thesis above the outline. For the sake of clarity or consistency, rewrite any items you wish.

    a. The following scrambled items are on the topic of college students and politics. We suggest that you use the mixed outline for this particular Practice—put the main points, using roman numerals, in complete-sentence form, and the subordinate points in topic form.

        1. Students often do not know or understand the issues in important political campaigns.
        2. Average student load: 15 to 18 semester hours
        3. Foreign policy too complicated for students
        4. Students are immature in their political judgments.
        5. Local issues usually unfamiliar to students
        6. Many laws understood only as a personal affair ("how it affects me")
        7. College students have neither the time, the knowledge, nor the

maturity to be politically active outside the university.

8. Containment of communism complex historically
9. Preparation—two hours for each hour spent in class
10. Limited knowledge of national social issues
11. The Middle East a complicated issue
12. Students too hasty in their judgments
13. Many students work 10 to 20 hours a week to make money.
14. Students prone to use politics as an exciting drug
15. National issues only superficially understood
16. 60 hours total per week excluding time for relaxation
17. Students need all their time for study classwork, and (in some cases) earning money.

b. For the following items on the subject of clocks as a hobby, we suggest that you use the sentence outline.

1. Clocks vary in materials and type.
2. Clocks are easy to repair.
3. My mother likes my clocks and proudly shows them off to friends.
4. I sell some clocks to dealers.
5. Thousands of old clocks need repair.
6. It's easy to get information on repair.
7. Clock-repair tools are readily available and inexpensive.
8. I make about $90 a month doing repair work.
9. If you want an interesting and profitable hobby, take up clock repair.
10. Types of movements show interesting variations.
11. There is a service gap in clock repair.
12. The "time side" of the clock movement is the same in almost every clock.
13. Clocks reflect a nation's culture.
14. Clocks are interesting.
15. Clock repair is profitable.

2. Pick out the thesis from the list of items in Practice **1a** and respond to it by answering, qualifying, or attacking it. Put your response in a thesis and write an outline of 15 to 20 items. Use whatever outline form you feel comfortable with.

3. Write a theme using the outline you prepared for **2**.

4. After you have decided on a specific thesis, create an outline based on the card system suggested on pp. 32–33; and then write the theme from the outline. Do not be afraid to modify your thesis and your outline as you write. Remember that both thesis and outline are only aids to writing. If your theme takes a legitimate turn (in responding to the assignment) that is not represented in your thesis and outline, change them. In your outline, keep at least your major headings in the full-sentence form.

4 Developing Themes: Seven Strategies

As we have indicated in previous chapters, writing situations are not all alike. Each of them tends to present its own problems. For this reason you need to investigate every situation carefully and create a special *stance* that will work best for it.

But while stances and writing situations may often vary greatly, your choices of methods for developing themes and papers are somewhat more limited. Let's consider some typical choices. Assume, for the sake of this discussion, that you have a subject and a stance. You are the student member of your college Student Union's governing board. The other six members are from the faculty and the administration. You want greater student representation on the board, and you are addressing your request to the vice-president of the college. In supporting your thesis, you have seven main strategies (or several combinations of these) for developing the ideas in your request.

1. *Personal experience* — an account of your term on the board and the meaning of your experiences there.

2. *Definition* — an extended definition of the term *governing board* in relation to your particular college Union.

3. *Cause and effect* — an analysis of the reasons why you believe the board would be more efficient and serve the students better if it had greater student representation. You claim, in other words, that certain causes would have certain effects.

4. *Process* — an account of the step-by-step procedures of the board in gaining a particular *end point* (the governing of the Union).

5. *Analogy* — an extended comparison designed to clarify the nature of the Union and its problems. The comparison, in this case, might be made with the Stadium Committee, which successfully maintains a 50 – 50 ratio between student and nonstudent representatives.

6. *Classification* — an analysis of certain groupings of governing bodies in the college, such as college senates, athletic supervisory boards, fraternity councils, dormitory councils, etc.

7. *Comparison-Contrast*—an explanation of how the Union is more (or less) efficiently administered than the Union at X College.

How can you consider these strategies of development and how should you make your choices among them?

First, bear in mind that each strategy is simply a way of supporting a thesis, of making a point that you wish your reader to consider carefully. If, for example, you use personal experience and recount your experiences on the board, you do so mainly to convince your reader that it needs more student representation. Or, if you choose the comparison-contrast strategy, it should serve the purpose of making your reader agree with this thesis, or at least of having him see the point you are trying to make.

Second, as you choose a strategy, let the other elements of your writer's stance (your *role* and your *reader*) help you in your choice. For instance, if your reader does not have personal knowledge about college student unions and how they are run, one solution might be to write a paper using the *process* strategy to help him understand the problem. If, on the other hand, he is familiar with the Stadium Committee but not the governing board of the Union, you can draw an analogy to convince him that the Union should be governed like the Stadium.

Whether your choice is a good one often depends on the nature of your subject. Certain subjects seem to call for certain methods of development; for example:

1. Subject: Trying out for a play
   Thesis: Even though I study the lines beforehand, whenever I read for a part my voice control is poor because a tryout is an unusual acting situation.
  Strategy: Personal experience

2. Subject: "Pass/fail" courses
   Thesis: "Pass/fail" courses are an educational opportunity to study a subject without having to face the pressure of a conventional grading system.
  Strategy: Definition (of the term)

3. Subject: Nervous headaches
   Thesis: My husband's headaches are caused by the pressures of having to meet strict course deadlines.
  Strategy: Cause and effect

4. Subject: Running for student office
   Thesis: There are three important steps in running for student office: applying, campaigning, and developing a constituency.

5. *Subject:* Hand guns
   Thesis: Like automobiles, hand guns are dangerous but controllable mechanisms.
   Strategy: Analogy

6. *Subject:* Nonflowering house plants
   Thesis: Of the nonflowering house plants, succulents and cacti are the easiest to grow in a dry climate.
   Strategy: Classification

7. *Subject:* Two science-fiction movies
   Thesis: *Star Wars* is a movie with a thin plot, unconvincing characters, and bizarre situations; *Close Encounters of the Third Kind* is a film with a strong plot, realistic characters, and situations based on actual happenings.
   Strategy: Comparison-contrast

Proper use of the seven strategies can help you express your ideas precisely and efficiently, and after you have learned to employ them you will find that writing most themes and papers is much easier. You may—and you should—use the strategies in combination. (We separate them here in our discussion only so that you can see more clearly how they work.) In dealing with the subject of running for student office, for example, it is likely that you could use the personal experience of others along with process. In managing the subject of hand guns, you might need to employ the strategies of definition, analogy, and comparison-contrast. While you will probably use one of the strategies as the main unifying principle behind your theme, you will often employ some of the others in creating your supporting material.

Strategy 1
Personal Experience

Any personal experience theme you write is likely to be a narrative. Such papers are usually short, from 500 to 1000 words. Since you cannot describe your whole life in so few words, you must limit your subject and narrow your thesis considerably. Essentially, there are two kinds of personal experience themes.

The first kind deals with a *single thread* of happenings in your life—something that is woven into the fabric of your past and is important to you. Your "thread of happenings" may have to do with a hobby, a personal relationship, an idea, the result of an accident, an ambition, a physical defect. What the thread is does not matter, so long as it can be traced for a period of time and has some significance.

In such a paper, you cover only those events and persons that relate closely to the thread you are discussing. Here are three examples of subjects and thesis statements:

a. *A hobby:* For many teenagers, repairing a car is only a hobby, but for me it became in high school a full-time paying job that allowed me to go to college.
b. *A relationship:* Because I was the only woman in my crowd who wanted to be a doctor, the members of the Women's Liberation Group looked to me for leadership.
c. *An ambition:* Computer programming in my spare time in high school gave me the incentive to work in a field I hadn't previously considered as an occupation.

The second kind of personal experience theme is one in which you concentrate on a *particular event* that has had an influence on your life. But you cannot simply narrate something that happened to you and call the result a theme; the event must be explained and analyzed. In other words, it is not only the event itself that you need to develop but also your later reactions to it. Here are some examples of thesis statements for this kind of theme:

a. The last time my grandmother came to visit, she made me realize how many "faults" I had acquired since the last time I saw her.
b. I saw Henry Mancini play only once, but that one concert spurred me to become a pianist.
c. Falling off a horse and breaking a leg was an interesting experience, but it has done nothing whatever for my character.

You are the best authority about yourself. You know more about your own experiences and their effect on your life than anyone else. If you keep in mind the following advice about personal experience themes, you will find that writing them will give you an opportunity to use some genuinely creative techniques.

Choose a "thread" or an event that has a point. Each of us has had at one time or another a friend or acquaintance who goes on and on about his experiences. But his stories never get anywhere. Our reaction to them is, "So what? Why are you telling me all this?" In order for you to avoid this kind of reaction from your reader, narrow your thesis so that your theme has meaning for you *and* your reader.

Make your experience come to life. Use dialogue if you wish to show an interaction or conflict between people, but don't overuse it so that your theme reads like a film script. Describe the scene or situation with detail, using sensory impressions of touch, smell, sight, hearing, and taste. Try to build some suspense if possible. Use vivid words to show emotional and physical response. (See pp. 126–138 for more advice on vivid writing.)

PRACTICE

1. The two student themes below are examples of the two kinds of personal experience papers. The first one centers on an important event. The second one describes a "thread of happenings." Study the themes and judge how well the writers use detail and organization to tell the reader about themselves.

An Unforgettable Experience

[1]During the summer between my seventh and eighth grades in junior high, my parents sent me to a YWCA camp at Grass Lake. I was happy to go because I liked all the activities of boating, swimming, and crafts that would be provided. Although I did not know any other girls who were going to that particular camp, I felt confident that I would soon make friends. I imagined that the camp experience would be free and joyous; it was to be my first summer away from home and my expectations of youthful pleasures, happiness, and shared enthusiasms were great. When I arrived I was assigned to a cabin with five other girls. Nothing occurred during the early hours to make me less enthusiastic. Although none of my cabin mates were very friendly, I felt that any reserve would disappear in the camp experience.

[2]During the first week the girls in my cabin were polite to me and boisterous and friendly to each other. They all had one common experience—all were members of the same junior-high school and its swim team. It was obvious that they were a tight little clique, and since I did not belong to it, I was only a person who did not really exist for them.

[3]I became the minority of one. I could never understand their allusions and jokes; I was made to feel that my presence was tolerated and, finally, even to feel that I was intensely disliked. I have never been wholly sure of what I represented to the girls. In some way I seemed to threaten them, their amusements, their activities. Although they shunned me, they could not seem to forget my presence and I could never be sure of a peaceful hour totally free of annoyance.

[4]For some reason, witless enough, I continued to hope that at least one of the girls would change her attitude toward me and that I could have one friend. After six weeks, all of my attempts to make friends had been rebuffed. One day one of them took me aside and suggested that all of us sneak out and go swimming from the rowboat while the other campers had their cabin rest period. To say that my heart leaped at the suggestion seems silly now, but that is what happened. I knew that it was against the rules, but I was willing to take the chance because I felt that then the rest of the summer would be golden and warm with friendship.

[5]On the lake that afternoon, we swam freely around the rowboat, one girl always staying in the boat. Finally, I was the last person still in the water and, as I started to climb back into the boat, one of the girls took off her shoe, a brown loafer, and began hammering at my fingers where I

clutched the side of the boat. I tried to hang on; I was terrified and quickly reached a point of hysteria and exhaustion. She beat at my fingers until my hands bled and I cried for help. The others watched passively although with quiet satisfaction. I knew that I would die, that I would drown without any one of them attempting to stop it. I pulled my hands away and began the long swim to shore. The girls in the boat rowed after me, their pursuit giving me the strength to swim as fast as I could. When the boat moved along side of me, my instinctive response was to attempt to dive deep into the water, anything to get away from them. One of them caught hold of me by the strap of my bathing suit and pulled me into the boat. I could not look at any of them and when we reached shore we all went silently to our cabin. I walked slightly apart from the rest.

6Since we had broken the rules about leaving camp without a counselor, I could not report my experience to anyone. All I could do was hide in my cabin, nursing my injured fingers until I could get my parents to take me home. I had little to say to the counselors or any other girls. In a few days I left with my parents.

7I do not know, looking back, what there was in me, in the projection of my personality, that affected the other girls so that they hated me enough, if hatred it was, to wish me harm. It was my first experience with irrationality and savagery. I dream of it still.

My Life with Snakes

1Let me say first that, like the typical layman who knows nothing about reptiles, I had always been scared stiff of snakes. On my grandparents' farm I always kept far away from the "slimy" creatures when my grandfather encountered them while we were making hay. I operated on the theory that you could never tell when one of the darned things was going to turn out to be a rattler, and even if he didn't, who wanted to fraternize with a snake anyway? With that kind of background, imagine my feelings when in my high-school zoology class I found a snake cage next to my seat. It didn't help my concentration on the subject to look out of the corner of my eye and see an unblinking-eyed green snake darting his forked tongue in my direction.

2When we got to the study of reptiles, I could hardly help being interested if only out of self-preservation. Our teacher listed a number of common misconceptions about snakes and administered antidotes of factual information. He ended one day's lecture by inviting any of us who were interested to come in after school and watch the snakes being fed. I figured I had nothing to lose so I attended, probably out of the same motivation that causes people to watch movies such as *Frankenstein* — morbid curiosity.

3The feeding session turned out be far less morbid and sensational than I had supposed, although it was interesting. Land snails, worms, and small frogs were forcibly pushed into the mouths of the snakes, which tended to lack appetites in captivity. I found out that feeding took place infrequently because of the fact that snakes have a low rate of metabolism and can therefore live a long time on little food. I asked a lab assistant about the use of the forked tongue and was told that it was more or less an aid to the sense of smell. Perhaps thinking I was more interested than I was, the lab assistant invited me to accompany him on a field trip the next Saturday. Several of us bicycled to a nearby stone quarry, where we were lucky enough to find a red milk snake, very rare in our area.

⁴The interest I had discovered spread to other reptiles and amphibians, and I was soon on the trail of turtles and frogs as well as snakes. I found myself reading a great deal about *herpetology* (the science of reptiles and amphibians) and getting more and more engrossed in the field. My mother became dismayed as our basement filled with cages of live crawling things and neatly labeled jars of specimens preserved in alcohol.

⁵By the time I was a senior in high school, I realized that this interest was too strong to remain a mere hobby. I made plans to go to college and major in zoology. When I complete my undergraduate work, I would like to get an M.S. degree and then seek work in a museum.

⁶I often think about the casual way in which I found my life work. If I had not gone to the zoology room to watch the snakes eat, I might have spent the whole semester loathing the snake whose cage was near my dissecting table and then gone on to forget all about him, never coming to know about the field that is now my deepest interest.

2. Using what you have learned from this section, write a brief personal experience theme of 500 to 1000 words. Limit your subject and be specific. Center your theme on a *significant* thread or event in your life. But do not merely narrate an anecdote or a story.

3. Here are introductions from personal experience essays that students have written. Choose one, adapt it to your own experience, and write an essay using the adaptation as your introduction.

   a. I'm the patient, easy-going type, calm in emergencies, afraid of nothing, indifferent to change. In my judgment it would take a lot to get me rattled. That's why I can hardly believe that I could get so irritated with another person's irresponsibility (or some other trait), but I did.

   b. Sometimes I find it hard to believe that I am the same person who sat, two years ago, in Teacher X's class. No one who knew me during my obnoxious but popular days would believe it either. No one who had not been there to see my_____conduct in the classroom could see how much I have changed. In the past, I have been too ashamed to discuss the matter, but I will remember it forever.

   c. Let's get one thing straight right away: I am not a fighter. I am a peaceful person, who has always enjoyed being a _____.

   d. It's high time someone debunked the Great Beauty Parlor Myth. The notion persists that women go hippity-hop to the beauty shop for the sheer joy of it.

   e. Marriage is (is not) one of my main goals in life.

Strategy 2 Definition

[handwritten: 189 Patorn Exposition 2A Virtono]

[handwritten: assignment 45-53 for mon.]

[handwritten: 250 WORD PAPER DUE MONDAY]

Consider this student's paragraph:

It is now fashionable for attacks to be made on 24-hour visitation in college dormitories. Usually such attacks are made on the grounds of morality. Yet the question is really not one of morality but of *privacy*. A private person is one who is sheltered from the public and from other people, who may not intrude upon him without permission. *Privacy* involves a certain amount of seclusion and isolation; one can't be private in Folsom Stadium. A dorm room is private in the same way that a man's home, which he has paid for, is private. What people do in both homes and dorm rooms is a matter of their *privacy,* not of public morality.

In this paragraph, we find many of the typical characteristics and uses of definition:

1. Definition works in a context of an event, situation, disagreement, etc. Notice that the student's definition of *privacy* takes into account the reader's knowledge about controversial co-ed dormitories. You will hook your reader if you relate your definition to his experience.

2. Definition clarifies an ambiguous situation by clearly explaining the key term (or terms) your essay is based on. You ordinarily define in order to support a thesis convincingly and to get your reader to see the point you are trying to make. In the paragraph above, the writer is taking a student's role and is moving toward a defense of 24-hour visitation, the argument being directed at a typical opponent of the plan.

3. Definition *explains, limits,* and *specifies;* the rest of this section shows you how.

4. Definition is a part of the writer's attempt to give a truthful account of what a thing, act, or idea is really like. *Defining is another strategy for getting at the truth.*

PRACTICE

1. After you have read the following passage, answer the questions given after it for class discussion.

¹Ernst Haeckel, a 19th-century zoology professor, created the word. While promoting Darwin's theories of evolution he hammered together two Greek fragments, and *oecology* had its beginning. In recent years few words have been so ill-used as the professor's brainchild.

²After Haeckel coined it in 1869, *ecology* (the initial *o* was soon dropped) lay around quietly for a time. Then botanists rummaging in the academic attic discovered it and put it back in service. *Ecology* then, and theoretically still, is the study of the relationships between living things

and their environment and the effect of various life forms on one another. Take any animal or plant as an example, and other animals and plants constitute an important part of its environment, *e.g.,* fox and rabbit, woodpecker and oak. Ecology is a science of the present, the immediate. In the time it takes for one to say DDT, patterns and relationships change and new ones are created. Since the subject in its entirety is beyond our present powers of comprehension, scientists in the field have sensibly avoided calling themselves ecologists.

[3]It is too late to finger the responsible individuals, but in the mid-1950's media men trying to sound scientific or scientists trying to sound like media men seized the tender word and fragile concept and began to peddle it publicly. The age of pop ecology had begun. It was a fad, like keeping gerbils. All sorts of people—politicians, preachers, boy scouts, revolutionaries, ad men, fashion designers, corporate executives, housewives, teachers—went out and got themselves a little ecology. Sometimes the faddists collected two ecological concepts, bred them, so to speak, and began to sell or give away the mongrel offspring.

[4]In 1950, for example, the *Readers' Guide to Periodical Literature* included only four references under the subject heading Ecology. Twenty years later there were four dozen such listings. By 1965 few publications did not feel obliged to make a passing reference to the magic word. Like an all-purpose seasoning, ecology was sprinkled on essays about poverty, racism, dope smuggling, military strategy, professional football, etc. Suddenly there were ecology T-shirts, soaps, executives, fund-raisers, lawyers, lobbyists. Civil disturbances in the name of ecology popped up all over the landscape like mushrooms after a warm spring rain.

[5]A society for the prevention of cruelty to words and ideas should be established, though it is, no doubt, too late to save ecology. We have trifled with it to the point that it has become an irrevocably loose and fallen word. However, while the intellectual atrocity is still fresh, there is perhaps some value in recalling how we have heartlessly overworked and mutilated this interesting and useful concept.—Bil Gilbert, "Gospel of False Prophets"

a. Most definitions of any length contain a thesis. What is Gilbert's thesis? Where is it located? Why?

b. Why does Gilbert bother with relating the history of the term *ecology?*

c. We listed four "characteristics and uses" of definition. In light of these, discuss paragraph 2 in detail.

d. Does paragraph 3 contribute to Gilbert's definition? To his argument? Why or why not?

e. What do expressions like "peddle it publicly" and "mongrel offspring" contribute to the essay?

f. Can you think of other words that need "a society for the prevention of cruelty to words"? What do such words have in common?

g. What is the *context* of Gilbert's definition? Is it literary? Philosophical? Social? Political? Historical? Why might his context be important?

h. What is Gilbert's writer's stance?

i. Are you convinced by Gilbert's argument? Why or why not?

2. Consider question **f** above. Write a paper on a word (or words) that you think needs "a society for the prevention of cruelty to words."

TECHNIQUES OF DEFINING

Now that you know something about definition, here are five practical techniques for getting the ordinary jobs of defining done. We will keep our discussion of each quite brief. All of them could be expanded by adding more examples and details.

Definition by Negation

This method of definition entails explaining what something is *not*. A *bucket* is not a "scoop." *Cool* is not "hot." *Liberty* does not mean "license." *Education* has little to do with "training." Negative definitions are useful because they allow you to narrow your general area of definition. You can use them at the beginning of an extended definition to cut out inapplicable areas of meaning, as the writer does in this definition of *humanities:*

> At this point a definition is in order. Negatively, the humanities are those areas which are not included in the sciences and the social sciences. But I like to be positive. The humanities, then, embrace — and I think the word appropriate — literature, languages, history, music, art, and philosophy. Originally the humanities meant only the classics; the list of subjects has been properly lengthened. In broader terms, the humanities acquaint man with the thoughts, creations, and actions of his predecessors through the ages and mankind around him. They tell him about his roots and his origins and his neighbors. They impel him to ask questions and to seek answers to them: Who am I? Where have I come from? What is the meaning of life? What can I do to become and remain an effective, responsible member of society? They have to do with making man more human. — Charles Keller. "The Wave of the Present"

Definition by Classification (Logical Definition)

In defining by classification, you put the term to be defined in its *class* (of things, people, activities, or ideas). Then you explain how the term *differs* from other terms in the same class. Examples:

Term	Class	Differences
Epic [is]	narrative poetry	"of exalted style, celebrating heroic adventures, mythical or historical, in poems of considerable length." — *Oxford Companion to Classical Literature*
Bucket [is]	a domestic carrying utensil	deep and round, with a curved handle that fits into the hand, used for carrying fluids, especially water and milk.
Liberty [is]	a human condition, mainly political and mainly negative	that has to do with those freedoms that are neither social, nor religious, nor private; it consists simply of being let alone by the people who have the temporary powers of government.

For logical definitions to be useful, neither class nor differences should be too broadly stated. The class for epic is *narrative poetry*, not simply *poetry*. The class for bucket is *domestic carrying utensil*, not just *domestic utensil* or *carrying utensil*. The list of differences should be complete enough so that the term is clearly distinguished from other terms.

Definition by Illustration or Example

You can sometimes employ, implicitly or explicitly, *illustration* or *example* to aid in your definition. That is, you can define a thing by giving an example of it. What is an epic poem? *The Iliad, The Odyssey,* and *Paradise Lost* are examples. What do I mean by "a great baseball player"? I mean someone like Joe DiMaggio or Rod Carew. Defining by illustration or example gives you a simple but incomplete meaning; consequently, you should use this method with at least one of the others.

Definition by Synonym

There are no perfect synonyms. Every word is at least slightly different from every other word. But it is possible to define a word by using another word that is similar in meaning. Examples: A *herald* is a "forerunner." *Honor,* in various senses, may be "homage," "reverence," or "deference." *Cool* may mean "composed," "collected," "unruffled," "nonchalant," "unfriendly," or "not warm." Like defining by illustration or example, this is a specialized approach that you should ordinarily use with at least one of the other methods.

Definition by Operation

You define by operation when you state what something does or how it works: a bucket is a round, deep container, hung from a curved handle, that is used for carrying water, milk, etc. Liberty allows one to say or do what he pleases without injuring others. Education is an attempt to discipline the mind so that it can act intelligently on its own.

If sufficiently detailed, the operational definition is valuable because it gives you a practical check on the reality or truth behind a definition. For example, the word *traitor* has been defined as "someone who deserts his country." This is a limited operational definition. But the definition does not take into account the possibility that one's country might be, like certain dictatorships, deserving of desertion. This last idea gives us an *operational check* on the definition of *traitor* and allows us to add a clause to the definition: A traitor "is someone who deserts his country when his country both needs and deserves his allegiance." Observe that the added clause is itself operational. If someone does not accept our operational check on the definition of *traitor*, we can ask him to provide his own check, and then we can argue the matter with him.

AVOID ERRORS IN DEFINING

Many errors are caused by the writer's not limiting his definition sufficiently. Consider this definition, which is both logical and operational: "A belt is a thing that a man wears around his waist to keep his trousers up." As a class, *thing* is not limited enough; for it does not take into account what sort of "thing" a belt may be. One can hold up his pants with rope, but that fact does not make the rope a belt. On the other hand, the rest of the definition is too limited because it does not take into account that women often wear belts to hold up "trousers" and that belts have many other uses. The process of limiting in the logical definition should be done in two steps—first limit the *class*, then limit the *differences*.

Perhaps the commonest errors in defining are made by writers who do not realize that their definitions must fit reality. The final question to ask yourself is: Am I telling the truth about this word? If you define *monarchy* as a "contemporary government ruled by a king for his own selfish purposes," you are in danger of being untruthful; for this definition would fit badly, to give only one example, the English constitutional monarchy. The writer who defined *individualism* as "the need of every person to be honored by others" not only blurred the meaning of *individualism* but also stated an untruth about the nature of an important idea. If a student defines *fraternity* epigrammatically as "a snob co-op," is he really being truthful about the fraternities on his campus and about fraternity life in general? The fraternity man may answer that the definition does not fit fraternity life as he knows it, that the definition is not "true." This does not mean that the point is unarguable; it means rather that the students are going to have to agree on the reality behind their definitions before they can get anywhere with their debate.

SOME FINAL SUGGESTIONS FOR DEFINING

In most instances, you will use definition in one of two ways. In the first way, you define a term at the beginning of a theme and then go on to develop your ideas by different methods. In the second, you devote much of your theme to an extended definition, part of which may actually supply your thesis. Sometimes you will need to combine these two ways.

Common to both of them are certain useful practices you should follow:

1. If a term you use is likely to cause confusion, define it when you first use it. If the term is important to your theme and its thesis, define it in the introduction. Don't make your reader guess at what you mean by a particular word or phrase.

2. Look to your dictionary for help, but don't use it as a crutch. Do not merely quote dictionary definitions because they are easy to copy into a theme. Before using them, make sure that they apply to your theme and to the situation you are discussing.

3. Understand the techniques of defining and how they work. Keep in mind, for example, that defining by negation is particularly useful for cutting out inapplicable areas of word meanings.

4. Make your definitions reasonably complete by using as many techniques of defining as are necessary. Remember that the techniques work very well in combination.

5. Run an "operational check" on your definition. Be sure that the definition fits reality — that it is *true*.

Most of your defining will be rather informal. Perhaps for many themes you will need no more than a few words in the first or second paragraph stating how you are using a particular word or phrase. For example: "By *teachers' union* I mean an organization similar to a trade union in which the workers organize to protect their economic interests."

But some themes will require a more detailed or extended definition, as in this early paragraph of a student's paper:

Before I continue, I must explain how I am using *courage* in this paper. As G. K. Chesterton wrote, the idea of courage is "almost a contradiction in terms. It means a strong desire to live taking the form of readiness to die." This paradox is inherent in true courage, which is not fearlessness or ordinary heroism—for a person who knows no fear has no choices to make. Nor is courage mere physical bravery coming from a stout heart (*courage* goes back to an ancient Latin word meaning "heart"). Courage is a form of choice-making. When someone is afraid, and still makes a choice to perform an act of bravery, he is being courageous.

PRACTICE

1. Define each of the following items by (1) indicating its general class or category, and (2) providing specific differences (examples or details) that distinguish it from other items in its class.

house	tennis
pond	yellow
anger	surgeon
noun	democracy

2. Write a brief analysis of each definition given below. What are the techniques of defining being used? Do you see any errors in defining? How would you improve and rewrite any definition that you consider weak or unrealistic? (You may wish to check your dictionary as you go along.)

    a. *Shortening* is something you put in a cake to make it better.
    b. *Marriage* is the ceremony of uniting two people in holy wedlock.
    c. A *dog* is a canine.
    d. *Integration* is the getting of people together for political freedom.
    e. A *thermocouple* is a temperature-sensing instrument made of two dissimilar metals.
    f. Technology is simply the knack of doing things with objects that are not part of your body. If you try to crack a nut with a rock, you are employing technology.—an ad for an electronics corporation from the *Wall Street Journal.*
    g. A book is *obscene* if it is totally without redeeming social importance and appeals entirely to the reader's prurient interest.
    h. When we come to accurate measurement, we find that the word "hard" has dozens of slightly different meanings. The most usual test of hardness in steels is that of Brinell. A very hard steel ball of 10 millimetres diameter is pressed onto a steel plate for 30 seconds with a load of 3 tons. The hardness number decreases with the depth of the indentation.—J. B. S. Haldane, *A Banned Broadcast and Other Essays*
    i. [What is meant by *life*? A thing is *alive* when] it does a minimum of

four things: it eats "foreign" substances which differ to a greater or lesser degree from its own body tissue. Then it "digests" these substances, and assimilates them into its body, which produces some waste material that is ejected. Furthermore, it "grows": it increases in size and bulk up to a certain point, which is different for different life forms. Finally, it "propagates": it produces, or reproduces, its own kind. — Willy Ley, "Life on Other Planets"

j. The idea that, since democracy is defective, it ought to be abolished, is an example of the commonest error in political philosophy, which I call "utopianism." By "utopianism" I mean the idea that there is a perfect constitution, and politics could be perfect. The last of our democratic duties which I shall mention is to avoid utopianism. Politics are and always will be a creaking, groaning, lumbering, tottering wagon of wretched makeshifts and sad compromises and anxious guesses; and political maturity consists in knowing this in your bones — Richard Robinson, *An Atheist's Values*

3. Below is a statement that contains definitions and a thesis. Write a response to it; agree or disagree with the writer wholly or in part. Include your own thesis and definitions in your response. Use as many of the techniques of defining as you think are necessary.

[1] . . . Our appetite for Getting There First has helped us to greatness as a Nation, but it also tempts us into national habits which threaten to pull us apart.

[2] An everyday example is the desperate quest for TV programs that are "relevant." But what people call "relevance" is not really that at all. What they are talking about most of the time is not the relevant but the topical

[3] *Topical* (from the Greek word "topos" for place) means that which is special to some particular place or time. "Topics of the Day" are the events which, having just happened, are peculiar to that day. We like to read or hear about them because they remind us that we are alive, that there is something special to our lifetime. The topical reinforces our mood with an exclamation point, but does not enlarge or illuminate. Hear this! See that! That's what we say when we point to something topical. On TV, characteristic statements of the topical are the video-taped clips of the day's events offered staccato on the news. The topical event — an earthquake, an airplane hijacking, a hotel fire or an assassination — is announced and diffused, but seldom explained at the time.

[4] The *relevant* is something quite different. "Relevant" comes from the Latin "relevans," which means lifting or raising. To show the relevance of something is to lift it above the current of daily topics, to connect it with distant events and larger issues. The search for relevance is a search for connections that don't at first meet the eye, that will be just as valid — and even more interesting — tomorrow and the day after.

[5] A topical fact becomes every moment less newsworthy. But a historical event is always growing in historical significance. The American

Revolution became more interesting after the French Revolution, and both became still more so after the Russian Revolution and after the Chinese Revolution and after President Nixon's visit to Communist China. . . .

⁶What we need are fewer talk shows, fewer interviews and discussions, fewer odd-ball quizzes, fewer celebrity say-so's. And fewer newscasts.

⁷We need programs that bring us less of the "up-to-the-minute" stuff, which every passing minute makes obsolete, and more knowledge. Fewer "situation comedies" and situation tragedies, but more comedy and more tragedy. Fewer reports of today's catastrophe, fewer cliches of today's "burning issues" and deeper visual documentation.

⁸In a word, what we need are more programs about something, and fewer programs about everything. More programs about how something really happened, how the world has changed and is changing. More about people who do things and make things, about how they're done and made, and less about people who say the kooky and do the ridiculous.

⁹TV will help bring us together—by shared knowledge and common understanding. TV will then be less a solvent and more a cement in our American community. That is what we have tried to offer in "Getting There First."—Daniel J. Boorstin, "Too Much Too Soon."

4. Definition skills are especially important when you must write a discussion of something that you know well but your reader does not. For instance, if you are writing a proposal to air-condition a house and you wish to explain why the house requires a 36,000 BTU central unit, you should define *BTU* (British Thermal Unit) in some fashion so that the owner will be convinced that he needs the particular unit you recommend.

Pick a subject you know fairly well and write a theme on it in which you define terms that the ordinary reader may not be familiar with—your subject can be anything from clarinet playing to fixing engines. Pick a stance, and convince your reader to do or believe something. At the beginning, define any terms necessary to your thesis.

Strategy 3
Cause and Effect

Cause and *effect* (or simply *causation*) refers to a specific relationship between events in time. If you fail to look both ways before crossing a street and get hit by a car, the *cause* is failing to look and the *effect* is getting hit. If a doctor tells you that you have a broken leg from the accident, the broken leg is the effect of getting hit by the car, which is the cause. An event (in this case, the accident) can be *both* a cause and an effect of other events.

RECOGNIZING THE SIGNS OF CAUSATION

In order to identify and determine whether or not a cause-and-effect relationship is logical, you should look for certain signs. Two of the most common are:

The Sign of Association. Suppose you find two events, A and B, in association. Their being together could imply that A causes B, or vice versa. However, B must ordinarily occur whenever A does—otherwise you probably don't have a genuine cause-and-effect relationship. For instance, hair should bleach when a strong solution of peroxide is applied to it; the cook should burn his hand every time he touches a very hot skillet handle.

The Sign of Time-Sequence. If B comes after A in time, this fact may imply a causal relationship. If a student stays up all night studying, the fatigue he suffers the next day is an effect signaled by time. But determining time-sequence is so tricky that a special name has been given to the fallacy of misinterpreting it. The fallacy is called *post hoc* (short for *post hoc, ergo propter hoc*—"after this, therefore because of this"). You create the *post hoc* fallacy if you say that A causes B merely because B comes after A. In other words, if the 8:30 train comes after the 8:15 train, you cannot say that the earlier train "causes" the later one.

In brief, the signs of causation are no more than signs—they are not proofs. To avoid making fallacies in thinking about causation, you must take each sign and investigate it carefully. Never assume that a causal relationship exists until you find proof.

Here are four types of cause-and-effect sequences that you should be aware of:

One cause ———————————————→ One effect

One cause ———————————————→ Two or more effects

Two or more causes ———————————————→ One effect

Two or more causes ———————————————→ Two or more effects

In most situations, more than one cause or effect is involved. Drug addiction, for example, may have several causes, and these causes may have more than a single effect.

PRACTICE

Prepare some notes for class discussion on the short autobiographical piece below. (1) Look for any *signs* of causation. (2) State any reasonably clear *causes* you find, and any reasonably clear *effects*. Do you find any of the four *classes* of causation operating in Bettelheim's account? (3) What is Bettelheim's *thesis*?

[1]Families can take many forms as long as they serve the needs of children. A few years ago, I studied the Israeli *kibbutzim*, the collective communities, for a short time. Here children do not live with their parents; they are raised in groups. One of the most important factors in the lives of the children, though, is that they constantly visit both parents at work. And when the children come, everybody stops working and explains to the children what they're doing and why it is important to them and to the community. Through that experience, the child gains respect for the work of the parents. People have wondered how *kibbutz* children grow up so well when their parents are distant figures. The answer is that, while there are only a few basic needs, there are many ways to satisfy them.

[2]A child need not be raised by his biological parents. Freud made so much of the Oedipus complex or Oedipal situation that many people believe a male child *must* have a jealous desire for his mother and an envious hatred for his father in order to grow up normally. But there has been much argument among anthropologists about whether or not this Oedipal relationship really exists in all societies. As I see it, the chief thing is to understand the basic principle underlying the Oedipus phenomenon, which is applicable to any family structure. The human infant for many years is entirely dependent upon and in the power of some individual or individuals. If you're in someone's power, for better or worse you have to come to terms with that person. If the person doesn't abuse his power, you come to love him. But in whose power the child is, and with whom he has to come to terms, can vary greatly.

[3]Consider my own history. Today, I teach psychoanalysis at the University of Chicago and, of course, my students read Freud on the subject of how all-important a child's mother is. After I've let them expound on the subject, I try to open their minds a bit more by telling them some of my personal story. During my early childhood, the person who fed me, took care of me and was with me most of the time was not my mother but a wet nurse. This was a custom among the upper-middle classes in Vienna at the time. The nurse was a peasant girl in her late teens, who had just had a baby out of wedlock. She left the baby with relatives and hired herself out to suckle the child of a well-to-do family. To make sure she gave a lot of

milk, she followed the folklore formula of drinking a lot of beer. So my entire care as an infant was entrusted to a girl who had little education, was by our standards a sex delinquent, was a little high on beer most of the time and was so devoid of maternal instinct that she left her own child. I am the deplorable result.

⁴The reasons why a relationship that, according to theory, should have been unpromising worked so well were that the girl had no interest other than me; she took good physical care of me and, being a peasant, was without undue fastidiousness about diapering and toilet training; the beer kept her relaxed and happy; she didn't discipline me excessively and didn't overawe me intellectually. It was not an idyllic upbringing but it certainly was adequate. And because my nurse was awed by my father, I learned to look up to him by observing her. Thus I acquired respect for him without his having to discipline me directly. My father was a very gentle man, very secure in himself, so convinced of his inner authority that he never needed to make a show of it. I didn't have continual fights with my parents, because the dos and don'ts came from the nurse, somebody who wasn't much of an authority. An infant learns very early what the power relations are in his family and these hold the key to his development.

⁵My father was a good model for me. As a child, I visited him at his place of work. I spent many hours there, watching him, more often just playing. The pace of life was still leisurely enough to permit my father to drop what he was doing and explain things to me. I saw other strong men work hard. Their respect for my father and his for them, without my being aware of it, made a deep impression on me. Such experiences make identification with his father seem worth while for a boy.—Bruno Bettelheim, "The Roots of Radicalism"

SUGGESTIONS FOR WRITING CAUSATION THEMES

Causation themes are among the most demanding you will write, mainly because you should do a good deal of thinking before you start. For many subjects (particularly for those relating to social and political matters), causes and effects are ambiguous or indistinct, leaving you unsure about the truth of a matter. And so your thesis has to be carefully limited and qualified. Also, for many subjects you have the reactions of your reader to worry about because your analysis of a cause-and-effect relationship might be controversial, and your reader may not agree with you. For example, in discussions about causes and effects in race, religion, sex, and government, some readers will object to your thesis or your conclusions.

But to look at the brighter side of all this, causation is one of the most interesting and important of the strategies of development. Everyone likes to speculate on the why of things—and without such speculation we could not improve our society. We've got to know why pollution occurs, why slums exist, why some strains of corn grow better than others, why women have been discriminated against in athletics, and so on.

When planning a causation theme, you should remember this advice:

1. *Investigate your subject thoroughly, either from firsthand experience or from research.* Identifying the causes and effects in a subject that you know firsthand can be easy to do. Your dissatisfaction with your roommate, for instance, may be based on the fact that he won't do his share in keeping the apartment clean. The cause is his laziness or carelessness. The effect is your anger and frustration. But identifying the causes of pollution in Los Angeles is much more difficult because pollution is a complex problem, and without doing research, you will not know enough to write about the subject.

2. *Make up your mind about how deeply you want to analyze a cause-and-effect relationship.* Bettelheim did not feel that it was necessary to go into a long discussion of why it was a custom in Vienna to hire wet nurses or why mothers didn't nurse their own children in upper-class families. Neither did he explain at length why men in families like his held so much authority. These causes and effects might be interesting, but his purpose was to show why his wet nurse was an acceptable authority for him as a child; and the other subjects were not relevant to his discussion.

3. *Qualify your generalizations carefully when you draw cause-and-effect relationships.* Do not hesitate to use qualifiers such as "it seems to me," "it may be," or "the evidence points to." In most cause-and-effect relationships, you deal in probabilities rather than certainties, particularly when you get out of the realm of scientific subjects.

4. *Be sure that your time sequence is accurate and inclusive.* This is especially true when you are explaining scientific causes and effects. You should present the chronology of the steps as they actually occur, and you should include every important link in the chain of events in order to ensure the accuracy of your paper. Here is an effective explanation of why Mexican jumping beans jump:

> A simple examination reveals the secret of the fascinating twisting, turning and jumping of the beans. Inside each bean is a tiny yellow caterpillar, the larvae of a small moth. How does it get there? The moth lays an egg in the flower of the spurge shrub. In time the eggs hatch and the larvae are said to work their way deep into the blossom, where they are eventually encased in the seeds.
>
> The caterpillar devours a large part of the inside of the seed, so that it occupies about one fifth of the interior of its little home. To move the bean, the caterpillar grasps the silken wall of the bean with its legs and vigorously snaps its body, striking its head against the other end of the bean

and sending it this way or that. The bean may actually travel several inches at a time, or leap in the air. Some people call them bronco beans because of the way they jump.

A jumping bean may keep up its antics for as long as six months. Then the caterpillar finally emerges from its house and becomes a moth. — "Why Mexican Jumping Beans Jump," *Watchtower*

5. *Separate "sufficient" from "contributory" causes.* An event may contribute to a cause, but it will not be sufficient in itself to create an effect. Failing to add baking powder or soda to biscuit dough is *sufficient* cause for the dough's failure to rise. A *contributory* cause to the flat biscuits might be a distracting phone call you had just when you were about to add the leavening agent. However, it isn't the phone call that caused the biscuits to be flat, but rather your forgetting to add the soda or baking powder. So you separate the phone call (*contributory* cause) from the lack of leavening agent (*sufficient* cause).

6. *Do not ignore immediate effects in a chain of multiple effects.* Note this description of the multiple effects of the cholera organism.

For centuries, men had known that cholera was a fatal disease, and that it caused severe diarrhea, sometimes producing as many as thirty quarts of fluid a day. Men knew this, but they somehow assumed that the lethal effects of the disease were unrelated to the diarrhea; they searched for something else: an antidote, a drug, a way to kill the organism. It was not until modern times that cholera was recognized as a disease that killed through dehydration primarily; if you could replace a victim's water losses rapidly, he would survive the infection without other drugs or treatment. — Michael Crichton, *The Andromeda Strain*

A diagram of this chain of cause and effect might look like this:

Cholera organism (first cause)
    ↘ diarrhea (first immediate effect)
        ↘ dehydration (second immediate effect)
            ↘ death (ultimate effect)

In this case, the failure to investigate the implications of an important immediate effect led to disastrous consequences.

7. *Much of what we loosely call "cause and effect" is actually "correlation."* In the process of identifying causation, researchers study samples to see if they can establish a pattern from which a generalization can be drawn about why something occurred. For example, from many medical experiments, researchers have discovered that there is a *correlation* between high cholesterol level and heart disease. They do not conclude that high cholesterol level *causes* heart disease but that a significant *correlation* exists between the two. You may use correlation in an analysis of cause and effect, but do not identify as causes what may only be correlations.

1. Discuss the accuracy and validity of the cause-and-effect relationships in these statements:

   a. Beauty is what sells the American car, and the person we are designing it for is the American woman. We figure that 80 percent of all car purchases are really decided by women. They like the comfort and beauty of modern auto interiors.

   b. The state's experiment in the abolition of capital punishment is going badly. During the first six months of the trial period, murders are up an estimated 20 percent and there has been a rash of sex crimes against children. Two child rapists last week got life imprisonment — which practically means, in this state, parole after twenty years.

   c. *Statistic:* If you change jobs very often, your chance of having a heart attack is two or three times greater than if you stay at one job for a long time.

   d. Why do people who in private talk so pungently often write so pompously? There are many reasons: tradition, the demands of time, carelessness, the conservative influence of the secretary. Above all is the simple matter of status. Theorem: the less established the status of a person, the more his dependence on jargon. Examine the man who has just graduated from pecking out his own letters to declaiming them to a secretary and you are likely to have a man hopelessly intoxicated with the rhythm of businessese. Conversely, if you come across a blunt yes or no in a letter, you don't need to glance further to grasp that the author feels pretty firm in his chair. — William H. Whyte, "The Language of Business"

2. Describe certain effects of each of the following causes (modify the cause, if necessary):
   a. If I decide to sell my car, then. . . .
   b. If I get married this month, then. . . .
   c. If I decide to quit school and go to work full-time, then. . . .
   d. If my parents are unable to help pay my tuition next fall, then. . . .
   e. If I can move into an apartment, then. . . .
   f. If I change majors, then. . . .

3. Discuss the following student theme as an example of cause-and-effect writing. Why does the writer start her paper with a definition?

   [1]Student-watchers have long identified a common type on campus — the "joiner." I don't mean the person who belongs to the band and the Pi Phis, and maybe in her junior year joins an accounting honorary. Nor do I mean the engineer who belongs to a mere three organizations. Nothing so limiting works for the true joiner, who may belong to six or eight organizations, and who may pop up in student government as well. What makes the joiner join?

²First, he likes the limelight. Most of the groups he belongs to are visible. On the dorm council, he can be seen writing petitions, or collecting the petitions of others. In the marching band, he performs before thousands of people. In his fraternity, he is the treasurer who hounds people for money and makes long reports in meetings on the state of fraternal economy.

³As these remarks imply, he likes to run things. My sister is a joiner, and one can be sure that any group she belongs to she is president or leader of. If the group has no important office to fill, she will run it by indirection, volunteering to do this or that job, writing any necessary letters or memos, being the first one at the meeting and the last to leave. No job is too small for her to take on cheerfully. By the end of the semester, any group she joins discovers that she has become its chief bottle-washer and major spokesman. She has fulfilled her desire to control events and people.

⁴Finally, the joiner joins because he must have something to do with himself. He is a bundle of energy, and his personality needs *activity*. Have you ever seen the joiner sitting alone, perhaps in the Union, just reading a book? Sam, on the men's side of my dorm, is a joiner; and for all the time I have known him, he has never been alone. People in the dorm say that Sam even goes to the bathroom with somebody. He belongs to eight organizations, and will someday be president of the country—if he can just decide which political party to join.

4.   Occasionally, it is necessary and rhetorically useful to organize a cause-and-effect theme or paragraph by introducing the effect first, then giving an explanation of the causes. Note how the writer in the following excerpt explains why the poor have more garbage than the rich. After studying the organization of the paragraphs, write a paper in which you give the effects first, then the causes.

¹. . . low-income neighborhoods in Tucson discard 86 percent more garbage per week per household than do high-income areas, and 40 percent more waste than medium-income districts. There is a trick to that statistic. There are more people per household in low-income areas. But, even dividing on a per person basis, the poor produce more garbage than the middle class and only slightly less than the rich.

²Why? It's not so hard to figure out. The rich buy antiques, the poor buy and throw away cheap or used furniture. The rich give their old clothes to the "Goodwill," the poor buy them there, wear them out and throw them away. And it is the poor and the working people who discard most of the packaging waste. They are the ones who drink soft drinks and beer and eat low-cost canned vegetables and canned stews, fish sticks, pot pies, and T.V. dinners. And, if they eat out at all, it is at McDonalds or Burger King or Kentucky Fried Chicken, with the packaging which that entails. It is the rich who have their food flown in fresh daily from Florida

or Spain. It is the rich who eat in the fancy French restaurants with all those superb dishes prepared from scratch, sans packaging and sans disposable dinner ware. — Judd Alexander, "Truth and Consequences"

5. Using the essay by Bettelheim (pp. 55–56) as a model, describe a personal relationship that has made a lasting impression on your life. Describe the causes and effects of this relationship.

6. Pick a subject concerning your hometown. Write a theme discussing the possible cause-and-effect relationships in the subject. Possible broad subjects: crime, education, religion, prosperity, government, sports, race relations, culture, economics. (Be sure to narrow your topic.)

Strategy 4   Process

WHAT IS PROCESS?

Process is a writing strategy that describes a series of steps leading to a particular end point. One of the two basic kinds is the *artificial* process, which traces the development of a situation or set of circumstances created by human beings. The manufacture of gasoline is such a process:

Steps in Process	1. Heat the raw petroleum.
	2. Cool the resulting vapor into liquid.
	3. Use further refining processes.
	4. Blend liquids and treat chemically
	to get
End point	grades of commercial gasoline.

The second kind of process is natural, one which occurs in the world around us. An example of a natural process can be found in the preparation of birds for migration. They begin by losing some of their feathers and growing new ones, taking many trial flights, and eating a great deal to store up fat. The steps and end point in this process are:

Steps in Process	1. Molting
	2. Trial flights
	3. Building a reserve of fat
	to get
End point	ready for migration.

Here are examples of both types of process. Read each and answer the questions at the end.

[1]The marriage flight is one of the most important days in the life of an ant colony. Its date varies according to the species but, in the case of the *rufa,* it falls between May and September. On one day—and on only one day in a single season—the reproducers must leave the nest, and workers chase out any reluctant ones.

[2]They fly out on an August morning and, in the air, they mingle with the sexed ants from neighboring nests. A pursuit begins until each female offers herself to a male on a neighboring tree. Then, in turn, the males mate with her and, in so doing, they accomplish the only act for which they were created. The next day, they all will be dead and many of the females as well. Of the surviving females, some may return to their original nests. Others will be adopted by nests in need of a queen or big enough to require more than one.

[3]Finally, others will go out alone and found a new nest. The female digs herself in about five inches below the surface of the earth and carves out a cell for herself with no exit. There she lays her eggs. Some of them will become larvae, but not all—most of them serve for food for their mother and for the larvae which she chooses to raise. If winter falls, the larvae must wait until the following spring before they become ants. On the other hand, if workers are born before the cold weather sets in, they immediately begin to dig galleries, the beginning of a future nest. They start foraging for food, and the normal life of an ant-nest has been founded.—"Ants," *Realities* magazine

[1]Periodic checks of the bicycle should take place before every trip, every night on the trip, and every morning in case you were tired and missed something. Here's how to do an on-road check:

[2]Pick up the bicycle by the handlebars; let the whole weight of the machine hang momentarily from the bars, and give them a shake. Bounce the bike down firmly on its front wheel. Kick the nearest crank. Hit the seat with your hip. Clamp the brakes shut and push the bike forward, hard. Kick the rear wheel with the brakes off.

[3]Straddle the bike. Kick the other crank. Bounce down firmly on the seat. Slide forward, trap the front wheel between your feet or calves, and twist the handlebars. Then check to make sure you're in a low or intermediate gear, start rolling, and run methodically through all the gears, making sure—as you always should—that you're not getting into low gear sprockets at one end while using high gear at the other. Listen for scraping, tinkling, and sawing sounds.

[4]All of this takes two minutes. It inspects all vital areas of the machine, including handlebar clamping, headset and front-axle bearing adjustment, crank and spindle bearing adjustment, seat post clamping,

brake adjustment, rear wheel alignment and rear hub bearing adjustment, seat clamping, stem clamping, and pedal and gear shifter operation.

⁵And while riding, continue to listen for metallic noises. A newly respoked wheel creaks for a while. New brake blocks squeal during the first few applications even when properly toed-in. A new saddle creaks. Other than that, if your machine is being operated properly, all you should hear is wind noise, tire hum, and the purr of the chain running smoothly and reassuringly over the sprockets. Any loud metallic noises or thumps and bangings behind you mean either that something has fallen off or that a junkman is catching up to you.—Ajay Budrys, "The Self Reliant Bicycle Camper"

a. Which process is *natural*, which is *artificial*? In what ways are the processes fundamentally different?

b. Number and identify the *steps* in each process; state each *end point*.

c. In a process paper, there are usually certain transitional "signals" (*first, later, after this, before,* etc.) which help the reader discriminate among the various parts of the process. List the signals in the examples. Do most of the signals fall into any particular class or type?

d. Describe the writer's stance in each passage. The two kinds of process ordinarily have different writer's stances. Explain why this should be so.

SUGGESTIONS FOR WRITING PROCESS THEMES

When you write a process of the types we have described, you are essentially describing how something is done. In the artificial process, you often give directions to a specific person or group (people who want to learn something about checking a touring bicycle, for example), and your writer's stance is clear and precise. You are the "expert" who is showing the "nonexpert" how to perform an operation of some kind. Keep in mind that your reader may know little about your subject and that he may need definitions of terms and clear signals showing how the steps are separated. You may wish to speak directly to the reader and address him as *you*.

In addition to giving directions, the artificial process can also inform. Although the writer of the following three paragraphs doesn't expect her reader to take her directions seriously, she is actually informing us for the purpose of entertainment.

¹You can play cars with any size garage and driveway. We use a double garage with a basketball hoop on the front of it. The driveway is two-laned for about twenty feet, then narrows into a single lane to the street. To play on a board this size you need a minimum of three cars, although four or five are preferable. We have, in fact, five cars in the driveway just now, though we've always thought of ourselves as a one-car family.

²The station wagon is the family car and all we ever needed until the boys started playing cars for real. . . .

³The game begins when someone asks, "Will you please move your car so I can get mine out?" or "May I have your keys so I can move your car so I can get mine out?" The first player to find his or her car keys wins points but is not necessarily able to move first. According to the rules, no car is allowed to pass *over* another. Cars must move out of the driveway in whatever sequence is necessary to allow the player originating the request to gain access to the street. Since the Buick is a stationary piece on the board, so to speak, the game may become complicated and full of interest. After one car moves out, the others must return to somewhere near their original positions without hitting the Buick, or the lawn mower.
—Pat Lubar, "Playing Cars"*

The natural process is somewhat more difficult to write because you have to look carefully at the sequence of events in order to find the steps and the end point. Your writer's stance is usually less clear and definite. But you can succeed with such a paper if you remember you are really just explaining something to your reader that he would like to know. As before, you are the "expert"; but in this case neither you nor your reader is directly involved in the process. You are both standing off from it—watching it and trying to understand how it works. Instead of addressing the reader, it is good to use the *"who* (or *what*) does *what"* formula: "The female [*who*] digs herself in [does *what*]. . . ."

PRACTICE

1. Here is part of a magazine article written by a doctor describing a process. Is this a natural or artificial process? Identify the steps and the end point.

   ¹At 11 p.m. on Dec. 22, 1963 fire broke out aboard the Greek luxury liner *Lakonia* as it cruised the Atlantic near Madeira, and passengers and crew were forced into the water. The air temperature was over 60°, the sea almost 65° and rescue ships were in the area within a few hours. Never-

theless, 125 people died, 113 of these fatalities being attributed to hypothermia, the lowering of the body's inner heat, perhaps no more than 6° from the normal 98.6°. . . .

²The moment your body begins to lose heat faster than it produces it, hypothermia threatens. As heat loss continues, the temperature of the body's inner core falls below normal. Hands and arms (the extremities most needed in order to survive) are affected first. When body temperature drops to 95°, dexterity is reduced to the point where you cannot open a jackknife or light a match.

³According to recent research by the Mountain Rescue Association, the body reacts in a series of predictable ways when inner-core temperature falls. At 2.5° below normal, shivering begins, an automatic body process to create heat. But it takes energy to shiver—comparable to what is expended sawing wood—and the heat loss continues. The more the core temperature drops, the less efficient the brain becomes. Although you may have a pack on your back with a sleeping bag and food in it, you may not have the sense to use them.

⁴If the core temperature drops to 94°, you will stop shivering but every now and then will experience uncontrollable shaking. Your system, automatically getting rid of carbon dioxide and lactic acid, also releases blood sugar and a little adrenaline, giving you a surge of energy, which causes the violent shaking. This last desperate effort by the body to produce heat utilizes a tremendous amount of energy.

⁵"Now," you think, "I must be getting warmer because I am not shivering anymore." By this time you are pretty irrational. If someone were to ask you your name and telephone number, you probably wouldn't know them, for the brain has become numb.

⁶If nothing is done, death usually occurs within 1½ hours after the shivering starts. In fact, a shivering person can go from fatigue to exhaustion to cooling beyond the recovery point so quickly he may perish before rescuers can build a shelter or get a fire started.—J. Clayton Stewart, "Growing Cold by Degrees"

2. Discuss this process theme written by a student. Note especially the transitional signals to indicate the steps.

Flying Time

¹When a freshman biology student is confronted with a collection of bottles stoppered with wads of cotton and filled with swarms of insects, he can be sure that fruit fly counting time has at last arrived. Because they multiply rapidly, fruit flies are often used to illustrate certain Mendelian concepts of heredity. In the experiment, flies possessing certain characteristics such as red eyes, long wings, or black bodies are mated with flies possessing similar or opposable traits. The results of these matings are supposed to prove that an orderly dominance of certain traits over their opposites exists and can be predicted. I interject a note of doubt at this point because Mendel, the originator of the theory of genetics, ne-

glected to take into account the well-meaning but slipshod efforts of fledgling zoology students to prove such a theory correct. Indeed, for the freshman biology student, the purpose of counting fruit flies is less to learn a scientific process than simply to fulfill an assignment.

²Confronted with a bottle bearing an illegible label, students are supposed to etherize the insects inside. This is done by pouring ether into the cotton covering the mouth of the bottle until the student becomes extremely drowsy and finds that his lab partner has slumped to the floor. In the time it takes the student to revive his partner, the fruit flies will have succumbed to the ether.

³The fruit flies are then shaken out onto a piece of white paper, where they are divided first according to sex. It is at this point that the first departure from Mendel's theory usually arises. Sometimes students counting the parental stock will, after an intensive search, find no females among the flies. At this point the harassed instructor must check the students' calculations. If he too can find no females, he usually mumbles something about their being stuck in the soft food at the bottom of the bottle and hurries out of the room on the pretense of getting a drink of water.

⁴Having surmounted many similar obstacles, the students finally separate all the flies into from eight to sixteen small piles, each of which contains flies possessing a certain combination of characteristics. At this point someone usually suffers a sneezing fit, and the flies are blown to the four corners of the room.

⁵After all the insects have been found, the windows are closed. Kleenex is distributed, and another count is made. The results of this final count are tabulated, and it is found that the ratio of offspring types bears, if the student uses his imagination, at least a slight relation to Mendel's observations.

⁶The students must then capture the fruit flies, which are beginning to flit around the room, and leave the lab at the insistence of their instructor, who, no doubt, spends the remainder of the period thanking God that the exercise on genetics is over.

3. Pick one of the following topics (or a similar one) and write a process paper. Suggestions:

Decide if you are giving directions or making an explanation (is your process artificial or natural?). Then choose the writer's stance that is most appropriate.

Determine the end point or purpose of the process.

Determine the relevant, main steps of the process that lead to the end point or purpose. State the steps clearly, and use transitions.

If possible, keep to a clear chronological sequence of events in the process, but avoid irrelevancies.

    a. How to start and operate a gasoline lawnmower.

    b. How to understand the growth of a tree.

c. How to start a car using another car's battery.
d. How a volcano is created.
e. How the human knee works.
f. How to keep a beard looking trim.
g. How a tornado creates destruction.
h. How to learn to play a guitar the quickest way.
i. How to stand up on water skis.

Strategy 5 Analogy

An *analogy* is basically a comparison — ordinarily an extended comparison — between two things usually thought of as unlike. Here is an analogy from a student paper:

[1]A tank truck usually holds between 4,000 and 6,000 gallons of gasoline. Depending on the tanker and the oil company, there are three to six individual compartments which hold 600 to 900 gallons of gasoline apiece. The tank that contains the compartments is elliptically shaped to distribute the pressure equally and to allow a more complete flow of air when the gasoline is delivered.

[2]Until recently the only way to load a tanker was to climb up on top, where the openings to the compartments are located. You can easily picture this by visualizing six pop bottles lined up in single file on a table. A man wants to fill up bottle three, so he takes the cap off. He then inserts a small hose into the neck of the bottle and turns on a faucet which is connected to the hose.

[3]A gasoline tanker is loaded in a similar way, but on a much larger scale. A man climbs on top of the tanker and opens a particular compartment by removing the cap. He then takes a hose with a four-foot metal pipe extension, about three and a half inches in diameter, and inserts the pipe down into the "bottle" (the compartment hole), which measures four inches in diameter. A pump is then turned on, allowing the gasoline to flow into the compartment.

LITERAL AND FIGURATIVE ANALOGIES

This analogy explains something relatively unknown (loading a tanker) by using your knowledge of something *known* (filling pop bottles). The example is a *literal* analogy because the two things being compared are real and existing. In the pure literal analogy you make an extended comparison that is real and true at every point. Here is an analogy between a wristwatch and a small clock:

Watch	is analogous to	Clock
Watch spring (A)	is similar to	Clock spring (A)
Watch movement (B)	is similar to	Clock movement (B)
Watch stem (C)	is similar to	Clock stem (C)

In order for this analogy to work properly, the watch and the clock must be literally comparable at each point (A, B, and C). For instance, if the stem of the watch and the stem of the clock are not comparable, then the analogy is only two-thirds accurate. The analogy is not false in this instance; it is simply imperfect.

The *figurative* analogy also explains something, but it uses figurative comparisons—extended metaphors, similes, and personifications. These figures of speech, explained more fully on pp. 149–151, clarify, dramatize, and sharpen the main point of your paper. Figurative analogies are most often used in supporting roles, rather than as the basis for an entire theme. Because both items in a figurative analogy are "knowns," its function is not so much to explain one of the things, but to make the reader see that thing in a new and fresh way. Observe how a figurative analogy (in italics) acts to dramatize the plight of the modern individual:

> The present universal collapse of mankind is no more than the outcome of two frightful wars. One need not be a great prophet to foresee that within a century or two mankind will have rediscovered a decent image of itself. But meanwhile *mankind is like a filthy, bloodstained drunkard who looks at himself in the mirror and is surprised to find he looks so horrible. According to some, mankind should go on looking at itself in the mirror; according to others, mankind should replace the mirror with a picture of a clean, sober man. Few think it would be better if mankind had a brush-up and a rest. And even those who think this are not prepared to give up either the mirror or the picture.*
> —Alberto Moravia, "When Art Becomes Propaganda"

Observe how the figurative comparison is "expanded" through the passage.

SUGGESTIONS FOR WRITING ANALOGIES

In making effective analogies, you should first understand which of the two kinds of analogies you are using. Your whole paper will be thrown out of kilter if you think you are constructing a literal analogy when actually your points of comparison are partly or mainly figurative. You can mix types of analogy as long as you are aware of the mixing, and as long as the mixing does not seem incongruous or invalid to your reader.

When you construct a literal analogy, make sure that the compared points are really comparable, and cut out or explain any points that cannot be logically compared. Be certain that the familiar or known side of the analogy is really familiar and known to your reader. It would be useless to explain a mineral crystal-lattice structure by reference to analytic geometry if your reader knows nothing about analytic geometry. Furthermore, do not try to stretch an analogy too far. Like the fabled camel which first put his nose in the man's tent, then his head, and finally his whole body, pushing the man out of the tent, metaphor tends to creep sneakily into analogies. What starts out to be literally explanatory can become as unreal and metaphorical as a fairy tale, and no more convincing.

Use figurative analogies cautiously. They are interesting but sometimes difficult to use well and are often misleading to your reader. One danger is that you may take them more seriously than their use warrants and expand them to the point of silliness: "The heart of the nation is in Washington," wrote a politician. "Its brains are in the fifty states, and its conscience is in the Supreme Court."

Although the figurative analogy can lead you astray, carefully employed it is a splendid rhetorical device. C. S. Lewis has given three conditions for the proper employment of the figurative analogy:

1. The figures or metaphors should be well chosen by the writer.
2. The reader must be able to understand the figures.
3. Both writer and reader should understand that figurative language is being used.

Here is an effective figurative analogy that fulfills these conditions:

> All scientists are not alike. Look at any laboratory or university science department. Professor Able is the kind of man who seizes an idea as a dog seizes a stick, all at once. As he talks you can see him stop short, with the chalk in his fingers, and then almost jump with excitement as the insight grips him. His colleague, Baker, on the other hand, is a man who comes to understand an idea as a worm might understand the same stick, digesting it a little at a time, drawing his conclusions cautiously, and tunneling slowly through it from end to end and back again. — John Radar Platt, "Style in Science"

For contrast, here is an effective literal analogy:

Repeats the statement he plans to refute by analogy.

> [1]A letter in *Time* magazine a few weeks ago from a reader who opposes gun laws was typical of the kind of illogical thinking that supports such arguments The letter said: "A gun has no will of its own. A gun does only what its owner causes it to do. The root of the problem is within the human heart. Cure the cause rather than treat surface symptoms "

Replaces *gun* with *automobile* and extends analogy in order to generalize about automobile laws.

2 Let me transpose this argument to a similar term to demonstrate how absurd it is: "An automobile has no will of its own. An automobile does only what the driver causes it to do. The root of the problem is within the human heart. Cure the cause rather than treat the surface symptoms." Therefore, dispense with automobile laws. No more speed limits, no more traffic signals, no more registration of cars, no more tests for drivers, no more fines or jail terms for offenses.

Extends analogy between guns and automobiles; concludes with point of the comparison.

3 Instead, we try to reform and change human nature. We work at making most people kind and considerate and attentive and model citizens. Meanwhile, what happens on the streets and highways? Slaughter, that's what happens. While we slowly "cure the human heart," we speedily kill thousands of human bodies. —Sydney J. Harris, "Gun Lobby Arguments Are Absurd"

PRACTICE

1. Discuss each of the analogies below. Is the analogy figurative or literal, or both? Is the comparison consistently made? Do the differences between the two elements being compared weaken the analogy? Is the "known side" of the analogy familiar enough to you? How could the analogy be improved (if at all)?

   a. Not letting students evaluate their teachers and curriculum is like an architect not allowing the prospective homeowner to assist in the design of his house. In both cases the person giving the assistance is untrained, while the architect and the teacher are highly skilled professionals. The student and owner both have ideas which would help the curriculum and design, respectively.

   b. **1** For a long time now, since the beginning, in fact, men and women have been sparring and dancing around with each other, each pair trying to get it together and boogie to the tune called Life. For some people, it was always a glide, filled with grace and ease. For most of us, it is a stumble and a struggle, always trying to figure out the next step, until we find a partner whose inconsistencies seem to fit with ours, and the two of us fit into some kind of rhythm. Some couples wind up struggling and pulling at cross purposes; and of course, some people never get out on the floor, just stand alone in the corners, looking hard at the dancers.

   2 That's the way it's always been, and probably, always will be. The only difference now is that for the past few years a group of noisy people have been standing over next to the band and yelling above it, "Hey, listen everybody! You don't have to dance to the old tune any more! You can make up your own tune! You can make up your dance steps! *The man doesn't even have to lead any more!* Forget the band!

This is a whole new movement! It's called *you can make your Life whatever you want!"* — Jay Molishever, "Changing Expectations of Marriage"

c. The other pitfall blocking the path of the New Left is the culture's skill at amiably absorbing all manner of rebels and turning them into celebrities. To be a radical in America today is like trying to punch your way out of a cage made of marshmallow. Every thrust at the jugular draws not blood, but sweet success; every hack at the roots draws not retaliation, but fame and affluence. The culture's insatiable thirst for novelty and titillation insured LeRoi Jones television interviews, Norman Mailer million-dollar royalties, and Paul Goodman fat paychecks as a government consultant. Yesterday's underground becomes today's vaudeville and tomorrow's cliché. — Jack Newfield, "A Prophetic Minority"

d   A judge in Madison, Wis., has ruled that a 15-year-old boy who raped a schoolgirl was reacting "normally" to the community's sexual permissiveness and the provocative clothing that women now wear. Think of the possibilities if his reasoning becomes a precedent: Anyone who sports a costly fur is asking to be mugged for extravagance or cruelty to animals, and the understandably aroused mugger will be permitted to stay at home, as the young rapist was. Burglars can gain sympathy from the law if they break into homes that look as though they cost $100,000 and up — the fancier the facade, the greater the sympathy. A homely face is asking to be punched, no penalty attached. And certainly no one could be punished for assaulting a judge who delivers foolish opinions from the bench. — editorial in the *Chicago Tribune*

e. Probably you have to go down several coal mines before you can get much grasp of the processes that are going on around you. This is chiefly because the mere effort of getting from place to place makes it difficult to notice anything else. In some ways it is even disappointing, or at least is unlike what you have expected. You get into the cage, which is a steel box about as wide as a telephone box and two or three times as long. It holds ten men, but they pack it like pilchards in a tin, and a tall man cannot stand upright in it. The steel door shuts upon you, and somebody working the winding gear above drops you into the void. . . . When you crawl out at the bottom you are perhaps four hundred yards under ground. That is to say you have a tolerable-sized mountain on top of you; hundreds of yards of solid rock, bones of extinct beasts, subsoil, flints, roots of growing things, green grass and cows grazing on it — all this suspended over your head and held back only by wooden props as thick as the calf of your leg. — George Orwell, *The Road to Wigan Pier*

f.   [1]For over twenty years, my father has worked on an oil seismograph crew. We all know about the big seismographs that detect and measure earthquakes. The oil seismograph is a small portable electronic instrument that detects and measures artificial earthquakes. The purpose of the instrument is to find geological structures that may contain oil. I have worked for the past two summers on a seismograph crew. Here I wish to explain how the seismographic instrument works.

²Let me begin with an occurrence that should be familiar. Imagine yourself standing near the base of a large cliff. If you shout at the cliff face, you will get an echo because the sound waves bounce back from the so-called "interface" where air meets rock. The sound waves travel at 1100 feet per second. You can find out how far you are standing from the cliff by measuring the time it takes for your shout to travel from you to the cliff and back again, and then by solving a simple formula for distance.

³The function of the oil seismograph is to find out how far down in the earth the horizontal layers of rock are. To discover this distance, the oil seismologist digs a deep hole (usually 100–200 feet) in the surface of the ground—the purpose of the hole I will explain later. At the bottom of the hole, he explodes a heavy charge of dynamite. Ground waves travel from the explosion down to the layers of rock. At each major interface between the layers, the waves bounce back to the surface. The explosion is similar to shouting at the cliff. Just as sound travels through the air at a certain speed, ground waves travel through the earth, although much faster. Ground waves bounce from rock interfaces as sound waves bounce from a cliff face. And the seismologist can determine distance just as you can determine the distance between you and the cliff.

⁴Why does the seismologist dig a hole to explode the dynamite? Much of the ground surface is covered with what geologists call *weathering,* that relatively loose covering of soil, sand, clay, etc., that usually goes down to the water table. This weathering has a disastrous effect upon seismic waves in the ground; it slows them up and even disperses them. To explode a dynamite charge on top of the ground would be like shouting at a cliff face through a bowl of mush —no matter how loud you shouted, little of your voice would get through. So the seismologist drills through the weathering and plants the dynamite charge below it. Usually the weathering has a bad effect only on the waves at the point of explosion; the *reflected* waves will travel through the weathering to the instruments on the surface.

⁵In the interests of accuracy, I should add that the analogy between air waves and seismic waves is partly literal and partly figurative. The principles are similar but the conditions are different. Air waves are relatively constant in speed because the medium varies little. Seismic waves, by contrast, increase in speed with depth, and the increase is irregular and difficult to measure. Also, seismic reflections vary in ways that no one completely understands. But the analogy is, in a basic sense, revealing and accurate enough to explain to a beginner how an oil seismograph works. — student theme

2. Write a paragraph or theme using one of the following theses and the analogy that it suggests; or you may use a thesis and analogy of your own choice. Specify your writer's stance.

a. *Thesis:* The state of _____ should pass the Equal Rights Amendment.

 Analogy: Discriminating against an able, intelligent woman because of her sex is equivalent to putting her in a cage.

b. *Thesis:* Everyone interested in politics should work within his own party.

 Analogy: Political activity is like gardening.

c. *Thesis:* Dissident groups should have a constructive plan for improvement.

 Analogy: A revolution tears down the building of government without putting anything in its place.

d. *Thesis:* Being able to drive a car makes a young person feel like an adult.

 Analogy: Passing one's first driving test is similar to an initiation rite.

e. *Thesis:* Every citizen should make an effort to avoid littering the nation's roadsides, parks, and cities.

 Analogy: Destroying the nation's environment is like burning down your house.

3. The powerful and prosperous Roman empire was said to have fallen for the following reasons: (a) the rise of despotic one-man rule; (b) the lowering of the prestige of the government; (c) the devaluing of the currency and increasing taxation; (d) the creation of a welfare state; (e) the rise of military control over civil government; (f) the expansion of bureaucracy; (g) the lowering of public morality; (h) the inability of the military to repulse foreign invaders. Write a theme in which you argue by using analogy that the United States is (or is not, or partly is) going the way of ancient Rome.

Strategy 6   Classification

Classifying or grouping things is a natural way to think. Young children playing with rocks separate large ones from small ones, rough ones from smooth ones. As they grow older, they become more sophisticated in their classifying, and they begin to group their playmates into those they like to play with and those they don't. When they enter school, they separate their school clothes from their play clothes. Then as they learn to use abstractions in their thinking, they identify subjects in school that they are interested or successful in. In every one of these classifications, the grouping is made according to a *ruling principle:* rocks classified according to *size* or *smoothness;* friends classified according to *amiability;* clothes classified according to *use;* school subjects classified according to *success* or, perhaps, *interest.*

Although classifying is a process "natural" to human beings, it is useful to remember that classes as such do not exist in nature itself. We create classes and systems of classification to help us understand our world.

THE "RULING PRINCIPLE"
IN CLASSIFICATION

Classifying is the act of grouping things, persons, activities, ideas, etc., according to their similarities and differences. By the time you are of college age, you are so accustomed to classifying and to being classified, that you are scarcely aware of the process. Yet classification affects nearly every part of your life. To mention only a few of the possibilities, you may be classified in religion as a believer, nonbeliever, or agnostic; a Christian or non-Christian; a Protestant, Jew, or Catholic; a Methodist, Baptist, or Episcopalian; etc. In politics, you are Republican, Democrat, or Independent. In school, you are a freshman, sophomore, junior, senior (or unclassified). In a university, you may be placed in the College of Arts and Sciences, Engineering, Education, etc. If you are in Arts and Sciences, you may be classified as an English major, math major, or psychology major, etc. (In classifying, the *etc.* is important!)

A *classification,* to define the term more accurately, *is a significant and informative grouping of things, persons, activities, ideas, etc.* The key words here are *significant* and *informative.* We classify in order to use information, and the most informative classifications are those based upon significant groupings. If, in order to understand them, we separate the students in a particular composition class into two groups, men and women, we have made a classification, but it does not seem significant nor does it satisfy our curiosity about the students.

To make such a classification useful, we must apply a significant *ruling principle,* which is a unifying idea or point of view used in the act of classifying. The division of a composition class into men and women is based upon a ruling principle of *gender,* which, as we have seen, is not a particularly significant grouping here, and thus will not prove to be very informative. Other ruling principles of varying significance might be *athletic ability, religion, major field, interest in composition,* etc.

In the passage below, observe that there are two ruling principles, cloud *formation* and *altitude:*

> [1]Clouds are classified according to how they are formed. There are two basic types: (1) Clouds formed by rising air currents. These are piled up and puffy. They are called "cumulus" which means piled up or accumulated. (2) Clouds formed when a layer of air is cooled below the saturation point without vertical movement. These are in sheets or foglike layers. They are called "stratus," meaning sheetlike or layered.
>
> [2]Clouds are further classified by altitude into four families: high clouds, middle clouds, low clouds, and towering clouds. The bases of the latter may be as low as the typical low clouds, but the tops may be at or above 75,000 feet.—Paul E. Lehr, R. Will Burnett, and Herbert S. Zim, *Weather*

As with the other strategies of development, classification is created by the writer *for a specific reason.* In the classification of clouds, the writers' aim was to explain cloud formations to a reader who is not a scientist and who knows very little about clouds.

A diagram of another classification may help you visualize how this device works. Note how the following discussion of different types of kisses might be diagrammed.

> If one wishes to classify the kiss, then one must consider several principles of classification. One may classify kissing with respect to sound. Here the language is not sufficiently elastic to record all my observations. I do not believe that all the languages in the world have an adequate supply of onomatopoeia to describe the different sounds I have learned to know at my uncle's house. Sometimes it was smacking, sometimes hissing, sometimes sticky, sometimes explosive, sometimes booming, sometimes full, sometimes hollow, sometimes squeaky, and so on forever. One may also classify kissing with regard to contact, as in the close kiss, the kiss *en passant* [in passing], and the clinging kiss . . . One may classify them with reference to the time element, as the brief and the prolonged. With reference to the time element, there is still another classification, and this is the only one I really care about. One makes a difference between the first kiss and all others. That which is the subject of this reflection is incommensurable with everything which is included in the other classifications; it is indifferent to sound, touch, time in general. The first kiss is, however, qualitatively different from all others.—Soren Kierkegaard, *Either/Or*

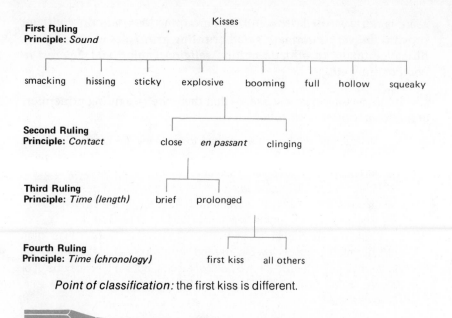

**First Ruling
Principle:** *Sound*

Kisses

smacking   hissing   sticky   explosive   booming   full   hollow   squeaky

**Second Ruling
Principle:** *Contact*

close   *en passant*   clinging

**Third Ruling
Principle:** *Time (length)*

brief   prolonged

**Fourth Ruling
Principle:** *Time (chronology)*

first kiss   all others

Point of classification: the first kiss is different.

PRACTICE

Prepare the classification below for class discussion. Outline the writer's stance. In what way is Viorst's classification significant and informative? What is her ruling principle of classification? How successful is this piece of writing?

[1]So if eating is not the most important thing in life, why are you eating again? Why, after all those promises and privations, have you once more become a diet drop-out? Are you morally as well as physically flabby? Are you weak of will, irresolute of purpose? Are you so undisciplined, so infantile, so *greedy,* that you can always be counted upon, sooner or later, to cave in at the sight of a Hershey bar with almonds, a freshly baked loaf of rye bread, a creamy, winy, buttery coquille St. Jacques?

[2]The answer, of course, isn't nearly that simple. There are many different kinds of diet drop-outs, each with her own *raison d'eat.* I have divided them into four categories: the alcoholic, the psychologist, the biologist and the out-and-out quitter.

[3]The alcoholic eater, like her drinking counterpart, is doomed from the moment she first slips off the wagon. Let her munch a single salted peanut and she's got to go on to devour the entire can. Let her nibble the tiniest forkful of cherry cheesecake and within minutes all that's left is a faint pink smudge. In the life of the alcoholic eater there is no such thing as a taste or a sip, a spoonful or a slice. As soon as she succumbs to the seduction of "just one bite," she's had it.

[4]When the psychologist goes off her diet, it's really her mother who's making her do all the eating. Her conversation is full of references to early-childhood traumas and the inexorable forces of the unconscious. "I'm

having an anxiety attack," she says from behind her butterscotch sundae. "I'm feeling rejected. I'm searching for love."

[5]The biologist who returns to full-time eating talks knowingly about sodium intake and metabolic rates and insists that she is not failing her diet but vice versa. "No matter how little I eat," she observes as she ladles the gravy onto her mashed potatoes, "everything I put in my mouth turns to fat."

[6]The out-and-out quitter quits her diet because she can no longer endure reaching for a green-pepper ring when what she really wants to reach for is a mousse. She awakens in the night racked with hunger pains that no amount of celery stalks can assuage. She is sick of unpersuasive food substitutes such as mock potato pudding made with cauliflower, mock sour-cream sauce made with cottage cheese, mock malteds made with neither malt nor ice cream and mock Bloody Marys made with neither vodka nor gin. The will that has sustained her through lunch after lunch of beef bouillon with cucumber garnish slowly leaks away, and a life without éclairs no longer seems worth living.—Judith Viorst, "A Dieter's Lament"

SUGGESTIONS FOR WRITING A CLASSIFICATION PAPER

Here are some suggestions for writing the classification paper that you will find useful.

1. Make sure your classification has a point. Don't try to write a classification paper without a specific stance.

2. Be consistent with your ruling principle. You may change your principle if, after having investigated your subject thoroughly from one angle, you wish to investigate it from another. Note that the classification of clouds used two ruling principles. If you were studying political systems, for example, you might use several different ruling principles: (a) time-sequence or history, (b) causes and effects, (c) types of systems, (d) philosophies of systems, (e) success of systems, to name just a few.

3. Avoid artificial or illogical classifications. Simply chopping your subject into parts will not necessarily give you a valid classification. If you divide your composition class into (a) men and (b) good students, you have made a classification that is artificial and probably useless.

4. Avoid most either-or classifications. For instance:

Voters are either left-wing or right-wing.
Financiers are either successful or unsuccessful.
Rhetoric students are either good writers or poor writers.

By its very structure, each of these either-or classifications probably distorts the truth because it omits certain members of the total group—those who would fall somewhere between the extremes of "left" or "right," "successful" or "unsuccessful," and "good" or "poor." Among a group of rhetoric students, for example, there are likely to be writers who are "excellent," "good," "fair," "poor" and and (perhaps) "terrible."

PRACTICE

1. Read the following student essay and identify the ruling principles used in the classification.

Classes of Conservatives

[1]Before coming to the University, I barely knew what a conservative was. Since I have been here, I have met or seen and heard many campus conservatives, and have become very interested in them. To put my thoughts into order about them, I intend to classify them according to several different principles, which will become clear as I go along.

[2]No definition of a *campus conservative* can be very satisfactory— there are too many varieties. Generally, he is a person who is an "aginner"; he is "agin" whatever is new or untried. He likes the old, partly because it is old, and partly because it *has* been tried. He usually does not think much anyway; he is too busy talking.

[3]We can first classify campus conservatives by what they do and say. There are two groups in this classification: religious and political conservatives. Religious conservatives are rather quiet and neither do nor say much. Whether Catholic, Jewish, or Protestant, they regularly attend religious services but customarily avoid public arguments or testaments of faith. On the whole campus, I know of only one religious conservative who regularly writes angry letters to the school newspaper. By contrast, the political conservatives—mostly Republicans and Birchers— are noisy in speech and full of action. The Young Republicans are always hiring a hall or writing letters to the paper. The Birchers, followers of the John Birch Society, are Republicans gone berserk; and they are noisier and more active, if possible, than their Republican friends. It has been said that when a Republican goes crazy, he goes not into an asylum but into the Birch Society.

[4]Perhaps we can more significantly classify conservatives by grouping them according to what they want. What are they after? Do they have a program? Again, it seems that there is a natural division between religious and political conservatives. Although both are, at bottom, concerned with salvation, one hopes to save the world by religion, the other by politics. Since religious salvation is an inward, spiritual thing, the religious conservatives have less a program than an expressed desire for each person to try to save his own soul.

⁵Of the political conservatives, the Republicans have the clearer program. They want less government interference in economics and private life, and they hope to get this by legislation. The Birchers want the same, only more so. Sometimes they appear to wish that government might be done away with entirely. They also appear to wish that their desires be satisfied by fire and lightning. They are religiously fanatic; and in their fanaticism — if in nothing else — they overlap with religious conservatives. But I know of only one person who is actively both a violent religious and political conservative; he is the letter writer I spoke of earlier.

⁶What can be learned from these classifications? The most important point that can be drawn is that except for the Birchers, the campus conservatives are relatively reasonable both in what they do and what they want. The Birchers, as a class, are outside the normal political groupings on the campus. Their thinking and actions are dangerously unrelated either to conservative principle or to common sense.

2. Make a significant classification of the following items. Give the ruling principle of your classification. Use the heading *etc.* if an item doesn't fit your classifying system.

    a. *Time,* table, book, chair, magazine, divan, *Sports Illustrated,* newspaper, bookcase, *Fortune.*
    b. Truck, station wagon, automobile, luxury car, "semi," convertible, pickup, sports car, compact, economy car.
    c. Left-winger, Southern Democrat, socialist, communist, right-winger, Democrat, Republican, independent, middle-of-the-roader.
    d. Poet, novelist, journalist, editorial writer, TV commentator, textbook author, social philosopher, newspaper columnist, writer for *True* magazine, writer on college paper, literary critic.
    e. Thugs, robbers, rascals, killers, arsonists, scoundrels, shoplifters, murderers, burglars, assassins, car thieves, rapists, traitors, villains.
    f. Various kinds of *rights:* moral, natural, political, original, acquired, absolute, relative, property, liberty, equality.
    g. Presidents, governors, prime ministers, mayors, kings, princes, queens, despots, princesses, commissars, dictators, rulers, wardens, magistrates.

3. Choose a topic that can be classified, and write a theme. Be sure to keep in mind the following: (1) choose the ruling principle(s) by which you plan to classify; (2) identify your purpose in classifying (Your reader should not read your classification and say, "So what?"); (3) choose a writer's stance that suits the ruling principle and the purpose of the classification.

    Here are some possible topics (modify when necessary):

    a. There are distinct kinds of people who patronize laundromats / sporting-goods stores / pizzerias / delicatessens; *therefore.* . . .
    b. I have encountered many types of / people / ideas / since coming to college. *My conclusions are.* . . .

c. The subjects in my major field can be divided into several categories; *consequently.* . . .

d. The parents of successful children fall into several categories, but
the most important category is. . . .

e. The summer and part-time jobs available to a college student have
certain characteristics, *so when you look for a job.* . . .

Strategy 7
Comparison — Contrast

Comparing means "showing likenesses"; *con-
trasting,* "showing differences." In the comparison-contrast theme,
you show likenesses and differences between two or more (but usually only two) persons, ideas, actions, or things *for the purpose of
making a point.* We emphasize "making a point" because you customarily employ the strategy of comparison-contrast to convince the
reader of an idea you have—that A is *better* than B; more *interesting*
than B; more *useful* than B; etc.

PLANNING THE
COMPARISON-CONTRAST THEME

For several reasons, the comparison-contrast
theme requires particularly strong control of thesis and organization.
First, you usually have more basic material to work with—two subject
areas instead of the customary one. Consequently, you should rigor-
ously narrow your thesis so that you can cover the subjects in the assigned number of words. Next, you have to know a good deal about
both subjects. Finally, as we have already mentioned, your theme
must have a point to make beyond the obvious one of simply comparing and contrasting. Here is a trap that students often fall into: They
describe the two subject areas, giving plenty of detail for both but
omitting the point and thus leaving the reader wondering why the
theme was written in the first place.

Consider this sample thesis: "High-school band was for me more
interesting musically than college band has been." The idea that the
writer had in creating this thesis was not merely to write about her
experiences in high-school and college bands, but rather to make a
specific point regarding her attitudes toward them. The key phrase is
"more interesting musically," and it is this idea that will control her
whole essay and make her comparing and contrasting *significant.*

Read the following student essay, and prepare the questions at the end for class discussion.

Motorcycles and Mopeds

¹When I go back to school next semester, I will need a more reliable means of transportation than buses, bicycles or friends' cars. So I'm going to buy a vehicle which will take me when and where I want to go. After examining the various advantages and disadvantages of cars, buses, taxicabs, airplanes, trains, and submarines, I have found that either a motorcycle or a moped will best suit my need for an inexpensive and convenient means of transportation. The problem is to find out which one is better suited for me.

²My first problem in considering a means of transportation is its cost, including the initial investment, insurance, and gas. The lowest starting price for a new motorcycle is usually around $495, which is definitely out of my price range at the moment. On the other hand, I find that new mopeds, priced at around $320, are more nearly what I can afford. Since drivers of motorcycles in my state are required to carry liability insurance, I would have to pay an additional $45 to $50 if I bought a motorcycle. Mopeds can be driven without liability insurance.

³I will have to pay for my own gas, which means that I will need a vehicle that will run on the least amount of gas possible. Motorcycles average 50 to 75 mpg, while a moped can get from 100 to 200 mpg.

⁴I do not need a vehicle capable of high speeds. What I want is one that can keep up with city traffic, which usually travels (on the streets I wish to use) between 20 and 30 mph. Motorcycles have large motors with complicated transmissions that allow them to travel at speeds of at least 45 to 50 mph. Mopeds run on a simple two-horse motor. The state law limits them to a maximum speed of 30 to 35 mph, which is fast enough for me.

⁵Since parking places are hard to find in the university lots, the motorcycle would be less convenient than a moped because I can park a moped in a bicycle rack. Furthermore, I can ride the moped on the university bicycle paths. For getting to and from classes easily, the moped would definitely be more convenient than the motorcycle. Another convenience of the moped is that in my state I don't need a special license, an automobile license being adequate.

⁶After comparing the motorcycle and the moped as a means of inexpensive and convenient transportation, I think that the moped better suits my needs. I would advise any student in my position to buy one instead of a motorcycle.

a. For what significant purpose was the comparison-contrast made? What is the writer's thesis?

b. Does the writer have a clear writer's stance? Explain your answer.

c. Outline the essay. (Note that each paragraph discusses a different topic in the comparison-contrast: Those topics might be major headings, I, II, etc.)

d. Discuss the emphasis given to motorcycles and to mopeds in the essay.

e. Discuss other ways the writer might have organized his material.

f. Particular transitional words are useful in writing comparison-contrast papers. Point out these transitions in the essay and suggest other terms the writer could have used.

ORGANIZING COMPARISON-CONTRAST THEMES

The writer of the essay on motorcycles and mopeds had strong control of his thesis and organization. He made the comparison-contrast in order to consider his need for better transportation, and that purpose was made clear. Note that he did not try to include irrelevant items such as bicycles and automobiles. He covered both items under consideration completely so that the paper was not primarily about mopeds even though that vehicle was his final choice. His transitional devices (such as *on the other hand* and *furthermore*) help the reader follow the organization of the material.

There are three basic methods of organizing a comparison-contrast paper. In the "block" method, you first discuss one item thoroughly, then go on to the second, giving about equal time to each. In the second method, you list all the similarities between the two items, then all the differences. In the "point-by-point" method, you discuss one point or feature of each item, then go on to the next, and so on. The following list shows how the three methods are organized. A and B stand for the two items being compared; and we assume that your theme has four paragraphs, although it may have more.

	"Block"	*"Similarities-Differences"*	*"Point-by-Point"*
1.	introduce subject	introduce subject	introduce subject
2.	discuss A	discuss similarities between A and B	discuss point 1 of A and B
	(transition)	(transition)	(transition)
3.	discuss B	discuss differences between A and B	discuss point 2 of A and B
4.	conclude	conclude	conclude

In the three models on the following pages, you will see how the writers used these methods for organizing their writing. The second and third examples are student themes.

"Block" Method

Introduction [1]I think there's something wrong here, but I can't exactly put my finger on it. I recently bought quantities of two fluids.

Discussion of A (gasoline)
1. Source [2]The first fluid was gasoline. Gasoline is derived from crude oil, which is found deep under the ground in remote sections of the earth. Enormous amounts of money are risked in the search for oil. Once it's found, a great deal more money is expended to extract it from the earth, to ship it to distant refineries, to refine it, to ship it via pipeline to regional distribution points, to store it, to deliver it to retail outlets and then to make it available to the retail consumer. . . .

2. Supply [3]As far as we know, the earth's supply of crude oil is limited. Once it's gone, it's gone. There may be other substances fermenting under the soil that will prove of value to future civilizations, but for the here and now our oil supplies are finite. . . .

Discussion of B (soda pop)
1. Source [4]The other fluid was sweetened, carbonated water, infused with artificial fruit flavoring. Some call it soda pop. It's made right here in town. As far as we know, the raw materials exist in unlimited supply. Most of it falls from the heavens at regular intervals. . . .

2. Supply [5]Almost all of it, by processes chemical and natural, will recycle back into the system. It will become sewage, will cleanse itself, will evaporate and will rain down again from the heavens at some undetermined time and place. It will come back. We can't really get rid of it. . . .

Conclusion
Thesis [6]Soda pop costs $1 for a gallon of the stuff. When you further consider that roughly a third of the cost of gasoline is taxes, that means that soda pop costs almost three times as much per gallon as does gasoline. — Robert Rosefsky, *Chicago Daily News*

"Similarities-Differences" Method

Introduction [1]What was it like for a girl to be brought up by two bachelors? When I was ten, my mother (a widow) died, and I had no one to look after me except her two brothers, Arthur and Alan. Both were in their early forties at the time. Arthur had been married once, long ago, and his wife had left him; Alan had never married and was, peo-
Thesis ple said, a woman hater. Being brothers, they had sever-

al traits in common; but they were also very different. And that fact showed up in their treatment of me.

Similarities between A (Alan) and B (Arthur)
1. Attitude toward work

²For instance, neither of them wanted me to work while I was going to high school. They were brought up to believe that a woman's place is in the home or, at least, in the trailer at the edge of town where we all lived. When they found out I took a job at a local drive-in, Alan bawled me out and made me quit, while Arthur, the more sociable of the two, made a personal visit to the manager to give him hell for hiring such a young kid. Both of them could not understand why I could not get by on the $5.00 a week they gave me for spending money. And besides, they said that the job was interfering with my "schooling."

2. Attitude toward school

³School was another thing they were concerned about, and probably with good reason. They always wanted to see my grade reports, although they were never quite sure when they were issued. And I tried to keep them in the dark about that as much as possible. Arthur, who thought he was better educated than Alan, always wanted to help me with my homework. Just to get him off my back, I sometimes let him. About the only thing he seemed to remember from his school days were the names of the capital cities of all the states, which, of course, did not help me much. Arthur was always concerned with long-term results, continually asking "Are you going to pass this term?" "Are you going to graduate?" I think he was a little surprised when I did. But, if it had not been for their concern, I probably would not have made it past my junior year.

Differences between A and B
1. Attitude toward dating

⁴But in other matters involving me, they had quite different attitudes. Alan was very protective of me as far as boys and dating were concerned. Arthur, however, encouraged me to date because he wanted me to have a good time while I was young. Alan treated me like a young Farrah Fawcett-Majors who was luring every male for miles around. When male friends would stop by, he would always grill them as if they were sex maniacs, while Arthur offered them a beer and talked sports, always managing to put in a good word for his niece. Alan was so protective that he sometimes would drive me to parties or dances, and sit outside a teen den in his pickup, waiting until I came out after the last song died away.

2. Attitude toward drinking

⁵Their concern for me also showed itself in their attitude toward drinking. Alan did not drink much, but Arthur was an alcoholic. He not only drank, he liked other people drinking. He made me my first salty dog. He taught

me that any sort of sweet stuff with bourbon was the devil's idea. Alan disapproved greatly of all this. But he was incapable of attacking his own brother, who could charm people with ease. Alan would, when I was seventeen, take a beer out of my hand if I was drinking one—only one!—with Arthur, and pour it down the sink. After Alan had gone to bed, Arthur would go to the refrigerator and get me another one. I was never more than mildly interested in alcohol, however; the sight of Arthur drunk and sick was enough to make anyone cautious.

Conclusion (with an anecdote that emphasizes their similarities and differences)

⁶Even though they were alike in some things and different in others, my uncles took care of me. When I graduated from high school last year, they came to the ceremony in the pickup. Alan wore his best and only suit, which had been out of style twenty years ago. Arthur was dressed like a king, and was so drunk he had to be carried out in the middle of "Pomp and Circumstance." A strange "family," but they are all I have—and many times all I need.

"Point-by-Point" Method

Introduction

Thesis

¹Fast-food restaurants are quickly becoming the most popular dining-out spots for Americans. Because of this popularity, people should know a little bit more about what to expect in these establishments. A comparison of two fast-food places I have worked in shows that they have several similarities and differences in the way they cook and serve their hamburgers.

Discussion of point 1 (assembly-line process) of A (Jack's) and B (Willie's)

²In both restaurants (let's call them "Jack's" and "Willie's"), the customer approaches the counter where he gives his order to a "server." After the cook fills the order, the server gives the customer his food. The customer goes to the next station, where he picks up his plastic eating utensils and pays his bill. He then sits down to a table that should have been cleared by its previous occupants. The whole operation runs smoothly without waiters; and, of course, there is no tipping.

Discussion of point 2 (meat)

³The preparation and cooking of the meat are different in the two restaurants. At Jack's the meat is frozen in patties and cooked while frozen. If the management knows that the lunch or dinner hour will be rushed, the cook may prepare as many as two or three hundred hamburgers ahead of time and keep them warm under a heat lamp. Some hamburger gourmets believe that ground meat cooked this way is gray and greasy. However, if customers want fast service, advance preparation of food has an obvious advantage. At Willie's the meat is

fresh ground and the burgers are cooked to order. The disadvantage here, obviously, is that the customer has to wait for his food. But cooking meat fresh, some believe, results in a juicier sandwich because the juices have not escaped, something which happens when a hamburger sits under a heat lamp. Burger gourmets also believe that the freezing process dries out ground meat.

Discussion of point 3 (garnishes) [4]At Jack's the hamburgers are served either plain or with "everything," and there are no exceptions. This allows more burgers to be cooked and sold, but it certainly discourages the customer who wants only mustard and relish, for example. At Willie's, everything is custom-made because individual orders are processed as they are received. And there is an "extras" table where customers can get additional helpings of catsup, mustard, onions, pickles, and tomatoes. This, of course, takes more time, but the customer gets what he wants.

Conclusion [5]So, whether you want your hamburger good and very fast, or fast and very good, you can certainly find a restaurant that will satisfy you.

PRACTICE

1. Here is an examination of the qualities young people in a Mexican village look for in a spouse. What method of comparison-contrast is used here? Explain. Respond to the excerpt by writing a comparison-contrast paper based on similar experiences you have had with your friends, family, and community.

   The qualities looked for in a spouse vary considerably between boys and girls. In selecting a wife, boys generally choose a girl for romantic reasons, beauty, or personality. Girls tend to be more realistic about selecting a husband and will often refuse to marry a boy who is known to drink, chase women, be violent, or be lazy. However, status factors are very important in marriage. It is usual for boys to seek out a girl who is poorer and who has the same or less education, so that "the man can be boss" and his family need not be ashamed before her. Tepoztecan boys tend to "respect" and avoid having affairs with girls from the more important and prosperous families, for fear of incurring reprisals from the parents of such girls. Girls, on the other hand, seek to improve their economic status with marriage, and it is rare for a girl to marry a man with less education. As a result of these attitudes, the daughters of the families in the upper economic group in the village have difficulty finding husbands. They tend to marry later, and to marry more educated men or men from the outside. Occasionally a wealthy girl in her late twenties will marry a boy poorer than herself rather than remain unmarried.—Oscar Lewis, *Life in a Mexican Village*.

2. Analyze the following comparison-contrast. What is the method(s) of organization? Is it an effective piece of writing? Why? Write a comparison-contrast paper about two people you know.

¹The seismic shocks that dealt death and destruction to Managua, capital city of Nicaragua, evoke this commentary on the lives of two Americans. One is Howard Hughes, the fabulously rich recluse, whose incredible compulsion to escape the real world has long fascinated a credulous press. The other is Roberto Clemente, star of the 1971 World Series and named to the National League All-Star team 12 times in his 18-year career.

²While the mystery of Howard Hughes has never been solved, such facts as do emerge show him to be a vain and selfish person, utterly devoid of compassion and with but little recorded evidence of useful service to mankind. By contrast, Roberto Clemente was a humanitarian and activist who worked with underprivileged youth and rebelled at injustice of any kind. To Howard Hughes, people are simply a commodity that a rich man can buy or sell; to Roberto Clemente, people were flesh and blood — to be helped when in need, to be uplifted in times of depression and despair.

³When the Managua earthquakes rocked the city, Howard Hughes was taking his leisure in a hotel hideaway. According to *Time* magazine, an admiring Hughes aide described this weirdo's actions as follows: "Cool, so cool." *Time* adds: "The phantom of high finance ducked through falling debris and spent his 67th birthday camping out in a nearby field. Looking for more comfortable surroundings, Hughes summoned a jet and flew off to London where he took over a whole floor of a hotel at $2,500 a day." In London, the *Daily Express* quoted another Hughes henchman as saying that his boss now felt "life has been passing him by . . . he's going to change that." The U.S. Embassy stated that Hughes would have to appear personally and pay $12 to renew his expired passport. "That's what every American has to do," said an embassy spokesman, "and it will be the same for Hughes." If Hughes has complied with this slight formality, no British or American cameraman has detected him in the act.

⁴While escapist Howard Hughes was fleeing the scene of tragedy where an estimated 6,000 were killed and another 20,000 injured, Roberto Clemente decided that he could be of assistance. The native of Puerto Rico headed a relief committee that gathered tons of supplies for victims of the earthquake. But fate decreed that the Pittsburgh Pirate hero would be killed on a mercy flight when his chartered DC-7 crashed. Puerto Rico's Gov.-elect Rafael Hernandez Colon proclaimed that "Roberto died in moments in which he was serving his fellow man. Our youth loses an idol and an example. Our people lose some of their glories." Gen. Anastasio Somoza, whose family has ruled Nicaragua for more than 30 years, paid this tribute: "Roberto Clemente died as a hero, leaving his family in order to aid humanity."

[5]But what can be said of Howard Hughes, other than here was a man who could have remained on the scene, could have used his great financial resources to help provide for the stricken, and could have made his presence felt in the only compassionate act he is known to have committed. So, Hughes now feels that "life has been passing him by." How touching. A life of utter selfishness has few rewards. There are a few biblical quotations that apply to persons such as Hughes, but I fear they would be incomprehensible to this victim of his own self-hypnosis.

[6]As we mourn Roberto Clemente and pay him tribute, let the wretched Hughes hasten to embrace his miseries wherever he may choose to rot.—John S. Knight, "Tragedy Spotlights Contrasts of Two Americans"

3. Pick two words or phrases that are often used in comparable ways. Write a comparison-contrast in which you show the likenesses and the differences between the meanings of the two. Suggestions:

Fashion—Style
Pathetic—Tragic
Persuasion—Force
Civil disobedience—Dissent
Amateur—Professional
Politician—Civil servant
Student—Teacher
Man—Woman
Movie—TV program
Blocking—Tackling
Housewife—Career woman

Writing Better Themes

Writing Better Themes

5 Organizing Clear Paragraphs and Themes

The Promise Pattern

There are many ways to organize a piece of writing. The most frequently used — and for many purposes, probably the best — employs what we call the *promise pattern*. You "promise" your reader at the beginning of your theme that you will tell him certain things, and as you write you fulfill your promise. The promise pattern is most easily seen in a typical paragraph. (Much of what we say here concerning the organization of paragraphs applies generally to complete themes also.)

Near the beginning of the following paragraph about surviving in the desert, the author makes a promise (note italics) to his reader:

> These few examples make one thing clear: for anyone who has to survive in the desert, the heat of the day, both cause and effect of the lack of water, is the chief danger. *Temperatures reach an amazing height.* In Baghdad the thermometer in the hot summer months often climbs to 150°F., occasionally even to 180° and over (in the sun). In the Sahara near Azizia (Libya) temperatures of 134° in the shade have been recorded, and in July 1913 that was also the temperature in the Great Salt Lake Desert (also in the shade). But if the thermometer is put in the sand there at noon during the summer, the mercury goes up to 176°. On the side of Highway 91, which goes through the Mohave Desert, it has sometimes been 140° in the shade at noon; in the evenings the thermometer sinks to a "low" of 90°. In Libya, Montgomery's and Rommel's soldiers sometimes fried eggs on the armor plate of their tanks. — Cord-Christian Troebst, *The Art of Survival*

In the rest of the paragraph after the italicized sentence, Troebst keeps his promise — to discuss and illustrate amazingly high desert temperatures.

Before we continue, a word about terms.

A theme promise = a theme's *thesis*
A paragraph promise = the prargraph's *topic idea*

As you probably remember from high school, the *topic idea* of a paragraph is its main, controlling statement, which is often expressed in a *topic sentence*. The topic idea of Troebst's paragraph is expressed in the italicized topic sentence, *Temperatures reach an amazing height*. Some paragraphs need two or three sentences to express their topic ideas (or promises), while a few paragraphs have no topic ideas at all. A paragraph that contains no topic ideas may fulfill the promise made in a preceding paragraph, or it may provide a transition between paragraphs.

Consider the promise pattern in the two paragraphs below. In an earlier section (not given here) the writer promised his reader that he would relate how immigrant Jews lived in a big American city. In the first paragraph, he keeps that promise; in the second he makes and keeps another:

Previous topic idea developed (promise kept)

¹The Jews in Lawndale cut down the trees for firewood and tramped out the grass in the parking strips. They removed the doorknobs and the light fixtures from the flats they rented and sold them for junk. They allowed the drains in their sinks to become clogged with debris, and when you went into their kitchens, you would see the sink full of water to the brim with fishtails and other remains of food products floating in it. I know because my aunt owned her house in Lawndale for some time after she had moved out of it and gone to Oak Park, and when I was in my teens I used to go in and collect the rent for her.

Transition from previous paragraph

New topic idea (promise)

²Obviously this was a situation ideally calculated to inspire racial and religious prejudice. But the dreadful mistake which many persons made was that they supposed that these people were behaving as they did because they were Jews. *The truth of the matter is of course that they were behaving thus because they were peasants. They had not yet learned how to live in an American city.* They, or their fathers, had come from Polish and Russian villages (most of the older members of the community had not even learned to speak English), and when they first came to America they had been herded into slums where it would have been impossible for anybody to live in any other way than they were living. They were now in the first stage of their escape from the slums, but they did not yet know any better than to take the slums with them. All this was straight sociological conditioning, and it had nothing whatever to do with their

Promise kept

being Jews. I am sure that most of us would have been astonished if we had been told that their children and grandchildren would have made their adjustment with complete success and that, long before the date at which I am writing, some of these would have made important contributions to American welfare and become distinguished citizens in music, science, philanthropy, and many others areas of our corporate life.—Edward Wagenknecht, *As Far As Yesterday: Memories and Reflections*

It is important to understand that when you make a promise to your reader you set up an expectation. Suppose you make this statement near the beginning of an essay: *The problem of recreation at Windsor College is not as great as the administration believes.* Immediately your reader perks up his ears (he may have thought it was a great problem), and he expects you to show him in some detail why the problem is not as great as some people think. If you wander off into another subject (like academic achievement, for instance), or do not give details concerning your thesis/promise, you will fail to satisfy his expectations. He will then say you haven't done your job of communication—and he will be right.

Idealized, the promise pattern for a typical theme looks like this:

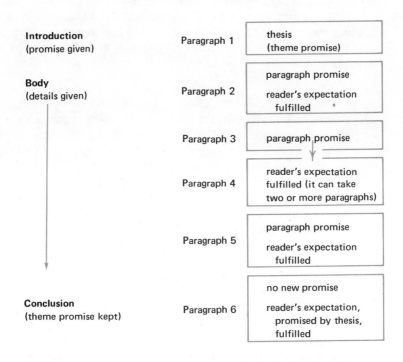

Introduction (promise given)	Paragraph 1	thesis (theme promise)
Body (details given)	Paragraph 2	paragraph promise / reader's expectation fulfilled
	Paragraph 3	paragraph promise
	Paragraph 4	reader's expectation fulfilled (it can take two or more paragraphs)
	Paragraph 5	paragraph promise / reader's expectation fulfilled
Conclusion (theme promise kept)	Paragraph 6	no new promise / reader's expectation, promised by thesis, fulfilled

PRACTICE

1. The following sentences from student themes were written to act as statements of promise. For class discussion, answer these questions. (a) What do these statements promise the reader? (b) Can each promise be reasonably fulfilled by the writer in a paragraph? In a theme of 500–1000 words? (c) If you answered *yes* to either part of (b), explain briefly how *you* might go about fulfilling the reader's expectation for each statement.

    a. Ballet is becoming one of the most popular art forms in America today.
    b. The history of war proves that human beings can never get along.
    c. The American luxury car is less popular now because its snob appeal is gone and it costs too much to repair and operate.
    d. Contrary to what many students think, our chemistry lab has more expensive equipment than the beginning student needs.
    e. There are no good Chinese / French / Italian restaurants in my hometown.

2. Using the idealized promise pattern as a guide, read the following essay and look for the writer's employment of the pattern. What is his theme promise? His paragraph promises? Locate each paragraph promise and explain its location in the paragraph. Are the "reader's expectations" fulfilled? Explain specifically why or why not.

    [1]The actual process of riveting is simple enough—in description. Rivets are carried to the job by the rivet boy, a riveter's apprentice whose ambition is to replace one of the members of the gang—which one, he leaves to luck. The rivets are dumped into a keg beside a small coke furnace. The furnace stands on a platform of loose boards roped to steel girders which may or may not have been riveted. If they have not been riveted there will be a certain amount of play in the temporary bolts. The furnace is tended by the heater or passer. He wears heavy clothes and gloves to protect him from the flying sparks and intense heat of his work, and he holds a pair of tongs about a foot-and-a-half long in his right hand. When a rivet is needed, he whirls the furnace blower until the coke is white-hot, picks up a rivet with his tongs, and drives it into the coals. His skill as a heater appears in his knowledge of the exact time necessary to heat the steel. If he overheats it, it will flake, and the flakes will permit the rivet to turn in its hole. And a rivet which gives in its hole is condemned by the inspectors.
    [2]When the heater judges that his rivet is right, he turns to face the

catcher, who may be above or below him or fifty or sixty or eighty feet away on the same floor level with the naked girders between. There is no means of handing the rivet over. It must be thrown. And it must be accurately thrown. And if the floor beams of the floor above have been laid so that a flat trajectory is essential, it must be thrown with considerable force. The catcher is therefore armed with a smallish, battered tin can, called a cup, with which to catch the red-hot steel. Various patented cups have been put upon the market from time to time but they have made little headway. Catchers prefer the ancient can.

[3]The catcher's position is not exactly one which a sportsman catching rivets for pleasure would choose. He stands upon a narrow platform of loose planks laid over needle beams and roped to a girder near the connection upon which the gang is at work. There are live coils of pneumatic tubing for the rivet gun around his feet. If he moves more than a step or two in any direction, he is gone, and if he loses his balance backward he is apt to end up at street level without time to walk. And the object is to catch a red-hot iron rivet weighing anywhere from a quarter of a pound to a pound and a half and capable, if he lets it pass, of drilling an automobile radiator or a man's skull 500 feet below as neatly as a shank of shrapnel. Why more rivets do not fall is the great mystery of skyscraper construction. The only reasonable explanation offered to date is the reply of an erector's foreman who was asked what would happen if a catcher on the Forty Wall Street job let a rivet go by him around lunch hour. "Well," said the foreman, "he's not supposed to."

[4]The most curious fact about a riveter's skill is that he is not one man but four: "heater," "catcher," "bucker-up," and "gun-man." The gang is the unit. Riveters are hired and fired as gangs, work in gangs, and learn in gangs. If one member of a gang is absent on a given morning, the entire gang is replaced. A gang may continue to exist after its original members have all succumbed to slippery girders or the business end of a pneumatic hammer or to a foreman's zeal or merely to the temptations of life on earth. And the skill of the gang will continue with it. Men overlap each other in service and teach each other what they know. The difference between a gang which can drive 525 inch-and-an-eighth rivets in a working day and a gang which can drive 250 is a difference of coordination and smoothness. You learn how not to make mistakes and how not to waste time. You learn how to heat a rivet and how not to overheat it, how to throw it accurately but not too hard, how to drive it and when to stop driving it, and precisely how much you can drink in a cold wind or a July sun without losing your sense of the width and balance of a wooden plank. And all these things, or most of them, an older hand can tell you. . . .
—"Skyscrapers: Builders and Their Tools," *Fortune* magazine

3. Write a theme using the promise pattern.

Writing Successful Paragraphs

A paragraph is a collection of sentences that helps you fulfill your thesis (theme promise). Itself a small "theme," a paragraph should be clearly written and specific; and it should not wander or make irrelevant remarks. Each paragraph should be related in some way to the theme promise. Here are suggestions for writing successful paragraphs.

1. Since a paragraph is usually part of a larger piece of writing (theme, research paper, report, etc.), use your outline to help you construct paragraphs that support the theme promise or thesis. Your outline will show you whether your paragraph contains the promise or if it will support a previously stated promise.

2. After you have decided on your paragraph promise, jot down all the facts and details that will support it. Arrange these ideas in a logical form and sequence, with your details and *specific* examples fulfilling the paragraph promise. Consider this paragraph written by an ex-cigarette smoker describing his withdrawal symptoms:

Promise **Joints, muscles, and calves hurt** **General aching**	*My body was sicker than I thought it could be.* The joints in my arms and shoulders and the muscles in my chest and my calves hurt so badly the first night I hid in the dark and cried. That pain lasted only one day, but for at least a week I was always aching somewhere. My mouth, nose, throat, stomach, and each tooth were deprived of smoke and nicotine, and their reactions lasted
Results of deprivation in mouth, throat, nose	much longer. I kept arching my mouth wide open as if adjusting cheap store-bought teeth. My throat was sore as if I had smoked too much, perhaps from inhaling too hard on an absent cigarette. I blew my nose needlessly. It is staggering how many parts of me—phalange, organ, membrane, and hair—wanted a smoke, each in its own
Nausea	sore way. For two full weeks I was nauseated. Peanuts and Irish whiskey are as good a way as I found to calm this sick desire of the body for tobacco. The cure, however, is expensive.—Budd Whitebook, "Confessions of an Ex-Smoker"*

3. Get to the point of your paragraph quickly and specifically. Don't waste time or words in stating your paragraph promise. Consider this good example of getting to the point—the writer is explaining the ancient Romans' technique for conquering their world:

> The technique of expansion was simple. *Divide et impera* [divide and conquer]: enter into solemn treaty with a neighbouring country, foment internal disorder, intervene in support of the weaker side on the pretense that Roman honour was involved, replace the legitimate ruler with a puppet, giving him the status of a subject ally; later, goad him into rebellion, seize and sack the country, burn down the temples, and carry off the captive gods to adorn a triumph. Conquered territories were placed under the control of a provincial governor-general, an ex-commander-in-chief who garrisoned it, levied taxes, set up courts of summary justice, and linked the new frontiers with the old by so-called Roman roads—usually built by Greek engineers and native forced labour. Established social and religious practices were permitted so long as they did not threaten Roman administration or offend against the broad-minded Roman standards of good taste. The new province presently became a springboard for further aggression—Robert Graves, "It Was a Stable World"

Graves makes his promise in the first nine words, in which he mentions the "simple" technique the Romans had for "dividing" and "conquering" in order to expand their empire. Suppose Graves had started his paragraph this way:

> The technique of expansion was interesting. It was based upon a theory about human nature that the Romans practically invented. This theory had to do with how people reacted to certain political and military devices which . . . .

Do you see what is wrong? Since the beginning sentences are so vague, the paragraph never gets going. The writer can't fulfill a promise because he hasn't made one. Another example of a poor paragraph beginning:

> The first step involves part of the golf club head. The club head has removable parts, some of which are metal. You must consider these parts when deciding how to repair the club.

Specify the beginning of this paragraph and get to the point quicker:

> Your first step in repairing the club head is to remove the metal plate held on by Phillips Screws.

This solid, specific paragraph beginning gives your reader a clear promise which you can fulfill easily without wasting words. (Observe, by the way, that establishing a writer's stance—as we did in the last example—can help you write clearer paragraph beginnings.)

4. Experiment with other useful organizational patterns for the promise paragraph—such as *time* and *space*. Read this student theme.

A Trial

Introduction

[1]About two years ago, my brother was charged with armed robbery, and I attended all the sessions of the trial. Three days stand out in my memory as being the most difficult of my life—the first day, the day the jury brought in the verdict, and the day my brother was sentenced.

Space

[2]The first day I became acquainted with the unfamiliar surroundings of the courtroom. When our family entered, it was full of spectators sitting in rows at the back of the court. We sat on two benches near the front. My brother and his lawyer sat on the left side of the room, facing the judge. The prosecuting attorney sat at the right front. The jury sat in a box along the wall on my right. As I sat there, I could feel all the eyes in the courtroom moving back and forth along the row where we were sitting. Whenever I glanced up I saw people smiling at us, but I knew what they thought. If someone laughed, I felt ashamed, and when someone whispered, I was offended.

Time

[3]On that first day, a young man told the jury that he recognized my brother. He pointed to him and said, "That's the man. That's him!" The girls who worked at the place he supposedly robbed were the next witnesses, and they said they were unsure of his identity. That first day I had to get used to the humiliation of the prosecuting attorney and the witnesses talking about my brother and the robbery.

Time

[4]The day the jury returned and announced the verdict of guilty, I felt a lump in my throat. I did not want to cry in front of all those people. Instead, I cried inside. I could see a tear on my father's face, and that made my agony worse. My mother was shaking her head and tears trickled down her cheeks. A few days later, my brother was sentenced to a term in the state penitentiary. This time I could not hold back the tears. It seemed that the pool of tears I had cried inside were now rushing up at once. They kept flowing. I tried to wipe them away with my hands, but I couldn't. Crying uncontrollably, I rushed past the people sitting behind us to the restroom to clean my face, but all I could find were rough paper towels that wouldn't absorb the tears. I stayed in the restroom, crying, until they took my brother, handcuffed, downstairs to the jail.

5. Avoid fragmentary paragraphs. A fragmentary paragraph does not develop its topic or fulfill its promise. A series of fragmentary paragraphs jumps from idea to idea in a jerky and unconvincing fashion:

> [1]My freshman rhetoric class is similar in some ways to my senior English class in high school, but it is also very different.
>
> [2]In my English class we usually had daily homework assignments that were discussed during the class period. If we were studying grammar, the assignments were to correct grammatical errors in the text. If we were studying literature, we were supposed to read the material and understand its ideas.
>
> [3]In rhetoric class, we do basically the same things, except that in the readings we are assigned, we look much deeper into the purpose of the author.
>
> [4]In my English class. . . .

Fragmentary paragraphs are often the result of a weak writer's stance.

6. Don't allow any paragraph to be a collection of unrelated statements. Notice that the following paragraph contains at least six paragraph promises, none of them properly supported.

> Peter Benchley's best-selling novel, *The Deep,* like his enormously popular book, *Jaws,* has come to the screen as a thrilling underwater epic. In brief, the story revolves around a honeymooning couple who dive in the reefs of Bermuda looking for the wreck of a sunken ship. What they find lures them into a terrifying struggle for survival. None of the actors — Nick Nolte, Robert Shaw, Jacqueline Bisset, Lou Gossett — had ever attempted an underwater dive. Nearly 11,000 practice attempts made them professionals. The set of *The Deep* was the largest ever constructed underwater for a film. Jacqueline Bisset was born in England and began her career as a model. She is considered one of the most beautiful women in films today. Nick Nolte gained fame in the successful *Rich Man, Poor Man* TV series. He lives far from the deep on a five-acre estate and enjoys his collection of old cars, dogs and horses.

7. Avoid irrelevancies in your paragraphs. The italicized sentence does not fit the development of this paragraph:

> We need a better working atmosphere at Restik Tool Company. The workers must feel that they are a working team instead of just individuals. If the men felt they were part of a team, they would not misuse the special machine tools, which now need to be resharpened twice as often as they used to be. *Management's attitude toward the union could be improved too.* The team effort is also being damaged by introduction of new products before their bugs have been worked out. Just when the men are getting used to one routine, a new one is installed, and their carefully created team effort is seriously damaged.

As with the fragmentary paragraph, the problem of irrelevancies in a paragraph is often the result of a vague writer's stance. The paragraph above does not seem to be written for any particular reader.

1. Prepare some notes for a class discussion of the following paragraphs. Center your analysis of the paragraphs on the *promise pattern*. How well do the paragraphs get to the point and fulfill their promises? Do the authors need a different stance? What suggestions for improvement, if any, would you make? Optional: Rewrite the first paragraph, which is from the middle of a theme on body surfing.

The physical sensations of body surfing are pleasurable. The cold water is invigorating. The churning water is exhilarating. The activity makes me feel more alive and receptive to the sensations I receive. The activity also relieves tension. Besides feeling the power around me, working for me, I like to smell and taste the salt water. It reminds me of the difference between the world on land and the ocean world and its vastness. With my experiences in skin diving I can see the beginnings of its vast depths. Standing on the beach I can see its vastness as it disappears over the horizon. It all combines to overwhelm me. I respect the ocean for its vastness and beauty and am somewhat awed by its majesty. Body surfing is a way of escaping the everyday world and entering a more perfect, ideal one.

[1]In this confusion, with cigar butts lying about, his large assortment of pipes scattered on whatever would support them, matchboxes everywhere—he was a large consumer of matchboxes, for he struck an incredible number of matches in order to keep a cigar or a pipe alight—and with the air filled with the decaying smell of tobacco, he passed his working hours in supreme contentment. He enjoyed writing, even though it was always difficult for him, and he enjoyed wrestling with ideas. He could not afford a large and extensive library, and at no time did he possess more than a thousand books. But in a hundred notebooks he preserved the important passages from the books he had read in the British Museum, and the library therefore represented only a part of his available literary resources. He was an inveterate note-taker, and the habit grew even more pronounced as he grew older.

[2]What Marx did not know was that this mode of life was slowly killing him. It was not only that he smoked too much, but he spent eight or nine hours a day breathing tobacco smoke in a room where, except on calm summer days, the windows were permanently closed. He was taking less and less exercise, and less and less sensible food, for now that he was reasonably affluent he was indulging himself more and more with highly seasoned foods. The only physical exercise came from the Sunday walks on Hampstead Heath, but these were neither so frequent nor so prolonged as in the days when he was younger. Sometimes he would go for a short stroll on Hampstead Heath in the evening.—Robert Payne, *Marx*

2. In order to save electricity, assume that you must get rid of every appliance in your home. Using *time* organization, write a paragraph in which you describe your decision about which appliances must go first — down to the very last one.

3. Write a paragraph, organized by *space* on:

    a. The stage as it appeared to you the first time you were in a play
    b. The college registration procedure the first time you registered
    c. Your first visit to your dormitory room or apartment
    d. Your mouth after your dentist applied braces
    e. Your car after it was wrecked
    f. Your _____ before/during/after _____

Non-promise Paragraphs

If you read typical modern paragraphs, you will find that most of them are organized on the promise pattern. But there are two broad classes of paragraphs that writers organize somewhat differently — the *suspense paragraph* and the *transitional paragraph*.

SUSPENSE PARAGRAPHS

We call them *suspense paragraphs* because the writer does not put the topic idea near the beginning. He places it later, near the middle or even at the end, a technique which allows him to concentrate on details and keep you in suspense as to what they add up to. He holds back his point in order to make it more dramatic, interesting, or emphatic. This kind of paragraph is often called the *inductive paragraph* because it develops from the particular to the general. (It is the reverse of the promise paragraph.) Here is an example:

> For instance, there is a current impression that it is unpleasant to have to run after one's hat. Why should it be unpleasant to the well-ordered and pious mind? Not merely because it is running, and running exhausts one. The same people run much faster in games and sports. **Details and examples** The same people run much more eagerly after an uninteresting little leather ball than they will after a nice silk hat. There is an idea that it is humiliating to run after one's hat, and when people say it is humiliating they

Topic idea (point) mean that it is comic. It certainly is comic; but man is a very comic creature, and most of the things he does are comic — eating, for instance. *And the most comic things of all are exactly the things that are most worth doing —* such as making love. A man running after a hat is not half so ridiculous as a man running after a wife. — G. K. Chesterton, "On Running After One's Hat"

Here is another suspense paragraph, written by Alistair Cooke, who had been asked to write about the American oil industry, a subject he knew nothing about. He panicked until he found an old man in Texas who knew "more about oil than anybody."

Details and examples

Topic idea (point)

I went to see the old man, and right away he said, "What do you know about oil?" Absolutely nothing, I said. "Fine," was his comment. I sat with him for one day, and went over the fields for another; and in forty-eight hours he took me step by step over the history and practice of the industry. It was like sitting at the feet of Aristotle and having your mind rinsed out at frequent intervals with such drafts of common sense as "A play has a beginning, a middle, and an end." I went off on many more expeditions after that, and remember with pleasure the tricks of a couple of Irishmen growing spray orchids in an Oregon hothouse, or tramping out at night into the mountains of Arizona with an infrared lamp to spot strategic minerals embedded in the rocks like petrified tropical fish. *From all these safaris and interviews I came to the tentative, but for me amazing, conclusion that the first-rate businessman in this country is more precise, more imaginative, watchful, and intelligent about his trade than 90 per cent of the writers and academics who despise him.* — Alistair Cooke, *Talk About America*

TRANSITIONAL PARAGRAPHS

The transitional paragraph, which usually acts as a bridge between two other paragraphs, is often found in a fairly long piece of writing. As the short italicized paragraph below illustrates, it can prepare the reader for a plunge into a new topic.

There was, however, a darker and more sinister side to the Irish character. They are, said a land agent on the eve of the famine, "a very desperate people, with all this degree of courtesy, hospitality, and cleverness amongst them."

To understand the Irish of the nineteenth century and their blend of courage and evasiveness, tenacity and inertia, loyalty and double-deal-

ing, it is necessary to go back to the Penal Laws.

    The Penal Laws, dating from 1695, and not repealed in their entirety until Catholic emancipation in 1829, aimed at the destruction of Catholicism in Ireland by a series of ferocious enactments. . . .—Cecil Woodham-Smith, *The Great Hunger: Ireland, 1845–1849*

In the longer transition, a writer may sum up what he has been saying before he introduces a new subject, and so he gives his readers a chance to catch up before he goes on to a new topic. Example:

    So far, we have spoken only about that portion of the stellar population that falls within the main sequence. All these stars, as we have seen, are very much the same. They differ mainly in their stages of evolution, which in turn is a result of their mass and the speed at which they use up their original fuel supply. But what happens to a star after it has used up its allotment of hydrogen? Can we find examples of such stars that have reached old age in their life cycle? Or can we find examples of stars that are still in their babyhood as far as the stellar cycle is concerned?—John Rublowsky, *Life and Death of the Sun*

PRACTICE

1. Write a *suspense* (inductively organized) paragraph on one of the following topics:

    a. a description of a problem, with your solution at the end
    b. a series of details reporting an event in college life, with a generalizing explanation at the end
    c. a series of statements or descriptions building up to a prediction

2. Do a complete rewrite of an old theme, concentrating on paragraph organization and, if appropriate, using transitional paragraphs.

How to Arrange Your Ideas

    Figuratively speaking, ideas come in different sizes and shapes. Some are smooth and familiar; some are jagged and strange. Some are unimportant; some are important; some of small value; others very valuable. Since your ideas in a theme may vary in certain ways, it is wise to arrange them in a pleasing and understandable fashion. A reader does not like to have ideas simply thrown at him in whatever order occurs to the writer.

It is likely that you know more about your theme subject than your reader does. Much of your material may be unfamiliar to him. A capable writer is often much like a professional guide in a jungle who leads his group of travelers toward an objective by avoiding wild animals, pitfalls, and quicksand traps. It is easier to lose a reader on the page than a fellow-traveler in a jungle. Here are a few suggestions that can help you become a more experienced guide through such dangers.

START WITH A SIMPLE OR FAMILIAR IDEA

If your subject warrants such treatment, you can plan the total theme to *lead* the reader from a simple (or familiar) idea to a more complex (or unfamiliar) one. Be sure that he understands each idea before the next is introduced. In the following two examples, each writer uses this strategy.

Familiar detail: beach ball

[1]To help us get a better picture of this solar system let us imagine a model of it reduced some five billion times. In this model, the sun is a beach ball about twelve inches across. Now, how far away would you imagine the planets to be from the sun on this scale? . . .

Familiar details: dust specks and pinhead

[2]Mercury, the closest planet to the sun and as small as a speck of dust in this scale, would be forty-two feet away. Venus, the second speck, about twice as big as Mercury, would be seventy-eight feet away. Earth, about the size of a pinhead next to the twelve-inch beach-ball sun, would be one hundred eight feet away; Mars, fifty-four yards; Jupiter, one hundred eighty yards; Saturn, three hundred forty yards; Neptune, one thousand eighty yards; and more than a mile away, tiny Pluto would move along its slow orbital path around the sun.

Application of familiar detail to scale of solar system

[3]Beyond this model of the solar system, the nearest star, on this same beach-ball scale, would be four thousand miles away. And farther still, the nearest galaxy would be almost four million miles out.—John Rublowsky, *Life and Death of the Sun*

First paragraph of article

[1]Most studies of atmospheric diffusion carried out heretofore have relatively little relevance to air pollution. The theoretical studies have been concerned (with some exceptions) with ideal situations which are sufficiently simple to be solved, at least approximately, and the experimental investigations have been carried out in situations which approximate the idealizations as nearly as possible in order to test the theory.

[2]Perhaps I should interrupt myself long enough to explain to nonspecialists just what is meant by *atmospher-*

ic diffusion. In the old days when people took cream in their coffee it was simple to illustrate from their daily experience. If poured into the coffee very slowly and not stirred, the cream would remain a long time where it was poured, and only slowly mix with the dark brown brew. Stirring with a spoon creates an irregular motion we call *mechanical turbulence,* which speeds up the horizontal and vertical spread of the cream and its rapid mingling with the coffee to form a uniform mixture. This spread and mixing is the process known as *diffusion.*

Application of *knowns,* by analogy, to "atmospheric diffusion"

[3]If the cream were poured first and then the coffee, the tendency of the light cream to rise to the top and the heavy coffee to sink would create convection, which would further tend to mix the two, even in the absence of mechanical stirring. In this case we speak of the stratification as *unstable,* whereas when the heavier fluid is at the bottom we say it is stable. The degree of stability and the amount of mechanical turbulence are the factors which determine the rate of diffusion in the atmosphere.—Morris Neiburger, "Where Is Science Taking Us?"

In the first example, Rublowsky gives his readers a relevant familiar detail (the beach ball) and works from it in order to lead us to a partial understanding of the vast distances in the solar system.

Since the second example is the beginning of Neiburger's article on *atmospheric diffusion,* he explains the term here in his introduction. To do so, he needs to define related terms — *mechanical turbulence, diffusion,* and *stability.* Instead of throwing these words at the reader without explanation, he uses an analogy: the familiar act of putting cream in one's coffee. After the reader has understood how diffusion and turbulence work in familiar liquids, he can better understand how they work in the atmosphere.

USE A GRADED ORDER OF IDEAS

In a piece of writing you may deal with ideas or actions that vary in interest, importance, usefulness, practicality, and value. For example, there are five ways to leave our college town when vacation starts and one could "grade" them according to

— how expensive they are
— how fast they are
— how dangerous they are
— how practical they are
— how interesting they are
— how reliable they are

Here is an example of a student's graded order using the organizing principle of *reliability.*

> For you new students who have not yet fought the battle of the student exodus, let me suggest the best way to get out of town before Christmas. Hitchhiking is illegal and dangerous—not very reliable. Planes are fast, but they don't go to enough hometowns, and airports get snowed in this time of year. Somewhat more reliable is the train, but the locals recently have had a nasty habit of running six or seven hours late. A car is better than the train, if you have one or know someone who does—and he happens to be going your way. The most reliable transportation for the average student is the bus. Buses aren't crowded and they are inexpensive. Also they are surprisingly fast, since if you plan ahead you can get an express bus that does not stop at small towns.

It is customary when employing any graded order to go from the "least" to the "most"—for example, from the *least reliable* to the *most reliable,* as in the paragraph above. You should follow this pattern partly because you want to get the less important ideas out of the way quickly so that you can get on with the more important ones. Also, you build up interest if you leave your best point until last. If you give your reader your best idea first he may quit reading in the middle of your paper. However, there are exceptions to this convention, as you can see in this example:

> [1]A good deal has been written about the values of owning a foreign car, but few people have given much thought to the realities of such ownership. Advertisers bombard us with facts about "fabulous gas mileage," but **Least important (gas mileage)** miles-per-gallon (so far as expense is concerned) is the least important thing to an owner of a foreign car. Of greater importance, since it eats into his mileage "savings" is the high initial cost of an import, which is often four or five hundred dollars more than that of the cheaper American makes. **Most important (repair costs)** More important still is the fact that parts and repair often cost so much that the import owner finds himself spending more on his car than the owner of a much bigger American automobile.
>
> **Transition** **Most comfortable (in city)** [2]Similarly, Americans often fool themselves about the comfort of the import, which, it is true, rides and parks like a dream in the city. But the car that gives a comfortable ride in town, that parks in a very small space, that turns on a dime, and is easy to get in and out of is a differ- **Least comfortable (in country)** ent vehicle on the highway. Anyone who has driven a light foreign car a few miles in a crosswind can sympathize with the Californian who drove his import to Denver and there promptly traded it off for several thousand pounds of power-steered, power-braked metal monster from Detroit before he started his trip home.

Write a theme in which you use a *graded order* to explain an unfamiliar process, device, or activity. Where you can, help your reader by moving from simple or familiar ideas to more difficult ones.

Introductions and Conclusions

An effective introduction ordinarily does two things: (1) it catches the reader's interest ("hooks" him, as journalists say), and makes him want to read on; (2) it tells him what the theme is about by stating the thesis and defining any unfamiliar terms.

An effective conclusion rounds off the paper. As you will see in the following examples, a conclusion often "matches" its introduction by referring to or restating the writer's thesis or his "hook." If the rest of the paper has been planned carefully, conclusions often seem to write themselves. Here are examples of two effective introductions and conclusions.

Introduction

Hook [1]Very few people would sit at the TV for hours to watch a cargo of potatoes take off from planet earth in a spaceship. Yet a single potato orbiting the sun could hold infinitely greater significance for the future of humanity than would the landing of a man on the moon. For a man on the moon can tell us nothing new about injecting happiness into life on earth. *But a potato in solar orbit* **Thesis** *might lead to the secret of how all growth — hence life itself — is regulated.*

Conclusion

References to material in the article [2]The last of the comments above concern Professor Brown's experiments principally. They convey some sense of the values inherent in orbiting a potato around **Allusion to thesis** the sun. NASA has not yet set a date for this expedition, but a "Spudnik" has been designed and if the conventional scientific opposition to innovation can be overcome, the chosen potato may take off next year. — John Lear, "The Orbiting Potato"

Introduction

Hook: a quotation

[1]Heywood Broun, watching a breadline in 1932, is said to have remarked with cynical sympathy, "Poor people wouldn't be such a bother if they didn't starve so publicly." Since the end of the Depression, and especially in recent years with the development of more sophisticated welfare programs, poor people have been much more discreet about their starving.

[2]Occasionally, the public peace of mind is elbowed by a news story indicating that something may not be quite right — a Mississippi family is reported to have eaten a cat; some Kentucky coal miners are seen eating only potato peelings for lunch; in Washington, D.C., pensioners scramble for discarded lettuce and cabbage leaves behind one of the largest markets. But most poor people are not observed in their ingenuities, and, in any event, the Government lists only 1,279 deaths from "malnutrition" and 197 deaths from "hunger, thirst, and exposure" in 1965, the last year for which there are statistics.

Thesis

[3]*This, coupled with the natural optimism of Americans, has pushed into public faith an almost religious tenet — a second miracle of the loaves and fishes — called Nobody Starves in America, with the alternate title, No Adult Is Completely Broke for Long.*

Conclusion

[4]If change does come, it will probably take some powerful motivating emotion to achieve it. But there is hope for that, too. When Robert Kennedy returned from his safari into Mississippi's shanty jungles, he told of seeing people who eat one meal every two days, but he described the results only as "extreme hunger." For politicians, "starvation" is a smut word. They don't like to come right out and say it exists in this country — so it

Reference to thesis

becomes "hunger" or "malnutrition" — and even less do they like to see that which the taboo word describes; it embarrasses them. Testifying before a Senate group about swollen bellies and running sores and all the cottonpatch grotesqueries he had seen, Kennedy several times became so embarrassed he laughed. The last best hope of "extremely hungry" folks is that that discomfort will spread. — Robert Sherrill, "It Isn't True That Nobody Starves in America"

There are as many ways to write introductions and conclusions as ways to write themes. A short, blunt beginning may make both an effective hook and promise: "The amateur productions in the University Playhouse are poorly directed this year." One-sentence conclusions are occasionally worth trying, although you should be wary of using conclusions that are too brief, for they may leave the reader with a feeling of having been let down.

Here are some ideas for writing introductions.* You might start with:

- An apt quotation
- A literary allusion
- A story or an incident relating to your subject
- A statement that shows how interesting your subject is
- A question that limits your subject; the answer to the question is your theme
- A statement of a problem that readers should know about
- A simple statement of thesis that limits your subject
- A definition of an important word or phrase relating to your subject
- The historical background of your subject (be brief)
- A statement that popular ideas about your subject are wrong and that you intend to refute them in a specific way
- A statement that your subject needs new examination; your theme is the examination
- Pertinent facts about your subject
- Combinations of some of these methods

For a conclusion, you might end your theme with:

- An allusion to the hook of your introduction
- A reference to the question, definition, statement of thesis, historical background, etc., that you started the theme with
- A restatement of your thesis
- A brief answer to the question you raised in the introduction
- A brief statement of the solution to the problem you raised in your introduction
- A new question that relates to your theme, a question that gives the reader something to think about (but be careful not to introduce an undeveloped idea)
- A summary of the main points in your theme (this can be dull and redundant, but often useful if materials are complex)
- A punchy, single sentence—don't punch too hard
- A new story or incident that relates to your subject

Avoid these errors in writing introductions:

- Writing a vague or ambiguous introduction, leaving the thesis of the paper unclear
- Failing to define terms that the reader is not familiar with; some terms should be defined if you are using them in a special sense

*We are indebted to John Conlee for his suggestions regarding introductions and conclusions.

- Writing an introduction that is too long; for most short papers, it is a mistake to write more than a one-paragraph (or, at most, a two-paragraph) introduction

And these errors in writing conclusions:

- Failing to fill out a conclusion, leaving the reader hanging
- Adding irrelevant or unnecessary details
- Adding an undeveloped idea; a conclusion is not the place to develop or introduce ideas

Transitions

Transitions are those words, phrases, and paragraphs that point forward and backward. They are the reader's signposts; without them he might easily get lost. The simplest and most obvious transitions are those that count in order: "This is my *first* idea. . . . Now for the *second* idea. . . . *Third*, I think. . . ." Less obvious are those transitions that do not so much lead the reader by the hand as smooth his way: "*It is certain that* the reactor could not have blown up so easily if. . . . *Nevertheless*, the men in the black suits were blowing up the bridge. . . . *Moreover*, the two physicists could not agree on what to do."

Here are some typical transitional words and phrases:

- To explain ideas: *for instance, for example, such as, specifically, in particular, to illustrate, thus*
- To count or separate ideas: *first, second, third* (but not *firstly, secondly, thirdly*), *moreover, in addition, another, furthermore, also, again, finally*
- To compare ideas: *likewise, similarly, in the same way* DO NOT USE LIKE
- To contrast or qualify ideas: *however, on the other hand, on the contrary, but*
- To show cause or effect: *as a result, consequently, therefore, thus*

Such a listing could continue indefinitely, for under special circumstances hundreds of words and phrases that are not ordinarily thought of as being transitional (like pronouns and certain key words) can be used to link words, ideas, or sentences. As an example, here is a brief passage taken from the middle of a magazine article (linking expressions are in italics):

¹Today it is no secret that our official, prison-threat theory of crime control is an utter failure. Criminologists have known *this* for years. When pocket-picking was punishable by hanging, in England, the crowds that gathered about the gallows to enjoy the spectacle of an execution were particularly likely to have their pockets picked by skillful operators who, to say the least, were not deterred by the exhibition of "justice." We have long known that the perpetrators of most offenses are never detected; *of*

those detected, only a fraction are found guilty and still fewer serve a "sentence." *Furthermore,* we are quite certain now that of those who do, receive the official punishment of the law, many become firmly committed *thereby* to a continuing life of crime and a continuing feud with law enforcement officers. Finding themselves ostracized from society and blacklisted by industry *they* stick with the crowd they have been introduced to in jail and try to play the game of life according to *this set of rules. In this way* society skillfully converts individuals of borderline self-control into loyal members of the underground fraternity. . . .

²What might deter the reader from conduct which his neighbors would not like does not necessarily deter the grown-up child of vastly different background. The *latter's* experiences may have conditioned him to believe that the chances of winning by undetected cheating are vastly greater than the probabilities of fair treatment and opportunity. *He* knows about the official threats and the social disapproval of *such acts.* He knows about the hazards and the risks. *But despite all this "knowledge,"* he becomes involved in waves of discouragement or cupidity or excitement or resentment leading to episodes of social offensiveness.

³*These episodes* may prove vastly expensive both to him and to society. *But* sometimes they will have an aura of success. Our periodicals have only recently described the wealth and prominence for a time of a man described as a murderer. Konrad Lorenz, the great psychiatrist and animal psychologist, has beautifully described in geese what he calls a "triumph reaction." *It* is a sticking out of the chest and flapping of the wings after an encounter with a challenge. All of us have seen *this primitive biological triumph reaction* — in some roosters, *for example,* in some businessmen and athletes and others — and in some criminals. — Karl Menninger, "Verdict Guilty — Now What?"

Organizing by "Creative Repetition"

Repetition, we are told, is an evil in writing; and it seems that we are told this practically from the time we begin to write. Yet the skillful writer instinctively recognizes that carefully repeating certain key words and phrases can help tie his ideas together. The mathematician Norbert Wiener begins his discussion of Brownian motion in this way: "To understand the Brownian motion, let us imagine a *push-ball* in a field in which a *crowd* is milling around. Various people in the *crowd* will run into the *push-ball* and will move it about. Some will *push* in one direction and some in another."

To use repetition creatively, you repeat certain words or phrases in order to keep the reader's mind firmly on the subject. Sometimes you change the grammatical form slightly in order to prevent the repetition from becoming a bore. Here is how one excellent writer of nonfiction employs creative repetition in examining business jargon.

[1]Its signal characteristic, as the reader and all other critics of businesese will recognize, is its uniformity. Almost invariably, businesese is marked by the heavy use of the passive construction. Nobody ever *does* anything. Things happen—and the author of the action is only barely implied. Thus, one does not refer to something, reference is made to; similarly, while prices may rise, nobody raises them. To be sure, in businesese there is not quite the same anonymity as is found in federal prose, for "I" and "we" do appear often. Except when the news to be relayed is good, however, there is no mistaking that the "I" and "we" are merely a convenient fiction and that the real author isn't a person at all but that great mystic force known as the corporation.

[2]Except for a few special expressions, its vocabulary is everywhere quite the same. Midwesterners are likely to dispute the latter point, but a reading of approximately 500,000 words of business prose indicates no striking differences—in the Midwest or anywhere else. Moreover, in sounding out a hundred executives on the subject, *Fortune* found that their views coincided remarkably, particularly so on the matter of pet peeves (principally: "please be advised," "in reference to yours of . . . ," "we wish to draw attention," "to acknowledge your letter"). The phrases of businesese are everywhere so uniform, in fact, that stenographers have a full set of shorthand symbols for them.

[3]Because of this uniformity, defenders of businesese can argue that it doesn't make for misunderstanding. After all, everybody knows the symbols, and, furthermore, wouldn't a lot of people be offended by the terseness of more concise wording? There is something to this theory. Since businesese generally is twice as wordy as plain English, however, this theory is rather expensive to uphold. By the use of regular English the cost of the average letter—commonly estimated at 75 cents to $1—can be cut by about 20 cents. For a firm transmitting a million letters a year, this could mean an annual saving of $200,000. Probably it would be even greater; for, by the calculations of correspondence specialist Richard Morris, roughly 15 per cent of the letters currently being written wouldn't be necessary at all if the preceding correspondence had been in regular English in the first place.—William H. Whyte, "The Language of Business"

Whyte employs *businesese* as a catchy technical term, and so he doesn't need to vary the word. Every time he refers to the "sameness" of business prose, however, he varies the word or phrase: *uniformity, quite the same, uniform, this uniformity.* Each use of this "word-idea" is just close enough to the last to keep the reader on the track of the essay's main point. Whyte's article is over twenty-five years old, but it is still the standard discussion of businesese, a fact which says something about the effectiveness of creative repetition.

1. For discussion prepare some notes on the organization of the two passages below. Describe the writer's stance in each. How well does each writer keep his *promise* to the reader and fulfill the reader's expectations? Consider both the paragraph promises (topic ideas) and the theme promise (thesis). Where is the thesis stated? Where are the topic ideas in each paragraph?

    Do the writers use any special techniques for arranging their ideas? Discuss their use of introductions, conclusions, and transitions; and of organizational devices such as creative repetition. To save space, both passages have been cut.

    ¹You don't have to be a farm boy to know what barbed wire is; even the most citified of us has gotten our britches caught at one time or another on the prickly barbs that fence off farm and other property across the breadth of this nation. But to most of us, barbed wire is simply barbed wire.

    ²Not so. At least not to the growing number of collectors taking to the field in search of century-old wires. More than five hundred different types of barbed wire have already been found, identified, and priced. And new varieties are turning up all the time — some of them patented and readily identifiable, some of them not. . . .

    ³Almost certainly part of the mystique of barbed-wire collecting is the allure of the Old West itself. As thousands of miles of wire fences crisscrossed the vast western expanses in the last century, they brought the men who favored the open range into conflict with those who bought and fenced the land. In the end, the open range men were run into the dusty earth, and fences of barbed wire were built around them. The wire that men died over could not entirely escape the romance of the times.

    ⁴But if the story of barbed wire is almost as old as the story of the American West, wire collecting itself is still in its infancy. Indeed, little attention was paid to the rusty, prickly barbed fence until ten years ago, and the biggest surge of interest has come only in the past four or five years. There are presently collectors' associations in at least ten states, and all of them hold annual shows, lasting up to three days, where "bobbed" wire is traded, bought, sold, or sometimes simply talked about by wire enthusiasts. . . .

    ⁵One word of warning that all serious and responsible collectors should remember: never cut a standing fence without permission. In Texas, for instance, as in some other states, fence cutting is still a felony. If you must have a sample of a standing fence, talk to the owner about taking a piece and replacing it with a splice of new fence. Some wire hunters carry a coil of new wire in the back of their car so that they'll be prepared for just such a circumstance.

    ⁶Having discovered an enticing old fence in the Estancia Valley east of Albuquerque, New Mexico, one enterprising collector and a couple of

his friends went a step further. They loaded their pickup with an eighty-rod roll of new barbed wire and set out to replace an old and worrisome fence free of charge. The ranch owner was delighted, and the wire buffs gladly traded four hours of their time for the privilege of snipping the nearly five hundred yards of yesterday's fence into thousands of "trade" pieces.

⁷Such a find obviously gluts the home market, but trades by mail and at distant shows are still profitable. Since hardware stores of the 1880s carried only a few of the many wires available, wire fencing that is common in one area is often a rarity in another. Of course, when too much of a certain wire is found, as sometimes happens, the price does drop.

⁸"Just like the Spur Wheel," one wire buff said. "It was a $5 wire once. Then someone found a whole fence full of it in Nebraska and knocked the price down to $2." But, with the growing number of collectors entering the field against a fixed supply of old fencing, the same aficionado predicts, unhesitatingly, that Spur Wheel will soon be a $5 wire again.—Richard Holben, "The Wire That Won the West"

¹Three seconds after you leap from the Golden Gate Bridge, perhaps the most popular location for suicide in the western world, you hit the water 226 feet below at about 75 miles an hour. The trip is nearly always one-way: It's cold down there, fierce crosscurrents pull a body under in seconds, and the water is 300 feet deep. Only 10 out of the more than 500 people who have jumped since the bridge opened in 1937 are around to tell the story.

²Each year more and more people are doing it, or trying to, and the experts agree that an antisuicide barrier is needed at once. It is not about to happen: A special committee studying the question in San Francisco has just voted against the idea, unanimously, after spending $27,000 on the design and testing of a model. "Much as I hate to say it," sighed Edwin Fraser, bridge district president, "we have to forget it until it's more financially feasible." A barrier would cost between $1 and $2 million and it seems the city has other priorities.

³The committee chairman said mail was running strongly against the barrier anyhow. It was not just the expense: The view would be ruined, and besides, folks would only find another place to do it. San Francisco is full of skyscrapers.

⁴"It's nonsense to say that blocking the bridge will merely send suicides elsewhere," says Dr. Richard Seiden, a psychologist at the University of California at Berkeley. "It is the bridge itself that's fatally attractive." The great russet span of the Golden Gate Bridge, with its sweeping, soaring lines poised over the sparkling blue water, is a glamorous place, and nearly all the suicides choose to jump from the landward side, facing the amphitheater-like ring of cities around the bay.

⁵Six survivors of the leap agreed with Dr. Seiden when asked: If they couldn't have used the bridge as backdrop for their attempt, they

wouldn't have tried at all. Each of them was in favor of the barrier; none has tried to repeat his act elsewhere. . . .

⁶For thousands, San Francisco is the end of the rainbow, the lovely dream-city where all the rootless, dissatisfied, lonely people come from elsewhere expecting that all their troubles will be cured. It does not work out that way and for some it is the final disappointment. If you cannot make it in this fun city, where can you make it?

⁷At least eight agencies and hospitals here are working to help the suicidal, with "hot lines" and crisis centers. But beyond that, doctors agree, there is a great need for more study, research, clinical investigation and social openness about suicide, and, of course, for that Golden Gate barrier. Says Dr. Seiden, "We really don't have to make it so easy."
—Charles Foley, "The Leap from Golden Gate Bridge"

2. After studying the major strategies in organizing paragraphs and themes, you should now be able to use all the skills you have learned in the chapter. Write a theme on a technical subject for a reader who knows little or nothing concerning the matter. *Technical* here refers to any subject that may have some mystery or complexity for the layman—for example, putting in golf, county primary elections, the balancing of tires on a car, the use of shorthand in secretarial work, etc.

In your theme concentrate on using the promise pattern, writing clear paragraphs, arranging your ideas clearly, and writing a good introduction and conclusion. Use transitions where necessary.

6 Improving Theme Content

Your theme's content is the *what* of it—the ideas, facts, descriptions, and details that you put into it to make it informative, truthful, and lively. Perhaps no problem in writing is more intriguing and challenging than this—how can you express accurately and interestingly to your reader the realities of experience, in all its complications and ambiguities? For one solution to this problem, see the following Practice.

PRACTICE

1. Here is how a skillful American author creates accurate, interesting content in his writing. Read John Gunther's description of his friend Albert Lasker, the great advertising man; then answer the questions at the end of the passage.

    ¹At about this period Lasker developed a minor idiosyncrasy which clung to him all his life, a passion for being shaved so close that the blood almost ran. He liked barbers and held that they knew more about what was going on in the world than members of any other trade. His various barbers loved him, but he terrified them. An extremely restless man, he would wriggle while in the chair, use the telephone, or dictate correspondence, muttering the while to the barber, "Closer! Closer!" He kept barber chairs in his office, in his house on the South Side, in Glencoe, and, later, in Lake Forest and Miami. Sometimes he took a folding barber chair with him when he traveled. Once he telephoned his Beverly Hills barber from a place far out in the California desert, instructing him to drop everything and come to him at once. The barber arrived, to find him being shaved in a perfectly satisfactory manner by a man on the spot. Lasker said, "Oh, I just wanted to talk to you, and find out what's going on." If he traveled beyond the reach of his own barbers, he would search out the best local talent available, and offer $10 for a shave. "That's too much," one recruit said. Albert replied: "Wait. It isn't too much for shaving *me!*"

    ²Lasker played golf and poker; also he worked. Few men have ever worked harder. Usually in the Chicago days he got to the office at 7:30 in the morning, and often did not leave till midnight. Late in 1912 he had a serious physical collapse. He records that he could not talk to anybody for five minutes without "bursting into tears." He went to Europe with Flora for five months, recuperating in various spas; another breakdown fol-

lowed, also marked by fits of uncontrollable weeping, and he spent some time in Mexico. Then his health cleared up to a degree, and for some years he was able to resume working fourteen or fifteen hours a day without worry or impediment. — John Gunther, *Taken at the Flood*

a. What does the passage tell about Lasker's character?

b. What is Gunther's attitude toward Lasker? What clues do you find in the passage concerning his attitude?

c. What *kinds* of description does Gunther depend on to make Lasker come alive for the reader?

d. Why is *wriggle* (fourth sentence) a key word in the passage? List other "key words" and explain your choices.

e. Why does Gunther write "for five months" in paragraph 2 instead of something like "for a brief period"?

f. What job do the initial sentences of the two paragraphs perform? Why are these sentences important to the *content* of the paragraphs?

g. Look up the terms *fact* and *generalization* in your dictionary. How many of each can you find in the paragraphs?

h. How would you find out if the episode concerning the Beverly Hills barber actually happened? Is it important that it "actually happened"?

i. Why are there quotation marks around "bursting into tears" in paragraph 2?

j. Why does this version of the last half of paragraph 1 seem dead?

Once he telephoned a favorite barber long-distance, asking the barber to come and shave him. When the barber arrived, he discovered that all Lasker wanted to do was talk to him. If Lasker traveled, he would look for a good barber and pay him more than he was worth for a good shave.

k. Describe Gunther's writer's stance.

2. After working through these questions, you probably have some tentative ideas about improving the content of your own themes. Draw up a brief set of "Practical Rules for Creating Good Content." Adapt them especially to your own problems in writing.

Be Factual

Being factual is a prime virtue in writing. The reader may forgive you at times for being ungrammatical, awkward, or wordy — but he will never forgive you for telling him something that isn't true. But how do you know that a thing, idea, or happening is "true," that it represents what we agree to call a *fact*?

Facts are that which we can *validate, corroborate,* or *verify.* Non-*facts* cannot be validated, corroborated, or verified. William James, in his essay "Pragmatism," commented:

> Truth lives . . . for the most part on a credit system. Our thoughts and beliefs "pass," so long as nothing challenges them, just as banknotes pass so long as nobody refuses them. But this all points to direct face-to-face verifications somewhere, without which the fabric of truth collapses like a financial system with no cash basis whatever. You accept my verification of one thing, I yours of another. We trade on each other's truth. But beliefs verified concretely by *somebody* are the posts of the whole superstructure.

A fact is a piece of truth, then, that exists because "somebody" has *verified* it—has read up on it, asked about it, looked at it (even heard, tasted, felt, or smelled it). Here is a list of facts expressed in short sentences:

> Blood is running from a cut on my face.
> The king is on his throne.
> This is a football.
> A leaf fell.
> I am holding a smelly tomato.
> The Common Market was a free-trade idea.
> Babies often get the croup.
> This piece of paper is clean.

Each of these might be considered a statement of "fact" if it has been verified. Genuine facts should be verifiable by more than one reasonable person or authority. If only one person sees a particular flying saucer, the saucer is for all practical purposes not a fact. If no one besides you sees a leaf fall, or sees the leaf on the ground, the leaf and its falling have not been verified. If people around you can't smell the tomato you are holding, never have heard of babies getting the croup, and can't agree that "this piece of paper is *clean*" then these statements are not to be considered factual.

Let's not argue about "people around you" having no sense of smell, being ignorant of both babies and childhood diseases, or never having seen a "clean" piece of paper. These are all possibilities, and should be taken reasonably into account for individual situations; they are a part of the process of verification. One does not ask a color-blind person, however "reasonable" he may be, to give an authoritative opinion on the distinction between a red dress and a green one. And of course one should always consult genuine authorities on a particular subject. Ask a pediatrician how often babies get the croup. Then it is likely that you will obtain the hard facts.

For there are hard facts and soft ones, the "hard" ones being relatively easy to verify and use, the "soft" ones being less so. Here are some typical hard and soft facts:

Hard (relatively)	Soft (relatively)
He has a skull made of bone.	He has a high IQ.
That family made $3,405.11 last year.	That family is poor.
Fires burn forests.	Brush fires preserve forests by burning out underbrush and saplings.
This car has a broken axle.	The axle broke because the driver abused this car.

Always inspect soft facts carefully before using them in writing. Some soft facts perhaps should not be used at all. For example, in measuring IQ one attempts to measure an essentially unmeasurable thing, intelligence. Get half-a-dozen people in a room to discuss *intelligence*, and they probably won't even be able to agree on what it is, much less on what "high IQ" means when applied to Joe Smith or Sara Jones. Soft facts resist solid verification.

GENERAL AND PARTICULAR FACTS

A *generalization* (or a *general statement*) is a remark about a class or group of things, actions, or ideas:

California produces more tennis stars than any other state.
Most stunt pilots use biplanes.
Dictators rule by fear.
Babies often get the croup.

As these statements suggest, the generalization itself can be a *broad* fact concerning a number of *particular,* individual facts. An important relationship between the particular and the general can be illustrated by this inverted pyramid.

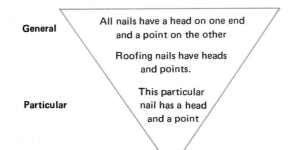

General — All nails have a head on one end and a point on the other

Roofing nails have heads and points.

Particular — This particular nail has a head and a point

As the diagram shows, the ideas of the general and the particular are relative. "Roofing nails have heads and points" is less general than "All nails have a head on one end and a point on the other," but more general than "This particular nail has a head and a point." Here is another example, working from the particular to the general, that uses single words instead of statements: "John" (referring to an actual young man, age ten) is a particular. "Boys" is more general. "Human males" is more general still.

General Statements and Value Judgments

General statements based on facts are usually more difficult to verify than particulars are.

"The English have produced great poets" can be considered a decent factual generalization based upon an examination of many particulars: the great English poets, from Chaucer on. Since the statement is also a *value judgment*—a statement of opinion about the worth of something— it is open to simple contradiction by someone using a different standard of judgment: "I don't think the English poets are as great as you say; I don't like Chaucer, for instance. The Italians have produced greater poets than the English have."

The value judgment is useful in expressing opinions or preferences: "The wine was excellent last night"; "Harding was a poor president"; "I prefer blondes." It is often hard, however, to prove that a value judgment has any factual basis unless a standard for judgment has been established.

Even general statements that are relatively free of value judgment can be troublesome when one tries to show that they are factual. The truth of "Babies often get the croup" hinges, according to one physician, on what *often* means. "Many babies do get croup," says he, "but *often* to me implies a majority. *Most* babies don't get the croup." "The Common Market was a free-trade idea" seems to be a clear-cut fact until one realizes that the idea of the Common Market was and is open to various interpretations and that definitions of *free trade* vary according to experts' views of political and economic history.

Inferences

When we draw a conclusion from one or more facts, we make an inference. General and particular statements of fact are often based upon inferences:

Yellow fever is transmitted by the mosquito. *(Beginning with the work of Walter Reed in 1900–1901, scientists have repeatedly shown that the mosquito carries yellow fever, a fact that we infer from repeated experiments.)*

Sally is allergic to penicillin. *(Every time she takes the drug, she breaks out in a rash. We infer a factual cause-and-effect relation between the drug and the rash.)*

Mexico is friendly to the United States. *(We infer this general fact after investigating many specific incidents concerning Mexico and the United States. In nearly every incident, either the government or the people of Mexico or both have indicated friendliness to us.)*

The man next door is laughing loudly. *(The voice is that of a man. The noise sounds like laughing. The noise is not soft or moderate, but loud.)*

Facts: A Summary

The difficulty of obtaining facts can be overdramatized. Don't fall into the trap of believing that factual material on most subjects is impossible to come by, even though it is true that some areas of human investigation — like the nature of political influence or of artistic inspiration — seem to produce very few facts indeed. The main thing to bear in mind is that facts exist because responsible persons (accountable, rational, and ethical persons) *say* they do, which is what we mean by "verifying" and "validating." When, in a certain area of investigation, the methods of verifying and validating change, or when responsible persons change their opinions, the facts may change also.

A generalization may be (or may imply) a decision, a summary, an interpretation, an opinion, or a value judgment. A generalization may also combine two or more of these. For the purposes of theme writing, we will assume that you will make your generalizations *after* you have inspected the facts available on your subject and *that your generalizations are based on the facts.* If you cannot find reasonably hard facts, you cannot generalize accurately.

PRACTICE

Read the passage below, and answer the questions at the end of it.

[1]Women throw books of poetry to him and propose marriage in dozens of letters each week. Fan clubs pay tribute to him throughout Western Europe. He has starred in two hit movies, one of them about himself, and earned more money ($10 million) than it cost to build the Spanish Armada. In July he became the fourth matador in this century to be allowed to spare the life of his bull. In August, he became the first in history to fight 31 *corridas* in one month. And, barring illness or injury, by this time next month the mop-haired lad who calls himself "El Cordobés" will have killed more bulls and been awarded more of their ears in more fights before more people in one year than any other bullfighter who ever lived.

[2]"A taurine odyssey," proclaimed one Madrid newspaper this month, and to his flocks of worshipers, some of whom have paid $65 a seat to watch him, the 29-year-old El Cordobés is the most exciting bullfighter who ever strode the sands. Brushing his great shock of sandy hair out of his eyes, he dances in front of the bull's horns, pulls its tail, turns his back on it, and usually manages to smear its blood all over himself. If the bull won't charge him, he charges the bull; and to keep things exciting, he will receive the bull standing up, on his knees and even sitting down. He has been gored 18 times. "He's the Picasso of the ring," exults one admirer. "He's finding fantastic new ways of expressing himself."

[3]Yet, to true *aficionados* of the world's only blood art, El Cordobés is the death of the afternoon. "He's like Chubby Checker playing Bach," sniffs one ardent detractor. "It's pop bullfighting."

[4]His vulgarity is only a minor concern of the critics; what shocks them is that, unlike Picasso, he has never really learned the tools of his trade. He handles the cape like a housewife flapping a bed sheet and uses the bright red muleta as if he were flagging down a train. Worst of all, he is so inept with the sword that about the only way he can be sure of killing the bull is to shoot it. He had to stab one bull 16 times this month before it would die, and twice within the past two weeks he has heard the rare warning of a bugle signaling that his allotted time for the kill had nearly expired. So badly did he butcher his opponents at one major fight this year that he needed police protection from the enraged crowd.

[5]More often, however, the crowd ignores his faults and cheers him for all it is worth. "The most interesting thing about El Cordobés' bullfights is the crowd," says António Diaz-Cañabate, one of Spain's most fastidious critics. "They don't care at all about bullfighting. They want to go mad in the physical presence of a fetish."

[6]And a fetish is what El Cordobés is. An orphan named Manuel Ben-tez who grew up on the streets of Córdoba and broke into bullfighting the hard way—by jumping into the Madrid ring from his seat in the stands— he is every Spaniard's dream of the poor boy who made good. He owns four ranches, a fleet of Mercedes and a six-seat private plane, and is building a seven-story hotel in Córdoba. With his serious young face, battered body and brilliant white smile, he has also become Spain's leading sex symbol, its contribution to the international beat generation.

[7]To the alarm of dedicated *aficionados,* El Cordobés' success has encouraged a group of imitators who threaten to transform bullfighting from a dramatic and highly emotional art into a crazy circus act. His imitators are even worse than he is. Significantly, one of them calls himself "The Disaster," another "The Assassin," and a third, whose outlandish caricature of the El Cordobés style has brought him warnings by bullfight authorities, fights under the name of "Little Banana." Last month at a town just outside Madrid, one young apprentice tried to introduce a new dimension to bullfighting by parachuting into the arena from a plane. Fortunately, he missed the bullring and landed in a garbage dump two miles away.—"Death of the Afternoon," *Time*

a. List three particular facts in the passage.
b. List three general facts (generalizations).
c. Make a guess as to where the general facts came from.
d. Are any of the six facts you found relatively "hard" or "soft"?
e. Suggest how the facts you found might be verified.
f. List three value judgments.
g. On what facts do these value judgments seem to be based? Are you convinced of the accuracy of the judgments? Why?
h. What weaknesses, if any, do you find in the writer's handling of factual material (be specific)?

LOOSE GENERALIZATIONS

You often hear the remark, "Oh, that's just a generalization." This is a misleading comment, for it implies that generalizations are by nature untrustworthy or somehow inferior to other types of statements. As we ordinarily use the term, a fact is "true" by definition; but a generalization is "true" only if the facts have first been found and properly used in drawing the general conclusion from them. A generalization, therefore, may be untrue, a *little* true, *partly* true, *mainly* true, or *entirely* true.

In order to make your statements as true as possible, you must avoid making careless or loose generalizations. A loose generalization is a faulty, or partly faulty, statement about a group or class of ideas, occurrences, things, persons, etc. Most loose generalizations are created by thinking carelessly about the subject and the available evidence. Here are some examples:

City children don't get enough sunshine.

Who says so? What city children? All over the world? What is meant by "city"? How much is "enough"? Who is an authority on *enough sunshine*? How does the writer know this? How many cities has he been in?

College students are working too hard and have no time for play or private thought.

Where? In the United States? In what sort of "college"? Ivy League? Big Ten? Small state college? Large junior college? All colleges in the United States? Could one person be an authority on this subject? What would he have to do to be an authority? What is meant by "working too hard"? By "no time for play or private thought"?

In France, people accept religion for what it is.

Has this writer been in France? When, and for how long? What sample of the population did he see? Did he talk to them about religion? What is meant by "religion"? By "people"? Eighty-year-old men? Young children? The clergy? (Catholic, Jewish, Protestant?) What does "for what it is" mean?

HOW TO QUALIFY A GENERALIZATION

You do not have to get *all* the facts before you can draw a reasonably truthful conclusion. Although some subjects require more facts than others for valid generalizing, for many subjects you can draw *tentative* or *qualified* generalizations. To *qualify* means to modify or to limit according to the evidence that is available. Take the three loose generalizations given above. Carefully qualified, they might read:

> Along Parsons Avenue in Chicago, where I lived for ten years, I saw a number of children who didn't get enough sunshine because they usually played indoors.
>
> The engineering students I know at Collins College have to take so many credit hours that they have only three or four hours a week for relaxation.
>
> When I was in Paris for three months last summer, I knew several young workingmen who were rather casual about observing the laws of their church.

It is wise to acquire the habit of using qualifying words and phrases where necessary, particularly when you are writing about people and their activities. But be wary of words that state an absolute condition, words like *always, never, continually, every.* Also be wary of implying these words in sentences like ["*All*] people love freedom," or ["*All*] women dislike men who smoke cigars." Here is a list of qualifying words and phrases that you can use with some assurance:

usually	nearly	some	generally
often	occasionally	sometimes	a few
a lot	many	a great deal	most
customarily	a little bit	ordinarily	almost all

To sum up: A generalization is an attempt to find out the truth about something—or a lot of somethings—and to state the truth in shorthand form. Imagine, for example, that we are trying to make a general, true statement about the total assets of the wealthy Mr. Jordan. We discover that he owns stocks and bonds, cash, houses, five automobiles, and two racing horses, with a total value of $300,000. He also keeps in a bank vault a number of gold bars worth about $285,000. We may generalize roughly that *half of Mr. Jordan's fortune consists of bar-gold.* If Mr. Jordan should be a vigorous buyer and seller of bar-gold, we might from time to time have to change our qualifying statements about his fortune, as follows:*

(100%)	Mr. Jordan's fortune consists *wholly* of bar-gold.
(99%)	*Practically all* of his fortune consists of bar-gold.
(95%)	His fortune consists *almost entirely* of bar-gold.
(90%)	*Nearly all* his fortune consists of bar-gold.
(80%)	*By far the greater part* of his fortune. . . .
(70%)	The *greater part* of his fortune. . . .
(60%)	*More than half* his fortune. . . .
(55%)	*Rather more than half* his fortune. . . .
(50%)	*Half* his fortune. . . .
(45%)	*Nearly half* his fortune. . . .
(40%)	*A large part* of his fortune. . . .
(35%)	*Quite a large part* of his fortune. . . .
(30%)	*A considerable part* of his fortune. . . .
(25%)	*Part* of his fortune. . . .
(15%)	*A small part* of his fortune. . . .
(10%)	*Not much* of his fortune. . . .
(5%)	*A very small part* of his fortune. . . .
(1%)	*An inconsiderable part* of his fortune. . . .
(0%)	*None* of his fortune. . . .

PRACTICE

The statements below have been represented as facts in student themes. Which statements do you consider factual? Upon what kind of authority? Which are loose generalizations? How can these be effectively qualified?

a. Abraham Lincoln was foully murdered by a crazy assassin on April 15, 1865.
b. In the history of censorship, no book has been banned oftener than the Bible.
c. Sharks do not eat people.
d. Leon ("Goose") Goslin batted .379 in 1929 and led the league that year in batting.
e. John's uncle was a geologist in 1937 in the state of Texas.
f. The motives of the United States in the Vietnam war were not imperialistic.
g. Football players are good students.

*This ingenious example involving Mr. Jordan's fortune has been taken from *The Reader Over Your Shoulder* by Robert Graves and Alan Hodge. Try as they might, Graves and Hodge could not make the qualifying phrases very precise. Phrases like *the greater part* and *a large part* are rather ambiguous even when they are presented in a "qualifying scale" like theirs. But the example does show that qualifying can be done with words and that a writer can qualify with a fair degree of accuracy. Incidentally, if Mr. Jordan were an American citizen, he would probably be in jail.

h. Lucille is a fair pool player.

i. Yesterday, the wind blew 28 mph from the southeast at 10:00 a.m.

j. The playwright Tennessee Williams got his name from having lived in Tennessee.

k. Robert De Niro is a better movie actor than Marlon Brando.

l. A window screen keeps all the flies out.

m. Sonic booms don't hurt you or your property.

n. By the year 2025, the human race will reproduce by cross-pollination.

o. The moon is a military base of great importance.

p. Evolution is true.

q. Humans evolved from apes.

r. Teen-age dance steps are immoral.

s. Bacon wrote Shakespeare's plays.

t. This sore muscle in my neck was caused by sleeping with my head at a wrong angle on the pillow.

u. "The music on the record player is Brahms' *First*." "You're wrong; it's Beethoven's *First*."

v. The Wolverine 8 is not selling because people think it's a compact car, and compacts are not as popular as they used to be.

w. If Freud had had a better upbringing, he would not have had all those silly theories about sex.

x. If lightning strikes your house, open a window in your basement so that the lightning will find its way out.

y. The cause of juvenile delinquency is parents.

Make Your Writing Informative and Lively

If a writer fails to present the contents of his paper effectively, he ordinarily does so for one or both of two reasons: (1) he does not give his reader enough specific information or facts; (2) he bores his reader.

These two reasons are closely related. If you pick out the most appropriate and convincing facts to support your thesis and your general statements, the problem of the reader's boredom is usually avoided. A reader likes factual examples and details because they give him a chance to picture situations for himself and to understand quickly what you are talking about. (See, for example, the character sketch of El Cordobés on pp. 121–122.) By contrast, note the lack of details and your corresponding lack of interest in the paragraph below (taken from a writer's first draft):

I learned very quickly last summer that there was one thing you had to understand immediately when you worked around a waterhole drilling rig: safety was the watchword. Rigs are dangerous. I had to be careful and watch my step. One of the other roustabouts forgot this, and he got badly hurt.

You get no clear idea of *danger*. You wonder what this is all about — why was "safety" the "watchword"? Why was a drilling rig "dangerous"? How and why did another roustabout get hurt? Here is the passage rewritten. The writer's specific material and facts are italicized.

During the drilling operation, a *rig* is dangerous at *three times:* when the *head driller* is *breaking out, putting pipe on,* or *drilling hard.* Take *breaking out (removing pipe),* for instance. The driller *signals* when he wants his *helper* to put his *wrench* on the *pipe.* When he is ready, he will *clutch-out* and throw the *rotary table* into *reverse.* After the table begins to turn, if the helper does not take his *hands* off the *wrench* he will get his *fingers cut off* because the wrench *slams* against the *drilling mast* with the force of 200 *horsepower* behind it. One *roustabout, Billy Lawe,* got careless one day and lost *three fingers* on his *left hand.*

Here is another example of dull, uninformative writing:

The Irish Penal Laws injured the Irish a good deal in the eighteenth century. The whole Irish way of living was changed. The laws were designed to keep the Catholics down in Ireland; Catholics were not free in matters of property, education, or religion. The Penal Code was very harsh.

By comparison, a good writer's description of the Irish situation contains more facts, and thus is more informative and stimulating:

In broad outline, they [the Penal Laws] barred Catholics from the army and navy, the law, commerce, and from every civic activity. No Catholic could vote, hold any office under the Crown, or purchase land, and Catholic estates were dismembered by an enactment directing that at the death of a Catholic owner his land was to be divided among all his sons, unless the eldest became a Protestant, when he would inherit the whole. Education was made almost impossible, since Catholics might not attend schools, nor keep schools, nor send their children to be educated abroad. The practice of the Catholic faith was proscribed; informing was encouraged as "an honorable service" and priest-hunting treated as a sport. Such were the main provisions of the Penal Code, described by Edmund Burke as "a machine as well fitted for the oppression, impoverishment and degradation of a people, and the debasement in them of human nature itself, as ever proceeded from the perverted ingenuity of man." — Cecil Woodham-Smith, *The Great Hunger: Ireland, 1845–1849*

Sometimes, however, facts and specific details alone do not stimulate the reader's interest. The material must also be presented vividly and vigorously, as in this satirical account of a Ku Klux Klan meeting held in 1922 (italics added):

Vivid words in description	Several hundred men, dressed in *white sheets* with *peaked hoods,* were *milling* around, their *trousers peeking out ludicrously* under the sheets. One of them kept
Speech accurately represented	*bawling,* "If there is anyone here who isn't a Klansman, or doesn't intend to be sworn in tonight, they will remain at the peril of their life!" The *snappy dresser* [described earlier as a "talkative Klansman . . . whose *breath smelled of rye*"] told the newspapermen that this *threat* was not meant to include them. He had a bottle of
Specific details	*rye* in one hand, and with the other he took a *.38 Colt revolver* from a *side pocket* of the car, examined it, and put it back. About *seventy-five sheeted candidates* for membership in the organization were lined up, and a spokesman ordered them to repeat after him the oath of the Ku Klux Klan, and then there was an *awkward pause.* It was time to light the *fiery cross,* but it couldn't be found. One
Speech	*hoarse voice* began shouting, "Where is the *fiery cross*? Where the hell is the fiery cross?" and a hundred others joined in. *Ten minutes later* the Klansman in charge of the fiery cross was found *asleep behind a tree* with an
Specific details	*empty whiskey bottle* beside him. During the search, a dozen Klansmen had come up to talk to the reporters. *Three* of them, in spite of their *robes,* were identified by *Bricker.* He recognized the *voices* of two of them and the *posture* of the other. The neophytes were finally sworn in, and as their voices were lifted in the *ugly responses,* the *snappy dresser* kept repeating, "Boy, that's one hell of an
Speech	oath those guys are takin'! They'll never forget it." The ceremonies were over before *eleven o'clock,* except for
Specific description	the *horseplay,* a few *fist fights,* and some *drunken singing.*—James Thurber, "The Gathering of the Klan"

The word picture that Thurber draws is so distinct and strikingly alive that the reader gets the impression he is there at the scene, seeing the "trousers peeking out ludicrously" under the sheets; watching the "snappy dresser" handle the ".38 Colt revolver"; hearing the "hoarse voice" shout; and smelling the "rye" on the Klansman's breath. No writer can create reality. He can only create the illusion of reality by choosing details, examples, and words that are strikingly alive—*vivid.* As the novelist Joseph Conrad wrote: "My task which I am trying to achieve is, by the power of the written word, to make you hear, to make you feel—it is, before all, to make you *see.*"

A basic strategy in writing vividly is: Don't just *tell* your reader — *show* him, too. General statements can explain a great deal, but they are often flat and colorless in comparison to the examples and details that *show* the reader what you have in mind. By showing, a writer can artistically work by implication and suggestion. Thurber did not have to state that he felt contempt for the stupid and cloddish Klansmen because every detail he put in his account shows us what he felt, and the reader can infer this feeling for himself.

Use the following list to check your themes for sound and lively content:

1. Generalize with care.

    a. Inspect your general statements. (Are they accurate?)

    b. Qualify your general statements, if necessary.

    c. Adapt your general statements to the reader. (The reader will seldom know your subject as well as you do. Make certain that he knows what you are talking about.)

2. Define your terms if necessary (see pp. 45–51).

3. Support your general statements with particular facts, examples, details; and present them as vividly as you can. (Don't simply *tell* your reader — *show* him, too.)

PRACTICE

1. Read the two student themes below. Analyze their content. Which theme is more convincing? Give specific reasons for your judgments, paying particular attention to the writers' use of informative, lively facts and details to support their theses.

A Lifeguard's Life

Thesis: A lifeguard's life is more arduous and less glamorous than most persons suppose.

    ¹Many people have a stereotyped idea of the lifeguard bravely rescuing a beautiful drowning girl. But this idea of the lifeguard is not always an exact one. In fact, an alert guard at an average-size public pool seldom is forced into the water to save a drowning person, and rarely is the drowning person a beautiful girl. During the two years I worked at a public pool as a lifeguard, only once did I find it necessary to make a swimming rescue, and then the victim wasn't even a girl.

    ²One of the lifeguard's duties, teaching nonswimmers and beginners how to swim, very often takes place in either very shallow water or on land where the learning swimmers will not be in any danger of drowning.

When the beginners are tested in deep water, they are kept close to shore. The lifeguard has a shepherd's hook (a long pole which is shaped into a hook at one end) which he uses to retrieve exhausted beginners who are floundering in the water. Swimmers who are learning more difficult strokes are usually good enough in the water that they can take care of themselves.

[3]The side of the average pool is usually only several yards away. Even weak swimmers can make this distance with some effort. Also, most of the pool is shallow water where drowning is almost impossible. Around the pool there is lifesaving equipment such as the ring buoy and shepherd's hook, which are used to extend the reach of the lifeguard. Anyone drowning near the edge of the pool can easily be saved by the hook or the buoy. The only area left for a possible swimming rescue is a small space in the very center of the deep end of the pool. An alert lifeguard can recognize the poor swimmers and restrict them to the shallow water. Sometimes small children in the shallow end find that they are in water over their heads. Their struggles attract attention, and they are usually picked out of the water by some larger person who is swimming nearby before the lifeguard can reach them.

[4]The nature of the average pool makes it practically unnecessary for the lifeguard to make swimming rescues. The stereotyped image of the lifeguard rescuing a drowning person is colorful but not exact. The true picture might be quite different.

[5]The darkly tanned body squirms in the hard, splintery seat of the lifeguard chair. Sweat trickles from his armpits under the searing heat of the midday sun. The screaming of young children and the splashing of boys dunking young girls echo back and forth in his weary head. A cry for help comes out of the conglomeration of sounds. The victim is only a chubby boy standing waist-deep in the water while two smaller boys splash him. Only the irritating sound of the whistle reminds the swimmers that the lifeguard is high upon his chair watching over them.

High Schools—Large and Small

Thesis: It is the purpose of this paper to explain some of the advantages that a small high school has over a large high school.

[1]There are definite advantages in attending a small high school. One of these advantages is the friendliness in a small school. By this I mean that the students know each other by name and usually know some personal information about each other, such as their grades, their activities, and their friends. With this information, one can understand the other students. One knows whether the person has initiative and a mind of his own or if he would rather let someone else do something for him.

[2]Another advantage is that a person in a small high school has a better chance to participate in athletics. For example, a person who is trying out for some athletic team in a large school must have a fairly high degree of natural ability in order to make the team or even to remain on the

squad. But in a small school, if a person has a little natural ability and there aren't too many others with a high degree of ability involved in these sports, this person has the chance to train, learn, and participate in these athletic endeavors.

³Another advantage of the small school is the various clubs and organizations to which a student can belong. Large schools have these same organizations, but the competition for membership is much greater.

⁴These are the reasons that I am glad that I attended a small high school.

2. Write a theme that uses many details and examples. Insofar as you can, avoid *telling* your reader; *show* him with specific detail—but avoid mere story-telling.

Use Description and Narrative

An excellent way of using details and facts to entertain, inform, or convince your reader is to describe a scene or narrate a series of events. Make sure, however, that the description and narrative are relevant to your theme and its development. And be careful not get so carried away with "describing and narrating" that your main ideas are buried under a landslide of detail or story.

DESCRIPTION

When you describe a thing, you give its qualities, nature, or appearance. The word *describe* comes from the Latin *describere* ("to copy" or "to sketch"), which implies that the thing described has a material existence. Customarily, the words *describe* and *description* have been used to refer to material things, although of course one may describe abstractions such as states of mind or moral attributes.

Behind every good description there is a point being made: the sunset is *beautiful*, the earthquake was *frightening*, the birth of a baby is *miraculous*, the political ideas of Theodore Roosevelt were *pragmatic*. Consider the point in the passage below, which describes the break-up of Ernest Shackleton's ship during his expedition to the Antarctic in 1915:

Sounds of the ice

¹There were the sounds of the pack in movement—the basic noises, the grunting and whining of the floes, along with an occasional thud as a heavy block col-

lapsed. But in addition, the pack under compression seemed to have an almost limitless repertoire of other sounds, many of which seemed strangely unrelated to the noise of ice undergoing pressure. Sometimes there was a sound like a gigantic train with squeaky axles being shunted roughly about with a great deal of bumping and clattering. At the same time a huge ship's whistle blew, mingling with the crowing of roosters, the roar of a distant surf, the soft throb of an engine far away, and the moaning cries of an old woman. In the rare periods of calm, when the movement of the pack subsided for a moment, the muffled rolling of drums drifted across the air.

Details (margin, paragraph 1)

Pressure of the ice (margin)

[2]In this universe of ice, nowhere was the movement greater or the pressure more intense than in the floes that were attacking the ship. Nor could her position have been worse. One floe was jammed solidly against her starboard bow, and another held her on the same side aft. A third floe drove squarely in on her port beam opposite. Thus the ice was working to break her in half, directly amidships. On several occasions she bowed to starboard along her entire length.

Details (margin)

Accumulation of ice on bows (margin)

[3]Forward, where the worst of the onslaught was concentrated, the ice was inundating her. It piled higher and higher against her bows as she repelled each new wave, until gradually it mounted to her bulwarks, then crashed across the deck, overwhelming her with a crushing load that pushed her head down even deeper. Thus held, she was even more at the mercy of the floes driving against her flanks.

Details (margin)

Ship's reaction to pressure of ice (margin)

[4]The ship reacted to each fresh wave of pressure in a different way. Sometimes she simply quivered briefly as a human being might wince if seized by a single, stabbing pain. Other times she retched in a series of convulsive jerks accompanied by anguished outcries. On these occasions her three masts whipped violently back and forth as the rigging tightened like harpstrings. But most agonizing for the men were the times when she seemed a huge creature suffocating and gasping for breath, her sides heaving against the strangling pressure.

Details (margin)

Comparison: ship like a dying "giant beast" (margin)

[5]More than any other single impression in those final hours, all the men were struck, almost to the point of horror, by the way the ship behaved like a giant beast in its death agonies. — Alfred Lansing, *Endurance*

The point behind the description is that the destruction of the ship was *terrifying,* and the descriptive details contribute to this point.

Point of View

Lansing wrote this description over fifty years after the expedition, a fact which partly controls his point of view. *Point of view* is the angle — psychological or physical (or both) — from which the writer views his subject. Lansing's point of view is that of the researcher, poring over old diaries and accounts of Shackleton's voyage and listening to the stories of the few survivors still alive. To re-create the incident, Lansing blends his point of view with that of the men inside the ship. You — the reader — hear, see, and feel what the trapped sailors heard, saw, and felt. Lansing's ruling principle is the terrifying physical effect of the ice on the ship and the terrifying psychological effect on the crew members. He presents his paragraphs in deductive fashion, following topic sentences with brilliant descriptive detail; we hear the weird sounds ("gigantic train with squeaky axles," "the moaning cries of an old woman"), and we feel the pressure of the ice ("she retched in a series of convulsive jerks," "her three masts whipped violently back and forth as the rigging tightened like harp-strings"). The climax of the passage occurs in paragraph 4, where the ship is described as a huge, dying animal fighting for life. All of these details give the reader an idea of the terror the sailors must have felt.

When writing description, do not lose control of point of view, your physical and psychological "angle." Here is a student's paragraph in which the point of view is fuzzy:

Point of view implied in *we*	As we strode through the alleyways between the houses, we met a few shy, ragged children who were gleefully playing with an equally ragged dog. From the
Details	stoop of his front door, a wrinkled old man with a red bandana wrapped around his head meditatively surveyed the distances beyond the mesa. In the distance,
Shift from *we* to impersonal *one*	one could discern the dim shapes of the farmers in their sparse corn patches. The rhythm of a woman grinding corn could be heard along the yellow street from within
Who is "hearing"?	one of the small apartments.

Although the student uses clear details, his shift in point of view blurs their effect. The reader may wonder how the writer saw "dim shapes in the distance," and heard *sounds* "along the yellow street," and knew at the same time that the dim shapes were farmers and that the sound came from a "woman grinding corn." This is not just a pedantic objection. Both description and narration demand a sense of reality in handling point of view. The reader should be made to feel that he is observing the scene in a natural way, the way he might observe it if he were there. The writer of this passage would have treated the scene more naturally and convincingly had he first described a dim shape in the distance, and *later* described it as a farmer. Also, the description would have been strengthened had the writer not recognized the noise from the apartment until he asked someone what it was, or until he went into the apartment to find out for himself. (These ideas on point of view can also be applied to the writing of personal-experience themes, discussed on pp. 40–41.)

The shifts in point of view in the student's paragraph are not particularly bad. Violent shifts, however, may cause the reader to feel that instead of being led into a scene he is being yanked into it. For instance:

> I was driving around that night, not thinking about anything particularly. I was completely unaware that before the evening was over I was going to witness the most horrible experience of my life. It was when I reached the top of the hill overlooking the valley where the accident occurred that I got an empty feeling in the pit of my stomach. It is strange what mixed thoughts run through your head when you see a bad accident.

Besides "telling" his reader too much and not allowing the details of the accident to speak for themselves, the writer shifts from the experience as it unfolded to his later reactions to the experience.

In the following passage from the same theme, the writer uses point of view accurately:

> I stepped out of the car and walked toward the ditch. Suddenly I heard a man's voice clearly over the muffled sounds of the crowd. The voice said: "Bring a flashlight over here!" A highway patrolman who was standing next to me turned the beam of his big flashlight down between the rows of corn. The voice kept speaking, and I could see by the patrolman's flash that it belonged to the county sheriff.

When the writer walked toward the ditch, he heard a voice. He accurately reports here the series of events as he saw and heard them: an unidentified voice spoke, the patrolman turned his flashlight toward the voice, the speaker turned out to be the sheriff.

The Pathetic Fallacy

Over a century ago, the writer-philosopher John Ruskin invented the term *pathetic fallacy*. In discussing the fallacy, he used two lines about death:

> They rowed her in across the rolling foam—
> The cruel, crawling foam.

In attacking these lines, Ruskin said: "The foam is not cruel, neither does it crawl. The state of mind which attributes to it these characters of a living creature is one in which the reason is unhinged by grief. All violent feelings have the same effect. They produce in us a falseness in all our impressions of external things, which I would generally characterize as the 'pathetic [emotional] fallacy.' "

Writers are guilty of the pathetic fallacy when, in trying to make a description vivid, they overstate and overwrite. For example: "I could count the rows of corn that were peacefully standing nearby, not aware of the appalling sight in their midst." Rows of corn are neither peaceful nor unpeaceful, aware nor unaware.

Our mention of the pathetic fallacy here is meant to be only a warning against writing that is overdone, sticky, or excessively emotional. We do not mean to imply that descriptive writing must avoid strong metaphor—if it is appropriate. Lansing's description of the ship behaving "like a giant beast in its death agonies" seems appropriate partly because of the unusual circumstances and partly because persons are accustomed to think figuratively of ships as living things. Unlike ships, rows of corn are prosaic; they will seldom stand the weight of metaphor.

NARRATIVE

A *narrative* is an account of an incident or series of closely related incidents that makes or illustrates a specific point. When writing a narrative, you need to ask yourself two questions: (1) Is the narrative relevant to my purpose? (2) Assuming that it is relevant, how can I tell it effectively? The first question you have to answer for yourself, as circumstances arise. To the second question we can suggest some partial answers.

In order to be effective, a narrative must get smoothly and quickly to its point and make that point dramatically. A narrative that dawdles along, introducing unnecessary people and irrelevant detail, is usually a failure. The reader will skip over it to get to something else. In writing vivid and convincing narratives, you should know how to compress certain details and expand others in order to give shape and emphasis to the incident you are relating. Here is how one writer uses narrative to emphasize the general ideas he is conveying:

From birth, the Fijians are in and out of the jungle. They understand the tangled greenery that covers the South Pacific islands the way a New Yorker understands Times Square. Their senses are sharper than the white man's and their strength and endurance are greater. There is very little left for them to learn about the jungle. Certainly the news, a year or so ago, that they were to be "trained for jungle fighting" by the Allies must have struck them as comical, though none of them ever said so. In fact, I was recently told by a New Zealand captain stationed at the Fiji camp on Bougainville that the men there had been unfailingly deferential and kind to their white tutors. They are a people with an extraordinary

Compressed description and historical account

	sense of humor, but they have an almost pathological aversion to hurting the feelings of a friend. However, at the end of their training, which took place in the Fijis, they allowed their sense of humor a fairly free hand. The

sense of humor, but they have an almost pathological aversion to hurting the feelings of a friend. However, at the end of their training, which took place in the Fijis, they allowed their sense of humor a fairly free hand. The

Story company of white soldiers who had trained them arranged to fight a mock battle with them in the bush. After dark, each side was to try to penetrate as far as possible into the other's lines. The main idea was to see how well the new Fiji scouts had learned their lessons. It turned out that they had learned them pretty well. During the night some of the white scouts worked thirty or forty feet into the Fiji lines, and figured they had the battle won, since they hadn't caught any Fijians behind *their* lines. When they came to check up at daylight, it developed that most of the Fijians had apparently spent the night in the white headquarters. They had chalked huge crosses

Climax of story on the tents and the furniture and had left one of the most distinct crosses on the seat of the commanding officer's trousers, which he had thrown over a chair around 4:00 a.m. — Robert Lewis Taylor, "The Nicest Fellows You Ever Met"*

The climax of the story nicely points up the ideas presented in the first part of the passage: that Fijians are at home in the jungle and that they have a sense of humor.

DIALOGUE IN DESCRIPTION AND NARRATIVE

Dialogue, the written representation of human conversation, is often useful when you wish to relate an incident or describe something — a state of mind, an attitude, a belief, etc. In most nonfiction works, writers use dialogue sparingly, compressing or reporting it indirectly when they can. In employing dialogue, you may find these suggestions useful:

1. Where it is possible, avoid unnecessary repetition of the speakers' names or unnecessary description of the way they speak. It is old-fashioned and tiresome to write:

"I see you in the corner," whispered Baker softly.
"How did you find me?" inquired Charles curiously.
"I smelled the pipe you've been smoking," purred Baker evilly.
"Oh!" exclaimed Charles alarmedly.

2. Present dialogue simply:

*Reprinted by permission; © 1944, 1972 The New Yorker Magazine, Inc.

I'll not forget my first—and last—meeting with that old Texan. He came striding down the line I had just surveyed on his property, pulling up my line stakes and tossing them over his shoulder as he came. When he got up to my surveying truck, he wasn't even out of breath:

"Get off my land."

"O.K., I will—in just a minute. If you'll just—"

"Get off *now*."

"Yes, sir, right now, just like you say."

And I did leave, as fast as possible.

3. Above all, remember to compress and shorten your dialogue whenever you can.

PRACTICE

1. Discuss the use of narrative and description in the passage below. Does the author's description have a point? How does he maintain a consistent point of view? (Durrell captured animals for zoos.)

He [Pious, a native] flicked the crocodile with the bag; it opened both eyes, and suddenly came to life with unbelievable speed. It fled through Pious's legs, making him leap in the air with a wild yelp of fright, dashed past the hunter, who made an ineffectual grab at it, and scuttled off across the compound towards the kitchen. Pious, the hunter, and I gave chase. The crocodile, seeing us rapidly closing in on it, decided that to waste time going round the kitchen would be asking for trouble, so it went straight through the palm-leaf wall. The cook and his helpers could not have been more surprised. When we entered the kitchen the crocodile was half through the opposite wall, and it had left havoc behind him. The cook's helper had dropped the frying pan, and the breakfast was all over the floor. The cook, who had been sitting on an empty kerosene tin, over-balanced into a basket containing eggs and some very ripe and soft paw-paw, and in his efforts to regain his feet and vacate the kitchen he had kicked over a large pot of cold curry. The crocodile was now heading for the forest proper, with bits of curry and wood ash adhering to its scaly back. Taking off my dressing gown I launched myself in a flying tackle, throwing the gown over its head, and then winding it round so tight that it could not bite. I was only just in time, for in another few yards it would have reached the thick undergrowth at the edge of the camp. Sitting in the dust, clutching the crocodile to my bosom, I bargained with the man. At last we agreed to a price and the crocodile was placed in the small pond I had built for these reptiles. However, it refused to let go of my dressing gown, of which it had got a good mouthful, and so I was forced to leave it in the pond until such time as it let it go. It was never quite the same again. Some weeks later another crocodile escaped and did precisely the same thing, horrifying the kitchen staff, and completely ruining my lunch. After this, all crocodiles were unpacked within the confines of the pool, and at least three people had to be on hand to head off any attempts at escape. — Gerald Durrell, *The Overloaded Ark*

2. Discuss the effectiveness of the description, narrative, and dialogue in the following passage.

¹I had been a pretty good lake canoeist in high-school but that was 30 years ago. David had never stepped into a canoe, so we went over the basics in the pool by Lost Bridge.

²When Harkey decided we were ready, we set off down the "Little T." He led us into each eddy. David and I made every mistake yet incredibly remained upright.

³Harkey repeated over and over: "Drive for the corner of the rock. Once across the eddy line, bow, plant your paddle and lean upstream. Stern, pry into the eddy and lean. Both drive forward until the bow almost touches the rock. Then, you can sit indefinitely while you decide what to do downriver."

⁴Slowly, we improved. Then, as we sat in one eddy, Harkey pointed downstream. "See the line where the river seems to disappear?" I nodded.

⁵"That's a fall. Never go over one until you've looked it over. Just below the Center is Wesser Falls — a Class Six. No one who has tried it wants to repeat the experience. One is dead."

⁶"Yet," Harkey continued, "while eating lunch one day, I saw a beach-bail plastic raft, carrying a 200 pound man with a beer can balanced on his belly, drifting right into Wesser! I dropped my fork and ran outside. 'Do you know what's below?' I yelled.

⁷" 'Is this a good place to take-out?' he asked.

⁸" 'Damn right it is,' I told him. He pulled over to the bank and we walked down to Wesser. He looked for a long time but didn't say a word. Then, still silent, he abandoned his raft, crossed the road and hitched a ride. We've never seen him again."

⁹We all laughed — but Harkey had made his point. We'll remember to scout every rapid first. — Charles Blair, "Those Slam-Bang Smokies Streams"

3. The passages in **1** and **2** contain material that might suggest ideas and techniques for your own writing. Write a descriptive or narrative theme using one of their successful methods.

4. How does each of the following three excerpts succeed or fail as a description? (The first two are one-paragraph excerpts.)

It was a beautiful day. The sun was shining, hitting the panes of glass in our motel window and causing the light to dance around the room like a graceful ballet dancer. My father woke me quietly, in a whisper, because my mother was still asleep. Today my father and I were going fishing together in the ocean! I was so excited I hurriedly put on my old faded blue jeans, my ragged red plaid shirt, and my shabby pair of sneakers. Soon we were on our way to the waterfront.

The waitress approached our booth over an old tired wooden floor. Her steps followed a well-worn path, and any previous illusion of her good looks disappeared as she neared. For her hair was coarse, and the bleach was beginning to fade at the roots. Her nylons had several runs, and her white uniform was dirty. Her eyes looked restless, and yet their look was dull and piercing. They seemed to be searching and asking questions, but when your glance met hers they shifted to say, "No, I don't have the answer to life." She stood there with her hands on her hips. Our condemning expressions turned quickly to embarrassment, and we quickly ordered to rid ourselves of her smirk.

[1]Tonight grandma is sleeping in an Indiana rest home. Each morning she packs, telling the nurse she is going back to the farm. She says she is going down the road to the bus stop to catch the Greyhound out of Indianapolis back to Coatesville.

[2]I asked her last spring if she was allowed to keep a bird in the nursing home, remembering the blue parakeet she kept in the farm kitchen.

[3]"Oh, I reckon I can keep what I want," she said. "You know I live out in the country and can do what I want."

[4]She sits in the maple chair, thin and pale, still wearing a pink flowered dress, as she did when we trailed her into the barn. Her new companions, more than 100 geriatric patients, silently wait for the Jell-O to be served. Outside, the Indianapolis slaughterhouses, factory smokestacks, and motels have replaced the grainfields. Grandma's hair is white, for winter settled into her mind a decade ago, but tucked in her wheelchair she believes it is a farm spring.—Linda Parker Silverman, "Roots"*

5. Take an old theme of yours with a subject that can be developed by description or narrative. Rewrite the theme, using several of the techniques discussed in this chapter. In your rewritten version, do you notice any "new" problem of unity?

7 Succeeding with Words

The actor and director Mike Nichols once called *creativity* "the second most unpleasant word in the English language—the first is *art*." He was asked why. "What I do," he said, "I prefer to call *work*."

Nichols' attitude toward language is so typical of craftsmen in every profession that it is worth comment. *Creativity* and *art*—along with *quality, function, viable, image, media*—are part of a large class of words that we call *drug words*. Their very use anesthetizes the mind almost instantly, causing it to stop thinking effectively for a time. "I believe in *quality* education," says the governor of a state; and thousands of brains—including his own—grind slowly to a halt, lulled by the abstract cliché. "The *media's* out to get me!" shouts a public servant with his hands caught in the taxpayers' pockets. A safe and anesthetizing word, it lays blame on people and institutions without naming any of them. Henry Grunwald remarks that the common use of *media* "obliterates" certain real differences: "It encourages the dangerous habit of not distinguishing a billboard from a painting, the telegraph from the radio, a magazine from a TV station, a large magazine from a small one. All sources of information become a great, shapeless monster."

Accurate Words

Behind Grunwald's observations lies a positive idea—that there are differences in the realities words represent. The idea can be expressed as a principle: The best writing uses *accurate* wording. One should call things by their right names, and not call a chair a "table"; a student's reasoned difference of opinion with his instructor an "act of rebellion"; a careless piece of writing "artistic" merely because it "expresses the author's personality." Accurate wording begins in clear thinking and in making clear choices about verbal possibilities.

The writer who says, "I know what I mean but I can't put it into words," is forgetting that, so far as writing is concerned, words *are* meanings. Before one can find an accurate word to put on paper, he must first have a clear idea of its meaning. In a theme on the novelist Joseph Conrad, a student wrote that "the plot of *Lord Jim* is unusually diaphanous." When his instructor objected to *diaphanous*, the student replied: "My dictionary says *diaphanous* means 'transparent.' What I meant was that Conrad's plot is clearly outlined in the novel." His instructor pointed out that the full meaning in the dictionary was "transparent as in gauzy cloth." A more accurate word choice, perhaps, for what the student had in mind could be found in what he had said to his instructor: "Conrad's plot is clearly outlined in the novel."

Notice that the change of wording in this example involves more than just a word-for-word substitution. It is a curious fact, and one well worth remembering, that you cannot always pull a "poor" word out of a sentence and replace it with a better one. Many times the "better" ones you try won't fit the context in either meaning or sentence structure. So you may have to back up to the beginning of the sentence — and sometimes to the beginning of the paragraph — and rewrite much of the material.

There is a two-way relationship between words and ideas. In the process of using words, of selecting some and discarding others, you are choosing or creating ideas and also, in a sense, evoking emotions and attitudes. In an autobiographical paper, one student explained how this process worked for her:

> What I had written in my first draft was this: "I have been expanding my ideas lately about being crippled." Then I paused because I did not know how to go on. I knew that my attitudes had changed about the accident and what it had done to me, but I could not put it into words. I pondered this problem for a while but couldn't find a solution. So I went to bed.
>
> The next day I looked again at my lonely sentence that began: "I have been expanding . . ." I scratched through the sentence and wrote: "At last I have accepted the fact that I am a cripple." For I suddenly realized that something had been happening to me over the past few months. I had been subconsciously learning to *accept* the fact that I will be crippled for life. This was the unformed idea that I had been trying to teach myself to put into words.

Like this student, as you hunt for words to express yourself, you are also thinking; and this thinking process may change the nature and goal of your hunting. But as far as your reader is concerned, it is the *result* of the search that counts. Since the reader wants to understand, he wishes above all for you to be both accurate and clear in your choice of words.

Suitable Words

When Harry Truman was president, he and his wife Bess visited a horticultural show. As he walked around, Truman kept praising the best plant specimens, saying, "My, you must use good manure on this." After a time, someone asked Mrs. Truman, "Couldn't you get the president to say *fertilizer?*"

"Heavens no," Mrs. Truman said. "It took me twenty-five years to get him to say *manure.*"

This anecdote illustrates a second principle of effective wording—that of *propriety*, or the *suitability* of word choice. Slang is suitable in some situations and for certain readers, but not for other situations and readers. Highly formal language is suitable in some circumstances, but not in others. To determine what is suitable, consider your *writer's stance:* your role as writer, your thesis, your reader.

It does not seem suitable to use *orthogeosyncline* in a paper on land forms written for the general reader, *predominant aspirations of our senior citizens* in a newspaper article on the problems of old people, or *I didn't like the damn movie* or *The movie was just great* in a magazine or newspaper review of a new film. Considering the writing situation and the reader, the first example is too specialized, the second too formal, and the third and fourth too casual or slangy.

To use words suitably is to use them responsibly, thinking as you write of your role, subject, and readers. Will they understand what you mean? Will they approve of your verbal "manners"?

PRACTICE

Consider the italicized words and phrases in the following sentences. Are they *accurate* and *suitable?* (Your dictionary may help you with some of them.) Rewrite each sentence to make the wording more effective.

a. There is just one more *thing she forgot to overlook.*
b. I'm in favor of *letting the status quo stay as it is.*
c. The student should not have his *curriculum of study preplanned* to make him *follow a role,* but rather have it *displayed* to *intensify* his already *inherent capacities.*
d. We were so *enervated* we lost any *moral* we had as a *real good* team.
e. From a letter: Well, the weather here is *crummy,* and the food *putrid.* The social events are too dull *to partake of.*
f. People don't *realize* all the time I spend on the job. I'm *insane* about work.

g. Sam's statement was loud and *formidable.* He *inferred* that no one should *belittle* a referee by throwing bottles of *alcoholic beverage* at him.

h. Can you give a *legible* description of the highlights of the *company's economic package?*

i. I can *do* that job of description *up right* if you will let me *discuss on* all the *facets* of the religion.

j. Written for a literary magazine read by students: Since Shakespeare's *optimum interest* was in tragedy, the critic *must of necessity utilize a functional analysis* of symbols *inherent* in the tragic plays.

Effective Words

You know that your words should be accurate and suitable. Here are a few more suggestions for making them so and for increasing the general *effectiveness* of your wording.

BE SPECIFIC

According to a recent newspaper story, county supervisors in Stockton, California, put up signs near a landfill where people were supposed to dump their garbage. The signs read "Foothill Sanitary Landfill Facilities," and people passed right by them looking for a place to dump their garbage. But an imaginative official saved the day, or Stockton might now be knee-deep in garbage. He put out new signs that read simply: "Dump."

Stocktonians knew what *dump* meant because it was specific—explicit, definite, particular. *Foothill Sanitary Landfill Facilities* was vague, indefinite, and general; and so the expression communicated poorly. If you are in doubt about whether your wording is specific, try placing it on a *specificity ladder:*

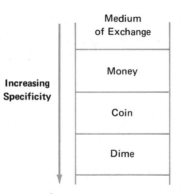

Increasing Specificity

| Medium of Exchange |
| Money |
| Coin |
| Dime |

As you step down the ladder from the top, you use words that are increasingly specific. Although *money* in the ladder above is a fairly general word, it is more specific than *medium of exchange. Coin* is more specific than *money,* and *dime* more specific than *coin.*

Here is another example of a specificity ladder. This time, we are considering a type of human conduct:

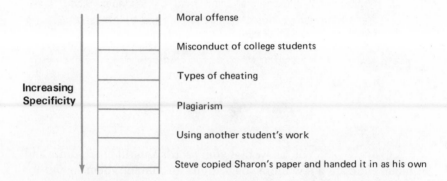

Increasing
Specificity

Moral offense

Misconduct of college students

Types of cheating

Plagiarism

Using another student's work

Steve copied Sharon's paper and handed it in as his own

What happens to your writing when you choose words from the bottom rungs of a specificity ladder? First, you will discover that your ideas seem to flow more smoothly and quickly because you are being definite about them and clarifying them as you go along. "What do I mean by a *moral offense?* I mean, in this instance, that Steve copied Sharon's paper and handed it in as his own." Of course you can mean something else by *moral offense*—a thousand specificity ladders could be constructed starting with that phrase on the top rung. Second, your reader will discover that you are "explaining" things to him as you write. This paragraph is vague and needs explanation:

> Why the student body should continue in this state of apathy is not really understandable. The practice and theory of politics are studied in the classroom but political habits on campus do not seem to benefit from such labor. Many a political figure has been invited to speak, only to discover that the students are not really interested.

The paragraph, made specific, explains the point better:

> Our student body is dull and slack-minded. All students here must take at least one course in history or political science that teaches them something about the theory and practice of American politics. Yet students have no interest in campus elections; only twenty percent voted in the Student Senate elections in October. It may be said that these student elections are not important. Perhaps. But nobody seems to care about national political affairs either. When Senator Rogers spoke here last week, the auditorium was two-thirds empty; and when he called for questions no student cared enough to ask one.

1. Construct specificity ladders using these words or phrases on the top rung. Where necessary, consult your dictionary.

> low-income individuals   physically fit
> effective leadership   brotherhood
> somebody's bad temper   beauty

2. Read the two passages below. Underline the specific words. As a reader, do you consider the passages successful? Why?

> [1]Thoroughbred horses eat well, work hard and, after the years and effort that have gone into improving the breed, their digestive tracts work at a truly magnificent pitch of efficiency. Under normal conditions we had 1,350 horses in the stable area at Suffolk Downs. And every morning we had 30 tons of manure to dispose of. Not to give the horses undue credit, it wasn't entirely the pure unadulterated product. The floors of stalls are covered with straw, and what you end up with is a sort of thatchy mixture. For decades mushroom growers bought all this stuff they could get. They came and got it and left their money behind. By the time I came to Suffolk the formerly eager mushroom men were in the process of converting to synthetic fertilizer. They were still willing to take the manure off the track's hands *if* we charged them nothing and shipped it to them. That cost us $100,000 a year.
>
> [2]It's a problem. It really is. The grooms muck out the stalls and pile the manure in front of the barns, and that's where the obligation of the horsemen ends. The track has the job of collecting and delivering it to railroad flatcars, a job we contracted out.
>
> [3]There was one phase of the operation that wasn't contracted out. After my son Mike graduated from high school he came to work at the track, and I handed him a shovel and pointed him in the general direction of the paddock. The thoroughbred is a high-strung animal, and once he is led into the paddock he seems to understand that something is about to happen. Mike's job was to stand there with his shovel and watch carefully. It made for a very active 20 minutes nine or 10 times a day. The boss' son should always start at the bottom, and I couldn't think of anything more bottom than that. — Bill Veeck, "Racing Has Its Dirty Side"

This passage is from Shakespeare's *King Henry V*. The boy soldier, Michael Williams, speaks to two of his friends and the disguised king, telling them that the king's war must be in a good cause.

> *Will.* But if the cause be not good, the king himself hath a heavy reckoning to make, when all those legs and arms and heads, chopped off in a battle, shall join together at the latter day and cry all 'We died at such a place'; some swearing, some crying for a surgeon, some upon their wives

left poor behind them, some upon the debts they owe, some upon their children rawly left. I am afeard there are few die well that die in a battle; for how can they charitably dispose of any thing, when blood is their argument? Now, if these men do not die well, it will be a black matter for the king that led them to it. . . .— Act IV, scene i, 140–152

3. Write a paragraph or two to a friend asking to borrow his car. Be very specific about your reasons for needing it.

4. Write a short paper supporting or attacking the candidacy of "someone" for "something"—for example, of someone who wants to be a student representative, a member of the tennis team, a teaching assistant, an aide in the admissions office, a secretary, bookkeeper, etc. Designate a reader or readership, and use specific words to describe the strengths or weaknesses of your candidate.

WATCH YOUR CONNOTATIONS

A word's *connotation* is what the word suggests or implies. Its *denotation* is its literal, neutral, or ordinary meaning.

A writer cannot control the connotations of the words he uses as well as he can control their denotations. But he should try. A reader often reacts to the suggestive coloring of a word more than to its neutral meaning. Matthew Arnold, the great Victorian critic, speaks to the point as he tells of reading this short paragraph in a newspaper:

A shocking child murder has just been committed at Nottingham. A girl named Wragg left the workhouse there on Saturday morning with her young illegitimate child. The child was soon afterwards found dead on Mapperly Hills, having been strangled. Wragg is in custody.

Except for *shocking*, the newspaper account seems rather flat, but Arnold reacts to the connotation of the girl's name. "Wragg!" he exclaims, "has anyone reflected what a touch of grossness in our race . . . is shown by the natural growth amongst us of such hideous names,—Higgenbottom, Stiggins, Bugg!"

Arnold continues, attacking the foolish optimism of nineteenth-century Englishmen who think that a world with miserable beings like Wraggs in it can be "happy":

And "our unrivalled happiness";—what an element of grimness, bareness, and hideousness mixes with it and blurs it; the workhouse, the dismal Mapperly Hills,—how dismal those who have seen them will remember;—the gloom, the smoke, the cold, the strangled illegitimate child! . . . And the final touch—short, bleak and inhuman: *Wragg is in custody.*—"The Function of Criticism at the Present Time"

Powerful writing this. Arnold's sense of moral outrage comes through in his choice of connotative words: *Grimness, bareness, hideousness, dismal, gloom, smoke, cold, bleak, Wragg.*

Let us consider more examples of connotation, particularly in contrast to denotation:

Word	Denotation	Possible Connotations
Housefly	Small, two-winged insect	Filthiness, uncleanliness, revolting to the senses— "O hideous little bat, the size of snot"—Karl Shapiro, "The Fly"
Prince	Nonreigning male member of a royal family	Wealth, glory, honor, gracefulness, courtesy
Strut	To walk stiffly	Egomania, vanity, swaggering, false pride, pretensions to glory; synchronized movements of a marching band

So long as you are reasonably accurate in your word choice, denotations shouldn't give you much trouble. But connotations, which supply much of the richness and vibrancy of language, may work against you if you fail to take into account what certain words suggest. To begin a critical analysis of a literary work with "The ingredients of this poem" could be a mistake because *ingredients* suggests to many readers flour, sugar, and shortening—the makings of a cake. "Susie has a beautiful *anatomy*" might suggest a number of things, ranging from corpses ready for autopsy to foldout pages in men's magazines.

Some words, four-letter obscenities, for example, are so furiously connotative that they are ordinarily banned from standard English. Around other words blow the violent emotional winds of social and political controversy. *Communist, reactionary, nigger, whitey, radical, sexist, queer, long-hair* are in most contexts so full of connotative static that their denotative message is lost. Many such expressions are no more than purrs and snarls. For *purr words* and *snarl words*, as S. I. Hayakawa has described them, are not meant to communicate meaning so much as to express emotional approval or disapproval: *filthy, dreamy, bastard, racist, fascist, darling, a great guy, true lover of democracy, authoritarian*, etc.

Unless you are deliberately trying to arouse the passions of your reader, you would be wise to search for less emotionally charged words than ones like these.

1. Used connotatively, what do these words suggest? Can you use any of them in a purely denotative or neutral sense?

red	spider	pus
redneck	ooze	slob
monster	creep (noun and verb)	cool
boss ["very good"]	weirdo	swinger

2. Discuss the uses of connotation in these two passages. How effective are the passages? Give reasons for your answer.

    > It was a crisp and spicy morning in early October. The lilacs and laburnums, lit with the glory fires of autumn, hung burning and flashing in the upper air, a fairy bridge provided by kind Nature for the wingless wild things that have their home in the tree tops and would visit together; the larch and the pomegranate flung their purple and yellow flames in brilliant broad splashes along the slanting sweep of the woodland; the sensuous fragrance of innumerable deciduous flowers rose upon the swooning atmosphere; far in the empty sky a solitary oesophagus slept upon motionless wing; everywhere brooded stillness, serenity, and the peace of God.—Mark Twain, "A Double-Barrelled Detective Story"

    > You want to know who I am? I am an American, a mother, a housewife, a keeper of the hearth, a helpmate to my man. I have been a schoolteacher and nurtured virginal minds; I've worked for the Red Cross and the Church, the saintliest institution in this holy land of ours. I refuse to complain about our wonderful country—"Love it or Leave it!" When the lefties complain that the country isn't fit to live in, that all we true Americans are interested in is loot and lucre, I answer: Take a hot bath, cut off that maggoty hair, and get to work! A man who won't work is a pig living off the bounty of these fruited plains.

3. Write three short angry letters, of paragraph length, to your college newspaper. In the first, use highly connotative language. In the second, use as little connotative language as you can. In the third, write a letter that combines or "averages" the connotative qualities of the first two. Which of the three letters is the most successful? The most "accurate"?

4. Write a paragraph to your worst enemy. Use "purr words." (Or write a paragraph to your best friend using "snarl words.") What is the effect of this technique?

USE FIGURES OF SPEECH CAREFULLY

"I see a *rat!*" she said, pointing to the little furry creature disappearing through a hole in the wall.

"I see a *rat!*" she said, pointing to her ex-husband sitting with a blonde at the next table.

The first rat is real or *literal,* a furry fact with four legs and a tail. The second one is not real or literal but *figurative.*

A figure of speech takes a fresh look at something; it is in effect a *re-perception.* In her novel *Memento Mori,* Muriel Spark re-perceives the dreariness of old peoples' lives in a hospital. Even when they sleep, their situation is hardly human; and she writes of "a long haunted night when the dim ward lamp made the beds into gray-white lumps like terrible bundles of laundry which muttered and snored occasionally."

Why are figures of speech used so much by writers? Because, in their re-perceptions, figures give life and vividness to writing. In his novel *McTeague,* Frank Norris describes a little, prissy old lady at a party: "Miss Baker had turned back the overskirt of her dress; a plate of cake was in her lap; from time to time she sipped her wine with the delicacy of a white cat."

Well-chosen figures of speech can turn workaday writing into brilliant prose. The literary critic F. L. Lucas describes in his book *Style* the bitterness and hatred in Jonathan Swift: "It is idle to wish, as Swift trots like a lean grey wolf, with white fangs bared, across his desolate landscape, that he were more like a benevolent Saint Bernard; he would cease to be Swift."

There are several types of figures of speech. Two of the most common are the *metaphor,* which implies or shows a comparison between two things usually considered as unlike ("She was a phantom of delight"); and the *simile,* which states the comparison by the use of *like* or *as* (old people who look "like terrible bundles of laundry"). Another rather common figure of speech is *personification,* which gives human attributes to inanimate objects, thoughts, and emotions ("Death is an amiable man wearing spectacles behind which there are no eyes"). Such distinctions are interesting and valuable for the scholar, but for the writer they ordinarily are not very useful. We have never heard of a writer who has separate stacks of similes and metaphors on his desk to be used, as the physician's prescription runs, "when necessary." Most writers pay no attention to the *type* of figure they are employing. Instead, they concentrate on making their figures of speech genuinely appropriate to their subject.

Suggestions for Using Figures of Speech

1. *Unless a figure of speech genuinely enlivens your prose, stick to a literal statement.* A syndicated sports columnist started a piece on college athletics with this: "The ivy stands out on the red brick walls as if it were varicose veins on a society matron's thigh." What an ugly, ineffective, and inappropriate image! Better he had used a literal statement: "The red brick walls are thickly covered with ivy."

2. *Be sure that your figure of speech is not incongruous or illogical.* "My weight has ballooned somewhat" is illogical — one's weight is a numerical figure and cannot *balloon*, although one's body can. "It is too early for the President to start honing his ulcer." Incongruous — one hones a knife, not a condition in the stomach lining.

3. *Avoid mixed metaphors.* Example: "*Huckleberry Finn*'s pivotal literary crescendo lies in the scene in which Huck refuses to turn Jim in." A *pivot* is one thing; a *crescendo* very definitely another; and a writer can't force the two of them to work together. Another example: "No satire can hold water unless it is salted with wit." First we are asked to believe that a satire can contain a fluid, then that one can put salt in it. These figures might have worked if the writers had dropped the second metaphor. Or perhaps they should have avoided figures entirely.

4. *Picture your figures of speech.* This advice, given by Jacques Barzun and Henry Graff in *The Modern Researcher*, helps you cut out those figures that are incongruous, illogical, mixed — or simply unnecessary. *Picture* these:

> Put your shoulder to the wheel, your nose to the grindstone, and your feet on the ground. ["Now try to work in that position," goes the old joke.]
>
> This restraint runs through the spectre of Chinese-American relationships. [Ever see a restraint running, much less through a ghost of a relationship?]

If you get a silly mental picture of your figure of speech, consider changing or dropping it.

5. *Do not use exaggerated figures of speech.* Sometimes writers become so attached to a figure which they think is novel and fresh that they fail to see that it overstates the situation. Let the figure slip up on the reader; don't slap him in the face with it: "The car cornered with the grace of a ballet dancer, its 300 howling horses straining like prize-fighters under the hood." "Nonsense," says the reader. A statement like "When he praised her, she grinned like a hungry tiger" is also an exaggeration. Better perhaps: "When he praised her, she purred." (It is possible that some people do grin like tigers; life often triumphs over metaphor. But in writing, as in life, overdoing it can be dangerous.)

A Final Note on Figures

Hard-and-fast rules for the use of figures are difficult to make. No sooner does an authority state that one must not mix metaphors than someone cites Shakespeare's "take arms against a sea of troubles." The figure, which is Hamlet's, is logically impossible, a fact that Shakespeare was surely aware of. Hamlet's allusion is to life, which sometimes is impossible. Use common sense in choosing figures. Every figure presents its own problems. For extraordinary situations, like Hamlet's, use extraordinary figures.

In general, let the figure fit the circumstance and clarify your prose, not fog it up. This is fog: "Professor Elspeth grades papers like an elephant stamping on gnats." The figurative language doesn't communicate. Professor Elspeth may grade peculiarly—but in what way? "When I sit down alone in my room to do my math homework, I feel like Daniel in the lions' den." Why Daniel? Where is the den? Who are the lions?

Perhaps the best practical suggestion for using figurative language successfully can be stated simply in two parts: (1) Strive for accuracy and a pleasant liveliness (figures should add to the precision of a statement, not detract from it); (2) don't exaggerate too much, or strain for effect.

PRACTICE

1. Underline the figures of speech in the following passages below. State briefly but specifically how well you think the writers have used the figures.

   a. "[Social] class is like a fur coat—soft and warm to wrap around you if you have it, a constant goad and affront if you're one of those left out in the cold."—Sara Sanborn

   b. At the end of Herman Melville's *Moby Dick,* the lone survivor describes the scene just after his ship has sunk: "Now small fowls flew screaming over the yet yawning gulf; a sullen white surf beat against its steep sides; then all collapsed, and the great shroud of the sea rolled on as it rolled five thousand years ago."

   c. "The society which scorns excellence in plumbing because plumbing is a humble activity and tolerates shoddiness in philosophy because it is an exalted activity will have neither good plumbing nor good philosophy. Neither its pipes nor its theories will hold water."
   —John Gardner

   d. Quotes from three U.S. senators:
   "It seems that many times when we want to change the water, we wind up throwing out the baby."—Mike Gravel

"I do not agree with those here or elsewhere that favor throwing out the baby because of dirty water."—Frank Denholm

"I say today, let us not throw out the baby with the bath water, let us not lose sight of the forest for the trees, let us not trade off the orchard for an apple."—John Pastore

e. He is pretty good at unravelling a complex issue or, as Seth Nicholson once said, "unscrewing the inscrutable."

f. A reporter on the 1975 Ali-Frazier fight: "Now, Frazier's face began to lose definition; like lost islands re-emerging from the sea, massive bumps rose suddenly around each eye . . . ."

g. The fans' hopes anchored on the fullback were knocked out from under them, and the road looked bleak for the team.

h. The poet Alexander Pope used the couplet form to encompass the roots of his neoclassicism.

i. A young and frightened soldier in battle views nature: "The red sun was pasted in the sky like a wafer."—Stephen Crane, *The Red Badge of Courage*

j. We played the pinball machines in those days with a lover's passion—so much energy we wasted on a clucking machine.

k. "If a man does not keep pace with his companions, perhaps it is because he hears a different drummer. Let him step to the music which he hears, however measured or far away."—Henry Thoreau, *Walden*

l. "Everything was coming up roses for a young west suburban married couple as long as two paychecks—his and hers—were rolling in. Then came the first of five children. And the cozy little two-paycheck dream world of Donald B. and his wife, Phyllis, collapsed into a rat race—slowly at first. Then the vicious circle of debt accumulation began to close in. When its grip was total, it embraced the young couple in $5,000 worth of debts."—*Chicago Daily News*

2. For each of the following words, create a figure of speech. Example: "*Dictionaries* are like watches: the worst is better than none, and the best cannot be expected to go quite true."—Samuel Johnson

art	rack	eternity
rock	pain	temperance
justice	chance	bump

What is the main difficulty you find in making your own figures?

3. Write a paragraph on a rather dull subject (eating breakfast, for example). Use many vivid figures of speech. Is your paragraph any better because of the figurative language? Do you detect a strain in your writing? How, if at all, can this be prevented?

4. Write a theme evaluating the figurative language of advertising in magazines that you commonly read. What types of figures are used most? Do the figures blur or clarify the ideas in the ads?

5. Write a theme on the use of figures of speech in a short story by a major writer, for example, "Figurative Language in Faulkner's 'A Rose for Emily.'" How does the author use figures to support the theme and characterization of his story?

USE STANDARD ENGLISH

By *standard English,* we mean the language that educated people generally accept as proper and suitable. It is the language used in technical reports, scientific documents, and business letters. It is found in reputable newspapers, magazines, and books—the words that you have just read are an example of standard English.

You should avoid two major deviations from standard English. In the first the writer picks words (usually polysyllabic ones) that are too heavy, abstract, or dignified—too formal. Example:

> Where the [primitive man's] shadow is regarded as so intimately bound up with the life of the man that its loss entails debility or death, it is natural to expect that its diminution should be regarded with solicitude and apprehension, as betokening a corresponding decrease in the vital energy of its owner.—Sir James Frazer, *The Golden Bough*

This sounds as if it were written by a man permanently dressed in a top hat and tails.

In the second deviation from standard English, the writer is excessively casual, slangy, or informal, as in these expressions:

enthused	rip-off	work like crazy	bozo
turkey	do it like now	have a ball	for sure
aced it	great setup	ivory-tower types	guy
screwed up	figured (thought)	got to me	real great

Your reader probably won't object to the suitability of your word choice unless you startle him with something that seems inappropriate. As long as you stay more or less in the broad area of standard usage, you should be safe enough. Don't be too formal or too informal. Neither address your reader as if you were delivering a sermon in St. Patrick's Cathedral, nor take him familiarly by the hand as if he were a bosom buddy, which he probably isn't.

PRACTICE

1. Prepare for class discussion a few notes on any deviations from standard English in the passage below. Prepare to defend or attack the writer's choice of words.

[1]Inevitably, sexual activity and taking drugs loom overlarge in the public picture: for, whereas unkempt hair, odd company and radical politics may be disapproved, sex and drugs rouse middle-class anxiety, a more animal reaction. The statistics seem to show, however, that quantitatively there are not many more sexual goings on than since the Twenties. The difference is that the climate has finally become more honest and unhypocritical. Sexuality is affirmed as a part of life rather than as the Saturday religion of fraternity gang bangs covered by being drunk. Since there is more community altogether, sex tends to revert to the normalcy of back rural areas, with the beautiful difference of middle-class prudence and contraceptives. (Probably, since there is less moralism, there are more homosexual acts, though not, of course, any increase of homosexuality as a trait of character.) In the more earnest meaning of sex, love and marriage, however, the radical young still seem averagely messed up, no better than their parents. There is no remarkable surge of joy or poetry— the chief progress of the sexual revolution, so far, has been the freer treatment of small children that I mentioned above. The conditions of American society do not encourage manly responsibility and moral courage in men, and we simply do not know how to use the tenderness and motherliness of women. The present disposition of the radical young is to treat males and females alike; in my observation, this means that the women become camp followers, the opposite of the suburban situation in which they are tyrannical dolls. I don't know the answer.

[2]Certainly the slogan "Make love, not war"—carried mainly by the girls—is political wisdom, if only because it costs less in taxes.

[3]The community meaning of the widespread use of hallucinogenic drugs is ambiguous. (Few students use addictives; again, they are prudent.) I have heard students hotly defend the drugs as a means of spiritual and political freedom, or hotly condemn them as a quietist opiate of the people, or indifferently dismiss them as a matter of taste. I am myself not a hippie and I am unwilling to judge. It seems clear that the more they take pot, the less they get drunk, but I don't know if this is an advantage or a disadvantage. (I don't get drunk, either.) Certainly there is a difference between the quiet socializing of marijuana and the alcoholic socializing of the fraternities, suburbs and Washington. Also, being illegal and hard to procure, the drugs create conspiracy and a chasm between those who do and those who don't. As usual, the drug laws, like other moral laws, fail to eradicate the vice they intend to eradicate, but they produce disastrous secondary effects.—Paul Goodman, "The New Aristocrats"

2. Read over an issue of your college paper carefully, marking any wording that deviates from standard English. Write a letter to the editor, giving him your evidence and your conclusions concerning the quality of usage in the paper.

BE IDIOMATIC

The term *idiom* has two meanings, both having to do with what is natural in language. In its first meaning, idiom is the "language peculiar to a people or to a district, community, or class." Thus we speak of the effect of Spanish idiom on the speech of Texans; of the difference between American idiom and British idiom; of French idiomatic use of adjectives (they typically come after the noun instead of before). This first meaning of idiom refers to the natural way a language works.

In its second, more limited, meaning *idiom* refers to particular expressions that are natural to the language but not ordinarily explainable by grammatical analysis. Examples:

drink your coffee up	make do	beat up [a person]
act your age	take to [someone]	keep house

Idiom is a sniffy old lady who is set in her ways. Arguments are useless; you simply have to go along with the particular idiom in its context. "Carl *is coming* to visit me, and he *is going* to stay a week." How can he be coming and going at the same time? One dictionary gives fifty-two meanings of the idiom *take up*—as in "He will *take up* bridge when he gets old." Do such usages make sense? Idiom merely smiles and says: "I don't *have* to make sense."

Idioms are found in every part of the language, but they are particularly evident in prepositional constructions, in which they influence the meaning at will (*from* will? *to* will?). Try changing the prepositions in the movie title, *The Sailor Who Fell from Grace with the Sea:*

The Sailor Who Fell *with* Grace *from* the Sea
The Sailor Who Fell *by* Grace *into* the Sea
The Sailor Who Fell *on* Grace *by* the Sea

English idioms are usually hard for foreign speakers to learn. A bridge player we know had as a partner an excellent player who was young, pretty, and French. After he made a terrible mistake and trumped her ace, he was astonished to hear her say in low, elegant tones—"I am mad about you!" Idiom reversed her meaning, for as it turned out she was mad as the devil *at* him.

To "be idiomatic," as our heading says, is to use the natural forms of the language. When in doubt about an idiom, speak it aloud and listen to the sound. What sounds right will usually be right. If you are still in doubt, see if your dictionary can help you. Most dictionaries have usage notes on common problems of idiom. Another good source is Theodore M. Bernstein's *The Careful Writer*, which has an alphabetical list of idioms that give trouble. Bernstein's book should be in your library's reference room.

PRACTICE

1. Each line in the poem below (and even the title) contains at least one idiom. Underline the idiom, and paraphrase it in a few words. Are your paraphrases generally longer than the originals? What does this tell you about the nature of idioms?

On Meddling with Idioms

At any rate they take heed
Although every now and then they don't.
Most set about to take notes
But some look down on such and won't.
A few fight shy of hearing
When I set about to speak—
By and large at least it seems so.
Off and on they say my points are weak.
I explain they'll not come in handy
But my pleadings don't catch fire.
And they all appear to watch out
In any event not to be inspired.
They make no bones about it
That it's I who set up the friction
When I mull over their papers
And meddle with their idiomatic diction.

—Richard J. Marince

2. In the sentences below, correct any idioms that are faulty.

a. He simply had a passion over oysters.
b. Judge Poofenverber cleared his throat and handed up the verdict.
c. The second danger of the job is that we work under extreme heat.
d. The young doctor's education was being frustrated because he couldn't practice in cadavers.
e. People are now declining from building homes in our town because we have no sewage system.
f. It was the most diverse information they had ever published.
g. A Japanese highway official writing for Americans driving in Japan: "When a passenger on the hoof hove in sight, tootle the horn, trumpet to him melodiously at first. If he still obstackle your passage, tootle him with vigor and express by word of mouth the warning, 'Hi! Hi!' "
h. He walked forth and back across the room.
i. "Amazing English idiom," said the German. "You make down a bed, make with your face, make over your mind, and make forward a story to keep us all happy."
j. "What did you choose that book to be read to out of for?"—quoted by Sir Ernest Gowers in his *Plain Words: Their ABC*

Ineffective Words

There are many causes of ineffective wording—lack of specificity, misleading connotations, distracting or exaggerated figurative language, nonstandard usage, unidiomatic choice of words. But ineffective word choice is often more than just a negative thing—a failure, say, to write specifically. Its causes are rooted in mental slovenliness and carelessness; and, in fact, carelessness breeds carelessness. One inaccurate or unsuitable word on page two seems to lead inevitably to a rash of slovenly and imprecise expressions on page three. Don't let the first ineffective word out of your mind and onto the page; and if it does get there, scratch it out before the infection spreads.

You also might try, as you edit your own prose, what a friend of ours calls his "editorial comedy routine." He reads his work aloud, and when he comes to a doubtful or inappropriate expression he tries to make fun of it:

Optimum   ("That's an optimistic mother.")
Counterproductive   ("We make an awful lot of counters in our factory.")
-wise   ("OK dollar-wise but not a good idea wisdom-wise.")

TYPES OF INEFFECTIVE WORDING

When the following types of bad wording appear, deal with them immediately:

1. *Vagueness:*

The second phase of the operation involves a new concept and a different attitude.

Phase, operation, involves, concept, and *attitude* are all so vague that the reader doesn't know what the writer is talking about.

A basketball team revolves around its center.

Vague—what is the exact relationship of the center to his team?

This part functions in the engine.

But what does the part *do* in the engine?

2. *Wordiness:*

The child's surgical past history in terms of her spinal condition showed a failure in correction.

Cut this to:

Surgery has not helped her spine.

All the huts, square in shape and few in number, had actually been blown away by the incredibly strong wind.

Cut this to:

All of the few square huts had been blown away by the strong wind.

3. *Redundancy:*

A redundancy has an implied repetition built into it:

continue to remain	protrude out	unite together
final outcome	original source	more preferable
complete master	habitual custom	new beginner
regularly consistent	projected forecast	necessary requirement

4. *Unnecessary Exaggeration:*

The honest truth

The truth is "honest," by definition. Just say "the truth."

Tom was literally a fireball in class.

Poor Tom must be pretty burned up. Say something like:

Tom knew all the answers.

An all-inclusive survey

You can't be inclusiver than inclusive. Write:

An inclusive survey

She was very furious.

It is hard to be more furious than furious; omit *very.*

The vice-president is very unique.

One can't be more unique than unique—"one of a kind."

5. *Clichés:*

Clichés are trite, tired, worn-out expressions. Cut them out, or rewrite. Here are a few:

hate with a passion	the die is cast
raining cats and dogs	the scales of Justice
pretty as a picture	straight from the shoulder
slick as ice	chip off the old block
poetry in motion	beat around the bush
hard as a rock	hot under the collar

In these sentences, identify the vagueness, wordiness, redundancy, unnecessary exaggeration, and clichés. Rewrite each sentence, making it specific and clear. Guess at its meaning if you have to.

a. The fact that the group of children has accomplished some worthwhile endeavor gives each member, in terms of the accomplishment, a happy sensation.

b. A good cooperative is a cooperating joint operation.

c. Social scientists have intimated that some of the personal reactions that penetrate into happiness college-studentwise are: satisfaction, achievement, affection, and belief.

d. Here at Wilson Motors, we are proud to say that much labor and concentration is poured into accomplishing a very superb product.

e. As we look down the avenues of life experience, what, ladies and gentlemen, do we see ahead for us living in this day and age?

f. Sanitation is a very important premium in a dormitory, personnelwise.

g. We must unite together to stop this false perversion of the undergraduate student.

h. The upsurges in the Gross National Product were caused by very ideal governing factors in the fields of railways, merchant marines, and canals.

i. Hamlet has been seen to be a neurotically disturbed personality who was all-consumed by hate.

j. First, in the youth, normally the gayer segment of our populace, there seemed to be a very wonderful glow, as if smugly possessing an insight of the wondrous events in store for the anxious world.

AVOID JARGON AND SHOPTALK

The worst misuses of language today are not in bad grammar, unsuitable wording, vulgarisms, "colloquialisms," or the like. They are in the growing employment of *jargon* like this:

Improved administration and management of the intervals in work related to the personnel coffee periods must be a constant aim in order that maximum utilization of labor from the minimum number of personnel may be achieved.

A possible translation: "Take shorter coffee breaks, and do more work."

Jargon is the opposite of plain English, which tends to employ the short, specific words: *take, break, work.* Nor is jargon the language of ordinary speech, which says things directly: "Do the best you can." Instead jargon puts such an idea into abstract polysyllables: "The maximum quality of your endeavors should be achieved."

The writer of jargon uses the worst possible writer's stance. Writer and reader and thesis all disappear in a babble of colorless words — *operation, implemented, in terms of, personnel, minimum* — dead words seemingly not written by or for living human beings.

Much jargon has its origins in *shoptalk*, the special language or terminology of a profession. *Head, lead, proof,* and *thirty* are the shoptalk of the newspaperman; *wheel, arbor, pivot, mainspring* the shoptalk of the watchmaker; *motif, symbol, archetype, protagonist* the shoptalk of the literary critic.

In defense of shoptalk, its users have long claimed that they cannot communicate in their businesses or professions without it, that a geologist, for example, could not talk to other geologists without saying *stratigraphic* eight times a day. This defense is not always convincing. As one geologist at the top of his profession wrote us:

> You can always tell an incompetent in geology by his language. The less he knows the more he throws in big words. He'll write "Pennsylvanian limestone strata" when all he needs is "Pennsylvanian rocks." He'll write *anticline* and *syncline* when *high* and *low* say the same thing.
>
> The main characteristic of the genuine expert in science is that in choosing words he writes both for other experts and for the nonspecialist, the man in the street. He knows that if he hits the man in the street, he will hit nearly everybody else he is writing for. Besides — and this is the important thing — *big words can hide a bad idea*. If you don't put your scientific notion in simple language, you may not know if it's any good. And we can't waste money and time on bad ideas.
>
> I have hanging on my office wall the motto:

kiss!
(Keep It Simple, Stupid!)

Avoid jargon and shoptalk when you can.

PRACTICE

G. K. Chesterton wrote:

> It is good exercise to try for once in a while to express any opinion one holds in words of one syllable. If you say "The social utility of the indeterminate sentence is recognized by all criminologists as part of our sociological evolution towards a more humane and scientific view of punishment," you can go on talking like that for hours with hardly a movement of the gray matter inside your skull. But if you begin "I wish Jones to

go to gaol [jail] and Brown to say when Jones shall come out," you will discover, with a thrill of horror, that you are obliged to think. The long words are not the hard words, it is the short words that are hard. There is much more metaphysical subtlety in the word "damn" than in the word "degeneration." — *Orthodoxy*

1. Try "thinking" the sentences below into clear and simple English that the man in the street would understand and appreciate. Use as many one-syllable words as possible, and check your dictionary when necessary.

   a. Sinistrality is a developmental anomaly of preferred laterality, and represents a mishap to the normal development of dextrality.

   b. The social-management concept of the disadvantaged necessitates our raising them above the poverty level.

   c. Mrs. Smith, in regard to your child's adenoids, our operation decision is one of contraindication.

   d. The Lord is my external-internal integrative mechanism. I shall not be deprived of gratifications for my viscerogenic hungers or my need-dispositions. He motivates me to orient myself towards a nonsocial object with effective significance. — Alan Simpson, president of Vassar College

   e. When industrial or commercial fraud and calculated complexity reach epidemic proportions, non-volitional expenditures are incurred to a level which often spur into being a mini-trade that counsels, for a price, consumers about avoidance techniques. These "cures," as with some debt-counsellors, are often as exploitative as the disease. — Ralph Nader, "Involuntary Economy"

   f. "Now, Mr. Barlow, what had you in mind? Embalmment of course, and after that incineration or not, according to taste. Our crematory is on scientific principles, the heat is so intense that all inessentials are volatilized. Some people did not like the thought that ashes of the casket and clothing were mixed with the Loved One's. Normal disposal is by inhumement, entombment, inurnment or immurement, but many people just lately prefer insarcophagusment. That is *very* individual. The casket is placed inside a sealed sarcophagus, marble or bronze, and rests permanently above the ground in a niche in the mausoleum, with or without a personal stained-glass window above. That, of course, is for those with whom price is not a primary consideration." — Evelyn Waugh, *The Loved One*

   g. As a nurse, I work with patients within a therapeutic milieu structure.

   h. We have escalated the interface in the demilitarized zone.

2. Rewrite the following passage in plain English, free of jargon and clichés.

   [1]Triteburg and its million residents invite you to a glorious convention and vacation in its crystal-clear and cool mountain air. With one foot

in its colorful past and the other in its bright future, Triteburg is proud of its rich heritage and its reputation as a fast-growing and progressive metropolitan center . . . a modern city with an ever-changing skyline set against the magnificent backdrop of the ageless mountains in the romantic atmosphere of Indians and pioneer miners.

²In Triteburg you will find an infinite variety of first-class accommodations—hotels, motels, highway hotels. In the nearby mountains are luxurious resorts, rustic cottages, and modern campgrounds. Dozens of fine restaurants offer menus to appeal to the most discriminating taste. Our convention facilities, available for groups of any size, are second to none.

³Triteburg's unique Hospitality Center can answer your questions about every vacation or convention need: Where to stay and eat . . . what to see and do . . . information about fishing, hunting, boating, or skiing . . . everything you need for the vacation of a lifetime or for a convention that you will long remember.

Shaping Better Sentences (I): Effective Structure*

What do these sentences have in common?

To everything there is a season, and a time to every purpose under the heaven. — Ecclesiastes

My mother was young and pretty when it happened, but she never married again. — Russell Moore, on the murder of his father

If you haven't got common sense, the best thing to do is not get out of bed in the morning. — Harry Truman

These sentences vary somewhat in tone, idiom, diction, and stance. This is not surprising, when you consider that they span three and one half centuries — the first one was written when William Shakespeare was still alive. Yet they have in common this fact: they are made by adding or accumulating certain sentence units. Such *addition*, as we will henceforth refer to it, can be found in a very large number of typical sentences, such as this one taken from a student paper:

Before he learned to cook soup and stew, Mike always threw leftovers away — a habit which cost him money in wasted food.

The Typical Sentence

The strategy of writing sentences through addition can be easily learned. The terminology is brief, simple, and reasonably consistent. Fundamentally, you write a sentence by setting down clearly separated *units of information* so that the sentence "accumulates" through the addition of parts:

---

*We have broken our discussion of the sentence into two chapters. Chapter 8 deals with basic problems in writing readable sentences, and Chapter 9 shows you how to revise and edit the sentence after you have written it. Some of the theory behind this material is based on the work of Francis Christensen.

Unit of Information	Type of Unit
Before he learned to cook soup and stew,	opener
Mike always threw leftovers away—	*sentence base*
a habit which cost him money in wasted food.	closer

We will discuss *openers, sentence bases,* and *closers* in the pages that follow. For the moment, it is enough to point out that the reader can easily understand each of the units of information about Mike as he moves his eyes rapidly along the masses of wording in the sentence. The units themselves are separated by punctuation, which helps indicate where they start and stop. The sentence also has a useful signal in the word *before,* which implies that a time relation will be expressed in the units to follow.

Our main purpose in this chapter is not to teach you how to analyze sentences, although we will perform a few simple analyses. Instead it is to show you how to *write* better prose by following certain basic rules for creating firm structure in your sentences.

As you read the material, also bear in mind that we are showing you how to write *and* punctuate at the same time. This is the easiest way to learn the basic rules of punctuation.

Sentence Bases

A *sentence base,* as the term implies, is the fundamental information unit of a sentence. The sentence bases in the following examples are in heavy type:

a. Because I startled it, *the cow mooed and ran away.*
b. *Cheryl and Sue danced and sang.*
c. *The girl in the long blue skirt standing by the bandstand sang a few bars of one of the earliest songs written by Paul McCartney after he left the Beatles.*
d. *Richard Nixon won the 1972 election,* a fact which did not surprise many people.
e. *The grass,* which was overfertilized, *is dying in the backyard.*

Here are the major characteristics of the typical sentence base:

1. A *sentence base* makes a complete statement. A base usually has no punctuation inside it. We will explain certain exceptions later. These statements are not sentence bases because they are not complete:

Because I startled it . . . .
. . . a fact which did not surprise many people.
. . . which was overfertilized. . . .

2. A sentence base can have something added: (1) to the front of it—an *opener*, as in a. above; (2) to the end of it—a *closer*, as in d.; (3) to the middle of it—an *interrupter*, as in e.

Here is a piece of professional writing that shows how sentence bases work; the bases are in heavy type:

> *The octopus has a remarkable trace of adaptability. Dumas determined that,* by patiently playing with them until he met some response. Usually, *octopi were most submissive when very tired. Dumas would release an exhausted octopus and let it jet away with its legs trailing. The octopus has two distinct means of locomotion. It can crawl efficiently on hard surfaces.* (Guy Gilpatric once saw an octopus let loose in a library. *It raced up and down the stacks,* hurling books on the floor, possibly a belated revenge on authors.) *Its method of swimming consists of inflating the head,* or valva, *with water and jetting the fluid to achieve moderate speed. Dumas could easily overtake the animal. The octopus discharged several ink bombs and then resorted to its last defense,* a sudden plunge to immobility on the bottom, where it instantly assumed the local color and pattern. Keeping a sharp eye out for this camouflage stunt, *Didi confronted the creature again.* At the exhaustion of its psychological warfare effects, *the octopus sprang hopelessly from the bottom, fanned its legs and dribbled back to the floor.*
> —Jacques Cousteau, with Frédéric Dumas, *The Silent World*

Since a sentence base gives your reader a unit of information, it is usually unpunctuated. Why break up a unit unnecessarily? Yet punctuation is sometimes needed in a base to explain certain ideas you want to present *inside* the unit—for example, a listing of two or three elements. In each of these examples, every part of the list is a part of the total base unit:

> Don't you loathe this <u>wretched</u>, <u>evil</u> man?
> I was <u>nervous</u>, <u>angry</u>, and <u>irritated</u>.
> The President <u>ordered out the Marines</u>, <u>sent two carriers to the island</u>, and <u>defied Congress to interfere</u>.
> The <u>Dodge</u>, <u>Chevy</u>, and <u>Ford</u> all crashed at the far turn by the wall.
> The <u>cold</u>, <u>congealed</u> porridge is not fit to eat.

Free Units in the Sentence

If your writing contains sentence bases only, after a while you will bore yourself and your reader. Your prose will be choppy, and you will discover that some of your ideas lack coherence or necessary information. For the sentence-base pattern tends to act like a stylistic cookie-cutter, producing "assembly-line" sentences that state ideas flatly without providing transitions or necessary explanation.

Therefore, to fill out many sentences, you will need to supply free units of information. A *free unit* has these characteristics: (1) it is incomplete and cannot stand by itself, as a sentence base can; (2) it is placed *before, inside,* or *after* the base it goes with; (3) it is usually punctuated at the "joint" where it fits the base. Such units of information are called *free* because they are "removable." When removed, the base can still stand as a complete statement. Of course, when you remove a free unit from its base, you usually change the meaning of the entire sentence. There are three kinds of free units (note punctuation):

1. Openers (placed before the base)

> After he got his $1.00 raise, *Wright yelled with joy.*
> In inspecting the car, *we discovered that it was powered by electricity.*

Openers add detail and provide transitions from sentence to sentence:

> For instance, *Belle Meade Hospital is now using only 65 percent of its available beds.*
> After the optometrist charged him $85 for his new glasses, *Jefferson swore he would never go back to him.*
> Lying there on the ground in the sun, its metal seeming a dull gray, *the .45 did not look dangerous.*

As in the last example, you can use two or more openers if they are necessary.

2. Interrupters (placed inside the base)

> *My roommate,* frustrated by my inability to manage our food budget, *began to scream at me.*
> *The work I enjoyed most*—I am speaking of part-time work—*was pruning trees for the city.*
> *Mr. McClean thought that his seven wives* (or some of them) *had married him just for his money.*

Interrupters explain and add detail to the ideas in a base:

> *My aunt,* who was the best friend I ever had, *died last week.*
> *Johansen's serve*—which was different from any I had faced before—*had a weird bounce on concrete.*
> *Mom* (being unsympathetic to my views on sex) *got up and left.*

3. Closers (placed after the base)

> *The owners said nothing about trading their aging quarterback,* probably because the team thought of the "old" man as their leader.

That pig is pretty agile—considering how fat he is.
We left the apartment early (making sure to leave a note for Roger).

Closers perform about the same job as interrupters. But because of their position, they can also supply afterthoughts, as in the last two examples. Or they can provide explanations:

The captain pulled on the bell rope, which suddenly broke off in his hands.
The weight of most of the trucks ran 15,000 pounds, less than the weight specified in the contracts.
You had better leave the door unlocked—just in case Jeanne returns tonight.
This has been a lovely birthday (much nicer than I had hoped for).

Sentence Signals

A *sentence signal* is a word placed at the beginning of a sentence. It helps the reader anticipate the direction your sentence will take. There are four general types of signals:

1. Signals of *time:*

While spraying the plant, he discovered mites on its leaves.
Before lighting the pilot light, be sure that the heat exchanger is clean.

2. Signals of *logical relation:*

Thus inflation continues to be a major problem in the Western democracies.
Because the ice was over two inches thick on the telephone poles, repairmen were unable to work in Sapulpa.

3. Signals of *similarity* and *contrast:*

Like the other teachers, she went on strike.
But the school board refused to grant pay raises.
Yet the Supreme Court seems determined to stay out of obscenity questions as long as possible.

4. Signals that *count* or *differentiate:*

First, let us define the term correctly.
Then, at this point, it is possible to see the precipitate in the tube.
Finally, all passengers should observe the no-smoking rule.

Sentence signals are small but important aids for the reader. Use them whenever they are appropriate.

The Sentence Base Rule

The sentence base rule is an important part of this chapter. It summarizes the techniques of sentence construction that we have been studying and points forward to the discussion of revising in the next chapter. Based on the work of competent writers, the rule makes three suggestions:

1. Break up your ideas into clear, *specific* units of information — sentence bases and free units (openers, interrupters, and closers).

2. Use punctuation to show where the units start and stop.

3. Where necessary, use sentence signals (*but, and, also, so,* etc.) to help your reader anticipate the direction your sentence will be taking.

Here are examples of sentences that illustrate the rule.

Sentence base by itself:

> *The Constitution does not provide for first- and second-class citizens.* — Wendell Willkie

Opener (with a sentence signal), followed by a base:

> When we Americans are through with the English language, *it will look as if it had been run over by a musical comedy.* — Finley Peter Dunne

Base with two interrupters:

> *Perhaps Brand and Cooke,* lacking interests that could absorb them, fuming like children over trifles, *simply invented their hate of each other in order to have something to feel deeply about.* — Richard Wright

Base with a closer:

> *There's a shipment of human parts come in downstairs* — hearts and kidneys and brains and the like. — Ken Kesey

Writers employ free units to break up a sentence in order to give it shape and clarity. For the reader's sake, they carefully signal the beginning and end of the units with punctuation marks. But punctuation is an art rather than a science, and a writer has choices about where *he* wants to put his punctuation signals. The great American historian Carl Becker wrote this sentence as a base unit:

> *The best-known and the most valiant defender of the freedom of mind was Voltaire.*

Since this has two ideas in it, Becker might have shortened the base unit and emphasized *and the most valiant* as an interrupting free unit:

> *The best-known*—and the most valiant—*defender of the freedom of mind was Voltaire.*

Is one version of the sentence better than the other? Probably not; however, they do create different emphases in the ideas expressed.

PRACTICE

1. Identify by name the units of information in each of the following sentences. Circle the punctuation marks that separate the units. Underline the sentence signals. How does each information unit help the reader understand the ideas expressed?

   a. In science, the credit goes to the man who convinces the world, not to the man to whom the idea first occurs. — William Osler
   b. Before I leave the dorm for vacation, I lock my stereo in the closet (a useless gesture, considering that the lock is breakable).
   c. Obviously, a stationary population—one in which the birth rate matches the death rate—is out of the question for many years to come. — David E. Lilienthal
   d. Dean McIntyre (he's the one who has been calling you long-distance) has also written a letter of congratulation about your award.
   e. Drug addiction is *not* increasing; in all probability, it has declined since the turn of the century. — William McCord
   f. She disagrees with you, but she respects your opinion.
   g. In the summer before the French Revolution, all of France was, it seems, gripped by a deep malaise, an underlying panic to which contemporaries gave the name of *la grande Peur*—the great Fear. — Adlai Stevenson
   h. She disagrees with you; she respects your opinion, however.
   i. He struggled in a wild frenzy of fury and terror, almost mad terror. — D. H. Lawrence
   j. The storm took the helicopter ten miles from the airport.
   k. Ten miles from the airport, the storm overtook the helicopter.
   l. For instance, violence—accidents, suicides, and homicides—accounts for fully three out of four deaths among males age 15 to 24, making the American death rate for this age group 62 percent higher than the Swedish rate.
   m. I was raised to farm work, which I continued till I was twenty-two. — Abraham Lincoln

2. For class discussion and writing practice, consider again the sentences in Practice 1. Pick out half a dozen of the sentences and write imitations of them. Use your own ideas, and modify or switch the units around if you wish. For instance, for e, you could write:

Highway accidents are not increasing; in all probability, they have declined since 1974.

Since 1974, highway accidents probably have not increased.

Highway accidents—judging from the evidence—have not increased since 1974.

Highway accidents seem to have decreased recently (since 1974, to be exact).

3. In each of these sentences, either the base or the free unit is missing. Supply the missing unit and write out the whole sentence.

    a. After I finished my car payments, _____.

    b. _____, although they could not dance easily on the sticky floor.

    c. _____ (who was leaning against the instructor's desk) _____.

    d. Because the stapler had run out of staples, _____.

    e. _____—leaving mud and silt six inches deep on Main Street.

    f. _____, which had been seen stalking a rabbit last Tuesday, _____.

    g. After _____, Henry can finish weeding the garden.

    h. The angry homeowner, who _____, yelled at the students when they were a block away.

    i. Margie will never graduate from college, no matter _____.

    j. To run for president of a sorority demands stamina, particularly _____.

    k. Ducks don't usually bite—except _____.

    l. That textbook (which _____) is the dullest I ever read.

Parallelism

An expert in expository writing was asked, "If you could pick one sentence device that is more important to clear sentence construction than any other, which would it be?"

He thought a long moment, and answered: "If I had to pick one—and mind you, there isn't just one—I'd have to say *parallelism*. It's impossible to talk sensibly about anything, from cardboard boxes to democracy to why people buy certain automobiles, without employing parallelism. You can't even make a laundry list without it. But parallelism is not only a clarifying device, it also makes for more interesting and effective prose. Imagine where Lincoln would have been without it: '. . . that this government *of the people, by the people, for the people,* shall not perish from the earth.' "

USING PARALLELISM

Parallelism refers to a listing of sentence elements which are: (a) roughly equal in importance or emphasis, and (b) written in the same grammatical form. Example:

Parallelism is *interesting, practical,* and *effective.*

Equal in importance and using the same form, the three italicized words in the list are parallel. We could make the list unparallel by changing the form of one of the words:

. . . interest, practical, and effective.
. . . interesting, practicality, and effective.
. . . interesting, practical, and to be effective.
. . . interesting, practical, and effectiveness.

As you look at the following examples of parallelism, observe three things: (a) that a parallelism of two items is ordinarily joined by the words *and* or *or* and has no punctuation; (b) that a parallelism of three or more items ordinarily has *and* or *or* before the last item; and (c) that in a parallelism of *three* or more items, commas separate the items.

Parallel items	Non-parallel items
Marge and Mary	Marge and pretty
Marge, Jim, or I	Marge, strong, or Jim
to study, learn, and memorize	to study, learning, and memorize
dusty, old, rickety, or messy	dust, old, rickety, or messy
light or dark	light or darkened
I came, I saw, I conquered.	I came, I saw, I will have conquered.

Parallel items can be anything from single words to full sentences. The items can be short:

rod and *reel*
rod, reel, and *bait*
I need a rod, I need a reel, and *I must have some bait.*

The items can be relatively long:

a new steel rod and *a rusty old reel*
a new steel rod, a rusty old reel, and *fresh wriggling bait*
I need a new steel rod with plenty of flexibility, I would like to replace the rusty old reel, and *I want the best possible bait for trout fishing in cool weather.*

In order to use parallelism well, you should know where it begins and ends in a sentence. In the examples below, we have shown the beginning and ending of each parallel construction with { }. (Note punctuation.)

a. {*You* and *Jim*}
b. {*You* and *Jim*} are hungry.
c. {*Jim*, *Mary*, and *I*} are as wet as drowned rats.
d. Like us, the others were {*hungry*, *cold*, *wet*, and *tired*} — although they had already rested for an hour.
e. The {*hunter*, *fisherman*, and *game warden*} were {*warm*, *cozy*, and *drunk*}.
f. She hated to {*study*, *memorize*, and *learn*}.
g. {*We stopped*, *we listened*, and *we trembled*}.
h. My son, {*cutting across lawns* and *avoiding the sidewalks*}, got to school early.

Parallelism allows you to state ideas easily, quickly, and economically. That sentence itself is an example of the generalization: ". . . to state ideas *easily*, *quickly*, and *economically*."

Using parallelism helps you write sentences that are more interesting and specific. It also gives your prose a pleasant strength and a musical rhythm. Many memorable sentences depend on parallelism:

a. {*Four score* and *seven*} years ago our fathers brought forth upon this continent a new nation, {*conceived in liberty* and *dedicated to the proposition*} that all men are created equal. — Abraham Lincoln
b. The Lord is {*my strength* and *my shield*}. — Bible, King James Version
c. A sudden violent jolt of corn likker has been known to {*stop the victim's watch*, *snap his suspenders*, and *crack his glass eye right across*}. — Irvin S. Cobb
d. We hold these truths to be self evident: {*that all men are created equal; that they are endowed by their creator with certain unalienable rights*}; that among these are {*life*, *liberty*, and the *pursuit of happiness*}. . . . — Thomas Jefferson
e. {*The energy, the faith, the devotion*} which we bring to this endeavor will light {*our country* and *all who serve it*} — and the glow from that fire can truly light the world. — John Kennedy

PRACTICE

Underline the parallel constructions in these sentences. Use { } to mark the constructions. For each sentence, ask yourself: Why is the parallelism interesting? What would the sentence be like without it? Why would the use of a different device probably weaken the sentence?

a. Even when he was 43, ancient quarterback George Blanda could still pass, kick, and run.

b. And the Lord went before them by day in a pillar of a cloud, to lead them the way; and by night in a pillar of fire. — Exod. 13:21

c. 			Last scene of all,
That ends this strange eventful history,
Is second childishness and mere oblivion
Sans [without] teeth, sans eyes, sans taste, sans everything.
						— Shakespeare, *As You Like It*

d. Feeling miserable, tired, and run-down, he reached for his jar of wheat germ.

e. Darting through the traffic — one foot on the gas, one foot on the brake, my hand jabbing the horn — I came suddenly on the repair crew blocking the road.

f. It was beautiful and simple as all truly great swindles are. — O. Henry

g. 			Down to Gehenna or up to the Throne,
He travels the fastest who travels alone.
					— Rudyard Kipling

h. The greatest of evils and the worst of crimes is poverty. — George Bernard Shaw

i. Any well-established village in New England or the northern Middle West could afford a town drunkard, a town atheist, and a few Democrats. — D. W. Brogan

j. I am tired and sick of war. Its glory is all moonshine. It is only those who have neither fired a shot nor heard the shrieks and groans of the wounded who cry aloud for blood, more vengeance, more desolation. War is hell. — William Tecumseh Sherman

AVOID FAULTY PARALLELISM

Note how the faulty constructions below are improved by putting parallel ideas in parallel form:

Faulty: A good hunting dog can {*find* the bird, as well as *bringing* him back to the hunter}.

Improved: A good hunting dog can {*find* the bird and *bring* him back to the hunter}.

Faulty: I think his report should be regarded as {*of poor construction* and *inconclusive*}.

Improved: I think his report is {*poorly constructed* and *inconclusive*}.

Faulty: In cooking the frozen hog dogs, {*the tongs were used* and *I also built a very hot fire*}.

Improved: In cooking the frozen hot dogs, we used {*tongs* and *a very hot fire*}.

Many examples of faulty parallelism are created by the writer's trying to jam too much into one sentence.

Faulty: Also predominant on a boy's mind during his high school years are the desire for sexual activity, the want for a car, experimenting with smoking and drinking, and the testing of authority.

Improved: During high school some boys can think only of {*smoking, drinking, sex,* and *rebellion*}.

Faulty: The church group voted on invitations to parents to meetings, decided why there was a necessity for the formation of a Youth Committee, and a Youth Sunday.

Improved: The group decided {*to form* a Youth Committee and *to establish* a Youth Sunday}. They also voted *to invite* parents to meetings. *(Two sentences.)*

PRACTICE

Underline the faulty parallelism in the sentences below. (a) Place { } around each faulty parallelism. (b) Rewrite the sentence, using correct parallelism and two or more sentences if necessary. (c) Put { } around your improved parallelism. (Don't be afraid to recast a sentence pretty thoroughly, but do try to keep its basic meaning.)

a. The quality of a comic strip exists in relation to the drawings, the language as well as the situations involved. (*Hint:* Employ a new subject for the sentence; for example: "A comic strip is only as good as its drawings. . . .")

b. Let's start to plan the recreation program, describe the advisor's job, and the budgeting for playground equipment.

c. With information from the library, and experiencing my accounting major, I can help explain course requirements to students who plan to major in accounting.

d. Maryanne says that her qualifications for the position are good and is excellent at dealing with the public.

e. The old Ford was creaky, cranky, and the starting of it was hard.

f. My girl friend said that she wanted a handsome man and lovable, and who makes a lot of money.

g. The politician said he was honest, of considerable legislative experience, was chairman of three important committees in Congress, and his ability to pay attention to his state's problems made his election necessary.

h. Because I dislike violent movies and also being a peaceful person, I refused to see *The Godfather*.

i. My experience shows the value of love perfectly by contrasting sex with spiritual.
j. The American worker's greatest flaw and possibly the most outstanding reason for his boredom is his too high expectations regarding his job.

Subordination

Subordination, as the term implies, makes sentence elements *unequal* in grammar or emphasis. Subordinated elements are not bases or main clauses; they can never stand alone:

> Jack Reiss, *who quit his job last week,* believed his boss was taking advantage of him.

The interrupter in italics is subordinated to the main part of the sentence, which can stand alone. The subordination here could be reversed:

> Jack Reiss, *who believed his boss was taking advantage of him,* quit his job last week.

Subordination covers a large number of possible variations in ranking the parts of sentences. Here are typical variations, with the subordinated elements in italics (note how many subordinate elements are *free* units):

Using a *clause:* See examples above.

Using an *-ing* phrase:

> Jack, *believing that his boss was taking advantage of him,* quit his job last week.

Using an *-ed* phrase:

> *Abandoned by his crew,* the captain of the vessel stayed by his post.

Using an *appositive* or "explainer":

> Carol, *our treasurer,* bought a new ten-speed bicycle.

Using a *descriptive phrase:*

> The children, *obviously anxious about their dog,* dashed into the street.
> *Before breakfast,* they swim for thirty minutes and jog a mile.

Subordination is often signaled by punctuation, but many subordinate clauses do not require punctuation:

The house *that Jack built* is falling down.
The woman *you saw* lives upstairs.

Subordination strengthens your prose by cutting unnecessary expressions, making relationships clear, and smoothing the flow of words.

> *Weak:* He came into the office. It was after lunch. He looked flustered.
>
> *Improved:* *Looking flustered,* he came into the office *after lunch.*

> *Weak:* They were disturbed by the laughter at the movie. They complained to the usher.
>
> *Improved:* *Because they were disturbed by the laughter at the movie,* they complained to the usher.
>
> *Improved:* *Disturbed by the laughter,* they complained to the usher.

> *Weak:* The student said that he had lost his research paper. This happened on Tuesday.
>
> *Improved:* The student said that he had lost his research paper *on Tuesday.*

PRACTICE

1. One way to get a feel for the art of subordination is to take sentences that use it and recast them into short, choppy ones. Pick a sentence with a fair amount of subordination:

    > He suggested instead that the Philosophical Society, after filling its glasses, should invite Mr. Freak of the senior class to give his imitation of two cats quarreling on a roof. — Stephen Leacock

    Rewrite, omit the subordination, and chop into small sentences:

    > He suggested something. The Society should fill its glasses. Then it should invite Mr. Freak. He is a member of the senior class. He should be asked to do something. It is to give an imitation. His imitation should be of two cats. They are quarreling on a roof.

    Work backwards, and create choppy sentences from these smooth ones:

    a. "It is useless to go to bed to save the light, if the result is twins." — Chinese proverb
    b. "I believe it stupid to torment [students] to write on topics that they know and care nothing about." — F. L. Lucas
    c. "Our grandfathers, particularly those living in and around Boston, were of the opinion that the English spoken in Boston was the 'purest' in the whole country." — Bergen and Cornelia Evans

2. Now that you have done Practice **1**, work "forward"—revise these choppy sentences for proper subordination. Perhaps you may need more than one sentence in your rewritten versions.

   a. The pilot was experienced. He had 1000 hours flying time. He brought the crippled plane into the airport. It did not have a scratch.
   b. This is the painting that Smith sold. It is very rare. Smith had wanted it for years. He paid $20,000 for it.
   c. She joined the company. Then we knew her better. We learned to like her. Her shortness of temper did not seem to matter.
   d. The snow got too deep. They could not drive in it. It stopped about midnight. They slept in the car. The engine was left running to keep them warm They ignored the danger.
   e. The football fans are middle-aged. They are having a picnic. The food is on the tailgate of a hundred station wagons. The martinis are ice-cold. Some fans will not see this game.

Variations on the Typical Sentence

Here are some interesting sentences:

Among those whom I like or admire, I can find no common denominator, but among those whom I love, I can: all of them make me laugh.
—W. H. Auden

These are the times that try men's souls: The summer soldier and the sunshine patriot will in this crisis, shrink from the service of his country; but he that stands it Now, deserves the love and thanks of man and woman. Tyranny, like hell, is not easily conquered; yet we have this consolation with us, that the harder the conflict, the more glorious the triumph. . . .
—Thomas Paine

The afternoons were long; sunsets were sad glories: allegorical wars between dark heroes and the lords of light.—Jack Vance

I had not known my father very well. We had got on badly, partly because we shared, in our different fashions, the vice of stubborn pride. When he was dead I realized that I had hardly ever spoken to him. When he had been dead a long time I began to wish I had. It seems to be typical of life in America, where opportunities, real and fancied, are thicker than anywhere else on the globe, that the second generation has no time to talk to the first.—James Baldwin, *Notes of a Native Son*

Sentences like these provide variety and drama. The techniques for writing them are relatively simple, and you might like to try them out yourself. Write a few sentences every day in which you imitate the sentence patterns and techniques discussed in the rest of this chapter. Create your own variations. Take off and fly a little. But don't worry about crashes — nobody ever got hurt from falling off a sentence.

TRY DIFFERENT BEGINNINGS

By varying the way your sentences begin, you can add variety to your writing almost automatically. Here is a sentence that follows the subject-verb-object pattern:

She has a new afro.

By introducing various kinds of beginnings, you can work variations on this:

With *object as subject:* Her afro is pleasing to look at.
With *change of subject:* Her new hairdo is an afro.
With *-ing subject:* Wearing an afro is a good idea.
With *infinitive subject:* To wear an afro is a good idea.
With *subordinate clause:* After she was paid, she got an afro.
With *-ing phrase:* Having been paid, she got an afro.
With *prepositional phrase:* About 4:00, she appeared in a new afro.
With *it/there:* It's true that she has a new afro.
　　　　　　　　There's a woman with a new afro.
With *that/what:* That she has a new afro is true.
　　　　　　　　What she wanted was a new afro.
With a *question:* A new afro? She has one.

EMPLOY INVERSION

Most sentences are written using this normal word order: "They did not say a word." In creating an *inversion*, or *inverted order*, you shift a sentence element into an *earlier* position in the arrangement of words: "*Not a word* did they say." An occasional inversion makes your writing more interesting and dramatic:

Normal order: He slid down the slope, scraping skin from his elbows.
Inversion: *Down the slope he slid*, scraping skin from his elbows.

Normal order: The vampire stalked through the castle, his eyes glowing.
Inversion: *Through the castle stalked the vampire*, his eyes glowing. (a double inversion)

Precisely because inverted sentences are dramatic, they should be used sparingly.

TRY A PERIODIC SENTENCE

For richness and suspense, use an occasional *periodic sentence*, which keeps your main thought suspended until the end, a position of emphasis. The periodic sentence has two virtues: (1) you can pile many ideas into its versatile and flexible structure; and (2) it holds the reader's interest like a detective story. How, the reader wonders as he reads through a periodic sentence, will it all turn out? Here are some examples (italics added):

> At that great moment in history, ranking with the moment in the long ago when man first put fire to work for him and started on his march to civilization, *the vast energy locked within the hearts of the atoms of matter was released for the first time in a burst of flame such as had never before been seen on this planet.* — W. L. Laurence

> Cleanliness is a great virtue; but when it is carried to such an extent that you cannot find your books and papers which you left carefully arranged on your table — when it gets to be a monomania with man or woman — *it becomes a bore.* — C. B. Fairbanks

> There is a homely adage which runs, "Speak softly and carry a big stick; you will go far." If the American nation will speak softly and yet build and keep at a pitch of the highest training a thoroughly efficient navy, *the Monroe Doctrine will go far.* — Theodore Roosevelt

USE QUALIFYING AND BALANCING DEVICES

In your writing you will sometimes need to qualify your statements. That is, you will need to limit the range of an assertion or include an exception to an idea expressed in the base. Suppose you write: "I like Wagner's music, even though some of it is excessively dramatic." Here you qualify the idea in the sentence base ("I like Wagner's music") with an idea in a closer that is introduced by the phrase *even though.*

In balancing ideas, you can use certain *signs of correlation* to indicate that the ideas are equal in importance and emphasis. Here are some typical signs:

> *Either-or:*   Sandy wants *either* strawberry *or* vanilla ice cream.
> *Neither-nor:*   We wanted to go swimming, but *neither* Judy *nor* Alice was able to go.

Both-and:	We went to Hawk Beach because the water there was *both* safe *and* warm.
Not only-but also:	Howells should be admired *not only* for his vivid storytelling *but also* for his knowledge of human beings.

Sometimes you will need to express *opposing* ideas that are equal in importance. So you should use a special kind of balancing structure known as *antithesis:* "Linda likes swimming but not baseball." Antithesis is an art beloved of satirists, preachers, and politicians: "Woolworth was not brave; he was a coward. He was not fair; he played favorites. He was not moral, but righteous; not honest, but slyly dutiful; not skillful, but lucky; not. . . ." Poor Woolworth. It is easy to get carried away by this sort of thing.

LET MEANING DETERMINE YOUR STRUCTURE

Surely, the most important suggestion of all is: *let meaning determine the structure of your sentences.* If your meaning demands a certain type of sentence or a certain construction, use that sentence or construction. A sentence expresses an idea. If your idea is one of cause and effect, for example, your sentence construction in some way must show cause and effect: "Since all children should be able to read, we must build schools to teach them." The *since* tied to the opener, which is in turn tied to the sentence base, helps give the reader a sentence that moves clearly from opener to period and that also neatly marries structure and sense. Of course there are other ways to state this idea: "We must build schools because all children should be able to read." Here, *because* signals the cause-and-effect relation. (Many cause-and-effect sentences should have either a *since* or *because* in them.)

As you allow the meaning to determine the structure of your sentences, you will combine several of the structures discussed in this chapter. For example, Tom dislikes baseball. Perhaps he dislikes football and tennis too. And he loathes swimming. To express these ideas accurately, you write something like: "Tom dislikes football, tennis, and baseball—but swimming he actually loathes." To express a rather simple set of ideas you have created a complex and interlocked set of constructions:

sentence base:	Tom dislikes football
parallel elements:	football, tennis, and baseball
signal:	but
inversion:	swimming he actually loathes.

All these guidelines end with a bit of practical and general advice: use different sentence structures and lengths. Occasionally sneak up on your reader with a sentence he does not expect. Don't plod along writing one *subject-verb-object* sentence after another. Make your sentences show a little sparkle and life—but remember that too much sparkle, like too much champagne, will only make your reader dizzy. Here is a sparkling bit of prose that illustrates many of the variations we've been talking about.

> It is curious to be awake and watch a sleeper. Seldom, when he awakes, can he remember anything of his sleep. It is a dead part of his life. But watching him, we know he was alive, and part of his life was thought. His body moved. His eyelids fluttered, as his eyes saw moving visions in the darkness. His limbs sketched tiny motions, because his sleeping fancy was guiding him through a crowd, or making him imagine a race, a fight, a hunt, a dance. . . . He sweated. He felt the passage of time and was making himself ready for the morning with its light and noise. And all that time he was thinking—vaguely and emotionally if he was intellectually untrained, in symbols, animals, and divinities if he was a primitive man, often in memories, sometimes in anticipations of the future, and far oftener than he himself would believe, forming intricate and firm decisions on difficult problems carried over from his waking life.
> —Gilbert Highet, *Man's Unconquerable Mind*

PRACTICE

1. Identify the sentence structures of the following sentences. Look for parallelism, inversions, periodic sentences, and qualifying and balancing devices.

    a. All animals are equal, but some animals are more equal than others.—George Orwell

    b. Though I speak with the tongues of men and of angels, and have not charity, I am become as sounding brass, or a tinkling cymbal. —1 Cor. 13:1

    c. In some sort of crude sense which no vulgarity, no humor, no overstatement can quite extinguish, the physicists have known sin; and this is a knowledge which they cannot lose.—J. R. Oppenheimer [Treat as two sentence bases.]

    d. All in green went my love riding / on a great horse of gold / into the silver dawn.—E. E. Cummings

    e. We must conquer war, or war will conquer us.—Ely Culbertson

    f. In the free billowing fender [of the automobile], in the blinding chromium grilles, in the fluid control, in the ever-widening front seat, we see the flowering of the America that we know.—E. B. White

    g. Through all his life one idea runs—"Avoid the intelligent men and embrace the mediocre."

    h. A man may be old, he may be ugly, he may be burdened with grave responsibilities to the nation, and that nation be at a crisis of its history; but none of these considerations, nor all of them together, will deter him from sitting for his portrait. — Max Beerbohm

2. Here are two famous passages, written about 300 years apart. How are they similar and different in their use of the sentence variations discussed on pp. 177 – 181?

[The Devil speaks:] I saw a man die: he was a London bricklayer's laborer with seven children. He left seventeen pounds club money; and his wife spent it all on his funeral and went into the workhouse with the children next day. She would not have spent sevenpence on her children's schooling: the law had to force her to let them be taught gratuitously; but on death she spent all she had. Their imagination glows, their energies rise up at the idea of death, these people: they love it; and the more horrible it is the more they enjoy it. Hell is a place far above their comprehension: they derive their notion of it from two of the greatest fools that ever lived, an Italian and an Englishman. The Italian described it as a place of mud, frost, filth, fire and venomous serpents: all torture. This ass, when he was not lying about me, was maundering about some woman whom he saw once in the street. The Englishman described me as being expelled from Heaven by cannons and gunpowder; and to this day every Briton believes that the whole of his silly story is in the Bible. What else he says I do not know; for it is all in a long poem which neither I nor anyone else ever succeeded in wading through. It is the same in everything. The highest form of literature is the tragedy, a play in which everybody is murdered at the end. — George Bernard Shaw, *Don Juan in Hell*

O eloquent, just, and mighty death! whom none could advise, thou hast persuaded; what none hath dared, thou hast done; and whom all the world hath flattered, thou only hast cast out of the world and despised; thou hast drawn together all the far-stretched greatness, all the pride, cruelty, and ambition of man, and covered it all over with these two narrow words, *Hic jacet* [Here lies]. — Sir Walter Raleigh, *The Discovery of Guiana*

3. Using the ideas supplied in the sentences below, create new sentences that employ the variations suggested in this chapter. Omit any sentences or sentence parts that seem irrelevant in your new sentences. But try to use as much of the detail as possible.

   a. I read *Dracula*. It frightened me. I did not understand some of it. After reading it, I dreamed of blood and castles. I did not understand much of the story

   b. Darwin College needs a new rugby field. The players are unhappy. The trustees will not vote the funds for it. The players are thinking of trying to raise money by charging people to watch the games for the rest of the season. The field is very bumpy and rough. It has a shallow irrigation ditch running through it.

   c. The desert is full of killers. The desert seems empty. The desert is hot, but the heat does not kill all life. Many forms of life live off other forms. Many inhabitants of the desert look like bugs from another planet.

d. His mother screamed when she first saw it. Spiders did not frighten him. He got a big black spider as a pet. He kept it in a coffee can. He was curious, not fearful. The spider was more afraid of him than he of it.

e. Censorship is wrong. Censorship at times is necessary. Society has certain rights. Individuals should be able to read or view what they please without censorship. Books that show pictures of people being tortured are an evil.

f. The child was bored. The professor was angry at being interrupted. The mother stayed in class with her child. The child ran out of paper and crayons. The student brought her five-year-old child to class.

g. She wanted to experiment with the new. She did not care for tales of failure in the past. She liked chemistry most of all. Tales of dusty kings bored her. She enjoyed working with figures and test tubes and chemical unknowns.

Shaping Better Sentences (II): Revising and Editing

Only the genius gets a sentence right the first time. Most of us write . . . rewrite . . . and then write again—trying to get the proper match between meaning and structure. Revision usually improves this match; but with revision, as with other techniques in composition, you need a plan—or a set of suggestions—in order to make it more purposeful. After writing a "bad" sentence, how do you fix it? In this chapter we will offer a number of suggestions for revision, all of them based on the following premise: as you inspect your own sentences, imagine that you are a cool, objective, and slightly negative editor who does not mind telling himself to rearrange, cut, and reword.

Suggestions for Revising and Editing*

1. *Think about what you've said.*

Many bad sentences are a result of the writer's failure to think about and visualize what he has written. Leo Rosten found a sentence in the *New York Times* that shows how such a failure can result in unintentional comedy:

> There is Mr. Burton growling and grousing and endlessly chewing the lips, ears, and neck of Elizabeth Taylor as the faithless wife of a dull ambassador with whom he is having a clandestine affair.

---

*Editors and instructors often hear this complaint from writers after they have rewritten a sentence: "But you changed my meaning!" The objection has some validity, but the response to it has more: "One cannot usually make a significant improvement in a weak sentence without changing the meaning." In fact, when writers revise or edit a sentence, they try to make *meaning* more exact at the same time that they improve *structure* and *word choice*. In the sentence, everything works (or does not work) together.

Rosten commented: "I am glad, in a way, that Mr. Burton was endlessly chewing the neck of Miss Taylor as the faithless wife of a dull
ambassador, because it probably wouldn't be fun to chew her neck as
anyone else; but who is the ambassador with whom Burton, it says
here, is having a clandestine affair?" Rosten quoted another sentence
from the *Times*:

Among her biggest gambles was during their tempestuous courtship.

Said Rosten: "I hate to be a spoilsport, gentlemen, but you just can't
'was' during anything."

2. *Check your stance.*

Is a weak writer's stance hurting your sentence? A student wrote
about a class project:

The availability of time is an important factor in the project choice.

The stance is vague here—no writer, reader, or clear point. Clarify the
stance and rewrite completely:

In choosing a problem for our project, we must remember that we have
only three weeks' time.

3. *Make your subject-verb relationship as clear and specific as
possible.*

A vague relationship helped make a mess of this sentence:

Parental *endeavors* (subject) in regard to education suggest (verb)
that . . . .

How can an endeavor *suggest*? Specify the subject and verb; then clarify the rest of the sentence:

Parents at Elm School now *insist* that their children be taught to read.

Here is another example of vague subject and verb:

One of the most important reasons for supporting the union *is* stable employment.

Edit this by changing both the stance and the subject-verb relationship:

Workers who want stable employment *should join* the union.

Or:

Do you want stable employment? Then [you should] join the union.

4. *Read your sentences aloud.*

Pedalling hard, she reached top of the hill.

That is a sentence one of us wrote several years ago. It went through our hands and the hands of an editor before the omission was found — by a proofreader reading the sentence aloud:

> Pedalling hard, she reached *the* top of the hill.

Since people read hundreds of words a minute, it is easy to miss all kinds of errors — dangling modifiers, misspellings, illogicalities, vague usage, careless punctuation, omissions. *The ear will catch what the eye will not.* Human beings spoke and heard language a million years before they wrote it, which is why the best editing often combines the talents of ear and eye and voice.

5. *Use the sentence base rule.*

Check back to p. 168 for a full explanation of the rule. Also see **6** below.

6. *Make sure your sentence openers logically fit the bases that follow.*

> *Faulty:* Like many specialities in engineering, you must learn . . . .
> *(dangling modifier)*
> *Improved:* Like many kinds of engineers, you must learn . . . .
>
> *Faulty:* To be considered for the debate team, the voice must be trained.
> *Improved:* To be considered for the debate team, you must first train your voice.

7. *Avoid "nouniness" and "preposition piling."*

Good sentences use no more nouns than are absolutely necessary. Abstract nouns are particularly troublesome. This sentence is "nouny":

> *Personality analysis* is the *determination* of *function defects* and *utilization* of their *cures.*

The sentence contains seven nouns — two of them used as clumsy modifiers: "*personality* analysis" and "*function* defects." This sentence is so bad it can't be edited; who knows what it means?

In a sentence, prepositions can multiply like rabbits. Such "preposition piling" occurs with nouniness and is a sign of it:

> English teachers agree that personal ownership and use *of* a good dictionary is a prime necessity *for* every student *in* obtaining the maximum results *from* the study of English.

Rewrite, cutting some of the nouns and altering others; for example, make *ownership* and *use* into verbs. Then the prepositions can be reduced from five to zero, the nouns from ten to three:

English teachers agree that students should own and use a good desk dictionary.

Here is a portion of a satiric essay on nouniness in modern prose:

Have you noticed the new look in the English language? Everybody's using nouns as adjectives. Or to put that in the current argot, there's a modifier noun proliferation. More exactly, since the matter is getting out of hand, a modifier noun proliferation increase. In fact, every time I open a magazine these days or listen to the radio, I am struck by the modifier noun proliferation increase phenomenon. So, I decided to write — you guessed it — a modifier noun proliferation increase phenomenon article. . . .

Abstraction is the enemy both of clear expression and easy understanding. And abstract is what these strings of nouns become. And very quickly the reader or listener doesn't know what the actual relationship is. Take "Reality Therapy," the name of a new book. Do you gather that the author uses reality as a means of therapy or that the goal of his treatment is facing reality or that he has worked out some sort of therapy which he applies to reality? Take a phrase puzzled over in *Newsweek*: "antenna television systems operation." Manufacture? broadcasting? consulting? The article said that somebody was going into that field and I still don't know where he's going. I suspect that the people who turn out these phrases might insist that they are seeking greater precision, as though each new noun pinned down the matter a bit more. Wrong. Another article like this one and we'll have a modifier noun proliferation increase phenomenon article protest campaign, but will you know what you've got? — Bruce Price, "An Inquiry into Modifier Noun Proliferation"

8. *Cut out deadwood — words and phrases that are not doing enough work in the sentence.*

The sample sentence in **7,** on using the dictionary, illustrates how to cut out deadwood. Here are more examples:

Poor: A woman who was present there saw the break-in.
Improved: A women there saw the break-in.

Poor: We are in receipt of your memo of August 14 making reference to football tickets sold by some of the players.
Improved: We received your letter of August 14 about football tickets sold by some of the players.

Poor: In relation to his idea, it does not seem to me to be a workable one.
Improved: I doubt that his idea will work.

Poor: A second area in which Jane should have a better knowledge involves rules of attendance.
Improved: Second, Jane should know more about rules of attendance.

9. *Rewrite to avoid monotony or lack of emphasis.*

> *Poor:* Many favorable comments are beginning to be made about fantasy movies by the critics. These comments are long overdue and welcome to students of film.
>
> *Improved:* Recently many critics have made favorable comments about movies. To students of film, these comments are welcome — and long overdue.

> *Poor:* I took the job happily when the head of the company offered me more money because of my long experience and also technical school training in the field.
>
> *Improved:* When he found out that I had both technical training and experience, the head of the company offered me the job with a higher salary. I accepted his offer happily.

The last two improved versions work well partly because they follow the three suggestions offered by the sentence base rule (p. 168).

10. *Change a vague or clumsy passive.*

The easiest way to understand the *passive* construction is to contrast it with the *active*, which follows the formula "Something does [something]":

Something	*does*	*[something]*
The wolf	howls at the moon.	
The wolf	bit	my ear.

The passive construction reverses the formula — "Something is done [by something]":

Something	*is done*	*[by something]*
The moon	was howled at	by the wolf.
My ear	was bitten	by the wolf.

The typical relationship between active and passive statements looks like this (the *agent* does the acting):

Active	*Passive*
[agent]	[agent]
The *wind* blew the flowers.	The flowers were blown by the *wind*.
[agent]	[agent]
Explorers found the cave.	The cave was found by the *explorers*.
[agent]	[agent]
The saw cut my *arm*.	My arm was cut by the *saw*.

These examples show the *complete* form of the passive, and every complete form will have all the parts mentioned. The shortened form of the *passive* (what we will here call the *short passive*) omits the *by* and the *agent*:

> The gift will be delivered.
> The police have been notified.
> The job was completed.
> The worker should be fired from his job.

Each of these four short passives can be made into a complete passive — if you know the agents. The complete passive of the last sentence, for example, might read:

> [agent]
> The worker should be fired from his job by the *supervisor*.

The passive is a minor sentence form. Skillful writers use certain other forms — particularly the active — much more often. The reasons are not hard to find. One is that the passive can be very awkward, as in "The moon was howled at by the wolf." A second is that the passive encourages vagueness, even dishonesty, because in its short form — without the agent expressed — the writer can fail to assign responsibility for an action: "The highway was blocked." But who or what blocked it? "The vice-president was discouraged from inspecting the firm's books." Who discouraged him?

A third reason why the skillful writer often avoids the passive is that in modern times it has become associated with jargon and gobbledygook:

> Currently utilized population estimates leave much *to be desired* in future planning.
> The experimental rationale *was explained* in the Foreword and *was* more fully *detailed* in Chapter 3.
> Psychological characterization *will be considered* as a major factor in the present analysis of Huck Finn.

Whenever a passive is wordy, awkward, unemphatic, or so gobbledygooky that a reader simply cannot understand it, there is a simple strategy for improving it. Make the statement active:

> *Poor:* A picnic table was located by Jim. (7 words)
> *Improved:* Jim located a picnic table. (5 words)
>
> *Poor:* The banquet was held during which speeches were made and songs were sung. (13 words)
> *Improved:* During the banquet, we heard speeches and sang songs. (9 words)

The solution to the gobbledygook passive is *never* to write a sentence like this in the first place:

> It has been decided that to maintain optimum learning conditions in the library, evening hours will be extended to 2:00 a.m.

But if a sentence like this sneaks up on you in a first draft, identify the agent(s) in the situation, and put the idea into one or more specific active statements:

> The library has announced that its evening hours will be extended to 2:00 a.m.
>
> Mr. Harlan Smith, Director of the Library, has announced that. . . .
>
> Mr. Smith announced today that starting Sunday the library will close at 2:00 a.m. Smith claimed that closing the library later will allow more students to use it.
>
> So that more students can use the library, it will close at 2:00 a.m. from now on.

11. *Change an unnecessary or clumsy expletive.*

The expletive sentence starts with *it* or *there:*

> *It is* a beautiful day in San Francisco.
> *There's* no fool like an old fool.

As these sentences demonstrate, the expletive is both normal and pleasant when properly used. But when it occurs in wordy or awkward constructions like the following, you should revise the sentence:

> *Poor:* For those who wish more heat, *there is* a heater switch on the dashboard.
> *Improved:* If you want more heat, turn the switch on the dashboard.
>
> *Poor:* At the feet of the corpse *it was* found that *there were* five empty jewel cases from three different robberies. (*Two expletives!*)
> *Improved:* At the feet of the corpse, the police found five empty jewel cases from three different robberies.

In both these examples, we edited and improved the weak sentences by shifting to active constructions. A lot of sentence editing works exactly like this: you look at the sick sentence; ask "What is happening here?"; and answer the question with an active construction.

Note: In order to balance our discussion of passive constructions and expletives, we need to point out that both have their place. The passive is useful for variety and is appropriate for statements in which the agent is either unknown ("My books were stolen in the library."), or understood ("The embezzler was paroled after serving five years."). The expletive is useful in beginnings: "There are a thousand ways to write an introduction"; or, "Once upon a time, there was a fair princess who loved a frog." Expletives are also useful in writing short, informal sentences: "It's a long way to Tipperary."

Yet all authorities recognize that the expletive and the passive have their dangers. So we say: Don't avoid the constructions entirely, but be wary of them—and edit them when necessary.

A Final Note on Editing

Recently, a student came in to see one of us about his writing problems, particularly about his weak sentences. We talked over several of them, bringing out ideas and possibilities hidden inside (or behind) them. In effect, we were "co-editors," identifying, analyzing, rethinking, and rewriting some of the troublesome constructions. You can do the same job by "talking" over your own sentences with yourself. Here are two of the student's sentences, with comments about their weaknesses:

Poor sentence: The students were accused of plagiarism, and they were told in terms of their careers in academia that they should not be too hopeful.

Comments: Stance and viewpoint are weak—*who* told the students? The two passive constructions are vague. Deadwood: *in terms of. Their careers* and *in academia* are not doing much work in the sentence either. Vague: *They should not be too hopeful.*

Edited sentence: After she accused the students of plagiarism, the Assistant Dean told them that they might be expelled.

Together, we created a clearer stance, cut out the deadwood, employed an opener, changed the vague passives to active constructions, and made the whole sentence more specific.

Poor sentence: The misuse of the environment must be improved in regard to the liquor industry.

Comments: Read the sentence aloud—we must *improve* our *misuse?* This says exactly the opposite of what the writer intended. He was probably thrown off the track by several weaknesses: the poor stance, the vagueness and deadwood in *in regard to the liquor industry;* the passive *misuse . . . must be improved.*

Edited sentence: Let's pass a law in this state abolishing throwaway beer bottles.

We changed the stance. Now the writer is addressing a more specific group of readers. We cut unnecessary words, changed the bad passive to an active verb, and substituted the more specific phrase *beer bottles* for the vague phrase *liquor industry.*

PRACTICE

Edit and rewrite these sentences.

a. The assassination of Lincoln had much speculation to it.
b. The fact that the new trainees at first do not get to do much work on

the actual engines should not give them a feeling of demotion.

c. It must be considered a possibility that the student nurse must be able to face physical damage, broken bones, cranial disorders, pregnancy, or even death.

d. It happened at the hour of three when there is much relaxing during the coffee break.

e. The nerve center of the oboe lies in its reed, and in its bore is its soul; the need of a good reed is the bane of the player's life.

f. Mr. Coleman announced his resignation this morning. He would have liked to have stayed a while longer.

g. "Don't expire before your license do."—from the Illinois State License Bureau

h. He only dislikes action pictures and neither does his brother.

i. The next point to make about idiom differences is one of the most difficult problems for many foreigners.

j. It is not believed that the critics show complete rationality in their judgments when they criticize the Fall Frolic.

k. After explaining my job to me, there was a car sent by the Head Ranger to take me to the office.

l. Our family has been really having huge difficulties with hard-core resentment on the girls' part, who have been claiming that we play favorites for the one boy.

m. Thus the continual success, interest, and the test of endurance are reasons why marathon racing is an important topic.

n. Although these statistics may look suspicious, it is because there is not a more specific breakdown of them.

o. President Carter should have begun to explore the possibility of détente with Congress as an explanation device for dealing with the problem of Bert Lance's credibility. (Break into two sentences?)

p. In response to the attack on my report on Adventure Playgrounds, I will prove to you, the newspapers, radio, and TV its validity.

q. Perched prettily on the branches, we watched the first robin of spring.

r. There have been several proposals which have since come forth about what to do with the dangerous crossing south of Fresno.

s. The exploration of student differences in response to the instructor's stimulus questions cause the students to return to the textbook seeking justification for their opinions and ultimately encourage the articulation of their personal views.

t. The loss of professors' credibility represents an indispensable foundation upon which authority structures are undermined.

u. The nation's domestic ills may keep, although there is a risk in deferring them.

v. Last year the campus had a great increase in narcotics arrests, most of them on a marijuana possession charge or for smoking marijuana.

Handling
Special Assignments

argument
   logical
    look at all
     evidenc
   Truth

Persuasive
an appeal to the emotions
   agreemt

10 Writing a Persuasive Argument

Situation One:

"I got gas for my car today—those *prices*! The big oil companies are sure out to get all they can out of the consumer."

"Well, it's not the oil companies' fault. They can't get enough oil for their refineries."

"I bet they've got *plenty* of oil! They just know they have the consumer where they want him. We've got to have fuel for our cars and houses, and they'll jack up the prices in this fake shortage, and then keep them there after the shortage is over."

"How do you know it's a fake shortage—are you an expert on the oil business or something?"

Situation Two:

Dear Sir:

I read your recent editorial in which you attacked the patriotic organization "Freedom Ringers" that calls people on the telephone and tells them how bad communism is.

I don't understand your point at all. Isn't telephoning a voluntary act? Who pays for the call? Not the man who owns the phone. Who is forced to listen? Any man has a recognized right of not listening to a Freedom Ringer.

Why does the telephone company yield to pressure? Is freedom of speech coming to an end in America?

Very truly yours,

Each of these situations involves *argument*, which is an attempt to convince or persuade. But neither situation represents a *formal argument*, as we use the phrase here. A *formal argument* is an orderly arrangement of carefully defined terms and properly qualified statements (backed by evidence) which support a single thesis. A formal argument is a written attempt to *convince* or *persuade* the reader that he should *believe* something or *do* something (or both).

It is possible to argue two or three theses in a long formal argument. But in practice, a well-made formal argument tends to have its own unity, so that even if you are arguing two or three theses, you will find that there is an implicit single thesis underlying or supporting them. It is important that a formal argument have evidence. Formally speaking, assertions such as these are not arguments:

> "The big oil companies are sure out to get all they can out of the consumer."
>
> "Any man has a recognized right of not listening to a Freedom Ringer."

The formal argument requires you to manage your writer's stance with unusual care. When such an argument is successful, both you and your reader feel that you have arrived at a conclusion more or less together, having agreed to believe in the thesis of the argument. As the writer, you *lead* your reader to agree with you not by force or deception but by the legitimate power of your persuasion.

What makes a formal argument *persuasive*? In most genuinely persuasive arguments there are five elements:

1. *A human approach.* The writer strikes the reader as an honest, believable person who has a genuine interest in his material and in his reader.

2. *Solid evidence.* The writer does not rely on mere assertion; he uses pertinent facts, details, statistics, or testimony from authorities to back up his statements.

3. *Good logic.* The writer makes the right *connections* between his pieces of evidence; he creates accurate generalizations and draws proper conclusions.

4. *An avoidance of fallacy.* The writer not only avoids logical errors, he also avoids irrelevancies, false appeals to emotion, or question begging. (These and other fallacies are explained in this chapter.)

5. *A clear argumentative organization.* The writer organizes his argument so that his reader can understand all its parts and how the parts relate to each other and to the thesis.

In the pages that follow, we will discuss each of these elements.

PRACTICE

Before we go on to discuss the major elements in persuasive argumentation, we should stop to look at all of them working in a particular argument (or not working — you be the judge).

The following passage is taken from a commencement address Mary Thibeault delivered at the Hartford College for Women in 1974. Ms. Thibeault is Assistant to the President of the college. The address was later reprinted in *Vital Speeches*. Prepare for class discussion a set of judgments based on the five elements of a successful argument.

The Hazards of Equality

[1]The first, and perhaps the most serious hazard is the temptation to make man the enemy.

[2]When Anita Loos, author of the classic socio-sexual analysis, *Gentlemen Prefer Blondes,* was asked about women's liberationists, she replied she was furious with them. "They keep proclaiming women are brighter than men and that's true, of course," says Miss Loos, "but it should be kept quiet or it ruins the whole racket." I'll register my own partial agreement with Miss Loos and the women's liberationists. I do believe that women, in general, are more acute about *some* things than *most* men. And I generally find it advantageous in the company of men to camouflage that superiority. I hope that *you* have learned by now not only that there are some differences between men and women, but also that you can join with me in saying, "Vive la difference." And I speak here not merely of a physical, but also, and most emphatically, of the temperamental, emotional, and psychological differences between men and women. The differences between male and female perceptions create, I believe, constructive tensions and broader dimensions that enhance life for men and women.

[3]Let me warn you, too, against indulging yourself in the blanket accusation that men have oppressed us. Rather, develop an awareness of the socio-economic and historical reasons for women's assignment to limited or subordinate roles in our social and economic life.

[4]Try to understand as well the not entirely happy role created for a man. He was socially programmed to say, "No wife of mine will ever work," and to see himself as the sole breadwinner for his family. These same social expectations lead this man to work to put his wife into a neo-colonial suburban house so that mowing the lawn in the summer, shovelling the driveway of the two-car garage in the winter, and meeting the demands of his job all year long will result in his just reward—an early heart attack.

[5]While the professional man is engaged in the struggle for professional success, his wife finds herself in what Betty Friedan calls "the sexual ghetto," with no one to talk to over three feet tall. So it is no surprise if some men in the world of work treat a woman they meet professionally as they treat their own wives and daughters. Having learned at home that women have little knowledge about anything significant, a man often does not know how to react when a woman at work is competent and forthright in discussing professional problems.

[6]This does not make man the enemy. He is, rather, a victim of the same attitudes that keep some women from exhibiting their competence.

[7]Those of us who have spent any time at a career know one unpleasant fact to keep us from thinking of man as the enemy. You sometimes discover that women can harbor the same attitudes attributed to a male chauvinist. In short, not all male chauvinists are men!

⁸So, misuse of authority is bad, no matter *who* does it, and sexual prejudice is a sin that may be committed by either sex.

⁹For example, I have heard some women say they do not want to work for a woman. Yes, I know they may have had one bad experience and hence condemn all women supervisors. They often say it to a man who may be the one to hire them. Since, in most cases, it is a man who holds the power to hire, promote, give raises and better titles and office space, this attitude is understandable. So, if you should become a supervisor, be prepared for some suspicion or even hostility from some of the women you supervise, and strive to be the kind of supervisor who recognizes talent, ability, and performance regardless of sex.

¹⁰A final reason why we must not let man become the enemy is that we want to live with him—as a brother, a father, or a husband. "Love thy enemy" may be a valid moral imperative, but who wants to *live* with an enemy?

Use a Human Approach

The *human approach* in argument involves a special adaptation of the writer's stance, particularly in regard to the relationship between the writer and his reader. The human approach has two basic aspects, closely interrelated. The first deals with the writer's *character* (his "ethical proof"), the second with the writer's *feeling for his reader* (his "you-attitude").

ETHICAL PROOF

From the time of the ancient Greeks, authorities in rhetoric have pointed out that the arguer's character is very important. The Greek word for "character" was *ethos*, and a writer (or speaker, in ancient times) whose work showed him to be honest, fair, and reasonable was said to be employing *ethical proof*. As Cato, a Roman, put it, an orator should be "a good man skilled in speaking."

When your good character appears in a written formal argument to your advantage, you too are employing the very old device of ethical proof. But such proof is not to be artificially displayed in an argument. Rather, you should emphasize your natural good qualities, and at the same time suppress any qualities—such as a tendency to jump to conclusions—that might injure your character or your believability in the eyes of your reader. Such suppression is not dishonest if it improves the truth and effectiveness of your argument.

As an example of ethical proof, consider these paragraphs from the end of John Kennedy's inaugural address:

Modesty and patriotism

[1]In your hands, my fellow citizens, more than mine, will rest the final success or failure of our course. Since this country was founded, each generation of Americans has been summoned to give testimony to its national loyalty. The graves of young Americans who answered the call to service surround the globe.

[2]Now the trumpet summons us again—not as a call to bear arms, though arms we need—not as a call to battle, though embattled we are—but a call to bear the burden of a long twilight struggle, year in and year out, "rejoicing in hope, patient in tribulation"—a struggle against the common enemies of man: tyranny, poverty, disease and war itself.

Concern for others

[3]Can we forge against these enemies a grand and global alliance, North and South, East and West, that can assure a more fruitful life for all mankind? Will you join in that historic effort?

Courage

[4]In the long history of the world, only a few generations have been granted the role of defending freedom in its hour of maximum danger. I do not shrink from this responsibility—I welcome it. I do not believe that any of us would exchange places with any other people or any other generation. The energy, the faith, the devotion

Selfless dedication

which we bring to this endeavor will light our country and all who serve it—and the glow from that fire can truly light the world.

[5]And so, my fellow Americans: Ask not what your country can do for you—ask what you can do for your country.

[6]My fellow citizens of the world: Ask not what America will do for you, but what together we can do for the freedom of man.

High religious and moral standards

[7]Finally, whether you are citizens of America or citizens of the world, ask of us here the same high standards of strength and sacrifice which we ask of you. With a good conscience our only sure reward, with history the final judge of our deeds, let us go forth to lead the land we love, asking His blessing and His help, but knowing that here on earth God's work must truly be our own.

In this brief passage, the admirable qualities of President Kennedy's character shine through *as an integral part of the argument*. This ethical proof, which really cannot be precisely described in the marginal notes, is woven into the texture of honest, clear arguments.

THE "YOU-ATTITUDE"

The *you-attitude* can be summed up like this: "As a writer, I am as interested in you [my reader] as I am in myself or my subject." *Example:* Joe Smith writes a brief argument addressed to his neighborhood Advisory Board, a group that acts as a go-between for the citizens of Valley Road subdivision and the City Council. He wants the two-way stop on Valley Road and Race Street to be replaced by a four-way stop. He writes this draft:

> The two-way stop at Valley and Race is at present a real danger to both pedestrians and drivers. Two accidents have occurred there within the last month. Valley feeds into the highway south, and drivers pick up speed two blocks north of the intersection. By the time they arrive at that point they are going quite fast. Race Street drivers or pedestrians (not to mention bike riders) often find it difficult to get across Valley Road safely.
>
> Let's ask the City Council to put a four-way stop at Race and Valley.

This is a decent enough draft, but there is no particular feeling for the readers or their problems. So, after receiving a bit of advice, Joe rewrites his draft, and creates a stronger you-attitude:

> Have you, as members of the Advisory Board, thought about making a recommendation to the City Council about the stop at Valley and Race? Most of you are my friends and neighbors, and I've heard you complain about that stop more than once. Rod Jensen's boy Greg nearly got run over on his bike the other day trying to get across Valley during the rush hour to deliver his papers.
>
> Do you think a four-way stop at Valley and Race might solve our problems? If you believe this might be the best solution, would you mind if I presented a more detailed plan for the stop (including costs) at the August 4th meeting? The City Council would probably be happier with an Advisory proposal if it came with a cost analysis.

Observe that ethical proof and an agreeable you-attitude support each other in evolving an effective human approach to an argumentative question. When Joe Smith refers (honestly and accurately enough) to the fact that his friends and neighbors are involved in the traffic problem and that Greg Jensen nearly got run over, he creates interest in the situation. He asks for the Board's judgment concerning the four-way stop instead of bluntly telling them that the stop is necessary. He gives them the impression (again honestly) that he has thought the matter through; he knows what the costs will be, and he will present the figures to the Advisory Board at the next meeting.

A common objection to the idea of using ethical proof and a you-attitude to support a "human approach" is that "they can be easily faked." Practically speaking, this doesn't seem to be the case. For one thing, the human approach does not ask you to create any aspect of your personality that is not already there; most writers have good sides and certain kinds of genuine interests in other human beings. The approach merely suggests that you make use of all possible avenues of rapport between you and the reader and that you try to show him the proofs of your character that truly exist, along with your genuine interest in him and his welfare.

PRACTICE

The following passage is a clear example of the use of ethical proof; the employment of the you-attitude is somewhat more subtle. The passage is taken from an argument against racial discrimination made by Henry Gonzales, U.S. Representative from Texas. Obviously Gonzales is addressing a wide and varied audience. Explain how he uses both ethical proof and the you-attitude.

[1]No man ought to either practice or condone racism; every man ought to condemn it. Neither should any man practice or condone reverse racism.

[2]Those who would divide our country along racial lines because they are fearful and filled with hatred are wrong, but those who would divide the races out of desire for revenge, or out of some hidden fear, are equally wrong. Any man, regardless of his ambitions, regardless of his aims, is committing an error and a crime against humanity if he resorts to the tactics of racism. If Bilbo's racism was wrong—and I believe that it was—then so are the brown Bilbos of today.

[3]Fifteen years ago as a member of the City Council of the city of San Antonio, Texas, I asked my fellow Council members to strike down ordinances and regulations that segregated the public facilities of the city, so as to end an evil that ought never to have existed to begin with. That Council complied, because it agreed with me that it was time for reason to at long last have its day. Eleven years ago I stood almost alone in the Senate of the State of Texas to ask my colleagues to vote against a series of bills that were designed to perpetuate segregation, contrary to the law of the land. I saw the beginnings then of a powerful reaction to racist politics, and I begged my colleagues to remember: "If we fear long enough, we hate. And if we hate long enough, we fight." I still believe this to be true. Since then there has been vast progress in Texas. I did not know how to describe to you the oppression that I felt then; but I can tell you that the atmosphere today is like a different world. Injustices we still have aplenty, but no longer is there a spirit of blatant resistance to just redress of just grievance. Yet despite this change in the general atmosphere, despite the far healthier tenor of public debate and public action today, I felt compelled almost exactly a year ago to address the United States House of Representatives on the continuing and alarming practice of race politics, and what I chose to call the politics of desperation.

Give Solid Evidence

Deep in the seventh tier of our university library, we were hunting for an elusive quotation in a book that didn't seem to exist. After about an hour, we decided to give up and headed for the stairs, which happened to be close to the study carrel of a friend. "Hey," he said, "Are you going home? You're going to get wet!"

"But it couldn't be raining—the sun was shining only an hour ago."

Our friend said nothing but merely pointed to a coat rack on which hung his dripping raincoat.

FACTUAL EVIDENCE

Appropriate cliché: "The evidence [a wet raincoat, for example] speaks for itself." But to allow it to speak for itself in your themes you must put it there in the first place. Always support your arguments with evidence—facts, figures, results of experiments, statements from authorities. As you write, check each important statement by asking: "Do I have evidence for what I am saying?" Of course, you will seldom, if ever, have perfect evidence, whatever that might be. Argument deals with the probable, not with the perfectly true. But for them to be persuasive, your statements—and your evidence—should be as solid (as "probably true") as you can make them.

PRACTICE

1. Taken from a longer essay, the following passage shows how evidence is ordinarily used to bolster an argument. The writer argues that many persons are wrong in their belief that the American worker is a robot victimized by the assembly line. Read the argument and prepare the discussion questions at the end.

[1]In this [the widespread notion that a majority of American laborers work on assembly lines], as in so many other respects, undue attention to Detroit and the automobile industry makes for gross distortion. General Motors is a huge corporation which fascinates our social critics. But GM, which has about one-third of its 550,000 employes on the assembly line, is not a typical firm and the automobile industry is not a typical industry. A much more accurate picture of what is fast becoming the typical manufacturing firm is provided by the Bendix Corporation, which has less than 10% of its 57,000 employes on the assembly line, while 50% are white-collared workers and 30% are professional and technical staff.

[2]And even this picture, taken by itself, is skewed, since the average American worker does not work for a manufacturing firm. Indeed, a majority of blue-collar workers are now outside manufacturing—they are in

transportation, construction, utilities, trade, etc.

³More and more, as the American economy becomes a "post-indus-
trial," service-oriented economy, fewer and fewer people are engaged in
blue-collar factory work, in blue-collar work of any kind, in manufacturing
altogether. The factory is following the farm as *yesterday's* typical place
of employment. Today, there are more insurance salesmen than blue-collar steelworkers in America, and the insurance "industry" as a whole
probably employs more people than does automobile manufacturing.
There are more white-collar than blue-collar workers in the American
labor force, and by 1980 the ratio will reach an overwhelming 5:3. Moreover, by 1980, some 25% of these white-collar workers will be either in
the "professional-technical" category (teachers, engineers, scientists,
etc.) or in the "managerial" (public and private) category.—Irving Kristol, "Is the American Worker 'Alienated'?"

a. Irving Kristol is Henry Luce Professor of Urban Values at New
    York University and co-editor of the scholarly journal, *The
    Public Interest.* How are these facts important in your evalua-
    tion of his use of evidence?
b. How many separate pieces of evidence are there in the pas-
    sage? Make a list of them.
c. Why does Kristol object to General Motors as a *sample* of
    American industry?
d. In paragraph 1, why does Kristol write "10% of its 57,000
    employes" instead of "a small number of its large employe
    force"?
e. What is the purpose of paragraph 2? What does *skewed* mean?
f. There is an analogy in the first two sentences of paragraph 3.
    What is it? Can it be called evidence? Of what?
g. Is the evidence in paragraph 1 more, or less, specific than that
    in paragraph 3? Is paragraph 3 more, or less, convincing than
    paragraph 1?
h. Summarize Kristol's argument.

2. Write a brief, clearly reasoned argument responding to Kristol's
    statements. You may agree, partly agree, or disagree with him. Or
    you may make a different argument entirely. (What you write can
    depend largely on your work experience.) Choose an appropriate
    reader for your writer's stance. You may wish to address Kristol
    directly or to write for his typical reader, an educated American
    who requires more information about the subject.

AUTHORITATIVE EVIDENCE

For our purposes, an *authority* is a person who
knows what he is talking about. He can be a theoretical expert in his

special area of knowledge, someone who has had practical experience in the field, or both. As a professor of urban studies at a major university and an editor of a scholarly journal, Irving Kristol might reasonably be considered a theoretical authority on the American blue-collar worker. A man (let's call him Jim West) who has worked for a few years in a blue-collar job could be a "practical" expert on his type of job.

Kristol will know more theory and have a broader range of knowledge about the blue-collar worker than West, but West will know more detail concerning his particular job than Kristol. If you were writing a paper on the American worker, you might read Kristol to obtain theoretical knowledge and go to a man like West for practical information on, for example, operating a punch press. Of course, both of these authorities would know something about the other's "area" of knowledge. If you were writing on the alienation of workers, you could certainly take into account West's firsthand knowledge of blue-collar work. Your decisions about which authorities to use depend on the nature of your thesis.

It is wise to remember that all authorities, whether theoretical or practical, are limited to some extent in the type and quality of their knowledge. Furthermore, they may be limited simply by being forgetful, prejudiced, out-of-date on the evidence, or plainly dishonest.

As a writer, you can use authoritative evidence in two ways: (1) you can quote authorities to bolster your own argument; (2) you can act as your own expert or practical authority. From your reading and experience, you should have considerable knowledge that you can use authoritatively. Whether you use your own or others' ideas, consider the following questions as you evaluate the *quality* of authoritative opinion:

1. *Is the person an authority on the subject?* We tend to associate the idea of authority with well-known people in special fields, whether their opinions are authoritative or not. It is wise to accept the medical ideas of a famous pediatrician on babies, but when that same man gives advice on political matters, we should be wary. The opinions of glamorous or popular persons, like movie stars and sports figures, are seldom authoritative except in their own narrow fields.

2. *Is the authority unprejudiced and sensible?* Just being an authority does not make one free from prejudice or egomania. The pathologist Sydney Smith has written of a world-famous authority on pathology: "Spilsbury, like the rest of us, could make mistakes. He was unique, I think, in that he never admitted a mistake. Once he had committed himself to an opinion he would never change it." An expert can be as prejudiced or obstinate as anyone else.

3. *Is the authority up-to-date on his speciality?* In many fields, last year's knowledge is unreliable. The authority should demonstrate that he knows the latest information in his field.

4. *Does the authority have evidence on the question being discussed?* Unless the expert has seen and examined the evidence for himself, it is unlikely that his opinion is valuable. A psychiatrist recently diagnosed the mental ailment of a political agitator without ever seeing the man. Under these circumstances, the psychiatrist's opinion was probably not authoritative.

PRACTICE

1. The first passage below is part of a letter written by a physician to the science editor of *Saturday Review;* the second is part of a memo written by a college student. Prepare some notes for class discussion on how each writer uses authoritative evidence. Also discuss the writer's stance of each excerpt.

    [1]In "Fluoridation vs. the Constitution" [*Saturday Review, Apr. 3*] Professor Arthur Selwyn Miller stated that the case for holding fluoridation unconstitutional would be strengthened if there existed soundly documented medical evidence that fluoridation threatened the health of the population. My own research, as well as the research of others, strongly suggests that fluoridation constitutes a hazard to the health of a significant portion of the population.

    [2]I have been engaged in the diagnosis and treatment of allergy since the inception of this specialty in the early 1920s and have contributed to development of the discipline through clinical research. I established and directed allergy clinics in five Detroit hospitals. Currently, I am consultant in allergy at Harper Hospital, Detroit, and attending physician at Woman's Hospital, Detroit. I am a Fellow of the American Academy of Allergy, the American College of Allergists, and the American College of Physicians.

    [3]In 1953 I was first to report, in the *Journal of the American Medical Association* (vol. 151, page 1398), a new disease caused by smoking. This disease, which I termed "smoker's respiratory syndrome," simulates asthma and eventually leads to emphysema. I would not have recognized the illness in my patients had I not by chance suffered from it myself. Because I recovered upon ceasing to smoke, I began to take a closer look at some of my patients who, presumably suffering from allergic asthma, had failed to respond to the conventional treatment for that ailment. A large percentage of these patients recovered without treatment when they stopped smoking. Since publication of my article in *JAMA,* numerous physicians have corroborated my observation and have thus prevented chronic emphysema in their patients.—George Waldbott, M.D.

To: Director of Personnel, Cleardale Corporation
From: Bob Cooper, Part-time Summer Worker
Subject: The Problems with Morale and Productivity at Cleardale Corporation and How They Can Be Solved

[1]Recently, you asked me to respond to a questionnaire dealing with employee morale and productivity. The questions were short-answer and allowed only for a minimum of detail. I felt that I could not do justice to the importance of the problems by answering the questionnaire, so I decided to write this report. I will deal exclusively with those problems which lower employee on-the-job morale and productivity. Because I am here with the company only for the summer months, I feel that I can give an unbiased appraisal of the problems affecting employee morale and productivity—I do not work long enough every year to become either pro-management or pro-employee.

[2]My qualifications for pointing out those problems include three summers' experience at Cleardale. During this time, I worked in all departments of the plant and performed many unskilled jobs; also, I worked for three months as a quality control inspector. So, I believe that I have a good idea of the working conditions of the plant and a first-hand knowledge of the problems affecting them. My other experience includes several business courses in college dealing with employee motivation and productivity. I believe that this background provides me with the theory and the analytical techniques necessary to identify problems in the area of morale and productivity.

2. An authority is "a person who knows what he is talking about," someone who is either a practical or theoretical expert. We have never known a student who was not at least partially authoritative in *some* subject or area. Any job you have had, for example, gives you a degree of authority in writing an argument concerning it.

Write an argument in which you explain carefully why you are reasonably authoritative on a subject, and why your evidence should be considered valid. Create a specific writer's stance for your theme.

Use Good Logic

There is nothing complicated about the basic logic of rhetoric or composition. Such logic simply represents the operation of common sense, which interrelates two activities: (1) finding the *connections* between things; (2) *concluding* what, if anything, these connections mean.

INDUCTION AND DEDUCTION:
A DEFINITION

There are two kinds of logic, *inductive* and *deductive*. Whether you are conscious of doing so or not, you use them both a great deal, even when you do something as ordinary as bake bread, replace a defective fuel pump in your car, or put a cut rose in water to preserve it.

Suppose a man says to his wife: "Gee, honey, I hope the Pinkham's old dog doesn't get loose and bite one of the kids." Hidden in this remark is a fair amount of logic whose *connections* and *conclusions* we can outline by showing you the processes of induction and deduction.

Induction moves from facts to a generalization:

Fact: An old dog nipped the postman in 1971. **Inductive leap**

Fact: Our old dachshund got cranky and bit me twice. —————

Fact: Last year, a 15-year-old boxer mauled a neighbor's child.

Generalization: Old dogs can be dangerous

Deduction moves from a generalization to a conclusion. (This process can be illustrated by what is known as a *syllogism*.)

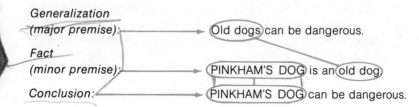

Generalization (major premise): ————→ Old dogs can be dangerous.

Fact (minor premise): ————→ PINKHAM'S DOG is an old dog.

Conclusion: ————→ PINKHAM'S DOG can be dangerous.

"Old dog" is the *middle term*—it connects the major premise to the minor premise. "PINKHAM'S DOG" is the *subject*—it connects the minor premise to the conclusion.

Refer to these examples as we explain inductive and deductive logic more thoroughly.

Induction is a logical process in which you make connections between particulars or facts in order to come to a generalization about them. Practically speaking, every induction has an *inductive leap*— the jump you have to make from a limited number of facts (of varying authoritative quality) to your generalization. If you see three old dogs, and they are all mean and cranky and bite, you can leap to the generalization that "Old dogs can be dangerous," which is not too long a leap—particularly if you don't want to get bitten.

The length of your inductive leap depends on the nature of the subject and how many "facts" you've got. The more old dogs that bite you can find, the smaller the leap to your generalization. If, in a period of twenty years, you hear of only two old dogs that bite, your leap is pretty large, and you may never make a good connection to your generalization. If you step off thirty bridges over streams and fall into the water each time, your inductive leap to "People who step off bridges fall into the water" is pretty small and can be easily made. But the leap, no matter how many "facts" you can muster, always exists. After all, it is always possible that someday you may step off bridge number 1,000,001 and just hang there in space.

Deduction is a logical process in which you make connections between a generalization *(major premise)*, a fact *(minor premise)*, and a *conclusion.*

Deductive reasoning can be most clearly seen in the *syllogism*, which is a three-sentence chain of reasoning. The classic syllogism in its full form has a broad major premise, a relatively narrow minor premise, and a conclusion drawn from these two premises. The *middle term* and the *subject* connect the parts of the syllogism.

In ordinary writing, deductive reasoning is most often expressed in the *enthymeme*, which is a compressed syllogism. Examples:

> An old dog like Pinkham's can be dangerous.
> Of course, Mike will die eventually; he's human, just like all of us.

Expanded into a full syllogism, the second enthymeme becomes:

Major premise:	All *persons* die.	*person* = middle term
Minor premise:	MIKE is a *person.*	MIKE = subject
Conclusion:	MIKE will die.	

Here is another example of an enthymeme:

> Since he is an elephant, Herbert eats peanuts.

And its full syllogistic form:

Major premise:	All *elephants* eat peanuts.	*elephant* = middle term
Minor premise:	HERBERT is an *elephant.*	HERBERT = subject
Conclusion:	HERBERT eats peanuts.	

USING INDUCTION AND DEDUCTION

Since induction moves from facts to a generalization, and deduction moves from a generalization to a conclusion, these types of logic have often been discussed as if they were two separate things. But actually they are interrelated, as this example shows.

> At a social gathering, a Frenchman remarked to a friend that all the long-haired men he had observed in the United States were political leftists.
>
> "Oh?" said the friend. "What about Jones over there—his hair is so long he's wearing it in a ponytail."
>
> "Of a certainty," said the Frenchman, "Mr. Jones is also a leftist."

The chain of reasoning the Frenchman created looks like this:

Induction

    Fact: A long-haired man is observed to be a leftist.
    Fact: Another long-haired man is observed to be a leftist.
    Fact: Yet another. . . .

|
[Inductive leap]
↓

    Generalization: All long-haired men are leftists.

Deduction (a syllogism)

    Major premise: All long-haired men are leftists.
    Minor premise: Jones is a long-haired man.
    Conclusion: Jones is a leftist.

Observe that the major premise of the syllogism is itself a conclusion inductively arrived at. As it turned out, Jones was not a leftist, leaving the Frenchman in a logical error. How can such errors be avoided in your handling of logic? The answer lies mainly in carefully managing logical *connections, generalizations,* and *conclusions:*

1. Make sure your inductive generalization is based on a sufficient number of reliable and authoritative facts. *Keep your inductive leap as small as possible.*

2. Check your deductive reasoning in the following ways: (a) Make sure that each premise is as accurate as you can make it. "All long-haired men are leftists" is a faulty major premise because it states a generalization that simply is untrue. You remember the minor premise in our sample syllogism on p. 207—"Pinkham's dog is an old dog." As it happened (this is a real-life example), Pinkham's dog was not old; he merely looked old because of his gray, mangy fur. (b) Expand each enthymeme into the full three-sentence syllogism to see if the connections and conclusions are properly made. (c) Do not shift your middle term. Examples of illogical shifts:

All *cats* meow.
My girl friend Sandy is a *cat.*
Sandy meows.

Men who commit murder should be severely punished.
That policeman just *killed a fleeing bank robber.*
That policeman should be severely punished.

In both examples, the writer has shifted the middle term. Sandy is not a real cat but a metaphorical one. A policeman who kills a fleeing bank robber is not considered by the law to have committed murder.

PRACTICE

1. After crash-landing on the planet Vark II, Captain Foubar of the Space Service found that he had plenty of water but no food. Raging with hunger, he explored the area near his ship, finding an abundance of small black flowers about six inches high. After eating two of the petals, he got rather sick and saw strange visions. His sickness passed in a few minutes, but he was still hungry and continued to explore the strange planet. He discovered a yellow weed that resembled a dandelion. He ate a little and found it reasonably good—at least it did not make him sick. He gathered about a pound of the yellow weed and took it back to his ship.

   The next day, he decided to try more of the black flower. After eating about a dozen petals, he became violently ill, and the visions this time were terrifying. In a desperate attempt to counteract the effect of the flower, he ate two yellow weeds. Almost immediately the sickness and the visions left him.

   Captain Foubar wrote down his experiences in the ship's log, using the classic inductive and deductive forms. He expanded each of his enthymemes into a syllogism. What did the captain write in his log?

2. Expand the following enthymemes below into the three-sentence form of the syllogism. Identify the subject and the middle term. If you can, rewrite the enthymeme to make it more reasonable.

   a. Phil shouldn't have married a girl with a personality so different from his; pluses and minuses cancel each other, you know.
   b. Any businessman who makes as much money as Leo does must be crooked.
   c. Judging from his antisocial behavior last night (talking against the government), Judson must have been either drunk or crazy.
   d. Booker can't be rich because he's signed up for Medicare.
   e. A typically modern, sexy novelist, Smith has written an evil book.
   f. Paley, make up your mind which side you're going to be on—people have to be either for us or against us. You sound like you don't believe in our position.
   g. As a college student, Joe should enlist because the army needs

superior minds.

h. Holden, you've got to get a job; no patriotic American should live on welfare.

i. *Laverne and Shirley* is not educational at all; why should it be on television?

j. Since Barber was definitely at the scene of the crime, he must have committed the murder.

k. Richard is too ignorant to have gone to college.

l. Only men who do valuable work for America should be elected to public office. I was in the Air Force for five years.

m. Yond Cassius has a lean and hungry look; He thinks too much: such men are dangerous. — Shakespeare, *Julius Caesar*

n. Jorgenson took the Fifth Amendment in a congressional investigation; therefore he is one of those undermining American democracy.

o. Since Professor Bunner does not publish, he must be a good teacher.

Avoid Fallacies

A fallacy is a weakness or an error in thinking or arguing. Fallacies are ordinarily caused by one or more of six basic human errors:

Oversimplifying
Jumping to a conclusion
Being irrelevant
Being too emotional
Deceiving oneself
Being dishonest

Of course, these human errors can never be totally eradicated from even the most well-reasoned argument. However, by being aware of such pitfalls, you can eliminate a great number of them from your thinking, thus making your arguments more persuasive and forceful.

RECOGNIZING AND CORRECTING FALLACIES

Here are descriptions of twelve major fallacies; for each one we suggest a method of improving the thinking or the argument. (The term *question,* when used in connection with fallacies, usually refers either to an argument's thesis or to one of its main points.)

Begging the Question

This fallacy is the mistake of assuming that some or all of a question or thesis is already proved — before the writer has proved it. To say that "Any person in the neighborhood who refuses to keep up his property should be prosecuted" begs two questions: first, whether refusing to keep up one's property is a bad thing for the neighborhood; second, whether failing to keep up property is covered by statute or is in any way illegal.

The statement that "The mistakes of teachers are buried on the welfare rolls" begs these questions: whether teachers make "mistakes," and whether there is a necessary relationship between teachers' "mistakes" and persons' ending up on welfare. Either of these questions or propositions might profitably be argued, and that is the point — they would have to be argued and *proved*. They cannot merely be assumed. Begging the question is an important fallacy because it often occurs at the starting point of an argument and thus renders the whole argument invalid.

Correction: Find the begged question and omit or prove it.

Rhetorical Question

The rhetorical question is usually a form of indirect attack. The attacker asks a loaded question to which he does not really want an answer. Such questions are inherently argumentative and often question-begging: "Mr. Webb, when are you going to stop being so bad-tempered?" Rhetorical questions are sometimes filled with emotion: "Is our do-nothing police force ever going to stop vicious murderers from roaming our streets at will?"

Correction: Customarily, omit the rhetorical question unless you have already proved the question. If you have satisfactorily proved that Webb is bad-tempered, you might inquire if he contemplates controlling his anger — but then the question is perhaps no longer rhetorical. It is worth adding that rhetorical questions are great fun, and it would be a pity to avoid them altogether.

Ad Hominem ("to the man")

In this fallacy, instead of attacking the argument, the writer attacks the person who made it. Examples: "You can't trust any statement made by that notorious socialist, Kurt Bleil." Or: "I won't work on the committee's proposal as long as there are psychologists on it. If Professor Ratmaze leaves, I will discuss the proposal."

Correction: Drop the attack on the man and consider the question, argument, or proposal at hand.

Stereotyping

In stereotyping, instead of describing persons as they actually are, the writer resorts to a trite description or cliché — every football player is big and stupid, every politician hypocritical and crooked, every movie star frivolous and shallow.

Correction: Check your description or generalization for accuracy.

Either-Or Fallacy

Writers commit this fallacy when they oversimplify a complex issue by assuming that there are only two sides to it. Either-or is one of the commonest fallacies, perhaps because all of us naturally think in either-or patterns: "You are either for or against me"; "She loves me, she loves me not"; "We should win the war or get out." Sometimes called the *black-or-white fallacy,* this error in logic is unusually dangerous because it is so easy to fall into and also because it gives no chance for alternatives.

Correction: Recognize any other possibilities or alternatives that may exist besides the two stated.

False Dilemma

A brother to the either-or fallacy, the false dilemma presents two (or sometimes three) firm courses of action, and then demands that the reader choose one. Examples: "Which are you going to buy, a new house or one that has been lived in?" (Maybe you don't want to buy a house at all.) "You can either come to my party or stay home." (Maybe you want to go to a movie.)

Correction: Point out that there may be other choices or actions than the ones offered.

Statistical Fallacy

Any misuse of figures, numbers, percentages, graphs, and so forth is a statistical fallacy. Most of these fallacies are created when a writer forgets this all-important fact: *in themselves, statistics prove nothing.* It is the writer who proves by using statistics. But statistics are not always meaningful. What, for example, is the meaning of the statistic that at age 24 engineers make an average of $3500 per year more than high-school English teachers? Such a statistic must be related to something and to somebody for it to have meaning.

Correction: Ask questions like, "Is the statistic accurate?" "Who says so?" "What does the statistic mean?" One might ask about the previous example: In what part of the country do English teachers and engineers make these salaries, and what are the living expenses there?

What is the authority behind these statistics? What is the basis for comparison (nine-months' salary vs. twelve-months' salary)? How sure is one of receiving this salary? (Are teachers laid off as often as engineers?) Is the comparison at age 24 significant? How do salaries compare at age 40? What have salaries to do with student interest in a profession? With working conditions? In other words, what is the question being argued? Is it the *right* question? Statistics have a way of distorting issues and propositions. "There are," Disraeli said, "three kinds of lies: lies, damned lies, and statistics."

Faulty Sampling

The flaw in many samples is that they are not representative of the group about which a generalization is made. A classic case of faulty sampling occurred in 1936 when the *Literary Digest* asked people in various parts of the United States whom they were going to vote for (Landon or Roosevelt) in the presidential election. The results of the poll said that Landon would win — but Roosevelt won by a landslide. The flaw in the sampling occurred because the *Digest* polled only persons whose names appeared in telephone directories. Taken in the middle of the Depression, this sampling omitted large numbers of people who did not have a telephone and voted Democratic.

Correction: Make sure that your sample is representative of the group under discussion.

Loose Generalization

A loose generalization is a faulty, or partly faulty, statement about a group or class of ideas, occurrences, things, persons, etc. Examples: "Large families make for happy children"; "All small automobiles save gas." In both examples, the writer has made careless and excessively broad statements about a group. Upon examining the evidence, it becomes obvious that some small cars are not "gas savers" — the phrase needs definition too. And one finds unhappy children in some "large families" (again a phrase needs definition).

Correction: Reason carefully from the evidence available. Examine broad statements for possible inaccuracy. When necessary, qualify your generalizations. (See pp. 124–125 for further discussion.)

Causal Fallacy

Three kinds of causal fallacy are important: (a) Mistaking the nature of a cause. Example: A boss believes that his employee does poor work because he is lazy, but the real reason is that he has difficult personal problems. (b) Failing to see that there is more than one cause. Example: "John is a fine violinist because he has great natural talent." Since John's parents required him to practice two or three hours a day for five years, there are probably at least two causes for his fine playing—talent and hard work. (c) Being misled by the order of events. If event B comes after event A, one should not automatically jump to the conclusion that A *caused* B. Example: Barbara started dressing neatly after her mother scolded her for being sloppy. Her mother congratulated herself, but the real reason for Barbara's neatness was a new boy friend who did not like sloppy girls. As you have seen in the discussion of cause and effect in Chapter 4, this common fallacy is called *post hoc* (short for *post hoc, ergo propter hoc*—"after this, therefore because of this").

Correction: Identify the true cause or causes in a situation, checking for the nature of the cause, multiple causes, and proper time-sequence.

False Analogy

In the false analogy, the writer tries to compare two things that are not comparable or fails to understand the nature of his analogy. Example: "The most successful public service in our town is the garbage collection which is managed entirely by three private firms. If we want to improve our other public services, like police work and fire prevention, we should consider using a number of small firms that compete in the same way that the garbage collection companies do." The analogy is doubtful because the "services" involved are not really comparable. For instance, garbage collection is a regular service that is fairly constant, while policemen and firemen provide services on a less regular and emergency basis. Emergency services tend to be distinctly different from nonemergency ones.

Here is another example: "It does not hurt to cut up your education by stopping to work for a year. Like those animals that grow a new leg or tail, you can re-learn what you have forgotten when you return to school." The comparison is figurative, but the writer is taking it literally. He has misunderstood the nature of his own analogy and so has rendered his conclusion invalid.

Correction: Check your analogy to see whether the two things being compared are comparable and in what sense they are comparable. Be very careful with figurative analogies. (See pp. 67–69 for further discussion.)

Ignoring the Question

Almost any form of irrelevancy can be identified as ignoring the question—the fallacy of failing to stick to the thesis of an argument or of wandering away from an important point of the argument. Accordingly, this fallacy often seems to be the result of other fallacies. For example, if one starts out refuting an argument by Jones but slides into a personal attack on him, the writer falls into both *ad hominem* and ignoring the question. Many cases of ignoring the question are created by carelessly forgetting one's thesis. If a writer begins to argue that all auto mechanics in the United States should be federally licensed, and then breaks into a condemnation of the Pinto as an unsafe car, he is ignoring the question.

Correction: Identify the question and rewrite, sticking to the question and omitting irrelevancies.

You may be surprised by the amount of truth in many statements that also include fallacies. Why do truth and fallacy often live happily side by side? One reason is that truths are seldom absolutes but rather mixtures of the true and false. Another reason is that half-truths can, superficially, be more convincing than "whole" truths. As Stephen Leacock ironically remarked, "a half truth in argument, like a half brick, carries better."

PRACTICE

In the following examples, identify the fallacy *by name* in two steps. First, determine which of the six basic human errors (p. 211) the writer made. Second, name the specific fallacy. In some examples, you may find more than one fallacy.

a. The freshman physics courses here at the university are bad. My physics instructor is a weak teacher; he does not know his material and is not interested in his students.

b. Juvenile crime in America is increasing. Over 1,000,000 youths are arrested every year. More than 55,000 youths are in jails. One-fifth of all youth is delinquent. Half the auto thefts, a third of the robberies, and a tenth of homicides and assaults in the United States are committed by youths. What is the cause? Society is to blame.

c. Grades are arbitrary. Students are in college to learn, not to get grades.

d. Making the sale of drugs a crime just makes using drugs more tempting. It is a fact that doctors have the money to satisfy this temptation and it is also a fact that doctors have a higher rate of addiction than people in any other profession.

e. I may or may not concede that some cops honestly try to maintain law and order. I will concede part of this, or all of this partly. If an old lady in respectable clothes falls down on the street, the cop will heroically try to help her, but the sight of an old bum on the same street brings out some atavistic desire in the cop with the cop mentality. The fakery of his charity reveals itself. He loves the old lady? Maybe; but, if so, only because it gives him a justification to beat up the old bum.—Nelson Algren, "Down with Cops"

f. A professor is like a tradesman. Like a plumber or electrician, the professor serves an apprenticeship so that he can learn a skill. Therefore, as the customer judges the worth of a tradesman's skill, we students should be able to judge the worth of a professor's teaching.

g. What are the other candidates afraid of? Mr. Bostwick says we cannot educate *all* of the children "because by definition not all children are educable." What kind of a Nazi remark is that? Is he going to tell us which of our children can be educated and which cannot be? Of course all children are educable; they are human, aren't they? Mr. Bostwick should put on his black armband and parade around like the Nazi he is — why (and we demand that he answer this question) is he afraid to educate *all* American children?

h. Our neighbor says about the new divorce law: "Divorce is only a symptom, and you don't cure a disease by treating its symptoms."

i. Before the end of the present century, unless something quite unforeseeable occurs, one of three possibilities will have been realized. These three are: The end of human life, perhaps of all life on our planet. A reversion to barbarism after a catastrophic diminution of the population of the globe. A unification of the world under a single government, possessing a monopoly of all the major weapons of war.

I do not pretend to know which of these will happen, or even which is the most likely. What I do contend is that the kind of system to which we have been accustomed cannot possibly continue. — Bertrand Russell, "The Future of Man"

j. From letters to the editor on the causes of alcoholism:
Alcoholism is caused by alcohol just as surely as tuberculosis is caused by the tubercle bacillus. — a doctor
Alcoholism is an act of the will; thus it is a sin, not a disease.
The real cause of alcoholism is in advertising. — the president of a County Beverage Board
The manufacturers and distributors of alcoholic beverages are almost entirely responsible for the problem.
The cause of alcoholism? People. — a clergyman

k. The bourgeois [middle-class] clap-trap about the family and education, about the hallowed co-relation of parent and child, becomes all the more disgusting, the more, by the action of Modern Industry, all family ties among the proletarians [the workers] are torn asunder, and their children transformed into simple articles of commerce and instruments of labor. . . .

Our bourgeois, not content with having the wives and daughters of their proletarians at their disposal, not to speak of common prostitutes, take the greatest pleasure in seducing each others' wives. — Karl Marx and Frederick Engels, *Communist Manifesto*

l. "Sexual permissiveness among America's college women hasn't changed much since 1930," a Stanford University researcher said Tuesday.

But the four-year study of 49 students at an unidentified Eastern women's college also showed "that American college students have evolved patterns of sexual behavior that will remain stable for some time to come," said Mervin B. Freedman.

Freedman, assistant dean of undergraduate education and a research associate at the Institute for the Study of Human Problems, reported his findings in the *Merrill-Palmer Quarterly.*—Associated Press news release

m. In the modern world we have no choice but to be atheists.

Use a Clear Argumentative Organization

In order for your argument to be persuasive, its organization must be clear enough so that your reader will have no doubts about what direction your thoughts are taking. There are basically three major kinds of organization in formal argumentation:

1. The *organization of fact*—in which you argue the truth (or reality) of an idea, opinion, occurrence, etc.;

2. The *organization of action*—in which you argue that something should be done, that an action should be taken;

3. The *organization of refutation*—in which you argue that another person's argument is wrong, invalid, or fallacious.

In practice, these three argumentative organizations often do not appear as distinct and separate forms. You may find yourself combining, for example, fact and refutation organizations in a single theme because you need them both to support your thesis. But the organizations can be most clearly understood if we discuss them separately. An argumentative organization is built around a thesis; accordingly, we will begin our discussion by distinguishing between the thesis of fact and the thesis of action. We will take up refutation later.

THESES OF FACT AND OF ACTION

The *thesis of fact* states that something is (or is not) true, or was (or was not) true. Of course the thesis may be qualified by stating that something is or was partly true. Any type of necessary qualification may be made. Examples of fact theses:

> Capital punishment is an uncivilized practice.
>
> Although it was tried only on a relatively small sample of the population, fluoridation seemed to prevent tooth decay in Sweetbrush, Indiana.

The thesis of fact is ordinarily a statement about the present, the past, or both.

The *thesis of action* states that a change must be made. Examples of action theses:

> We must do away with capital punishment in the United States because it is an uncivilized practice.
>
> Since fluoridation of drinking water prevents decay in children's teeth, the citizens of Sweetbrush, Indiana, should add fluoride to their drinking water.

The thesis of action is a statement about the future that is based upon a statement of truth, sometimes implied, about the present or past. This is a very important idea about the relationship between the two types of theses. The thesis of action must be based on a thesis of fact. In other words, you cannot argue for any kind of change in human affairs until after you have proved that there is a *need* for the change. As you will shortly learn, *fact* arguments and *action* arguments differ in both purpose and organization.

ORGANIZATION OF FACT ARGUMENTS

An organization of fact is simply a clear presentation and elaboration of a thesis of fact. You set down your ideas straightforwardly:

Introduction	State problem State *thesis* Define terms	Use most reasonable order
Body	First point + evidence Second point + evidence Third point + evidence Etc. Evaluate points and evidence (optional)	Use a graded order; e.g., from the weakest point to the strongest
Conclusion	Written to fit	

For a short paper, an introduction of one or two paragraphs is sufficient. In the introduction, be sure you tell your reader all he needs to know, especially about the thesis and definition of terms. In the body, separate the main points clearly so that your reader can tell them apart. Use any graded order that seems appropriate; a common one is suggested in the diagram above. (See pp. 105 – 106 for a further discussion of graded order.) It is natural and more convincing to save your strongest point until last. It may be unnecessary to evaluate the points and evidence, unless you are trying to prove something important about them. Write the conclusion to fit the whole argument. Don't try to argue a new point in the conclusion — this is usually unconvincing.

The following letter to a college newspaper is an example of a fact organization:

<table>
<tr><td>Introduction:
one paragraph</td><td>[1]When I was accepted by Ivy, I was very proud. This is a great private university, with a fine reputation all over the United States. But since coming to school, I have</td></tr>
<tr><td>Problem and
thesis stated</td><td>discovered one thing about the university that is injuring its educational program — its attempt to compete in big-time college football. I have heard students, and also the</td></tr>
<tr><td>Issues stated</td><td>administration, claim that football is necessary because the alumni want it, the students want it, or because Ivy needs it for prestige. None of these is a major issue; none of these issues is relevant to the educational problems created when Ivy tries to compete in football against state schools with large enrollments and low entrance standards. This competition is what I mean by</td></tr>
<tr><td>Term defined</td><td>big-time football. What I mean by injuring our educational program I will explain in the rest of this letter.</td></tr>
<tr><td>First point
+
evidence</td><td>[2]Contrary to popular belief, football players are not always more ethical than ordinary students. At Ivy, freshman players cause more than their share of the cheating problems. In two of my classes I have seen players cheat, but I have never seen other students cheat. Admittedly, this is a small sample. But it is an accepted fact that more players than non-players in the past four years have been brought before the Honor Council for plagiarism. This situation occurred despite the fact that players are outnumbered more than twenty to one by nonplayers.</td></tr>
<tr><td>Second point
+
evidence</td><td>[3]Cheating on this scale by a small group of students lowers both the moral and intellectual tone of the university. In order to limit cheating, instructors in some freshman courses have been forced to monitor exams more closely than ever. And freshman composition teachers are giving a large number of in-class themes, a practice that reduces the course to the level of a high-school offering.</td></tr>
<tr><td>Strongest point
left till last
(note transition)</td><td>[4]But however irritating and high schoolish these practices may be, they do not weaken our educational program as much as tutoring, the special attention that</td></tr>
</table>

Evidence many instructors give to football players both in the classroom and in their offices. Time and again, the instructor in my introductory literature class has had to stop to explain a simple literary interpretation to a hulking tackle. There are four such "students" in my class; they are noisy and disruptive; and my instructor, who is a tolerant man, has been forced to lower his teaching to fit them while the rest of us squirm with boredom. Moreover, when we go to his office—this has happened to me twice—there is the tackle, getting free advice on commas and semicolons, things he should have learned in freshman comp.

Conclusion ⁵It is hard to believe that a small group of athletes could injure the educational process in a major university. But that is what these players are doing. Many of them cannot meet our academic standards, but they are here anyway. This situation can only further weaken the fine educational program that Ivy has established and maintained for so many years.

Very truly yours,
John Cate

ORGANIZATION OF ACTION ARGUMENTS

As we explained earlier, an action argument must be based on a fact argument. This relationship determines an important part of the action organization. If you have not proved to your reader that there is a *need* for a change (fact argument), then you probably have to provide the argument of fact before going on to the argument of action. This would mean, practically speaking, that you would have to write two separate but related arguments. But we will assume here that the need for a change is evident, so that you have only to explain it briefly before beginning your argument of action. For this type of argument, here is a typical organization:

Introduction	State *need* for action (the problem)	Use most reasonable order
	State *thesis* (proposed action)	
	Define terms	

Body	Give as much *fact* argument as necessary
	Give details of proposed *action:* expand as necessary
	State why action is *practical*
	State why action is *beneficial*
	State why action is better than other proposed or possible actions (optional)

Conclusion

{ Written to fit (many writers state here why their proposed action will satisfy the need introduced at the beginning)

Here is an example of an organization of action: a letter to the same college paper, answering the preceding letter.

Introduction: one paragraph

[1]John Cate's recent letter about football players lowering the academic standards of Ivy centers on a small group of athletes who cause trouble in class, lower academic standards, and cheat. It is true that some of them were brought before the Honor Council this year. Yet there were only four athletes—all football players—

Problem (need for action) stated

involved in this group. They are the ones causing the trouble Mr. Cate is so disturbed about. To take care of only four players, he recommends that Ivy "get rid of big-time football. . . ." To put the case in the classic terms of argument, he has identified a need, but he has not suggested a practical solution. Ivy cannot condemn the whole football program because of four players. I suggest an effective solution to the problem. Ivy should ap-

Thesis of action

ply the same entrance requirements to athletes as to

Definition of term

other freshmen. By *entrance requirements,* I refer to the required College Board scores, high-school grades, recommendations from teachers, and interviews.

Paragraphs 2 and 3 give an argument of fact; the student must argue *fact* before he can argue *action*

[2]It is well known at the university that many freshmen players are recruited directly by the coaches or alumni. Such players are often athletes first and students second. In many instances, they had given no thought to coming to Ivy before a coach or an alum talked to them. Three of the four players Mr. Cate is so unhappy about are in this category. None of these three had good College Board scores or high-school grades. Their teachers did not recommend them for Ivy, and they should not have come here. But the Admissions Committee—manned almost entirely by instructors—voted to let these students in as special cases. This is not unusual. A number of students, and not just athletes, are let in as special cases. Some, for example, have high College Board scores but weak high-school grades.

[3]Mr. Cate mentions that over the past four years more football players than non-players have been brought before the Honor Council for cheating. He is right, but what he does not state is that in all but two of these cases the players involved were those that were admitted as special cases by the Admissions Committee. In other words, the players causing most of the trou-

ble are not "students" at all; they are sort of athletic appointees.

⁴The action to be taken seems obvious: Judge all of our proposed freshmen as *students*. Require all of them to pass our high entrance standards and ignore whether they are athletes. This is a practical solution because the Admissions Committee will only have to do what it has been supposed to do all along. Moreover, this solution will take care of Mr. Cate's problem; there will be few, if any, football bums infesting his classes and taking up his instructors' office hours. Also, my solution has the special attractiveness of allowing Ivy to continue its football program, which I think is a benefit to both the university and its students.

Why proposed action is *practical* and *beneficial*

⁵One final point: I play football. I also have a *B+* average. Only three of our varsity players are as of now in academic trouble. The fact that most of us do pretty well in our studies indicates that the need is not to get rid of football players but to get rid of certain students (who happen to be players) who should not have been allowed to enter Ivy in the first place.

Conclusion

Very truly yours,
Doug Cleary

ORGANIZATION OF REFUTATION ARGUMENTS

In the argument of refutation, you take someone else's argument and prove that it is, to some degree, wrong, invalid, or fallacious. An argument is like a tower made of rocks. If you pull out one of the rocks near the bottom, the whole tower is likely to fall. If you show that one important part of an opponent's argument is weak, his whole case may topple. Thus before you write a refutation you need to examine your opponent's argument to see if you can find any weak spots in it. Here are some possible weak points to look for:

1. *Faulty premises.* A premise is a basic idea, stated or assumed, on which an arguer builds his argument (or a part of it), or from which he reaches a conclusion. If you can show that your opponent's premises are faulty, you can probably refute his entire argument. Refuting his major premise is likely to cut him down on the spot. Even refuting one of his minor premises is a victory. Here is a premise from the first student letter:

Cheating on this scale by a small group of students lowers both the moral and the intellectual tone of the university.

If you can show that cheating by a small group of students does not "lower both the moral and the intellectual tone of the university," you have weakened his argument considerably.*

2. *Faulty definitions.* A *definition* is itself a kind of premise, a part of an argument's foundation. If your opponent has been careless in defining, you can answer as follows:

> Mr. Cate says that by *big-time football* he means competition against "state schools with large enrollments and low entrance standards." His definition is meaningless because Ivy does not compete against such schools. B_____ University, it is true, has 30,000 students but it also has high entrance standards — it admits only those from the top quarter of the high-school class. W_____ University has low standards but only 6500 students. We compete against only four state schools, two of which I have mentioned. The other two (J_____ College and M_____ University) do not fit his definition either. Mr. Cate's carelessness in defining throws doubt on his whole argument.

3. *Fallacies in logic or in presenting the argument.* See pp. 211–216 for a complete discussion of fallacies.

4. *Faulty use of evidence and authority.* Mistakes here are usually either those of using insufficient or irrelevant evidence, or using a wrong or doubtful authority. (For further discussion, see pp. 202–205.)

5. *Impractical or undesirable action (applicable only to action arguments).* In many areas of argument, there is general agreement by everyone concerned that something must be done — a definite need for action does exist. But your opponent's suggested action may be impractical, undesirable, or irrelevant. It may bring about greater evils than now exist in the situation. If you believe that your opponent's suggested action is wrong, it is your job to point out *specifically* what is wrong with it. You may also give your own argument of action. But strictly speaking, a refutation states only the flaws in an opponent's argument.

Before writing a refutation, analyze your opponent's argument. Isolate its parts, from the thesis to the premises to the evidence used. If you can show that his thesis is badly worded, vague, or perhaps not stated at all, you can shoot down his argument with a paragraph. You do not have to waste much time on an opponent who does not even know the main point he is supposed to be arguing.

In organization, your refutation might look like this:

*Sydney J. Harris wrote: "There is nothing more dangerous than a person with a good mind who begins to reason, logically and coolly, from insufficient premises: for his answers will always be valid, justified, rational — and wrong."

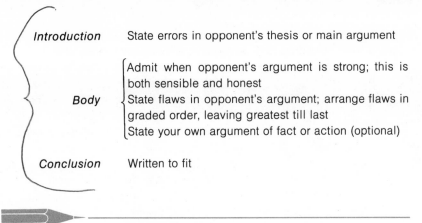

Introduction	State errors in opponent's thesis or main argument
Body	Admit when opponent's argument is strong; this is both sensible and honest State flaws in opponent's argument; arrange flaws in graded order, leaving greatest till last State your own argument of fact or action (optional)
Conclusion	Written to fit

PRACTICE

1. Of the following theses, which are of fact and which of action? For each action thesis, state the thesis of fact (the *need*, in other words) which would have to be proved before one could argue the action thesis. In each thesis, what terms need definition?

   a. The press should not be allowed to cover in great detail any important murder trials.
   b. Alcohol is a dangerous drug.
   c. The individual states in the Union should be allowed to determine their own educational policies.
   d. Poverty is a cause of crime.
   e. Help abolish poverty.
   f. Scientists should refuse to work on any type of nuclear weapon.
   g. Swimming is the best form of general exercise there is.
   h. Robert E. Lee was a more capable tactician than Ulysses S. Grant.
   i. Undergraduates planning to go to law school should not have to take a foreign language.
   j. I don't care whether you believe me or not, he's got four people on that motorcycle with him!

2. Analyze the organization of the following student argument. How successful is the argument? What is the writer's stance?

   [1]Resident Advisors (RA's) are a tradition at almost every college in this country, and ours is no exception. You can find at least one RA living on every floor of every residence hall ("dorm") on this campus. I myself am an RA for this semester; and if my experience is any indication, the college should abolish the RA system as soon as possible.

   [2]RA's are people selected by the Housing Division to perform many duties and services for an overwhelmingly ungrateful group of students each year. The basic "duties" of an RA are fourfold:

   a. To keep peace and harmony among the residents on the floor;
   b. To provide the residents with an atmosphere in which learning, in all forms, is a way of living;

c. To provide para-professional counseling if and when required;

d. To enforce college regulations if and when necessary.

³But what the residents really expect and want from their RA's are things like:

a. Being allowed to wake up their RA any time of the day or night just to talk or to let them into their room when they're locked out;

b. Having their RA pretend she didn't see the residents smoking dope or drinking beer;

c. Having their RA tell their roommate or neighbor to turn their stereo down when they're too scared to do it themselves;

d. Giving them light bulbs when theirs burn out;

e. Filling out maintenance forms when their air conditioning fails.

⁴And if an RA is not around 24 hours a day just in case somebody wants her services, then she's labeled a bad advisor who's "never around when you need her." On the other hand, if an RA is always on the floor ready to help, then she's called "nosy." So an RA can't win. And it's frustrating.

⁵But the worst part of the job is the fact that the student residents themselves don't want RA's, and they're very vocal about it. Residents are defensive about their privacy and they don't want any member of the college staff living among them. To them, RA's are unnecessary additions to college housing. And I think the students are probably right. *Any* responsible student on the floor could be assigned to supply light bulbs, maintenance reports, and spare keys. And with the current attitude of the residents, RA's don't usually get very many students coming in just to talk or get advice.

⁶As for enforcing regulations—it's more than a one-person job anyway. Residents generally work together to create and maintain the type of atmosphere they want to live in. No individual RA can either create or destroy the style of a living unit.

⁷As it stands right now, each RA receives free room and board, tuition and fees, and a monthly stipend of $50. That amounts to approximately $2200 per RA per academic year. With about 170 RA's on campus, the total cost comes to $374,000. I truly think that in the future we should use this money to give the students something they need and want. Resident Advisors are not needed or wanted. Is it worth $374,000 per academic year merely to keep a tradition?

3. Analyze the following refutation argument. How effective is it in refuting the issues it discusses?

¹Some civil libertarians have little doubt that not providing economic protection for childbirth is sex discrimination. Childbirth is as much a disability for a woman as a broken leg for a man, goes the argument.

²The point this ignores is that procreation is in fact a joint venture of both man and woman, usually conducted within the legal bonds of marriage and quite often as a planned, joyous process. The economic cost

involved is not usually borne solely by women but by man and wife. Thus, the failure of an employer to bear that cost does not strictly discriminate against women.

³There is, of course, an exception to this principle. If a single working woman has a child the economic burden can fall entirely on her shoulders. Thus, the public policy question moves into a new area: Whether full sexual equality implies that women should have economic protection for bearing children out of wedlock? Some women's rightists argue that there should be such protection. But that raises still broader questions about whether any further public policy measures should be permitted that might further weaken the family unit as a basic foundation for our society. If the family unit is to go—it has been disintegrating already to an alarming degree—what is to take its place? The state, perhaps?

⁴It should be kept in mind that this is not merely a question of employers and employes. If employers are to be asked to bear the substantial cost of childbirth disabilities, it is certain that in most cases this cost will be passed along to consumers of the products and services the employers provide. In other words, society, not employers, becomes ultimately responsible for such costs.

⁵It could of course be argued that the effect of childbirth disability coverage would be to strengthen families. This is not an idle argument. It is true that a very high proportion of young wives have jobs and further cushioning of the economic shock of childbirth might help young couples avoid the kind of adversity that sometimes undermines marriage. But this again is not a sex discrimination question—it is a question of public policy towards the family as a basic social unit.

⁶We have framed the argument in these terms to suggest that sex discrimination issues are not really as simple as protagonists on both sides would sometimes make them. They very often go to the heart of issues of social organization that have great relevance to a nation's future. They deserve more thoughtful treatment than simple "battle of the sexes" argumentation.

⁷We would hope that policy makers might give some thought to such questions when they frame their simple sounding proposals. But we would also admit that our hopes may well be in vain.—"Examining Sex Discrimination," *Wall Street Journal*

4. Make a few notes for a class discussion of the following argument, taken from a magazine advertisement. After you have discussed it, write an argument using an organization of fact or action that is based on some of the ideas in the ad. Sample thesis: *A majority of students at _____ College apparently feel an "obligation" to pay their own way, since over 55 percent of us are working our way through college.* Pick a specific writer's stance for your argument; for example, you might want to address Warner & Swasey directly.

For Every Right There Is an Obligation

¹If you kept telling a child about his rights and never about his duties, you'd soon have a spoiled brat on your hands. We're doing the same thing in this country but on a vastly more dangerous scale.

²The "right" of unions to strike for more pay but no obligation to earn it.

³The "rights" of new nations to independence but no obligation to prove they deserve it, no obligation to use freedom for the good of mankind.

⁴The "right" of young people to education but no obligation to pay their own way to get it.

⁵The "rights" of criminals and communists to flout the laws of our land, without any obligation to contribute to its worth and its freedom.

⁶Spoiled children grow into adult criminals, who have to be punished by the decent society they defy. Why wait?—advertisement by Warner & Swasey in *Newsweek*

11 The Research Paper

In writing the research paper, you will go outside your own experience and use mainly the ideas of others, usually authorities on the subject you have chosen. In most cases, the research paper is based upon library sources—books, periodicals, and newspapers—but you may also consult authoritative living persons. The research paper should not be for you a new or unusual rhetorical problem. You find and limit your subject, as you have always done. You evaluate and organize your materials and evidence and create a writer's stance, as you have learned to do. For most students, the only difficulty is how to mesh these activities with library research. How do you get into the maze of a library and safely get out, several days later, armed with dozens of neatly written note cards which can be turned into a footnoted paper?

It will help if you follow a series of steps in both your library research and your writing:

Research
    Step 1: Choose your subject.
    Step 2: Make your working bibliography.
    Step 3: Read, take notes, evaluate the evidence, create a stance, and look for a thesis.

Writing
    Step 4: Make an outline.
    Step 5: Write the paper.

Step 1: Choose Your Subject

If your instructor has not assigned subjects for the research paper, you should choose a subject that has interested you and that you will enjoy working with. Be positive and optimistic about the project. The following suggestions may help.

Joan Van Nord, Associate Professor of Library Administration, University of Illinois at Urbana-Champaign, acted as consultant for this chapter.

1. Consider your own special interest or academic major. Look through some of the dictionaries and encyclopedias in your major field. See "Special Reference Works" (pp. 269–273) for a list of some of the more important titles. For example, if you are a speech or drama major, look at *The Oxford Companion to the Theatre.* This book's discussion of *pantomime*, for example, might suggest to you a subject dealing with one aspect of that art.

2. Look through current magazines and newspapers. What kinds of subjects are being discussed? Do any of them interest you? Be wary of subjects so current that there is little or nothing in the library about them. Also, be wary of subjects that you feel strongly about. If you are emotionally involved in an issue, you will find it difficult to be objective and fair.

3. Consider broad subjects such as the *increase* in arson, divorce, abortion, airline crashes, or terrorist activities. Ask yourself the following questions about one of these subjects:

— What are some of the causes for the increase?
— What solutions have been offered?
— How successful have the solutions been?
— Are there other solutions that might work?
— What effect does the increase have on society?

(You can also ask the same questions about *decreases* in such problems or activities.)

Let us assume that you decide to look into one of the broad subjects suggested in **3**—*divorce.* As you think about the problem of divorce in American society, you wonder what has caused its increase in the last decade. This leads you—as you start working with your topic—to consider a subject dealing with changes in the family itself, particularly the American family.

Before you go further with the subject, you should see whether your library has material on it. The quickest way to find out is to run a brief check on three sources: (1) *reference books* (particularly encyclopedias); (2) the *card catalog;* and (3) a major *periodical index.* What you want to know is whether material on your subject really exists, and whether you can investigate the subject in your library.

REFERENCE BOOKS

Encyclopedias

The most efficient way to use a multivolume encyclopedia is to turn first to the index, which is contained in a separate volume. There you should find the main entry for your subject. Here are the index entries from the *Encyclopedia Americana* for *Family* and for some closely related subjects.

Subject entry ——————— FAMILY (biol.) 11–2
   Animal 1–860
   Genus 12–428
   Order 20–753
   Zoology 29–860
FAMILY (sociol.) 11–2
   Adolescence 1–177
   Adoption 1–179
   Africa 1–265, 266, 268, 294
   Ancestor Worship 1–800
   Anthropology 2–45
See *also* reference to ——————   Arab 2–144
related subjects   Asia 2–458 fol.
   Bachofen, J. J. 3–19
   Betrothal 3–632
   Birth Control 4–4
Subheadings for more ——————   Budget 4–699
specific subjects   Caste 5–775
   Child Abuse 6–450
   Child Welfare 6–464, 466
   Childbirth 6–467, 468
   China 6–501, 503, 504
   Clan 7–9
   Colonial Life 7–281
   Corporation 8–12
   Court of Domestic Relations (U.S.) 8–114
   Custody 8–355
   Divorce 9–210, 211
   Economics 9–603, 596
See or *cross* reference ——————   Egypt, Ancient 10–39
   Eskimo 10–575
   Europe 10–682, 683
   France 11–695
   Frontier Life 12–120
   Genealogy 12–382
   Greece 13–363
   Hawaii 13–869
   Heraldry 14–119, 124
   Home Economics 14–316
Volume number and page number,   Homosexuality 14–334
e.g., Volume 14, page 482 ——   Housing 14–482
   Incest 14–840
   Income Tax 14–852
   India 14–868, 874
   Indian, American 15–5 fol.
   Japan 15–699 fol., 706, 709
   Marriage 18–311
   Matriarchy 18–437
   Negro in America 20–73
   Pakistan 21–134b
   Patriarchal System 21–401
   Penates 21–496
   Philippines 21–753
   police intervention unit 22–325
   Population Control 22–411
   Poverty 22–496

   Primogeniture 22–590
   Roman Law 23–643, 645
   Sex Education 24–641
   Social Work 25–144
   Sociology 25–160
   Ten Commandments 26–470
   USSR 27–399
   United States 27–541
   Women's Liberation 29–111c
   See also Divorce; Domestic relations; Husband and wife; Marriage, History of; Women, Legal Rights of

FAMILY ALLOWANCES 11–7
   Canada 5–400
   Child Welfare 6–465
   Great Britain 13–252
Family at Gilje, bk. (Lie) 20–476
Family budget: *see* Budget, Family
Family Compact (Can. hist.) 5–487 fol.
   Mackenzie, W. L. 18–69
Family Compacts (Eur. hist.) 25–417
Family court (U.S.): *see* Court of Domestic Relations
Family Group, sculp. (Moore) 19–441
   Illus. 19–441
Family income plan (ins.) 17–430
Family of Acrobats with Ape, paint. (Picasso):
   Illus. 22–68
Family of Charles IV, paint. (Goya) 25–435
Family of Love (rel. sect): *see* Familists
Family of Saltimbanques, The, paint. (Picasso) 22–67
   Illus. 11–809
Family planning: *see* Birth Control
Family protection plan (ins.) 17–430
Family Reunion, The, play (Eliot) 10–241
Family Shakespeare (Bowdler) 4–362
Family Under the Bridge, The, bk. (Carlson) 17–571

In addition to the main entries, you may find a *See also* reference, which indicates there are other related subjects in the index that you should check. You may also find a *See* reference, which tells you that a particular subject is listed under a slightly different heading.

After checking the index entries for subjects that look promising, go to the volumes where the articles appear. From these articles, you can get a good overview of the subject. Also check the bibliographies that follow most articles of any importance.

Special Reference Works

Check any reference books in your subject to see if they give general information that might be useful. Be sure to examine the indexes and tables of contents of these books for ideas that might help you narrow your subject to a workable topic. (See the list of reference works arranged according to discipline at the end of the chapter.)

THE CARD CATALOG

The card catalog is an alphabetized collection of index cards that carry information on every book your library contains. For each book, you will find three types of cards: (1) author or main entry card; (2) title card; and (3) subject card. When using the card catalog for a preliminary investigation of your subject, check the subject cards first. If your subject is the *family,* here is the kind of card you might find:

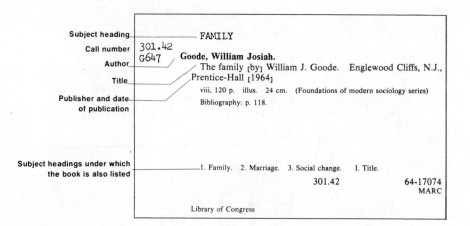

When you look for your subject in the card catalog, start with the most specific term you can think of. If you can't find that term listed, try a more general classification. For example, if you can't find *Divorce,* try *Family.* If you can't find *Shoplifting,* try *Theft.* If you can't find *Theft,* try *Crime* or *Criminals.* Analyze your subject from different angles, and consider closely related terms which might refer to it.

When librarians assign subject headings, they use as a guide either *Sears List of Subject Headings* or *The Library of Congress Subject Headings,* both of which may be shelved near the card catalog. Skim these reference books, looking for different headings, to see if you can find information on your subject.

Another way to find out what books on your subject the library contains is to check the *shelf list,* a listing of all the books in call-number order. After getting the call number of one book that deals with your subject, you can check the shelf list for books with similar numbers. If you are not allowed to go into your library's stacks, the shelf list can be a valuable way of finding other material on your subject.

Now is the time to see if the important books on your subject are actually in the stacks. If they are, check them out; if not, put a hold on them. If your library has open stacks, browse through all the books shelved together on your subject. Check their tables of contents and indexes. You may find pertinent or interesting material that can give you a new perspective on your subject.

PRACTICE

Where in your library's card catalog would you go to find the following information? (Indicate the drawer numbers in your answer.)

1. Books by Isaac Asimov
2. Information about cats
3. A history of Africa
4. The *Koran*
5. A biography of Ernest Hemingway
6. Twentieth-century American poetry

PERIODICAL INDEXES

Many periodical indexes are available for research; however, you will probably find the *Readers' Guide to Periodical Literature* most useful. (See the list of periodical indexes for several academic disciplines, p. 269.) The *Readers' Guide,* as it is most often called, lists recent articles published in 160 magazines. It is published twice a month, combined every three months into a larger volume, and then published yearly in one bound volume.

Most periodical indexes contain roughly the same format. To use an index efficiently, you need to be aware of the information presented in the front of each issue: (1) suggestions for using the index; (2) abbreviations of the periodicals indexed; (3) a list of the periodicals indexed; and (4) the key to other abbreviations. This information will tell you how to read references and abbreviations such as *Bull Atom Sci, jt, Ja, il, por,* and give you other important help in using the index.

To look up your subject, start with a specific term. If you can't find it, move to a broader subject. Periodical indexes use cross references in the same way encyclopedia indexes and card catalogs do.

Here are some of the entries for *Family* in a recent *Readers' Guide:*

FAMILIES of alcoholics. See Alcoholics families
FAMILIES of prisoners. See Prisoners families

Subject heading————————FAMILY
City families; excerpts; photographs; with text by S. Milgram. R. Banish. bibl il Psychol Today 10:59-63+ Ja '77

Title of article————————Family out of favor. M. Novak. il Harper 252: 37-40+ Ap '76
Happiness is. . .an empty nest; study by Norval

Author————————Glenn. J. Horn. Psychol Today 9:22+ Ja '76

Title of magazine————————Of blacks, whites and family stability. H. Hill. Current 188:11-12 D '76
Revolution in the American family; symposium. ed by J. Muchovej. il Am Home 79:46-7 Jl '76

Date of magazine————————What future for the American family? il Changing T 30:7-10 D '76

See *also* reference————————See also
Birth order
Childlessness
Children, First-born
Divorce
Family life
Fathers
Grandparents
Home education
Husbands
Marriage
Mothers
Parents
Single parent families

Subdivision of subject————————Religious life
Family spirituality: a kind of joy. R. Haughton. il New Cath World 219:80-4 Mr '76
FAMILY, Size of
Do you want children? D. Carlinsky. il Seventeen 35:122-3+ N '76
Eight is enough; excerpt. T. Braden. il Good H 182:163+ Ja '76
End of the IQ slump; theories of R. Zajonc. C. Tavris. il Psychol Today 9:69-72+ Ap '76
Families and intellect; scores to increase. Sci N 109:245-6 Ap 17 '76
Family configuration and intelligence. R. B. Zajonc. bibl il Science 192:227-36 Ap 16 '76
What life is like with 12 children. . .two. . .none. il U.S. News 81:57-60 O 4 '76
FAMILY budget. See Budget, Household

See reference————————FAMILY businesses. See Family corporations
FAMILY camping. See Camping
FAMILY corporations
Old values produce success for a family business; R. S. Graves bros. C. A. Cerami. il por Nations Bus 64:68-70+ Mr '76
Runing a family business for 274 years; J. E. Rhoads & sons, inc; interview J. E. Rhoads. il pors Nations Bus 64:30-4 Jl '76
Transferring power in the family business. L. B. Barnes and S. A. Hershon. bibl f il Harvard Bus R 54:105-14 Jl '76
What to do about relatives on your payroll. R. E. Levinson. il Nations Bus 64:55-6+ O '76
FAMILY counseling. See Counseling
FAMILY doctors. See Physicians
FAMILY farms. See Farm ownership
FAMILY finance. See Finance, Personal
FAMILY history. See Genealogy

After you have identifed the items in the *Readers' Guide* that may contain information on your subject, check the shelf list and card catalog to see if your library has the magazines in bound form. Unbound magazines may be listed in a Kardex file. Many librarians now have magazines on microfilm, in which case the microfilm number appears over the call number on the catalog card.

PRACTICE

In a recent issue of the *Readers' Guide,* look up one of these subjects: *Education, Publishers and Publishing,* or *Medicine.*

1. Is the subject subdivided? If so, what are the subdivisions? (See the sample on the preceding page.)

2. Are there *See also* references? List them.

3. What do the following abbreviations mean? *Ja, My, D, il, Good H, Clearing H.*

4. Look up one of the articles printed on your subject. Describe the process you went through to find the article in your library.

After you have surveyed your library's resources, you should be able to say whether you have chosen a workable subject. After checking the reference books, the card catalog, and a periodical index, you may discover that little has been written on your subject or that much of what has been written is not available in your library. In that case, you will have to change your subject.

On the other hand, so much may be published on your subject that you wonder where you can start to narrow it. For example, anthropologists, sociologists, and social historians have been studying the family for the last half century. If your library is very large, you could not cover all the "family" material in a year of reading. So you begin to narrow the subject by considering, for example, the changes in the modern American family and their effect on the increase in divorce. Ask yourself certain pertinent questions: What caused the recent changes in the family? What other effects of cultural change — like the rise of "individualism" — are in themselves causes of change in the family?

Every subject seems to have its own "shape" and logic. This means that we cannot give exact instructions on how you can proceed with the topic you have chosen. Simply remember that you will probably have to *narrow* and *unify* a broad, vague, clumsy subject down to a sharp point. You will know when you get to that "point" when you can: (1) ask a limited, specific question about your subject; and (2) answer the question in a single, specific thesis statement.

Step 2: Make Your Working Bibliography

At this point, many students start using short cuts, some of which may actually work. But unless students have done a lot of research and writing—and most freshmen have not—short cuts may lead only to errors and frustration. The best researchers are usually both careful and lazy, careful in taking all the steps but lazy in not wanting to repeat any of them unnecessarily. For instance, if you don't make your working bibliography cards accurately the first time, you may not be able to find some of your sources in the library. Or you may have to go back to look up a source before typing your final bibliography. The best rule is to do everything right—*once*.

Step 2 is really just Step 1 done in depth. You may have spent only a short time on Step 1, for your purpose was merely to find out whether material was available. Now you are going to make a working bibliography, do some reading, and take a few notes. Use three-by-five cards for your bibliography:

Author ——————

Call number ——————

Title ——————

Ross, Susan Deller   396
                      R889

The Rights of Women: The Basic ACLU Guide to a Woman's Rights.

Publishing information ——————
New York: Avon Books, 1973

Note about usefulness of source ——————
Book not only describes rights of women, but of minor girls as well.

Go slowly through those encyclopedias, other reference works, periodicals, and books that looked promising when you were searching for a workable subject. Take brief notes on the bibliography cards, indicating what you feel to be the particular usefulness of each source. If a source doesn't look helpful, abandon it.

In other words, even at this early stage, it is wise to anticipate Step 3 and start evaluating your sources and evidence. Begin with the most informative and most interesting sources. Skim through them and look for aspects of your subject that are repeatedly emphasized. This repetition often gives a clue to important developments in your subject. Don't get lost in a blind alley—a small part of a subject which one source treats voluminously but which the others ignore.

Step 3: Read, Take Notes, Evaluate the Evidence, Create a Stance, and Look for a Thesis

You may believe that the five elements in Step 3 are distinct operations that must be tackled separately. Actually, you can do several of them at nearly the same time if you are careful. By now, you should have some idea of what is the best source material available on your subject. And, by referring to your bibliography cards, you should be able to locate the material easily and begin your intensive reading and note-taking.

THE FORM OF NOTES

As you take notes, you should consider both their form and how they may be used in your paper.

Take notes on four-by-six cards, not on sheets of regular notebook paper, for they are too large to handle. Do not use three-by-five cards because you might mix them with your bibliography cards. *Put only one idea*—a paraphrase, summary, fact, or quotation—on each card:

> What American value today   quote, p. 39
> Individual, not family
>
> In most countries "the family is the central institution." However, in the United States, it is "the _individual_ that is the chief social unit. We speak of the individual vs. the state, individual achievement, support for disadvantaged individuals, the rights of individuals, finding ourselves as individuals.... The family is not currently a social unit we value or support."
>
> Bronfenbrenner, "The American Family in Decline"

The two-part title in the upper-left corner is useful because it tells you what is on the card without your having to read it. When you come to arrange the note cards before outlining your paper, such careful labeling will pay off. In the upper-right corner is a reminder that this material is quoted (a good way to avoid accidental plagiarism) and that it was taken from page 39. At the bottom, the card provides the author's name and the title of the book or article.

It is often more convenient to make photocopies of magazine and reference-work articles, especially when you cannot check them out of the library.

TAKING NOTES

This may seem like an odd place to discuss the use of notes — even before you have started to outline your paper. But we have discovered that students often go wrong later because they went wrong earlier. If you have a clear idea of what quotations and paraphrases are for, and how they should be eventually worked into your writing, you will be able to take notes more purposefully and avoid some common errors.

The quotations and paraphrases on your note cards provide much of the content — the material and the evidence — of your research paper. Such content comes from the work of other people who have written the articles and books you read. A note card is no more than a piece of paper on which you reduce the ideas of another person to manageable form.

As you take notes, bear this fact in mind: Students often use too much of others' work. Some research papers turn out to be no more than a loose sewing together of other writers' thoughts. A good general rule can be stated in two parts:

1. Use the materials and opinions of others mainly *as support* for your ideas, not in place of them.

2. When using sources, paraphrase as much as possible. A *paraphrase* restates a passage, using words *different* from those in the original. A *quotation* uses the *original* words of the passage. Quote only when the writer says something better or more vividly than you can, or when for the sake of evidence you choose to present the author's own words. Keep paraphrases and quotations short.

Obviously, these "rules" can be bent or broken when necessary.

ACCURATE PARAPHRASING

To illustrate paraphrasing, we will use this sample selection from Fletcher Pratt's *A Short History of the Civil War:*

In 1862 Abraham Lincoln was only the spokesman of an angry people, and no one realized more clearly than he that he did not have *carte blanche* from the nation—a fact which has been obscured by the halo that has since surrounded his name. To the majority he was at that time still the low, cunning clown, the President by hazard, and Chase, Stanton or Seward (according to whether one lived in the West, the Atlantic states or New England) the frequently thwarted brain of the administration. It must be remembered that the arrangement was then the normal one in American politics; the last seven Presidents had all been Merovingians ruled by some Mayor of the Palace. Lincoln's shambling gait, awkward movements and low jokes made him appear as the most inept of all the presidential ventriloquist's dummies. Beside him Zachary Taylor looked like a drawing-room fop and Franklin Pierce like a courtier. When he leaned over and patted the leg of a Congressman who was urging some unfeasible scheme and threw him off balance with the remark "My, my, what big calves you do have," the discomfited legislator could see nothing in it but a piece of *gaucherie*. Even the skill with which the President charmed Kentucky, Maryland and Missouri out of the rebels' lap made no impression. His part in the intrigues was largely secret and both Southerners and Northerners regarded the series of events as fortuitous. The surprising thing in the North was not that the border states remained in the Union but that so many of the others left it.

Here are two paraphrases of the passage:

Paraphrase 1

Abraham Lincoln did not have *carte blanche* from the nation. Even so, he was a very effective president who charmed many southern states out of the rebels' lap. He was the first president in many years to act on his own without being another powerful politician's mouthpiece; he was never just a political ventriloquist's dummy.

Paraphrase 2

According to Fletcher Pratt's *A Short History of the Civil War,* Abraham Lincoln's political skill during the early years of the war was a study in contrasts. While appearing to be a buffoon who made irrelevant remarks at the wrong times, a politician who became president only by accident, he was actually involved in partly successful attempts to save the border states. Since the power given him by the country was incomplete (in Pratt's phrase, "he did not have *carte blanche* from the nation"), he had no choice but to move slyly and by indirection.

You can see that Paraphrase 1 is not a paraphrase at all but rather a careless mixture of summary and unmarked quotation. A paraphrase like it is considered a form of *plagiarism* (see p. 241). Paraphrase 2 fairly states Pratt's ideas and honestly places words in quotation marks that the writer has taken directly from Pratt.

PROPER TECHNIQUES FOR QUOTING

Short Quotations

Always quote accurately. Short prose quotations (those of fewer than five lines) should be worked into your own material with smooth and coherent introductions. Here are two examples (we are assuming that footnotes are used to provide the sources):

> As Fletcher Pratt states, "the skill with which the President [had] charmed Kentucky, Maryland and Missouri out of the rebels' lap made no impression."[12]

> In light of our admiration of Lincoln, Fletcher Pratt's comment concerning the President's "shambling gait, awkward movements and low jokes"[13] may seem oddly inappropriate.

In the first quotation, the brackets indicate *editorial insertion* — words or phrases put into the quotation for the sake of grammar or explanation.

Long Quotations

Prose quotations of more than four lines are usually put in *block form*. That is, they are single-spaced (in contrast to your own material, which is double-spaced) and indented five spaces from the left-hand margin. And quotation marks are *not* used to set off the entire quotation. Here is an example of how a block quotation is set up in relationship to the regular text of a paper:

> It is very easy to forget that during much of his administration, Lincoln was an unpopular president. For one thing, as Fletcher Pratt points out, he did not look or act much like a president:
>
> > Lincoln's shambling gait, awkward movements and low jokes made him appear as the most inept of all the presidential ventriloquist's dummies. Beside him Zachary Taylor looked like a drawing-room fop and Franklin Pierce like a courtier. When he leaned over and patted the leg of a Congressman who was urging some unfeasible scheme and threw him off balance with the remark "My, my, what big calves you do have," the discomfited legislator could see nothing in it but a piece of *gaucherie*.[14]

Ellipsis Marks

An *ellipsis* is an omitted portion of a quotation. *Ellipsis marks* (three or four spaced periods) indicate the place in the quoted material from which the words were removed. Ellipses are usually made in the middle or at the end of the quotation. Here are two examples:

Pratt's comment on the political history of the time was: "It must be remembered that . . . the last seven Presidents had all been Merovingians ruled by some Mayor of the Palace."

As Fletcher Pratt states, "To the majority he was at that time still the low, cunning clown, the President by hazard. . . ."

The three periods in the first example indicate that a phrase has been removed from the middle of Pratt's sentence. The four periods in the second example indicate that material from the end of the quoted sentence has been omitted.

Four ellipsis marks are also used when a *full sentence or more* is removed from a quotation. The four periods in the following example represent the omission of a full sentence:

"Lincoln's shambling gait, awkward movements and low jokes made him appear as the most inept of all the presidential ventriloquist's dummies. . . . Even the skill with which the President charmed Kentucky, Maryland and Missouri out of the rebels' lap made no impression."

Ordinarily, you do not use ellipsis marks at the beginning of a quotation; that is, you do not write:

Pratt's opinion is that Lincoln was ". . . at that time still the low, cunning clown. . . ."

Instead you fit the beginning of the quotation smoothly into your own sentence without the ellipsis marks:

Pratt's opinion is that Lincoln was "at that time still the low, cunning clown. . . ."

PLAGIARISM

Plagiarism is using the ideas or words of another person without giving him proper credit. It is stealing, and it is to be avoided. Most colleges and universities define "plagiarism" in their student codes. If you wish further information, check the rules on written work in your own institution. Your instructor undoubtedly will give you more complete advice on this problem, which proves vexing to students and teachers alike.

PRACTICE

Read the following passage. Then, on five separate note cards, put down: (1) a quotation from the passage that is worked into your own sentence(s); (2) a longer quotation to be used as a block quote in a paper; (3) a one-sentence paraphrase of the entire passage;

(4) a quotation using an ellipsis inside one sentence; (5) a quotation using an ellipsis that "bridges" two or three sentences.

> There was a kind of family stability in the late 1940s and early 1950s. The extended family still existed in places; one out of 10 families had another adult relative living under its roof. After the shakeout year of 1946, the divorce rate was quite low, especially among families with young children. Only one mother in four was working outside the home. And fewer than four percent of all children born were illegitimate. Parents fought for a better education for their children, kicking off a school and college-building boom. Television, which became commercially available to households in 1948, was almost unknown. Mass magazines wrote of "togetherness" and radio soap operas featured families. Hollywood made films about young Andy Hardy, Shirley Temple, and young Dorothy from Kansas, who went to see the Wizard of Oz but longed to return to her family. — Urie Bronfenbrenner, "The American Family in Decline"

THESIS AND STANCE

As you read and take notes, you should also be evaluating evidence and looking for a thesis. With the *family* as your general subject, for example, you are struck by Bronfenbrenner's belief that in America the individual is "the chief social unit" (see the note card, p. 237). So you ask yourself questions: What promoted this individualism? How has individualism affected the family? What is the link between what promoted individualism and changes in the family? A fully developed answer to the last question can provide a workable thesis for a paper: "Recent court decisions and laws which protect the rights of the individual, particularly those of women and youth, have promoted the doctrine of individualism, thereby contributing to important changes in the American family." As a matter of fact, this is the thesis of the sample research paper (p. 254).

Now you may be wondering about assuming a particular writer's stance. Practically speaking, in your composition course, your role will be that of the student. Your reader will be your instructor, who represents that part of the general audience interested in your subject. In research papers for more advanced courses, your role will again be that of the student and your reader will be the instructor. But in these courses, you will be expected to demonstrate a firm grasp of a specialized aspect of the subject. Then you will probably not be writing for the general reader, but rather for an expert in the field.

Always remember that the goal in any research paper, regardless of the subject matter, is to convince your reader that your research is sound, your communication effective, and your conclusions valid.

Step 4: Make an Outline

After doing your research carefully and before beginning your outline, you should have three kinds of information: (1) bibliography cards that give accurate and brief descriptions of all your sources; (2) note cards that are keyed to the bibliography cards and that contain paraphrases and quotations of important material; (3) bits of information that you have retained from reading. In a general way, this last kind of information is of subtle but considerable help in writing a paper.

Set aside the bibliography cards, and group the note cards by title and subtitle. If you were writing on the subject of changes in the American family, you might discover that your cards fall into groups labeled "rights of youth," "rights of women," "increase in number of working women," and so on. In such groupings, you have the beginning of an outline. It will probably not be polished or final at this point, and you may make two or three more before you are finally satisfied with your organization. However, the preliminary outline should indicate any gaps in your research, perhaps requiring you to make another trip to the library. The outline might also show you where you can use your own experience and knowledge to tie up various aspects of your research.

In order to make sure that you have a firm grasp of the basics of outlining, refer to Chapter 3. Also see the outline for the sample research paper (p. 254).

Step 5: Write the Paper

Start to write your first draft, using mainly the material in your note cards. This material is your evidence. Make no statements unless you can back them up, either with an authority or with your own experience. Whenever you draw on material from a note card—whether a direct quotation or a paraphrase—*put a footnote number where you use the material in your first draft and the same number on the card.* If you don't do this, you may get hopelessly lost. If your first draft has twenty footnotes, you should have twenty cards numbered from one to twenty. (For the proper use of quotations and paraphrases, see pp. 238–241.)

In its final form, your paper may look pretty much like our sample on pp. 253–265. The footnotes are numbered consecutively, and they are placed at the bottom of each page. However, a more convenient method is to put them on a separate page immediately following the body of the paper. If at all possible, the paper should be typed, on 8½- × -11 sheets, on one side only, leaving top, bottom, and left margins of about 1½ inches and a right margin of about 1 inch. The pages are numbered in the upper-right corner, and the body of the paper (except for block quotations) is double-spaced.

If you have made your bibliography cards carefully from the beginning, all you do to make the bibliography is to alphabetize your cards for those books and periodicals you referred to in your paper, and type them into final form.

Footnote and Bibliography Forms

The forms used in documenting papers vary considerably from discipline to discipline. A footnote in a biology journal may not look very much like a footnote in a journal devoted to geology. Nor would a footnote in a journal of literary criticism necessarily look like either of these two. And there are even variations within disciplines. Many book and journal publishers that produce material on English literature and composition use the footnote and bibliography forms authorized by the Modern Language Association. These are the forms we recommend. In some instances, however, we have slightly modified them for the sake of simplicity. The important thing is to be *consistent*, no matter what system of documentation you choose.*

FOOTNOTE FORMS

A footnote gives the reader the source of the fact, paraphrase, or quotation you use in the paper. The footnote says to the reader: "Here is where I found this information in case you are interested in pursuing the subject further."

Books

The general rule is: Give author, title, place of publication, publisher, date, and page number, in that order. *Note:* In footnotes, as well as in the bibliography, be most careful in your placement of parentheses, commas, and other punctuation marks.

Note that the following footnotes are numbered consecutively, just as you would number them in your paper.

*There are several excellent paperbacks available which deal comprehensively with the problems of footnoting, bibliography, and the research paper generally. Two of the best are James D. Lester's *Writing Research Papers: A Complete Guide,* Second Edition (Glenview, Ill.: Scott, Foresman, 1976), and Kate Turabian's *A Manual for Writers of Term Papers, Theses, and Dissertations,* Fourth Edition (Chicago: Univ. of Chicago Press, 1973).

One author:

[1]John Smith, <u>Cigarettes</u> <u>in</u> <u>History</u> (New York: Smokin and Koffin, 1974), p. 45.

Two authors:

[2]John Smith and Sam Jones, <u>Smoking</u> <u>and</u> <u>Sex</u> (New York: Smokin and Koffin, 1972), p. 217.

Three authors:

[3]John Smith, Sam Jones, and William Rogers, <u>You</u> <u>and</u> <u>the</u> <u>Filter</u> <u>Tip</u> (New York: Smokin and Koffin, 1959), p. 80.

More than three authors:

[4]John Smith, et al., <u>Menthol</u> <u>Madness</u> (New York: Smokin and Koffin, 1969), pp. 29-30.

Et al. means "and others."

No author:

[5]<u>Ashes</u> <u>to</u> <u>Ashes</u> (Boston: Matchless Press, 1970), p. 193.

Editor:

[6]Frank Klink, ed., <u>A</u> <u>Good</u> <u>Cigar</u> <u>Is</u> <u>a</u> <u>Smoke</u> (New York: American Academy for Habits, 1972), p. 54.

or:

[7]<u>A</u> <u>Good</u> <u>Cigar</u> <u>Is</u> <u>a</u> <u>Smoke</u>, ed. Frank Klink (New York: American Academy for Habits, 1972), p. 54.

Editors:

[8]Frank Klink and Phoebe Tipp, eds., <u>A</u> <u>Pictorial</u> <u>Guide</u> <u>to</u> <u>Early</u> <u>American</u> <u>Ashtrays</u> (Chicago: Smith and Franklin, 1968), p. 102.

Translator:

[9]Roger Carp, <u>Smoke</u> <u>in</u> <u>the</u> <u>Dining</u> <u>Car</u>, trans. Phoebe Tipp (Boston: Nicotine and Tarr, 1945), p. 14.

Edition or revision:

[10]Franz Wiedemann, <u>A</u> <u>Psychoanalytical</u> <u>Approach</u> <u>to</u> <u>the</u> <u>Cigar</u> <u>Smoker</u>, rev. Phoebe Tipp and Frank Klink, 3rd ed. (Boston: Nicotine and Tarr, 1969), pp. 36-39.

The original author is Wiedemann; the third edition was revised by Tipp and Klink.

Article reprinted in a collection:

[11]Theodore Furber, "The Smoking Experience," The Chesterfield Review, 22 (1951), 84; rpt. in A Casebook on Popular Vices: Essays and Criticism, ed. Elroy Weede (New York: American Academy for Habits, 1966), p. 8.

Rpt. stands for reprinted.

Part of a book:

[12]Roger Carp, "Ode to a Cigarette," in Famous Poems on Smoking, ed. Phoebe Tipp, 4th ed. (New York: Tiparillo-Cigarillo, 1965), p. 313.

Reference Works

Although they are books, reference works that are alphabetically arranged do not need the publisher or page and volume number cited. The general rule is: Give author, title of article, title of reference work, and year of publication.

[13]Elroy Weede, "Smoking," Encyclopedia Tobaccoana, 1965 ed.

If the article is unsigned, begin the footnote with the title of the article.

Periodicals

The general rule is: Give author, title of article, title of periodical, volume number, date, and page number (omitting the p. for *page*), in that order.

[14]Thomas Puffington, "A Note on the Identity of the Marlboro Man," The Chesterfield Review, 36 (1965), 234.

If the article has no author, start the footnote with the title of the article. If the article has multiple authors, employ the same conventions used with books in listing the authors. If the periodical is paged anew in each issue—like *Time* or *Newsweek*—a slightly different form is used. The volume number is unnecessary; the full date is given, and p. or *pp.* is used before the page numbers.

[15]John Smith, "Smoking Up a Storm," Saturday Review of Smoking, 3 March 1966, pp. 17-18.

Newspapers

Use the same format as you would with a periodical that is paged anew with each issue; in addition, indicate the column number(s) of the article (use *col.* or *cols.*).

16James Menish, "Smoke Gets in Your Eyes," <u>Chicago</u>
<u>Daily News</u>, 8 May 1958, p. 20, cols. 4-5.

Government Documents, Commission Reports, and Pamphlets

Usually no author is given in these materials. Accordingly, the governmental or private agency should receive credit as author. The agency responsible for publication is given as publisher.

[17]Department of Health, Education and Welfare, <u>Pre-natal</u>
<u>Effects</u> <u>of</u> <u>Smoking</u> (Washington, D.C.: GPO, 1977), p. 66.

GPO stands for "Government Printing Office."

[18]U.S. Commission on Diseases of the Lungs, <u>The Unwitting</u>
<u>Victim--the</u> <u>Non-smoker,</u> Report IV (New York: American
Medical Assn., 1975), p. 10.

[19]"The Breathing Problem," Pamphlet (Urbana, Ill.:
Concerned Patients' Committee, Burnham City Hospital, 1976),
p. 3.

Interviews

Give the name of the person interviewed, his title and affiliation, the place, date, and kind (personal or telephone) of interview.

[20]Personal interview with James Carlson, Vice-President,
Acme Cigar Company, Asheville, N.C., 6 June 1973.

FOOTNOTES AS THEY MIGHT APPEAR IN A PAPER

The first time you cite a source in your paper, put down all the information about the source in the footnote. Use the full form. Every time you use the same source after that, include the name of the author or, if you don't know the name, the title of the source; then give the page number. Here is a list of footnotes as they might appear consecutively in a paper:

Footnote 1: First time Smith is cited.

[1]John Smith, <u>Cigarettes</u> <u>in</u> <u>History</u> (New York: Smokin
and Koffin, 1974), p. 45.

Footnote 2: First time Puffington is cited.

[2]Thomas Puffington, "A Note on the Identity of the
Marlboro Man," <u>The</u> <u>Chesterfield</u> <u>Review</u>, 36 (1965), 234.

Footnote 3: This footnote refers to the previous one, but to a different page in Puffington.

^{3}Puffington, 238.

Footnote 4: This refers to the Smith book cited in footnote 1. If *two* books by Smith were being used, however, you would give the title in each subsequent reference: e.g., Smith, *Cigarettes in History,* p. 47.

^{4}Smith, p. 47.

Footnote 5: This refers to Smith in the last footnote but to a different page.

^{5}Smith, p. 48.

Footnote 6: A new citation.

^{6}Frank Klink, ed., <u>A</u> <u>Good</u> <u>Cigar</u> <u>Is</u> <u>a</u> <u>Smoke</u> (New York: American Academy for Habits, 1972), p. 108.

THE BIBLIOGRAPHY

The bibliography is a list of all the sources you have used in the paper—those you have cited in footnotes. Your instructor may also want you to list all the sources you have read or consulted. If that is the case, you may add another section entitled "Sources Consulted but Not Used." You should check with your instructor to see what format he wants you to follow.

Arrange the entries in your bibliography in alphabetical order by the surname of the author. When no author is given, use the first word of the title; when the title begins with an article (*a, an,* or *the*) or with a preposition, use the second word. If you have two sources written by the same author, it is not necessary to repeat the author's name in the second entry. Instead, type ten hyphens, follow with a period, skip two spaces, and give the title:

> Klink, Frank, ed. <u>A</u> <u>Good</u> <u>Cigar</u> <u>Is</u> <u>a</u> <u>Smoke</u>. New York: American Academy for Habits, 1972.

> ----------. <u>Making</u> <u>a</u> <u>Hole</u> <u>in</u> <u>Your</u> <u>Habit</u>: <u>The</u> <u>Ice</u> <u>Pik</u> <u>System</u>. Chicago: Smith and Franklin, 1977.

Be aware of the slight difference between the use of commas and periods here and in the footnotes; also note that parentheses are not used to set off the place of publication, publisher, and date. In addition, the *first* line of each bibliography entry is flush to the left margin, while subsequent ones are indented about five spaces.

Books

The general rule is: Give author (last name first), title of book, place of publication, publisher, and date.

One author:

> Smith, John. <u>Cigarettes in History</u>. New York: Smokin and Koffin, 1974.

Two authors:

> Smith, John, and Sam Jones. <u>Smoking and Sex</u>. New York: Smokin and Koffin, 1972.

Three authors:

> Smith, John, Sam Jones, and William Rogers. <u>You and the Filter Tip</u>. New York: Smokin and Koffin, 1959.

More than three authors:

> Smith, John, et al. <u>Menthol Madness</u>. New York: Smokin and Koffin, 1969.

No author:

> <u>Ashes to Ashes</u>. Boston: Matchless Press, 1970.

Editor:

> Klink, Frank, ed. <u>A Good Cigar Is a Smoke</u>. New York: American Academy for Habits, 1972.

or:

> <u>A Good Cigar Is a Smoke</u>. Ed. Frank Klink. New York: American Academy for Habits, 1972.

Editors:

> Klink, Frank, and Phoebe Tipp, eds. <u>A Pictorial Guide to Early American Ashtrays</u>. Chicago: Smith and Franklin, 1968.

Translator:

> Carp, Roger. <u>Smoke in the Dining Car</u>. Trans. Phoebe Tipp. Boston: Nicotine and Tarr, 1945.

Edition or revision:

> Wiedemann, Franz. <u>A Psychoanalytical Approach to the Cigar Smoker</u>. Rev. Phoebe Tipp and Frank Klink, 3rd ed. Boston: Nicotine and Tarr, 1969.

Article reprinted in a collection:

> Furber, Theodore. "The Smoking Experience." <u>The Chesterfield Review</u>, 22 (1951), 75-86. Rpt. in <u>A Casebook on Popular Vices</u>: <u>Essays and Criticism</u>. Ed. Elroy Weede. New York: American Academy for Habits, 1966, pp. 2-11.

Part of a book:

> Carp, Roger. "Ode to a Cigarette." In <u>Famous Poems on Smoking</u>.
> Ed. Phoebe Tipp. 4th ed. New York: Tiparillo-Cigarillo,
> 1965.

Reference Works

Just take the information contained in your footnote and recast it slightly in the form for a bibliography entry.

> Weede, Elroy. "Smoking." <u>Encyclopedia Tobaccoana</u>. 1965 ed.

Periodicals and Newspapers

These forms are essentially the same as those for
footnotes, except for two important changes: (1) give the author's surname first, then his given name or initials; and (2) give the inclusive
page numbers of the article (not just the pages from which you took
material).

> Puffington, Thomas. "A Note on the Identity of the Marlboro
> Man." <u>The Chesterfield Review</u>, 36 (1965), 231-241.

> Menish, James. "Smoking Up a Storm." <u>Chicago Daily News</u>,
> 8 May 1958, p. 20, cols. 4-5.

Interviews

Give the name of the person interviewed, form of
interview, and date. If the person interviewed is not well known to
your reader, give his title in parentheses.

> Carlson, James (Vice-President, Acme Cigar Company). Personal
> interview. 6 June 1973.

PRACTICE

Listed below in a scrambled fashion are four
sources:

Wasson, Kyle: *Journal of Psychiatry;* (October 1954); pp. 201–215; vol.
22; "Notes on Insanity."

V. R. Belle; 1965; Harper & Row; *What Is Sanity?;* New York.

Rivers, Karen; pp. 10–15; "Craziness"; ed. J. B. Goode; Boston; *Psychoanalytical Interpretations of Fundamental Behavior;* Houghton
Mifflin; 1955.

Falk, Peter and J. Q. Stuart; Chicago; 1961; *Stanislavsky and the Normal
Mind;* Univ. of Chicago Press.

Using proper bibliographical form, unscramble each of the items and put them in alphabetical order. Then make ten footnotes from the above items, in this order: Belle, p. 74; Falk and Stuart, pp. 75–76; Belle, p. 74; Belle, p. 80; Rivers, p. 12; Wasson, pp. 214–215; Rivers, p. 13; Rivers, p. 13; Falk and Stuart, p. 1; Wasson, pp. 214–215.

Checklist for the First Draft

After you have written your first draft from your outline, use the following checklist to see if your material is as logically organized, clear, and accurate as you can make it.

Outline

1. Is your thesis placed at the top of the outline page so that it can be checked against the outline?
2. Do each of your first-level points (I, II, III, etc.) support the thesis?
3. Do your second-level points (A, B, C, etc.) support your first-level ones?
4. Are the items in the outline parallel in content and in form? Did you use complete sentences for all first- and second-level points? (The sentence outline is preferred for research papers, but your instructor may want you to use another form.)

Introduction

1. Is your thesis clearly stated?
2. Have you shown why the topic is important enough to interest your reader?
3. Have you defined any terms that the reader should clearly understand?

Body

1. Have you checked your reasoning in the paper?
   a. Are your generalizations supported by well-chosen evidence?
   b. Are your causal relationships logical?
   c. Have you checked your facts? Your sources?
2. Are your paragraphs unified and logical?
3. Have you used your sources properly?
4. Have you reviewed the material on paraphrasing and quoting (pp. 238–241)?

5. Have you used correct quotation, footnote, and bibliography forms?
    a. Did you give a complete footnote reference for the first time you used a source in the paper?
    b. Did you check the bibliography against your footnotes to see that you have included all sources?

Conclusion

1. Do you have a concluding paragraph which restates the thesis and rounds off the paper?
2. Have you introduced any new and significant ideas in the conclusion (usually a poor idea)?

Proofreading

1. Have you read the paper aloud at least once, listening and watching for anything that doesn't sound and look right?
2. Did you avoid shifts in tense and person?
3. Are your parallel ideas stated in parallel form?
4. Have you overused the passive voice?
5. Are your signals and transitions clear so that your reader can follow your organization?
6. Have you used words precisely and accurately?
7. Have you avoided errors in spelling, grammar, and punctuation?
8. Have you proofread for typographical errors?

Sample Research Paper

The sample research paper and outline written on the broad subject of the American family will show you the culmination of one student's efforts. The paper contains many of the techniques and forms discussed in this chapter so that you can see how they work together in an actual situation. Here are a few things you should note about the format of the paper:

1. The body is double-spaced, with block quotations single-spaced.

2. The outline, footnotes, and bibliography are single-spaced, with double spacing between each entry.

3. The numbers preceding each paragraph have been added so that you can refer to specific paragraphs when discussing the paper. (You should *not* use such numbers in your own paper.)

The Practice (pp. 266–267) not only should give you a better understanding of the principles and conventions illustrated in the paper, it should also help you apply them to your own efforts.

THE AMERICAN FAMILY--WHY IS IT CHANGING?

by

Diane Dellinger

English 100 Section 03

Rhetoric 10A, Section B3
Instructor: Mr. Lamboth

May 3, 1978

THE AMERICAN FAMILY--WHY IS IT CHANGING?

Thesis: Recent court decisions and laws which protect the rights of
the individual, particularly those of women and youth, have promoted
the doctrine of individualism, thereby contributing to important
changes in the American family.

I. The courts and law-making institutions protect certain rights of
   women and youth.
   A. Anti-discrimination laws have provided women increased
      opportunity for jobs and education.
   B. The courts and laws protect the rights of women and girls
      to control their own bodies.
   C. The rights of public-school students are also protected.

II. Because of the government's and the Supreme Court's increased
    concern for the individual's rights, thereby promoting the doctrine
    of individualism, the family is losing its hold on its members.
    A. Women are leaving the home.
       1. Many are entering the work force.
       2. Some are "running away" from home.
       3. The "empty house" can be hard on children.
    B. The increased number of working mothers and single-parent
       families is creating independent children.
    C. Traditional values have been supplanted by the value of
       individualism.

III. The values of individualism are influencing the future of the
     family.
     A. Many young adults are rejecting marriage as a way of life.
     B. Many young adults reject marriage because of society's values.
     C. Those who marry often see the relationship in contractual
        terms.
     D. In raising children, the "New Breed" family is stressing
        individualism.

THE AMERICAN FAMILY--WHY IS IT CHANGING?

[1]In the last decades we have seen a growing concern for the individual, the self. The tremendous interest in consciousness-raising and self-awareness arose in the sixties and is flourishing today. The youth movement of the sixties was at least partly concerned with the individual and his right to be independent from society's demands. The 1964 Civil Rights Act and other recent laws and Supreme Court decisions have provided for the protection of the rights of the individual. The concern for the rights of the individual has generally contributed to the rise of the doctrine of individualism in our society.

[2]Individualism can be defined in various ways. One of the most commonly accepted meanings is expressed in these words: "The ethical doctrine or principle that the interests of the individual himself are or ought to be paramount in determination of conduct."[1]

[3]This paper will show how the court decisions and laws which protect the rights of the individual, particularly those of women and youth, have promoted the doctrine of individualism, thereby contributing to important changes in the American family.

[4]Since 1964 the courts and law-making institutions, by protecting the rights of women in employment and education, have provided women with increased opportunities for jobs and education. Title VII of the 1964 Civil Rights Act prohibits sex discrimination in employment.[2]

[1]Webster's Third New International Dictionary, 1976.

[2]Susan Deller Ross, The Rights of Women: The Basic ACLU Guide to a Woman's Rights (New York: Avon, 1973), p. 39.

Through its enforcement agency (the Equal Employment Opportunity
Commission), this law has opened up employment opportunities for women
in fields where they had previously been shut out. Title IX of the
Education Amendments of 1972 Act prohibits sex discrimination in
education,[3] thereby encouraging women to train for professions that are
dominated by men. Law and medical schools, for instance, now recruit
women. As a result of better opportunities and better training, "for
the first time in history the job market is competing with the marriage
market."[4]

[5]The courts and legislators also protect the rights of women and
girls to control their own bodies. Many states have laws that allow
minors to have birth-control devices without parental consent.[5] The
Supreme Court decision of Roe v. Wade provided that "states may not
prohibit abortions during the first trimester of pregnancy."[6] This
ruling also applies to minors. For instance, in the state of Illinois,
a pregnant minor is considered "emancipated"; therefore, she can get
an abortion in the first trimester without her parents' consent.[7] Such
laws and court rulings have a profound effect on the control that a
family has on its members, particularly girls.

[3]Ross, p. 131.

[4]William M. Kephart, "Family," Encyclopedia International, 1972 ed.

[5]Ross, p. 201.

[6]Ross, p. 194.

[7]Telephone interview with Margaret Drickamer, Director, Champaign
County Planned Parenthood Assoc., Urbana, Illinois, 25 June 1977.

[6]The rights of public-school students are also protected by the courts. In 1969, the Supreme Court ruled that the First Amendment guarantees the rights of public-school students to express their views on controversial subjects.[8] In addition, the courts and state departments of education no longer accept arguments from school administrators that they are "empowered to act in loco parentis."[9] Other legal actions have restricted the power of schools to impose dress codes, inflict corporal punishment, and suspend students for misbehavior or truancy. Since public schools have traditionally tried to maintain the values of the family, the breakdown of the power of the school to discipline and control students contributes to a loss of family control.

[7]Because of our society's increased concern for the individual and his rights, thereby promoting the doctrine of individuality, the family is losing its hold on its members. Women, particularly educated women from the middle and upper classes, are frustrated with being housewives and are entering the work force in increasing numbers each year.[10] One-third of working women have children under six.[11] As a result of the anti-discrimination laws, which provide greater opportunities than

[8]Alan Levine, The Rights of Students: The Basic ACLU Guide to a Student's Rights (New York: Dutton, 1973), p. 16.

[9]Levine, pp. 14-15. In loco parentis is Latin for "acting in place of parents."

[10]Kephart says that women college graduates don't like being housewives, even though their jobs outside the home are often "routine clerical and office variety."

[11]Urie Bronfenbrenner, "Nobody Home: The Erosion of the American Family," Psychology Today, May 1977, p. 41.

before, educated women who are highly individualistic seek fulfillment,[12] but not (necessarily) by staying home with children.

[8]Many other middle-class, educated women are running away from
home, often leaving young children. In 1976, police reported 2,394
adult females missing in the Chicago area, many of whom were mothers
in middle- and upper-class families. Some of these women claim that
they left their families because they wanted to be independent and
not live by someone else's values.[13] One woman left three sons--ages
10, 8, and 5--to get a master's degree in social work,[14] a field which
(ironically) is often concerned with helping others resolve the problems of separation, divorce, and desertion.

[9]But what happens to the children of mothers who seek fulfillment
and individualism? Urie Bronfenbrenner says: "This whole way of life
[individualism] is fine if you're young, sexy, and full of verve. But
if you happen to be a child, or sick, or lonely, or old--and all of us
are at some time--you need somebody else. If that somebody else is
doing his own thing, he's not there."[15]

[10]The increase in the number of working mothers and single-parent
families is creating an independent youngster who is likely to grow up
with no particular commitment to the family. According to the most
recent statistics, one-sixth of all school-age boys and girls live in

[12]Bob Tamarkin, "Why Wives Are Running Away from Their Families,"
Chicago Daily News, 13 June 1977, p. 2, col. 3.

[13]Tamarkin, p. 2, cols. 3-4.

[14]Tamarkin.

[15]Bronfenbrenner, "Nobody Home," pp. 41-42.

single-parent homes.[16] Most of these single parents must work. Only

five percent of American homes have a relative other than a parent

living with the family;[17] consequently, there frequently is no one in

the house when children come home from school. Because pre-school

children are often sent to day-care centers, and young people may be

left on their own after school, they "develop a sense of independence

from their families."[18] Charles W. Hobart claims that the family relies

on the values of "being, knowing, caring, loving, unconditionally com-

mitting oneself."[19] It is obvious that many young people never see

these values in their families. But they do see what Bruno Bettelheim

calls a "preoccupation with self-fulfillment."[20]

[11]Our society has emphasized the rights of the individual more than

traditional values, and change for the sake of change has been a con-

stant theme in American life. As Michael D'Innocenzo remarks, "In the

face of such swift and extensive changes, it has been difficult for

parents to play a major role in shaping their children."[21] The courts,

[16]George E. Jones, "Can Carter Revitalize the American Family?"
U.S. News and World Report, 28 February 1977, p. 35.

[17]Urie Bronfenbrenner, "The American Family in Decline," Current,
January 1977, p. 40.

[18]Ira L. Reiss, The Family System in America (New York: Holt, 1971),
p. 411.

[19]Charles W. Hobart, "Commitment, Value Conflict and the Future of
the American Family," Marriage and Family Living, 25 (1963), 408; rpt.
in The Family and Change, ed. John N. Edwards (New York: Knopf, 1969),
p. 330.

[20]Jones, p. 35.

[21]Michael D'Innocenzo, "The Family Under Fire," Vital Speeches, 43
(1977), 433.

in allowing minors to have birth-control devices and abortions without parental consent, have overridden the traditional values of morality. According to Ira L. Reiss, a decrease in family control is associated with "premarital pregnancy" and "casual and occasional homosexuality,"[22] both creating stress not only for the existing family but also for future families.

[12]But what of the future of the family? How do young adults feel about marriage? How are new families raising their.children?

[13]Many young adults are rejecting marriage as a way of life. The number of unmarried adults living with a member of the opposite sex doubled between 1970 and 1975.[23] Entire apartment complexes in large metropolitan areas cater to young, unmarried adults (or "singles"), who share the interests and philosophy of individualism. The management of such complexes promotes the singles' way of life by providing entertainment, parties, and activities that appeal to them. Many cities have singles bars which cater to young adults, many of whom live alone. They are often pursuing a way of life they began in college, where a variety of living arrangements is possible. With the abandonment of in loco parentis, living arrangements in colleges and universities have become freer and more varied in the last two decades. Students may choose coed dormitories or apartments where they can live with whomever they choose, without fear of punishment by the administration. Due partly to the influence of court decisions, our society has encouraged an individual-

[22]Reiss, p. 411.

[23]Sandra Stencel, "The Family in Turmoil," Caravan (Champaign-Urbana Courier), 22 June 1977, p. 3, col. 2.

istic way of life for young adults, particularly those with college
educations and professional training.

[14]Some authorities believe that young adults, especially those who
are college-educated, reject marriage for two reasons: we have a youth-
oriented society, and individualists do not value families. Urie
Bronfenbrenner calls ours an "adolescent society" because of our preoccupation with "glamor, sex, violence, machismo."[24] Michael Novak says,
"In our society, of course, there is no need to become an adult. One
may remain--one is exhorted daily to remain--a child forever."[25] He
explains why young adults do not want children: "Children are not a
welcome responsibility, for to have children is, plainly, to cease being a child oneself."[26] The increased belief in the doctrine of
individualism prevents some intellectuals from marrying. Novak remarks:

> There are, perhaps radical psychological differences between
> people who center human life in atomic individuals--in "Do your
> thing," or "Live your own life," et cetera--and people who center
> human life in their families. There may be in this world two
> kinds of people: "individual people" and "family people." Our
> intellectual class, it seems, celebrates the former constantly,
> denigrates the latter.[27]

Michael D'Innocenzo goes even further by saying that individualists
avoid responsibility because they are selfish:

> Perhaps never before in America has the celebration of the
> imperial self, the I above everything and everyone else gone

[24]Bronfenbrenner, "Nobody Home," p. 45.

[25]Michael Novak, "The Family out of Favor," _Harper's_, April 1976,
p. 39.

[26]Novak.

[27]Novak.

so far. Selfishness is now being made into a perverted ideal.
An emerging view seems to be that if one gets beyond responsibility and connections, one may truly be free and thus open to
experience and ecstasy.[28]

[15]Those young adults who do marry often see the relationship in

contractual terms. Recently some friends of mine married after a long

series of discussions over their marriage contract. They specified in

legal terms the arrangements for doing the household chores, taking

care of finances, determining vacation plans, and managing future

children. Yet in dealing with such "legal" agreements, people cannot

live by contracts alone. As Nelson Foote says about the self-interest

inherent in the nature of contracts:

> Commitment to certain moral norms ultimately furnishes the struc-
> ture of any society, without which its members cannot organize
> and successfully conduct their various interdependent activities.
> Yet moral commitment based solely upon individual self-interest
> is a contradiction in terms.[29]

[16]According to a recent poll, almost half of young families are

raising their children by following the doctrine of individualism.

Pollster Daniel Yankelovich recently conducted a study of 1,230 families

with one or more children under 13. In a review of the study, called

The American Family Report: Raising Children in a Changing Society,

Time magazine states:

> It [the study] found that 43% of the parents belong to the
> "New Breed." They stress freedom over authority, self-fulfill-
> ment over material success, and duty to self over duty to others
> —including their own children. The study found that New Breed
> parents are loving but self-oriented, and they take a laissez-

[28]D'Innocenzo, p. 433.

[29]Nelson Northrup Foote, "Family," Encyclopaedia Britannica,
1960 ed.

faire attitude to their own child rearing. Says Yankelovich:
"It's not the permissiveness of the '50s, which was child-
centered and concerned with the fragility of the child.
Today, the parent says in effect, 'I want to be free, so why
shouldn't my children be free?'"[30]

[17]America seems to be going through a period in which the individual

receives great attention from the government and the courts. Even

though this concern for the individual helps many people become self-

sufficient, the effect on the family as a social unit--and particularly

the effect on young children--may be harmful. Yet the answer to the

problem of the family does not seem to be in more laws and more court

decisions but in a different attitude on the part of individuals and

society. This may occur almost automatically, as the younger individ-

ualists approach middle and old age, when the consequences of being

alone are most profoundly felt. Families have a way of nourishing

their members that no other human institution has, a fact which may

affect individualism more than any number of new court decisions.

[30]"Family: New Breed v. the Old," _Time_, 2 May 1977, p. 76.

Bibliography

Bronfenbrenner, Urie. "The American Family in Decline." Current, January 1977, pp. 39-47.

----------. "Nobody Home: The Erosion of the American Family." Psychology Today, May 1977, pp. 41-43, 45-47.

D'Innocenzo, Michael. "The Family Under Fire." Vital Speeches, 43 (1977) 431-435.

Drickamer, Margaret (Director, Champaign County (Ill.) Planned Parenthood Assoc.). Telephone interview. 25 June 1977.

"Family: New Breed v. the Old." Time, 2 May 1977, p. 76.

Foote, Nelson Northrup. "Family." Encyclopaedia Britannica. 1960 ed.

Hobart, Charles W. "Commitment, Value Conflict and the Future of the American Family." Marriage and Family Living, 25 (1963), 405-412. Rpt. in The Family and Change. Ed. John N. Edwards. New York: Knopf, 1969, pp. 325-338.

Jones, George E. "Can Carter Revitalize the American Family?" U.S. News and World Report, 28 February 1977, p. 35.

Kephart, William M. "Family." Encyclopedia International. 1972 ed.

Levine, Alan. The Rights of Students: The Basic ACLU Guide to a Student's Rights. New York: Dutton, 1973.

Novak, Michael. "The Family out of Favor." Harper's, April 1976, pp. 37-40, 42-44, 46.

Reiss, Ira L. The Family System in America. New York: Holt, 1971.

Ross, Susan Deller. The Rights of Women: The Basic ACLU Guide to a Woman's Rights. New York: Avon, 1973.

Stencel, Sandra. "The Family in Turmoil." Caravan (Champaign-Urbana Courier), 22 June 1977, p. 3, cols. 1-4.

Tamarkin, Bob. "Why Wives Are Running Away from Their Families." Chicago Daily News, 13 June 1977, p. 1, cols. 1-4, p. 2, cols. 1-4.

Webster's Third New International Dictionary. 1976.

Works Consulted but Not Used

Demos, John. "American Family in Past Time." <u>American Scholar</u>, 43 (1974), 422-446.

Farber, Bernard. "Family." <u>Encyclopedia Americana</u>. 1976 ed.

Goode, William J. <u>The Family</u>. Englewood Cliffs, N.J.: Prentice-Hall, 1964.

McCarthy, Abigail. "Our Fictions and the Family." <u>Commonweal</u>, 102 (1975), 520, 544.

Mead, Margaret. "Can the American Family Survive?" <u>Redbook</u>, February 1977, pp. 91, 154, 156, 159, 161.

Mousseau, J. Edward. "Family, Prison of Love" (Interview with Philippe Aries). <u>Psychology Today</u>, August 1975, pp. 53-58.

Young, Leontine. <u>The Fractured Family</u>. New York: McGraw-Hill, 1973.

"What Future for the American Family?" <u>Changing Times</u>, December 1976, pp. 7-10.

1. Check the student's outline against the body of her paper by putting outline symbols (I, A, B, C; II, A, etc.) in the margin of the paper where the various topics and subtopics are discussed. How well does the student follow her outline?

2. Why does the title page include so much information?

3. Explain the purpose of the first three paragraphs. Are all three necessary?

4. In the fifth paragraph, why is footnote 7 placed after *consent* rather than *emancipated*?

5. Explain how footnotes 9 and 10 help the reader. Why is the added information put in the footnotes rather than in the text?

6. Why does the writer use so much statistical evidence in paragraph 8?

7. Why are brackets placed around the word *individualism* in the quotation in paragraph 9?

8. Describe the organizational strategy of paragraph 9.

9. Why might paragraph 10 be called figuratively a "frame paragraph"?

10. In your opinion, does the first sentence in paragraph 11 need documentation? Why or why not?

11. Defend the inclusion of paragraph 12.

12. In what specific ways does paragraph 13 *remind* readers of the writer's thesis?

13. Why are the two quotations in paragraph 14 put in block form? Why does the writer indent the first line of one but not the other?

14. What does the writer's "lead" into the second block quotation in paragraph 14 imply about the organization of the material in the paragraph?

15. Do you object to the personal reference in the second sentence of paragraph 15? Why or why not?

16. Study paragraph 17, the conclusion. Consider each sentence separately as a statement. How convinced are you by each one? Why does the paragraph have no sources or footnotes?

17. Point out three transitional devices in the paper.

18. Why are there no page numbers given in footnotes 14, 26, and 27?

19. Here is the note card for footnote 13. Explain how the writer integrated the material into her paper.

Runaway Wives   p. 2, Cols. 3-4

Middle-and upper-class
need independence

In 1976, police reported 2394 adult females
missing in the Chicago area. Many of these
women are from middle-and upper-class
homes and they want to be independent.
They don't want to live by another's
values.

Tamarkin, "Why Wives Are Running Away
From Their Families"

20. Here is the note card for footnote 18. How does the student use the material on the card in her paper?

Day-care centers and independent activities   quote, p. 411
Encourages family independence

Reiss believes that as each member of a family
becomes more autonomous, he involves other
members of the family less and less. Because
of day-care centers for young children and
the autonomous lives of teen-agers, boys
and girls live "in ways that encourage them
to develop a sense of independence from
their families."

Reiss, The Family System in America

A List of Reference Works

GENERAL REFERENCE WORKS

Encyclopedias

Chambers's Encyclopaedia. 4th ed. 15 vols. Elmsford, N.Y.: Maxwell Science International, 1968.

Collier's Encyclopedia. 24 vols. New York: Collier, 1949–1951. (Continuous revision). Yearbooks.

Columbia Encyclopedia. 3rd ed. 1 vol. New York: Columbia Univ. Press, 1963.

Encyclopaedia Britannica. 1st to 14th eds. 24 vols. Chicago: Encyclopaedia Britannica, 1768–1973. Yearbooks.

Encyclopedia Americana. 30 vols. New York: Encyclopedia Americana, 1978. Yearbooks.

The New Encyclopaedia Britannica. 15th ed. 30 vols. (3 parts). Chicago: Encyclopaedia Britannica, 1974. Yearbooks.

Biographical Dictionaries and Indexes

Biography Index: A Cumulative Index to Biographical Material in Books and Magazines. New York: H. W. Wilson, 1946–date.

Chambers's Biographical Dictionary. Rev. ed. New York: St. Martin's, 1969.

Current Biography. New York: H. W. Wilson, 1940–date.

Dictionary of American Biography. 20 vols. New York: Scribner's, 1928–1937. Supplements to 1955.

Dictionary of National Biography. Ed. Leslie Stephen and Sidney Lee. London: Oxford Univ. Press, 1908–1909. Supplements to 1960.

International Who's Who. London: Europa and Allen & Unwin, 1935–date.

Webster's Biographical Dictionary. Rev. ed. Springfield, Mass.: Merriam, 1972.

Who's Who in America. Chicago: A. N. Marquis, 1899–date.

Almanacs

Facts on File. New York: Facts on File, 1940–date.

Information Please Almanac. New York: Simon & Schuster, 1947–date.

The World Almanac and Book of Facts. New York: Newspaper Enterprise Assn. 1868–date.

Atlases and Gazetteers

Columbia-Lippincott Gazetteer of the World. Ed. Leon E. Seltzer. New York: Columbia Univ. Press, 1962.

Goode's World Atlas. Ed. Edward B. Espenshade, Jr. 13th ed. Chicago: Rand McNally, 1970.

National Geographic Atlas of the World. 3rd rev. ed. Washington, D.C.: National Geographic Society, 1970.

Periodical Indexes

Humanities Index. New York: H. W. Wilson, June 1974–date.

Nineteenth Century Readers' Guide to Periodical Literature, 1890–1899. 2 vols. New York: H. W. Wilson, 1944. With supplements to 1922.

Poole's Index to Periodical Literature, 1802–1881. Rev. ed. Boston: Houghton Mifflin, 1891. Supplements to 1907.

Readers' Guide to Periodical Literature. New York: H. W. Wilson, 1900–date.

Social Sciences and Humanities Index (formerly titled International Index, now in two parts: Humanities Index and the Social Sciences Index). New York: H. W. Wilson, 1916–1974.

Social Sciences Index. New York: H. W. Wilson, June, 1974–date.

Newspaper Indexes

New York Times Index. New York: New York Times, 1913–date.

Official Index to the [London] Times. London: The Times, 1906–date.

Pamphlet Indexes

Vertical File Index: Subject and Title Index to Selected Pamphlet Material. New York: H. W. Wilson, 1935–date.

Bibliographies

Besterman, Theodore. A World Bibliography of Bibliographies. 4th ed. 5 vols. Lausanne: Societas Bibliographica, 1965–1966.

Bibliographic Index: A Cumulative Bibliography of Bibliographies. New York: H. W. Wilson, 1938–date.

Subject Guide to Books in Print. New York: Bowker, 1957–date.

Winchell, Constance M. Guide to Reference Books. 9th ed. Chicago: American Library Assn., 1976.

SPECIAL REFERENCE WORKS

Art

The Art Index. New York: H. W. Wilson, 1929–date.

Chamberlin, Mary W. Guide to Art Reference Books. Chicago: American Library Assn., 1959.

Encyclopedia of World Art. 15 vols. New York: McGraw-Hill, 1959–1968.

Myers, Bernard, ed. Encyclopedia of Painting. New York: Crown, 1955.

Business

Business Periodicals Index. New York: H. W. Wilson, 1958 – date.
McGraw-Hill Dictionary of Modern Economics: A Handbook of Terms and Organizations. 2nd ed. New York: McGraw-Hill, 1973.
Nemmers, Erwin E. and C. C. Jantzen, eds. *Dictionary of Economics and Business.* 3rd ed. Totowa, N. J.: Littlefield, Adams, 1974.

Drama

Baker, Blanch M. *Theatre and Allied Arts: A Guide to Books Dealing with the History, Criticism, and Technic of the Drama and Theatre and Related Arts and Crafts.* New York: H. W. Wilson, 1953. Rpt. 1967.
Cumulated Dramatic Index, 1909 – 1949: A Cumulation of the F. W. Faxon Company's Dramatic Index. 2 vols. Boston: G. K. Hall, 1965.
Hartnoll, Phyllis, ed. *The Oxford Companion to the Theatre.* 3rd ed. London: Oxford Univ. Press, 1967.
Ottemiller's Index to Plays in Collections. 6th ed. rev. by John M. Connor and Billie M. Connor. Metuchen, N. J.: Scarecrow, 1976.
Play Index. 3 vols. New York: H. W. Wilson, 1953 – 1968.

Education

Current Index to Journals in Education. New York: Macmillan, 1969 – date.
Education Index. New York: H. W. Wilson, 1929 – date.
Good, Carter V., ed. *Dictionary of Education.* 3rd ed. New York: McGraw-Hill, 1973.
Monroe, Paul, ed. *A Cyclopedia of Education.* 5 vols. New York: Macmillan, 1911 – 1913.
UNESCO. *World Survey of Education.* 5 vols. Paris: UNESCO, 1955 – 1971.

Film

Bawden, Liz-Anne, ed. *The Oxford Companion to Film.* London: Oxford Univ. Press, 1976.
Film Literature Index. Albany, N.Y.: Filmdex, Inc., 1974 – date.
Halliwell, Leslie. *The Filmgoer's Companion.* 4th ed. New York: Avon, 1975.
Manvell, Roger, ed. *International Encyclopedia of the Film.* New York: Crown, 1972.

History

Adams, James Truslow. *Dictionary of American History.* 2nd rev. ed. 6 vols. and Index. New York: Scribner's, 1942 – 1963.
Bibliography of British History. 3 vols. Oxford: Clarendon Press, 1928 – 1970.

Boehm, Eric H., and Lalit Adolphus. *Historical Periodicals*. Santa Barbara, Calif.: Clio Press, 1961.

The Cambridge Ancient History. 12 vols. Cambridge: Cambridge Univ. Press, 1923–1939. 3rd ed. 1970–1973.

The Cambridge Medieval History. 8 vols. New York: Macmillan, 1911–1936.

The Cambridge Modern History. 13 vols. Cambridge: Cambridge Univ. Press, 1902–1926.

Freidel, Frank, ed. *Harvard Guide to American History*. Rev. ed. 2 vols. Cambridge, Mass.: Belknap Press of Harvard Univ. Press, 1974.

The New Cambridge Modern History. 13 vols. Cambridge: Cambridge Univ. Press, 1957–1970.

Literature

Baker, Ernest A. *The History of the English Novel*. 10 vols. 1924–1939. Rpt. New York: Barnes & Noble, 1960–1961. Vol. 11, Lionel Stevenson. *Yesterday and After,* 1967.

Bateson, F. W., ed. *The Cambridge Bibliography of English Literature*. 5 vols. New York: Macmillan, 1941–1957.

Baugh, Albert C., ed. et al. *A Literary History of England*. 2nd ed. New York: Appleton, 1967.

Cook, Dorothy E., and Isabel S. Monro. *Short Story Index*. New York: H. W. Wilson, 1953. Supplements to 1976.

Garland, Henry, and Mary Garland, eds. *The Oxford Companion to German Literature*. Oxford: Oxford Univ. Press, 1976.

Granger's Index to Poetry. 6th ed. New York: Columbia Univ. Press, 1973.

Hart, James D. *The Oxford Companion to American Literature*. 4th ed. New York: Oxford Univ. Press, 1965.

Harvey, Sir Paul. *The Oxford Companion to English Literature*. 4th ed. Rev. by Dorothy Eagle. Oxford: Clarendon Press, 1967.

———, and Janet E. Heseltine. *The Oxford Companion to Classical Literature*. Oxford: Clarendon Press, 1937.

———, and Janet E. Heseltine. *The Oxford Companion to French Literature*. Oxford: Clarendon Press, 1959.

Holman, C. Hugh. *A Handbook to Literature*. 3rd ed. (Based on original by William F. Thrall and Addison Hibbard.) Indianapolis: Odyssey, 1972.

Hornstein, Lillian H., ed. *Reader's Companion to World Literature*. Rev. ed. New York: New American Library, 1973.

Kunitz, Stanley J., and Howard Haycraft. *American Authors, 1600–1900*. New York: H. W. Wilson, 1938.

The New Cambridge Bibliography of English Literature. 4 vols. Cambridge: Cambridge Univ. Press, 1967–1974.

Spiller, Robert E., et al. *Literary History of the United States*. 4th ed. 2 vols. New York: Macmillan, 1974.

Music

Apel, Willi. *Harvard Dictionary of Music*. 2nd rev. ed. Cambridge, Mass.: Harvard Univ. Press, 1969.

Grove, Sir George. *Dictionary of Music and Musicians*. Ed. Eric Blom. 5th ed. 9 vols. New York: St. Martin's, 1955. Supplement, 1961.

Oxford History of Music. 2nd ed. 8 vols. London: Oxford Univ. Press, 1929–1938.

New Oxford History of Music. 10 vols. London: Oxford Univ. Press, 1954–1974.

Thompson, Oscar. *The International Cyclopedia of Music and Musicians*. Ed. Bruce Bohle. 10th ed. New York: Dodd, Mead, 1975.

Philosophy

Baldwin, James Mark. *Dictionary of Philosophy and Psychology*. 4 vols. Rpt. Gloucester, Mass.: Peter Smith, 1960.

Encyclopedia of Philosophy. Ed. Paul Edwards. 4 vols. New York: Macmillan, 1973.

Political Science

International Political Science Abstracts. Oxford: Blackwell, 1951–date.

Laqueur, Walter, ed. *A Dictionary of Politics*. Rev. ed. New York: Free Press, 1974.

Plano, Jack C., and Milton Greenberg. *The American Political Dictionary*. 4th ed. New York: Praeger, 1976.

Psychology

Baldwin, James Mark. (See *Philosophy*.)

English, Horace B., and Ava C. English. *A Comprehensive Dictionary of Psychological and Psychoanalytical Terms*. New York: Longmans, 1958.

Grinstein, Alexander. *The Index of Psychoanalytic Writings*. 5 vols. New York: International Universities Press, 1956–1960. Supplements, 1964–1975.

Religion

Encyclopedia of Religion and Ethics. Ed. James Hastings. 2nd ed. 12 vols. New York: Scribner's, 1908–1927.

Hastings, James. *Dictionary of the Bible*. Rev. ed. F. C. Grant and H. H. Rowley. New York: Scribner's, 1963.

Index to Religious Periodical Literature. Chicago: American Theological Library Assn., 1954–date.

The Interpreter's Dictionary of the Bible. 5 vols. New York: Abingdon, 1972.

The Jerome Biblical Commentary. Comp. Raymond E. Brown, et al. Englewood Cliffs, N.J.: Prentice-Hall, 1969.

New Catholic Encyclopedia. 5 vols. New York: McGraw-Hill, 1967. Supplement, 1974.

The Oxford Dictionary of the Christian Church. Ed. F. L. Cross and E. A. Livingstone. 2nd ed. London: Oxford Univ. Press, 1974.

Peake's Commentary on the Bible. Ed. Matthew Black and H. H. Rowley. London: Nelson, 1962.

Universal Jewish Encyclopedia and Readers' Guide. Ed. Isaac Landman. 10 vols. New York: Ktav, 1939–1944.

Science

Applied Science and Technology Index. New York: H. W. Wilson, 1913–date. (Before 1958, see *Industrial Arts Index.*)

Clark, Randolph, and Russell W. Cumley, eds. *Book of Health.* 3rd ed. Cincinnati: Van Nostrand, 1973.

Jenkins, Frances B. *Science Reference Sources.* 5th ed. Cambridge, Mass.: M.I.T. Press, 1969.

McGraw-Hill Encyclopedia of Science and Technology. 3rd ed. 15 vols. New York: McGraw-Hill, 1971.

Van Nostrand's Scientific Encyclopedia. 5th ed. Cincinnati: Van Nostrand, 1976.

The Way Things Work: An Encyclopedia of Modern Technology. 2 vols. New York: Simon & Schuster, 1967 and 1971.

The Way Things Work Book of the Computer: An Illustrated Encyclopedia of Information Science, Cybernetics & Data Processing. New York: Simon & Schuster, 1974.

Social Sciences

American Indian Index. Chicago: J. A. Huebner, 1953–1968.

Biennial Review of Anthropology. Ed. Bernard J. Siegel. Stanford, Calif.: Stanford Univ. Press, 1959–1971.

Black Information Index. Herndon, Va.: Infonetics, 1970–date.

Encyclopedia of the Social Sciences. Ed. Edwin R. A. Seligman and Alvin Johnson. 15 vols. New York: Macmillan, 1930–1935.

Hoselitz, Bert F., ed. *A Reader's Guide to the Social Sciences.* Rev. ed. New York: Free Press, 1972.

Hoult, Thomas F. *Dictionary of Modern Sociology.* Totowa, N.J.: Littlefield, Adams, 1969.

International Encyclopedia of the Social Sciences. Ed. David L. Sills. 17 vols. New York: Macmillan, 1968.

McConaughy, John B., and Hazel Blanks. *A Students' Guide to United Nations Documents and Their Use.* New York: Council on International Relations and United Nations Affairs, 1969.

Miller, Elizabeth W. *The Negro in America: A Bibliography.* 2nd ed. Rev. by Mary L. Fisher. Cambridge: Harvard Univ. Press, 1970.

Terrell, John Upton. *American Indian Almanac.* New York: World, 1971.

12 The Literary Paper

What Is a Literary Paper?

A literary paper may be written on a single work (a play, short story, novel, or poem) or on several related ones. If you write on several works, they will probably have something in common—for example, all written by the same person or published in the same period. They may express similar themes or belong to a certain class of literature such as science fiction, nature poems, or antiwar plays.

Ordinarily, the point you make in the literary paper (the thesis you support) is made about the work itself rather than about the author, his historical period, the genre (the class or type of work), the literary background, or yourself. While these may be brought within the broad area of your subject, they are usually not emphasized in a purely literary paper. Of course, with your instructor's approval and assistance, and by working carefully from a thesis, you could write on one or a combination of these. Papers concentrating on author, period, genre, and background customarily require secondary sources and are therefore literary research papers, which may be outside the scope of your course or take more work than you are prepared to do. However, when assigned, the literary research paper often proves to be a stimulating and worthwhile project.

PRACTICE

Read the following literary paper, and prepare the questions at the end for class discussion.

"The Bride Comes to Yellow Sky" Is a Comedy

[1]Most of our class discussion of Stephen Crane's "The Bride Comes to Yellow Sky" centered on its allegorical meaning. Several students believed that the story is full of symbols showing a conflict between the values of America's West and East, the Eastern values being evil and treacherous. It seems to me that this interpretation takes the story far too

seriously. It also ignores the basic qualities and occurrences in the story, all of which point not to deep, serious meaning but to light comedy.

²The plot of "The Bride" is, in construction, like those of other Crane stories we have read, "The Blue Hotel" and "The Open Boat." It is carefully divided into dramatic scenes, and it could easily be staged as a play. The first scene presents the town marshal of Yellow Sky, Jack Potter, and his bride as they sit in the train waiting for its arrival at the marshal's town, Yellow Sky. They are honest and simple persons, not young, but too inexperienced to play the part of newlyweds without great awkwardness.

³The second scene is a partial flashback; it begins in time at the same moment as the first scene and its function is exposition: the men in the Weary Gentleman Saloon tell a drummer from out of town about the ancient gunman Scratchy Wilson, who is a superb shot but harmless except when he is drinking. "When he's sober," explains the barkeeper, "he's all right—kind of simple—wouldn't hurt a fly—nicest fellow in town. But when he's drunk—whoo!" Scratchy intends to shoot up the town, and the barkeeper boards up his place to ride out the storm.

⁴Crane shows us Scratchy for the first time in the third scene. The old gunman, drunk and blazing away with two six-shooters at various targets, including the saloon, is looking for a fight but cannot find one. He remembers his old enemy, the marshal, and staggers away to the marshal's house, where he yells for Potter to come out. In the fourth and last scene, the paths of the two men meet as Potter and his bride round the corner heading for their new home and come upon Scratchy loading one of his pistols. The gunman waves his weapon angrily at them until Potter introduces his new wife. At the sight of the two together and at the knowledge of their marriage, Scratchy's rage is gone, and he walks sorrowfully away dragging his feet. The comedy is ended.

⁵It is true that the language (in particular, Crane's metaphor and imagery) appears to be serious and symbolic, as it is in his other stories. When they first see Scratchy, Potter and his wife are afraid: "Potter's mouth seemed to be merely a grave for his tongue. . . . As for the bride, her face had gone as yellow as old cloth. She was a slave to hideous rites, gazing at the apparitional snake." In Crane's description of the couple's reaction to the Pullman, he employs one of his most significant images: "He pointed out to her the dazzling fittings of the coach; and in truth her eyes opened wider as she contemplated the sea-green figured velvet, the shining brass, silver, and glass, the wood that gleamed as darkly brilliant as the surface of a pool of oil."

⁶However, Crane's customary dramatic, ironic, and poetic techniques in this story are generally either overridden by comic effects or shaped for the ends of comedy. The marshal and his bride are more than faintly ludicrous on the train. The fear of the men in the saloon is comic, as is the sudden deflation of the bragging drummer who, after ducking behind the bar, has "balm . . . laid upon his soul at sight of various zinc and copper fittings that bore a resemblance to armor plate." Scratchy is

made out to be a holy terror, but his actions and appearance imply otherwise. He accurately and purposefully shoots in front of a dog instead of at it, and his major targets consist of pieces of paper and adobe walls. Dressed like a child's idea of a cowboy, in a maroon shirt and red-topped boots "of the kind beloved in winter by little sledding boys on the hillsides of New England," the old gunman is obviously a comic figure playing a childishly attractive game. Even when he faces Potter and his bride, Scratchy avoids shooting him; he merely talks about it, and although Potter is doubtful of his antagonist's harmlessness, the reader is convinced that the marshal is safe.

7Throughout "The Bride" Crane uses comic devices with great sureness. There is tongue-in-cheek understatement in his catalogue of the men drinking in the saloon: "One was a drummer who talked a great deal and rapidly; three were Texans who did not care to talk at that time; and two were Mexican sheep-herders, who did not talk as a general practice in the Weary Gentleman Saloon." Crane's favorite device is comic overstatement. The marshal's marriage is called an "extraordinary crime" that was "an important thing to his town. It could only be exceeded by the burning of the new hotel." Scratchy's drunken bellowing is called the "chanting [of] Apache scalp-music." In describing the actions of his characters, Crane uses echoes of and allusions to the epic to attain comic overstatement. The barkeeper becomes "the man of bottles." Jack Potter is not merely Scratchy's enemy; he is "his ancient antagonist." And when no one answers his challenges, Scratchy addresses the universe and calls "to the sky" like a hero out of Homer.

8Occasionally Crane employs a sort of visual comedy that is close to slapstick. The marshal and his wife in the Pullman are little better than two hayseeds, the butt of joking throughout the car. They are terribly embarrassed and self-conscious. The black porter looks down on and bullies them, laughing at them as they leave the train. Potter's trying to tip the porter without drawing attention to himself is perfectly constructed rustic slapstick comedy: "Potter fumbled out a coin and gave it to the porter, as he had seen others do. It was a heavy and muscle-bound business, as that of a man shoeing his first horse."

9All of these devices and scenes either anticipate or support the comedy of the confrontation of the "ancient antagonists" who have been involved in a burlesque of the Western feud. Holding a gun on the brave marshal, who is afraid to face the town when it finds out about his marriage, and who has just been caught skulking around back streets trying to get home without being seen, Scratchy works himself into a rage that disappears like a pricked bubble when the bride is mentioned. "No!" he says. And then in a splendid anticlimax he asks: "Is this the lady?"

10The feud that Scratchy has enjoyed so much is over. "I s'pose it's all off now," he says, and like a child who has lost something forever he walks away dragging his feet, making "funnel-shaped tracks in the heavy sand." But "The Bride Comes to Yellow Sky" is a comedy that implies a happy ending. Surely the marshal and his bride will live happily ever after; Scratchy Wilson, now that the object of his feuding attentions is no longer available, will undoubtedly reform and get religion; and even the dreadful wedding reception by the town that Potter was so frightened of will probably turn out to be no worse than an ice cream social at the Baptist Church.

a. What is the thesis of this paper?

b. Does the writer himself appear in the paper? Where and why?

c. What does the reader know *before* he starts reading the body of the paper?

d. How much plot summary does the paper contain? Where does the summary start and stop? (See p. 279 for a definition of *plot*.)

e. Why is some plot summary necessary in many literary papers? Can you give a rule of thumb about how much summary might be necessary in the "average" paper?

f. Analyze carefully the sixth paragraph. How does each of its sentences support the thesis stated in the topic sentence?

g. Write down the thesis of each paragraph. What does this list tell you about the writer's organization of the paper? Is there any paragraph that should have been left out?

h. What is the purpose of the final paragraph?

i. Why does the writer use so many quotations?

j. Explain the *form* of the quotations in the two sentences below. How are the quotations fitted into the sentences? (Before answering, you may want to read the discussion of quoting and paraphrasing, pp. 238–241.)

    a. The fear of the men in the saloon is comic, as is the sudden deflation of the bragging drummer who, after ducking behind the bar, has "balm . . . laid upon his soul at sight of various zinc and copper fittings that bore a resemblance to armor plate."

    b. Scratchy's drunken bellowing is called the "chanting [of] Apache scalp-music."

k. Explain the use of verb tenses in the sixth paragraph.

l. Does the writer make any general statements about Crane's story that leave you puzzled or unsatisfied?

m. The literary paper is a form of argumentation. In what ways is this paper an argument? Are you convinced by it? Why or why not?

Reading and Understanding the Literary Work

After reading the paper on "The Bride Comes to Yellow Sky" and learning something about the nature of literary papers, you should know a few things about literary works themselves.* A literary work of any merit says something significant and says it in a significant way. As you read a work, look for this "something" and "way" — the *content* and the *form* that, properly interrelated, create a work of literature.

Over the years, readers and critics have developed a set of terms that they use to help them read and understand the work. As you read this chapter, refer to the following Glossary, which explains only those terms that you will use most often when you analyze a work.

Brief Glossary of Literary Terms

Allusion — an indirect reference to a person, thing, idea, or action outside the literary work. For example, the title of John Steinbeck's novel *Of Mice and Men* is an allusion to Robert Burns' lines in his poem "To a Mouse":

> The best laid schemes o' mice and men
> Gang aft a-gley;
> An' lea'e us nought but grief and pain,
> For promis'd joy.

Character — a person in a story, poem, or play.

Characterization — the technique of making a fictional person seem "real." Characterization is created by (1) the actions of the person; (2) the person's comments about himself; (3) comments on the person by other characters; (4) authorial comments.

Climax — the major "high point" near the end of the *plot*, in which the *conflict* is usually resolved.

Conflict — a struggle between people or forces in a story. (Without conflict, there is no story.) Typical conflicts can be between two peo-

*Of necessity, our discussion in this chapter concerning literary forms and devices is brief and limited. For more detailed information on these subjects, see a text like Bernard Cohen's *Writing About Literature*, Revised Edition, Scott, Foresman, 1973, or Edgar Roberts' *Writing Themes About Literature*, 4th Edition, Prentice-Hall, 1973.

ple; between a person and his society or his environment (man against "machine," for example, or man against "nature"); between man and God (or the fates); between man and himself.

Exposition—that part of a story that introduces the characters, the setting, and (usually) the conflict. Exposition gives the background details necessary to the plot.

Image—a description, often poetic, which appeals powerfully to the physical senses. Example (from Tennyson's poem "The Eagle"): "The wrinkled sea beneath him crawls."

Irony—a literary device that expresses a discrepancy between appearance and reality. *Verbal irony* says one thing but means another. *Irony of situation* expresses an incongruity between what happens on the surface of a situation and what is actually taking place.

Narrative—a literary work or mode that describes an incident (or a series of closely related incidents), usually in chronological order.

Plot—the whole "story" of a play, novel, poem, or short story. *Plot* includes *exposition, conflict,* and *climax.*

Point of view—the angle from which the author presents a story. Point of view can be *omniscient* (all-knowing), *limited omniscient, first-person,* or *objective.*

Satire—a form of literary argument or attack that ridicules persons, ideas, or institutions in a scornful, ironic, and usually witty fashion.

Structure—the total form of a work. A literary structure is created by the interrelationship among devices such as plot, point of view, imagery, symbol, statement, and theme.

Symbol—a literary device which acts as itself while suggesting another thing (or many things). The American flag, for instance, can *symbolize* many different attitudes and ideas to different people.

Theme—the main point, idea, or statement of a literary work.

With the help of the terms in the Glossary, we will discuss two short poems that belong to different literary classes. The first poem can be called a *narrative*—it presents a dramatic scene and indirectly tells a story. The second one (p. 282) is *non-narrative*—it expresses the mood and thought of the poet rather than presenting an incident or a series of incidents.

THE NARRATIVE WORK

How Annandale Went Out

"They called it Annandale — and I was there
To flourish, to find works, and to attend:
Liar, physician, hypocrite, and friend,
I watched him; and the sight was not so fair
5   As one or two that I have seen elsewhere:
An apparatus not for me to mend —
A wreck, with hell between him and the end,
Remained of Annandale; and I was there.

"I knew the ruin as I knew the man;
10 So put the two together, if you can,
Remembering the worst you know of me.
Now view yourself as I was, on the spot —
With a slight kind of engine. Do you see?
Like this . . . You wouldn't hang me? I thought not."
　　　　　　　　— Edwin Arlington Robinson

"Wow," said a student after he read the poem. "What is *that* about?"

It's simpler than it looks on a first reading, we told him. Many works (poems in particular) have to be read more than once for their meanings to become clear.

You should carefully read the poem several times (at least once out loud), and look for clues. Note these elements: the title (what does it mean?); the fact that it is a speech; the two-part structure; the rhyme scheme; any significant or unusual wording (like *engine*, or *apparatus* for "man"). After we have inspected these and looked up *engine* in the dictionary, we are ready to analyze the poem.

In the poem a man is speaking, without interruption, to the police — or perhaps to other representatives of the law. He is telling them how Annandale died. He was Annandale's friend and doctor and was with him in his last moments. But the doctor makes a startling confession, particularly startling for a physician. He used an "engine," which our dictionary says can be "any mechanical appliance, instrument or tool," to kill Annandale. Perhaps the instrument was a scalpel (he apparently holds it up for the police to see) that he used to put Annandale out of his misery. "Surely you would not punish me for doing such a thing, would you?" asks the doctor. The answer seems to be negative, and you believe the doctor will go free.

Baldly stated, that is the "plot" of the poem. Yet Robinson has the doctor say so much more than this brief summary implies. Annandale, it would appear, is not just a dying man; there is something different about him. He is a "ruin"; the sign of him is not "fair"; he is a "wreck, with hell between him and the end." He is not even a human being any more—"They called *it* Annandale" who is "an *apparatus* not for me to mend." And what of the doctor, who is, we can guess, the only one left to attend Annandale? He calls himself a "liar" and a "hypocrite," one who can make the proper noises (and "flourishes") at the death of a friend. His listeners in the poem know that he has a bad reputation ("Remembering the *worst* you know of me").

The poem tells us in a fairly direct way that what might be called "a mercy killing" was performed by a physician capable of evil. But the poem indirectly tells us a different story. Annandale may be no better than the doctor. Most of the words that describe him have moral as well as physical connotations; we can guess that he is both a moral and a physical "wreck" and that his death is not one to weep over. Besides, what sort of man would have *this* doctor, who confesses that he is a liar and hypocrite, for a friend? And for a friend, the doctor is strangely objective, even coolly ironic: the dying Annandale was a "sight . . . not so fair / As one or two that I have seen elsewhere." Do not these men deserve each other?

The point or theme of this small dramatic poem is ambiguous. As a drama showing people in action, it tells us something about human beings. In the poem, a man who is no better than he should be, alone with a dying friend of similar character who is suffering greatly, takes the risk of committing a mercy killing. Yet there are hints that the dying man deserved to die for other reasons (the listeners do not seem to mind much that he was killed), and there is in the killing as much a feeling of retribution as mercy. Moreover, the doctor has no intention of paying for his crime: "You wouldn't hang me? I thought not." So the theme is a mixed one, a comment on the ambiguousness of friendship and retribution, and on the character of the speaker himself, who contains terrible moral opposites. The poem implies that a human being, like this physician, can be both good and evil and can balance such opposite characteristics with surprising grace and irony.

How is the story of the poem formed and shaped? First, and most obviously, it is a speech; technically speaking, a dramatic monologue. A man talks, revealing himself to others who themselves do not speak but who react "between the lines":

"Do you see? [*reaction*]
Like this . . . You wouldn't hang me? [*reaction*] I thought not."

The poet also shapes his story by putting it into the traditional pattern of the Italian sonnet, which is customarily made of two stanzas, the first asking a question or stating a problem, and the second answering the question or solving the problem. Robinson's poem uses a typical rhyme scheme for stanza one (*abbaabba*), but a somewhat unusual one for stanza two (*ccdede*). The complete structure (organization) of the story, then, is shaped by two basic elements: the dramatic monologue arranged into the pattern of the Italian sonnet.

It is typical of most literary works that, while the author wrote or created them, he is not necessarily in them. Edwin Arlington Robinson is neither the physician nor Annandale; and neither of them, so far as we can tell in this poem, speaks for the poet. We can infer, if we like, that the view of human beings implied in the poem (in its theme) is also Robinson's view; but we cannot infer that opinion directly from the poem. What Robinson "says" is the poem itself, there on the page. For what he believes about the Annandales of the world and their doctors we would have to turn to biographical materials. A literary work can tell us only so much.

How successful is "How Annandale Went Out"? Observe that we don't ask: "Do we like this poem?" A work can be successful but not very likable, or likable but not particularly successful. Our main interest is expressed in the questions: "In this literary work, did the author succeed in what he intended to do? If so, why? If he didn't, why not?"

We believe that it is successful. Robinson took a difficult, ambiguous narrative theme and shaped it carefully and dramatically, using two literary forms, the dramatic monologue and the sonnet. Form and content seem to work naturally together, without any feeling of strain. Ultimately, we *believe* in the poem. We believe that these men and their situation can exist, in all their moral ambiguity and dramatic irony.

THE NON-NARRATIVE WORK

Robinson's poem presents a short, dramatic scene that indirectly tells a story. Some literary works do not narrate stories as such, but are more concerned with the expression of certain emotions, attitudes, ideas, or philosophical positions. (Of course, many works both tell a story and deal with such abstractions.) The following poem, by Robert Frost, is an example of such a work. Read it several times and then examine the analysis of it written by a student.

Nothing Gold Can Stay

Nature's first green is gold,
Her hardest hue to hold.
Her early leaf's a flower;
But only so an hour.
5   Then leaf subsides to leaf.
So Eden sank to grief,
So dawn goes down to day.
Nothing gold can stay.

—Robert Frost

The Loss of "Gold"

¹When I read Robert Frost's "Nothing Gold Can Stay" for the first time, it seemed meaningless to me. Then I examined its structure, trying to see whether in Frost's development of his poem I could find hints of its theme. I noticed that the poet used a series of four couplets, *aa bb cc dd.* Each of the first two couplets presents its own completed idea regarding a condition of nature. Line 5 presents a conclusion to the ideas in the first two couplets, while lines 6 and 7 present analogies derived from the previous couplets. Line 8 is the conclusion to the whole poem. Examining the poem in this way, I concluded that the poet is concerned not only with spring but also with a universal truth about human life.

²The first line of the poem opens with a description of spring that forces the reader to think. The statement that "green is gold" is puzzling, but when one visualizes the very beginning of spring, one realizes that the green of the leaves is indeed touched with gold. Upon further consideration of the word *gold,* however, it becomes apparent that the poet means to present more than a colorful description. Gold is precious and so is early spring. The second line introduces the impermanence of spring—this "gold" is hard to keep. The line also brings out the essential intangibility of this "gold" quality—it is the "hardest hue to hold."

³The qualities presented by the nature metaphor are expanded in the third line. A leaf is not a flower, but a flower and a leaf have common characteristics: both are beautiful, both are delicate, and, particularly with a very young leaf, both are fragrant. The fourth line returns to the note of sadness, but more strongly this time. The flowerlike quality of the leaf only lasts "an hour."

⁴The spring metaphor is completed in line 5. The flowerlike, "gold" leaf, becomes an ordinary leaf. The idea of loss is emphasized by the poet's word choice: the leaf doesn't just *become* an ordinary leaf, it "subsides to" one.

⁵Lines 6 and 7 introduce new metaphors. The poet states that the quality lost by the leaf is like the innocence lost by man when he left Eden. The essential "flowerlike" quality of Eden was its simplicity and happiness. Eden "sank to grief," though, and the result is the modern world. So the metaphor has been generalized to include mankind, not just nature. The metaphor in line 7 compares the loss of the leaf's innocence to the loss of dawn in becoming day. Literally, dawn is more beautiful, more colorful, more ethereal than day; figuratively, day is a common metaphor for life, and dawn represents youth and innocence. Once more, the transition is a loss, a degeneration—dawn "goes down to day."

⁶The final line of the poem harks back to the first and expresses the theme that runs throughout the poem. The line is apparently nonsense: the color of an object cannot affect its durability. By now, however, "gold" has taken on many symbolic meanings in the poem: it is the beauty of spring, the glory of dawn, the innocence of youth. It is to the abstract ideas in the poem that the last line applies. The intangibles of life such as

beauty and innocence are precious (like gold), but they are fleeting; spring, dawn, and youth cannot "stay," but are lost with the passing of time.

[7]The poet has accomplished his purpose. The apparent incongruities of the poem have forced the reader to look at it more carefully and discover its broader meaning, rather than merely passing it off as a prettily worded description of spring.

QUESTIONS TO ASK ABOUT A WORK

To help you understand a literary work, read it carefully with certain questions in mind. (And remember to refer to the Glossary on pp. 278–279.)

1. What *happens* in the work?

If it is a story, who are the *characters*? What motivates them? (Why do they act as they do?) What is the *plot*? The events of the plot usually progress through a series of *conflicts* until a high point (the *climax* of the plot) is reached, in which the conflicts are resolved. There may be only one major conflict, or there may be several, with one usually predominating. A conflict can be physical or psychological, or both. In most stories, the climax does not come right at the end; time and space are needed at the conclusion to "tie up the loose threads" of the story.

Many literary works (poems, in particular) make statements rather than tell stories. Frost's "Nothing Gold Can Stay" is an example.

2. How is the work organized? What is its *structure*?

What gives it shape or form? If it is a story in the form of a play, does it have acts, and divisions and scenes within the acts? If it is a story, who tells it? (Some long stories are told by different persons, each giving his idea of the action and his views of the other characters.) If it is a poem, are meter and rhyme used to give it shape? Is there a stanzaic pattern? What special symbols, images, ideas, arrangements, or plot devices can help organize the work? A poem can ask a question, and then answer it. A short story can be filled with images of a particular color that symbolize certain attitudes or beliefs. A novel can refer time and again to an idea (like freedom, for instance). Stories within a story can be arranged, as in Chaucer's *Canterbury Tales*. Many works have several organizational devices that work together in a complicated fashion. In *The Scarlet Letter* Nathaniel Hawthorne organizes his story in several ways, chief among them the use of the three important scaffold scenes and the symbol of adultery (the scarlet A) that Hester Prynne is forced to wear on her bosom.

All of the elements that go to organize or shape a work create its structure, its total framework. A successful work tends to have its own, unique structure.

3. What does the work *say?*

What is its *theme* (its main point)? Authors tend to state their themes somewhat indirectly through symbol, imagery, allusion, action, characterization, irony, or satire. A symbol like Hester's scarlet *A* may tell the reader much about a work's theme. The important thing about this particular symbol, for instance, is not merely that Hester is forced to wear it because she committed adultery, but that it becomes for *her* a symbol of her rich, defiant nature. She decorates and embroiders it, and wears it proudly. To take another instance, through characterization Crane indirectly creates his comic theme in "The Bride Comes to Yellow Sky" (see pp. 274–277). Scratchy, the old gunman, wears clothes that little boys love to wear while at play, and when the feud he enjoyed so much is over, he walks away like a little boy, dragging his feet.

So, as you read, watch for the author's indirect statements that help you interpret the meaning of the work. For example, the title "How Annandale Went Out" probably contains an allusion to Macbeth's lines on the meaninglessness of life that begin: "Out, out, brief candle. . . . it [life] is a tale / Told by an idiot, full of sound and fury, / Signifying nothing." Is it possible that Annandale's doctor is telling his listeners, with bitter irony, that the momentous events he recounted really meant nothing after all, that human life means nothing?

Themes are often expressed through the indirection of irony. In an ironic statement, the doctor says that the sight of Annandale "was not so fair" as others he had seen. What he means is that the sight of Annandale was horrible, although it does not seem to fill him with horror, a fact which contributes to the poem's theme. In an ironic situation, events point two ways (appearance vs. reality): a beautiful girl graduates from college with high honors and with a shining future—but she is killed in a freak accident as she drives to her first job. It is an irony of *situation* that Annandale's doctor, who should be a saver of lives, deliberately takes one.

Satire is irony sharpened, pointed, and (usually) directed at people or ideas the author believes need reform or scornful instruction. The TV show *All in the Family* is partly a satire on bigotry and on a particular bigot, Archie Bunker. One may consider it an irony of situation that Archie is occasionally quite lovable, but this fact merely reflects the truth that a successful work in any medium seldom presents an issue that is totally black or white. The better the work, as a matter of fact, the more complex its theme appears to the reader. But the reverse is not necessarily true; a complex work is not always well-made or convincing. Perhaps the best literary complexity tends to mirror the real complexities of human life, rather than those of the author.

4. Where is the *author* in the work?

What is his *point of view*? If the work is fiction, from what angle does he present his story? Is he *omniscient* (all-knowing), able to present all the actions and speech of his characters, as well as their thoughts and feelings? Does he use the *limited omniscient* point of view, in which he mainly sticks to one character and sees events through his eyes? Does he employ the *first-person* viewpoint? Does he present events as they happen but without comment, as if they were simply crossing his range of vision? This kind of perspective, called the *objective* point of view, is most often used in plays but it also can be found in novels, short stories, and poems. Robinson's point of view in "How Annandale Went Out" is objective.

In nonfictional works, authors may take a variety of viewpoints or "positions," which often combine the physical and psychological. To describe a city, a poet may imagine himself on a hill, a point of view that will color and shape his statements about the city. In Tennyson's line, "The wrinkled sea beneath him crawls," the poet's point of view is physically the same as the eagle's; and that is why *wrinkled* and *crawls* seem so effective as images. The possible roles and viewpoints the poet, dramatist, or story writer may adopt are so many that you should consider each work as unique, and describe carefully the point of view of the author in that particular work.

5. Finally, how *successful* is the work?

Does the author accomplish what he set out to do? Why or why not?

Writing the Literary Paper

When your instructor asks you to write on a poem, play, novel, or short story, his assignment may well be related to one or more of these elements of literary study:

Element	Possible Assignment
1. *Character*	What is the cause of Hamlet's madness? (Not only is this a question of character analysis, but as the question is stated it also implies a cause-and-effect strategy of development.)
2. *Theme*	Defend or attack Golding's view of society in *Lord of the Flies*.

3. *Setting*	How does the setting of Conrad's *Heart of Darkness* influence the action?
4. *Structure*	Discuss how the two climaxes of Fitzgerald's *The Great Gatsby* support the novel's theme.
5. *Imagery*	Explain Frost's use of imagery in "The Road Not Taken."
6. *Symbolism*	What are the fertility symbols in Faulkner's *Light in August?* In what ways are the symbols used? How are they related to the theme?
7. *Style*	Defend the "repetitiousness" of stylistic patterns in Hemingway's *A Farewell to Arms.*
8. *Genre*	What is "The Bride Comes to Yellow Sky"? Is it a tragedy, a tragicomedy, a comedy? Give reasons for your answer.
9. *Point of View*	Is Leggett a reliable narrator in Conrad's *The Secret Sharer?* Does it make any difference whether he is or isn't?

Assignments on literary topics may implicitly or explicitly ask you to use some of the seven strategies of development. Here are some examples:

1. *Comparison-Contrast*	How are the characters Carol and Vida alike and different in Sinclair Lewis' *Main Street?*
2. *Definition*	Define Albert Camus' existentialist position (as presented through Meursault) in *The Stranger.*
3. *Cause and Effect*	What are the causes of Willy Loman's tragic end in Arthur Miller's *Death of a Salesman?*
4. *Classification*	What different uses does Poe make of sound in "The Raven"?

THE ASSIGNMENT

Themes and longer papers about literature usually fall into two types: those for which your instructor gives you the assignment, and those for which you create your own topic. In either case, you will find that certain techniques for responding to an assignment will be useful.

Let's assume, for a moment, that your assignment says no more than "Write on a literary work."

First, decide how large your *focus* should be on the work. In a large focus you consider a broad aspect of the whole work — its theme, for instance, and how the author develops and supports it. Or you might focus more narrowly on a smaller aspect — plot, character, style, imagery, or point of view. Even more narrowly, you could focus your paper on a single part of the work: an important scene in a play, a short significant passage in a story, or a grouping of six or eight lines in a poem.

You should then examine the theme, the fundamental meaning that the author is trying to express (mainly by indirection) through characterization, action, description, symbolism, imagery, and so on. You will discover that your own writing on a work will have deepest significance if you relate your discussion to its theme. If you decide to focus narrowly on the climax of a novel, consider relating it to the theme of the work. If you wish to focus on the structure of a work, ask yourself: "Why did the author choose *this* structure over the many others available to him? Does the structure fit well the theme he is trying to convey to his reader?"

These suggestions for broad assignments also apply well to more limited ones, because even though the limited ones will require you to narrow your focus on the work, you still must consider its theme directly or indirectly. It is particularly important to read carefully the assignments using limited topics. You should have a good idea of what your instructor expects. Words in the assignment such as *discuss, explain, analyze, define, compare, classify,* and *describe* give you direct clues to the kind of strategy you should choose before you write the paper. If the assignment begins with *why, how,* or *what* you have a hint that *causation, process,* or *definition* is important in answering the question. As you read, use such clues.

KNOWING THE WORK

You must understand the work thoroughly. *Read it carefully. Know what the work says.* Do not draw conclusions about it unless you can support them with specific evidence from the work. (See the paper on "The Bride Comes to Yellow Sky" for examples of the use of evidence.)

Take notes on the work as you read. Mark important passages that you can refer to when writing the paper; for instance, those passages that present the theme, show a particular trait of a character, reveal the author's point of view, or exemplify a stylistic device.

Finally, trust your instincts about a work. All literature is about people and written for people. Make use of your experience as you read. Mark passages and descriptions that seem particularly realistic or pertinent to your life and interests.

THE WRITER'S STANCE

The writer's stance for the literary paper is somewhat limited and unusual. In such a paper you should consider the reader as someone who knows the work fairly well. You might sum up your relationship with your reader as follows:

> I have read a work (that you also have read), and I have an idea about it that may have not occurred to you. I am going to explain this idea, giving you examples from the work to prove my point, and I hope when I am through that you will agree with me.

However, you will never state your intention as explicitly as this. Such a stance is essentially an argumentative one, and the literary paper is fundamentally a form of argumentation that depends for its success on a clear, specific thesis and strong proof taken from the work. For example, when you state that the scenes of violence in a novel are contrived and unbelievable, you should be prepared to prove that point, with specific examples from the text. When he finishes reading your paper, your reader should be able to say—"You have not only read the work carefully but have also made a solid, intelligent point about it. And your evidence taken from the work convinces me that you are right."

WHAT TO AVOID IN WRITING
THE LITERARY PAPER

As an interpretation of literature, your paper must be more than a summary of what goes on in the work. A summary of what a poet says (or seems to say) in a poem, of the action in a play, or of the plot of a novel or short story is often necessary to your interpretation and your argument. But such a summary is only the beginning, a foundation on which to build. Unless they specifically request them, instructors will not accept mere summaries as literary papers. Also be aware of the "chronology trap." It is difficult to write a successful paper on fiction by using a chronological strategy of development because it is so easy to fall into plot summary. If the outline of your proposed theme shows its development to be mainly chronological, start over and get a new focus on the work.

Do not push your interpretations of literature too far. It is often tempting, for example, to explain a character's motivation by writing down something that seems obvious to you at the time but is not based solidly on the evidence in the work. Is there, as has been argued, a homosexual relationship between Huck Finn and Jim in Mark Twain's novel? Read the novel with care and see if the *evidence* points to such a relationship. It has been claimed that some of the description at the beginning of "The Bride Comes to Yellow Sky" points to a theme about the conflict between the values of the decadent East and the innocent West:

> The great Pullman was whirling onward with such dignity of motion that a glance from the window seemed simply to prove that the plains of Texas were pouring eastward. Vast flats of green grass, dull-hued spaces of mesquit and cactus, little groups of frame houses, woods of light and tender trees, all were sweeping into the east, sweeping over the horizon, a precipice.

To argue that this descriptive passage implies a conflict of East-West values is probably pushing an interpretation too far.

Do not assume that there is one, fixed, "right" interpretation of a literary work. Professor Arra Garab comments: "Far too many readers labor under the delusion that there is a magical key to a poem or story, and if they could just find this key, the 'real meaning' would suddenly be revealed to them." As a reader, you should try for a *reasonable* interpretation, one that is firmly based on the evidence in the work. And a reasonable interpretation is not just a matter of opinion ("my reading is as good as yours because my opinion is as good as yours"). Any opinion stated about a work must be based on the facts in the work.

Finally, do not suggest in your paper that the literary work represents literal fact. Hawthorne's Hester Prynne, Marvell's Coy Mistress, Shakespeare's Macbeth, Robert Penn Warren's Willie Stark, the people and situations in T. S. Eliot's *The Waste Land*, Big Brother in George Orwell's *1984* — none of these has ever literally existed in the real world. It may be a temptation to write that "Holden Caulfield shows us what American life was like in the 1950s for a sensitive boy who hated hypocrisy." While it is true that Holden, the leading character of J. D. Salinger's *Catcher in the Rye*, may for many readers illuminate life in a way that sociological treatises never can, he and his experiences are not *literally* true. Although one may reasonably argue that great literature is more "real" than real life, that assertion does not make them the same thing.

PRACTICE

1. We would like you to act as a reader for two literary papers written by students. Each can be considered a successful example of student writing, although you (as a reader) might have a few suggestions for the writers. Discussing the paper in class might be a good idea, particularly after you have looked at the questions at the end of each paper.

The first paper was written in response to an informal assignment given by the student's instructor. The student had idly commented in the hall after class that he had just seen the movie *M*A*S*H* and that in some ways it seemed surprisingly different from the TV series. His instructor said: "I've never seen the movie, but I've read the book, which is different from the TV show. For your next assignment, why don't you write your paper on *M*A*S*H*? I'd like to know more about the three versions. And it doesn't have to be a heavily 'literary' paper."

The second paper was written in response to a formal assignment: "In a *brief* paper, analyze Ursula Brangwen's real motives regarding love and marriage in D. H. Lawrence's *Women in Love*. Use specific evidence from the novel to support your answer."

M*A*S*H — Will the Real Swampmen Please Stand Up?

[1] *M*A*S*H,* by Richard Hooker, has had an unusual life for a war novel. The book was made into a very successful movie, which was later turned into a popular TV series. Even though the paperback book has over "1,500,000 copies in print," to most people *M*A*S*H* is not a novel but a TV series that has been adapted from a movie.

[2] After encountering the three versions of the story, set in an American field hospital during the Korean War, I am a little puzzled — not by the success of each of the versions but by their differences. The book, movie, and TV show differ significantly from each other, yet each has been acclaimed by the public, which apparently does not mind (or is not aware) that it is being exposed to three different treatments of the same story.

[3] The novel centers on three Army surgeons (Hawkeye, Duke, and Trapper — the Swampmen). They are not regular army personnel, and they have little use for anybody in the regular army. They live in a hut they call "the Swamp." When they are not in the Swamp they are engaged in one of two activities: operating on wounded soldiers or giving the authorities fits. The book abounds in outrageous comedy: the Swampmen encourage the dentist to commit "suicide" because he believes he is impotent; they beat another service football team through trickery and guile; they talk back to a regular army colonel after he catches them putting golf balls on his office carpet: "You men are under arrest," the colonel boomed, when he stormed onto the scene. "Quiet!" Trapper said. "Can't you see I'm putting?"

[4] Yet the real theme of the novel has little to do with military service or with the endless conflict between draftees and the regular army. Rather the theme is that trained surgeons are dedicated to saving lives, no matter where they are working or under what conditions they are forced to operate. Medicine is not only the Swampmen's profession but their religion as well. The comedy in the book is secondary and often even perfunctory, sometimes barely funny. Hooker's style is flat; he tells every

joke and relates each comic scene in a stylistic monotone. The reader can pass right over a punch line because his comic scenes lack emphasis, energy, and pacing.

⁵But when Hooker (who is himself a doctor) brings the Swampmen face to face with death in their profession, the writing takes on life and passion. Their suffering and concern for their wounded patients are real and moving. Moreover, the descriptions of operations are very vivid:

> Hawkeye donned a pair of gloves, accepted a syringe of Novocain from a corpsman, infiltrated the skin and the space between the ribs and shoved the needle into the pleural cavity. Pulling back on the plunger he got air, knew he was in the right place, noted the angle of the needle, withdrew it, took a scalpel, incised the skin for one-half inch and plunged the scalpel into the pleural cavity. Bubbles of air appeared at the incision. Then he grasped the tip of a Foley catheter with a Kelly clamp and shoved the tube through the hole. A nurse attached the other end to the drainage bottle on the floor, a corpsman blew up the balloon on the catheter and now bubbles began to rise to the surface of the water in the bottle. Hawkeye dropped to his knees on the sand floor and as he began to suck on the rubber tube attached to the shorter of the two tubes in the bottle, the upward flow of bubbles increased as the lung was, indeed, expanding.
>
> "Crude, ain't it?" said Hawkeye.

The reader believes that these men are dedicated doctors, and that the author is basing his description on operations he actually witnessed.

⁶The movie is a different story—*literally*. From the unmotivated fight at the beginning between two soldiers to the last comic scene, the movie concentrates on comedy and burlesque. Scenes not in the book are given great emphasis, and they are wildly funny—the "unveiling" of Hot Lips in the shower, for example, or the still-life parody of the Last Supper at the dentist's "suicide" banquet. The movie is basically a comedy that happens to have a field hospital as a setting. Although the Swampmen are still dedicated doctors, their dedication is deemphasized while their antics and brawls fill up the plot. The book's comedy occurs only outside the operating room, but a great deal of the comedy in the movie occurs during the operations; horrendously, red blood spurts and spatters while the quips fly fast. The medical theme almost disappears under the weight of burlesque.

⁷The kind of medical dedication described in the book is seldom matched in the movie. In the book, Dago Red tells the Swampmen, "But you people in the Swamp have got to get over the idea that you can save everyone who comes into this hospital. Man is mortal. The wounded can stand only so much, and the surgeon can do only so much." It would be ludicrous for Dago Red to say this in the movie because the seriousness of the situation is not emphasized to that great a degree. But statements of this kind are made quite often in the TV version.

⁸The TV series appears to "average" thematically the book and mov-

ie. Certain episodes of the television show focus only on the humor and antics of the doctors while other episodes focus solely on the doctors' dedication to their profession. Like the movie, it sometimes mixes comedy and medicine in the operating room. Like the book, it takes medicine very seriously; the TV Swampmen desperately want to save lives, and they will move mountains to do so. Statements like Dago Red's quoted above are made quite often in the television series.

⁹Why are these versions of *M*A*S*H* different? One answer may be that they were written for different purposes and audiences. The foreword to the novel stresses the surgeons' work and the terrible strain they endure. When Hawkeye, Duke, and Trapper engage in crazy stunts in the book, it is in their spare time—to relieve them from the pressures of their grim life. In the movie, the comedy is its own excuse for being. I understand that when it first came out, people thought *M*A*S*H* was an antiwar movie, but the student audience I saw it with the other night just seemed to think it was hilarious. The TV version takes advantage of both antiwar sentiment and the viewer's simple desire to be amused. Of course the TV shows are much "cleaner" than the other productions; television morality prohibits some of the racier scenes and dialogue that are found in the book and movie.

¹⁰Of the three versions of *M*A*S*H*, I believe that the television version is the most successful and consistent. But I still wonder if war can ever be truly funny.

a. In the first two paragraphs of the paper, the author implies that he will use a particular rhetorical strategy. Does he successfully organize the paper according to this strategy?

b. Is the writer using a large or small focus in discussing the three versions of *M*A*S*H*? Explain.

c. How does the author bring himself into his paper? Describe his writer's stance, using the form: "I am a _____ who _____."

d. What facts or information does the writer assume that the reader already has?

e. How important is the plot summary in discussing the three forms of *M*A*S*H*?

f. In paragraph 3, the writer says that the "book abounds in outrageous comedy." Discuss the evidence used to support this statement. Consider paragraph 4 also. Are there any contradictions between paragraphs 3 and 4?

g. Analyze the long quote in paragraph 5 in relation to the statements in the rest of the paragraph.

h. How does the writer use the promise pattern (see pp. 91–93) in paragraph 6?

i. Does the last line of the paper fit the paper's thesis?

j. Do you consider the paper a success? Why, or why not? (Be specific in your answer.)

Ursula: Dominated or Domineering?

¹Ursula Brangwen, the leading female character in D. H. Lawrence's *Women in Love,* is a fiercely independent, self-possessed woman. She is contemptuous of men and marriage because she believes men try to control and possess her—she thinks marriage represents total submission. Ursula feels so strongly about her freedom that she interprets everything that affects her negatively as being an affront to her right to independence as a woman. She construes the words and actions of those around her in a way that enables her to become self-righteous and to assume the role of the persecuted woman. As Lawrence says of her: "She had a maddening faculty of assuming a light of her own, which exhausted the reality, and within which she looked radiant as if in sunshine."

²When Ursula sees Gerald Crich forcing his horse, a "lovely, sensitive" mare, to stand still at a noisy railway crossing, she criticizes him for it. After Gerald explains his actions, Ursula's fiery response concerning the mistreatment of animals sounds as if she were actually referring to the abuse of women:

"I have to use her," he replied. "And if I'm going to be sure of her at *all,* she'll have to learn to stand noises."

"Why should she?" cried Ursula in a passion. "She is a living creature, why should she stand anything, just because you choose to make her? She has as much right to her own being, as you have to yours."

³Ursula reacts in a similar manner when she sees Mino, Mrs. Birkin's male cat, box his mate with his paws. " 'Mino,' said Ursula, 'I don't like you. You are a bully like all males.' " When Birkin tries to explain the female cat's submission, Ursula says, " 'Oh, it makes me so cross, this assumption of male superiority! And it is such a lie! One wouldn't mind if there were any justification for it.' "

⁴After seeing Ursula become so self-righteous and defensive in these two situations, it is easy to understand how she is able to misinterpret everything Birkin says and does to mean that he wants to control her. For example, when Birkin says, " 'Adam kept Eve in the indestructible paradise when he kept her single with himself, like a star in its orbit,' " Ursula immediately interprets this as an expression of his desire to control a woman. " 'Yes—yes—' cried Ursula, pointing her finger at him. 'There you are—a star in its orbit! A satellite—a satellite of Mars—that's what she is to be!' "

⁵Ursula even takes Birkin's marriage proposal as another effort to make her concede to him. When, in her father's presence, he asks her to marry him, she refuses even to answer him. Finally, she says, " 'Why should I say anything? You do this off your *own* bat, it has nothing to do with me. Why do you both want to bully me?' " Ursula feels elated after she has rejected Birkin and embarrassed her father. She relishes the power she has over both men: "Ursula's face closed, she completed herself against them all. . . . She was bright and invulnerable, quite free

and happy, perfectly liberated in her self-possession."

[6]Ursula continues to believe that Birkin's idea of marriage is her total submission to him. She says at one point to Hermione: " 'I don't want to give the sort of *submission* he insists on. He wants me to give myself up — and I simply don't feel that I *can* do it.' " Actually, Birkin never does expect Ursula to do any such thing. But she continues to deceive herself into believing this for one reason. She wants to control and possess Birkin in the way that she claims he wants to control and possess her. Because she knows he will never submit to her, she continues to believe it is he who wishes to dominate her. Birkin is perfectly justified in thinking that Ursula

> was the awful, arrogant queen of life, as if she were a queen bee on whom all the rest depended. . . . She was only too ready to knock her head on the ground before a man. But this was only when she was so certain of her man, that she could worship him as a woman worships her own infant, with a worship of perfect possession.

[7]Ursula says she could not bear to surrender herself to Birkin. Yet, "She wanted to have him, utterly, finally to have him as her own, oh, so unspeakably, in intimacy. To drink him down — ah, like a life-draught." Because she is unable to do so, she accuses Birkin of doing to her exactly what she wants to do to him. Birkin says, " 'I tell you, you want love to administer to your egoism, to subserve you. Love is a process of subservience with you. . . .' "

[8]Ursula's intense pride and desire for freedom carry her to the point of wanting to control others. When she sees she cannot succeed, she transfers her motives to Birkin and acts on the defensive. Her constant self-righteousness turns out to be a self-serving act. Everything that she says Birkin is trying to do to her, she is actually doing to him!

a. What does the reader need to know in order to understand this paper? Would you, as a reader, recommend a plot summary for it?

b. Why doesn't the writer discuss the theme of *Women in Love*? Would the paper have been improved if she had done so?

c. Prepare a brief outline of the paper. Concentrate on topic ideas and transitions. Are the transitions of a particular kind? Do they help or hinder the reader's understanding of the paper? Describe specifically the organization of the paper. Should the writer have organized her paper in a different way? Why?

d. Discuss the paper as an argument. For example, are you convinced by the evidence presented that Ursula "construes the words and actions of those around her in a way that enables her to become self-righteous and to assume the role of the persecuted woman"?

e. Block quotations are usually not surrounded by quotation marks (see p. 240). Why are there quotation marks in the block quotation in paragraph 2? Discuss the convention of using double and single quotation marks in paragraphs 3, 4, 5, and 6.

f. Why does the writer use *four* periods in the quotation in paragraph 6 to show a deletion? Discuss the use of ellipsis marks (pp. 240–241) at the end of paragraph 7. Why couldn't the writer just end the quote with a period and quotation mark?

g. Does the writer quote "too much"? Give reasons for your answer.

h. In planning their papers, the writers on *M*A*S*H* and *Women in Love* obviously used different focuses. Compare and discuss each focus. Which paper would be easier to write? Why? Is one paper more convincing than the other? Give your reasons.

2. Write a paper in which you apply the principles of critical interpretation and judgment you learned in this chapter to this poem.

Reflections on a Gift of Watermelon Pickle
Received from a Friend Called Felicity

During that summer
When unicorns were still possible;
When the purpose of knees
Was to be skinned;
5   When shiny horse chestnuts
    (Hollowed out
    Fitted with straws
    Crammed with tobacco
    Stolen from butts
10   In family ashtrays)
Were puffed in green lizard silence
While straddling thick branches
Far above and away
From the softening effects
15   Of civilization;

During that summer—
Which may never have been at all;
But which has become more real
Than the one that was—
20   Watermelons ruled.

Thick pink imperial slices
Melting frigidly on sun-parched tongues

Dribbling from chins;
Leaving the best part,
25 The black bullet seeds,
To be spit out in rapid fire
Against the wall
Against the wind
Against each other;

30 And when the ammunition was spent,
There was always another bite:
It was a summer of limitless bites,
Of hungers quickly felt
And quickly forgotten
35 With the next careless gorging.

The bites are fewer now.
Each one is savored lingeringly,
Swallowed reluctantly.

But in a jar put up by Felicity,
40 The summer which maybe never was
Has been captured and preserved.
And when we unscrew the lid
And slice off a piece
And let it linger on our tongue:
45 Unicorns become possible again.
—John Tobias

3. The following tale, which takes place during the Russo-Polish campaign of 1920, is by Isaac Babel, a recognized master of the short-story form. Read it carefully and then write a paper on one of its outstanding features, for example, how a few well-chosen details establish the setting and tone, and present the character of the narrator.

My First Goose

[1]Savitsky, Commander of the Seventh Division, rose when he saw me, and I wondered at the beauty of his giant's body. He rose, the purple of his riding breeches and the crimson of his little tilted cap and the decorations stuck on his chest cleaving the hut as a standard cleaves the sky. A smell of scent and the sickly sweet freshness of soap emanated from him. His long legs were like girls sheathed to the neck in shining riding boots.

[2]He smiled at me, struck his riding whip on the table, and drew toward him an order that the Chief of Staff had just finished dictating. It was an order for Ivan Chesnokov to advance on Chugunov-Dobryvodka with the regiment entrusted to him, to make contact with the enemy and destroy the same.

³"For which destruction," the Commander began to write, smearing the whole sheet, "I make this same Chesnokov entirely responsible, up to and including the supreme penalty, and will if necessary strike him down on the spot; which you, Chesnokov, who have been working with me at the front for some months now, cannot doubt."

⁴The Commander signed the order with a flourish, tossed it to his orderlies and turned upon me gray eyes that danced with merriment.

⁵I handed him a paper with my appointment to the Staff of the Division.

⁶"Put it down in the Order of the Day," said the Commander. "Put him down for every satisfaction save the front one. Can you read and write?"

⁷"Yes, I can read and write," I replied, envying the flower and iron of that youthfulness. "I graduated in law from St. Petersburg University."

⁸"Oh, are you one of those grinds?" he laughed. "Specs on your nose, too! What a nasty little object! They've sent you along without making any enquiries; and this is a hot place for specs. Think you'll get on with us?"

⁹"I'll get on all right," I answered, and went off to the village with the quartermaster to find a billet for the night.

¹⁰The quartermaster carried my trunk on his shoulder. Before us stretched the village street. The dying sun, round and yellow as a pumpkin, was giving up its roseate ghost to the skies.

¹¹We went up to a hut painted over with garlands. The quartermaster stopped, and said suddenly, with a guilty smile:

¹²"Nuisance with specs. Can't do anything to stop it, either. Not a life for the brainy type here. But you go and mess up a lady, and a good lady too, and you'll have the boys patting you on the back."

¹³He hesitated, my little trunk on his shoulder; then he came quite close to me, only to dart away again despairingly and run to the nearest yard. Cossacks were sitting there, shaving one another.

¹⁴"Here, you soldiers," said the quartermaster, setting my little trunk down on the ground. "Comrade Savitsky's orders are that you're to take this chap in your billets, so no nonsense about it, because the chap's been through a lot in the learning line."

¹⁵The quartermaster, purple in the face, left us without looking back. I raised my hand to my cap and saluted the Cossacks. A lad with long straight flaxen hair and the handsome face of the Ryazan Cossacks went over to my little trunk and tossed it out at the gate. Then he turned his back on me and with remarkable skill emitted a series of shameful noises.

¹⁶"To your guns—number double-zero!" an older Cossack shouted at him, and burst out laughing. "Running fire!"

¹⁷His guileless art exhausted, the lad made off. Then, crawling over the ground, I began to gather together the manuscripts and tattered garments that had fallen out of the trunk. I gathered them up and carried them to the other end of the yard. Near the hut, on a brick stove, stood a cauldron in which pork was cooking. The steam that rose from it was like

the far-off smoke of home in the village, and it mingled hunger with desperate loneliness in my head. Then I covered my little broken trunk with hay, turning it into a pillow, and lay down on the ground to read in *Pravda* Lenin's speech at the Second Congress of the Comintern. The sun fell upon me from behind the toothed hillocks, the Cossacks trod on my feet, the lad made fun of me untiringly, the beloved lines came toward me along a thorny path and could not reach me. Then I put aside the paper and went out to the landlady, who was spinning on the porch.

18"Landlady," I said, "I've got to eat."

19The old woman raised to me the diffused whites of her purblind eyes and lowered them again.

20"Comrade," she said, after a pause, "what with all this going on, I want to go and hang myself."

21"Christ!" I muttered, and pushed the old woman in the chest with my fist. "You don't suppose I'm going to go into explanations with you, do you?"

22And turning around I saw somebody's sword lying within reach. A severe-looking goose was waddling about the yard, inoffensively preening its feathers. I overtook it and pressed it to the ground. Its head cracked beneath my boot, cracked and emptied itself. The white neck lay stretched out in the dung, the wings twitched.

23"Christ!" I said, digging into the goose with my sword. "Go and cook it for me, landlady."

24Her blind eyes and glasses glistening, the old woman picked up the slaughtered bird, wrapped it in her apron, and started to bear it off toward the kitchen.

25"Comrade," she said to me, after a while, "I want to go and hang myself." And she closed the door behind her.

26The Cossacks in the yard were already sitting around their cauldron. They sat motionless, stiff as heathen priests at a sacrifice, and had not looked at the goose.

27"The lad's all right," one of them said, winking and scooping up the cabbage soup with his spoon.

28The Cossacks commenced their supper with all the elegance and restraint of peasants who respect one another. And I wiped the sword with sand, went out at the gate, and came in again, depressed. Already the moon hung above the yard like a cheap earring.

29"Hey, you," suddenly said Surovkov, an older Cossack. "Sit down and feed with us till your goose is done."

30He produced a spare spoon from his boot and handed it to me. We supped up the cabbage soup they had made, and ate the pork.

31"What's in the newspaper?" asked the flaxen-haired lad, making room for me.

32"Lenin writes in the paper," I said, pulling out *Pravda*. "Lenin writes that there's a shortage of everything."

33And loudly, like a triumphant man hard of hearing, I read Lenin's speech out to the Cossacks.

[34]Evening wrapped around me the quickening moisture of its twilight sheets; evening laid a mother's hand upon my burning forehead. I read on and rejoiced, spying out exultingly the secret curve of Lenin's straight line.

[35]"Truth tickles everyone's nostrils," said Surovkov, when I had come to the end. "The question is, how's it to be pulled from the heap. But he goes and strikes at it straight off like a hen pecking at a grain!"

[36]This remark about Lenin was made by Surovkov, platoon commander of the Staff Squadron; after which we lay down to sleep in the hayloft. We slept, all six of us, beneath a wooden roof that let in the stars, warming one another, our legs intermingled. I dreamed: and in my dreams saw women. But my heart, stained with bloodshed, grated and brimmed over.

---

13 Writing for the Business World

"What sort of writing are you doing these days?" This was a question asked more or less at random of people working in business and government, many of them still in their twenties. Here is a shortened list of the writing jobs they mentioned:

announcements	long-range planning reports
procedures manuals	program reports
proposals	appraisals
requests for action	identifications of problems
instructions	activity reports
reports of meetings	budget reports
grievance reports	scientific papers

And: memos, memos, memos!
letters, letters, letters!

Business Writing: Five Emphases

So far as this book is concerned, the writing jobs listed above *do not represent new types of writing.* In writing for business, you are not going to learn five or ten new kinds of exposition or argument. From first to last, the items on the list simply represent adaptations of rhetorical problems and strategies that have already been discussed in the first ten chapters. But some of these strategies are more strongly emphasized, or more widely used, than others in "business writing," as the subject is often called. In such writing, you should place particular emphasis on:

Thanks are due to Professor Francis Weeks, Chairman of the Division of Business and Technical Writing, University of Illinois. Professor Weeks designed the course that we have been teaching and gave us much useful information on the problems of business writing. Professor Robert Gieselman of the same Division read and criticized the chapter, and we thank him for his help.

1. *A specific writer's stance.* Before you start writing a letter, memo, or report, you must be very sure of your role, thesis, and reader. If you are both a technician and an administrator, for example, you may be shifting roles almost hourly as you write memos, instructions, technical reports, budget proposals, or requests for action to readers as diverse as maintenance men, stock clerks, or company vice-presidents. If you don't "shift the proper gears" as you adapt your writer's stance, you may transmit the right information to the wrong reader. Even though they may be in similar income brackets and social levels, you don't often use the same stance in writing to a vice-president and a stockholder. It is likely, for instance, that the stockholder won't understand certain technical information that the vice-president would consider obvious.

2. *Clear word choice and sentence structure.* The bane of business writing is the jargonized sentence: "Pursuant to our agreement of the 12th in terms of clarification of repair data. . . ." Says one expert, "If we could just convince our people to avoid big words and empty jargon ['Pursuant to . . . in terms of clarification'], we could cut costs *by thousands of dollars a year* in typing time alone!" (The estimated average cost of dictating, typing, and sending a business letter in the United States today is $4.50, and we have seen estimates as high as $15.) An insurance company in the Midwest recently hired a writing expert to spend one day a week in its home office just to go over company letters and talk to writers. The expert found that he spends much of his time on the same problems of word choice and sentence structure that you studied in Chapters 7, 8, and 9.

3. *An organization that is easy to follow.* The most common organizational device in business writing is the promise pattern, which we explained at length in Chapter 5. If you do not remember this pattern in detail, review pp. 91–93 before reading further. Busy executives, managers, scientists, and technicians prefer a "stripped-down" promise pattern, in which all inessentials are cut. "Get it on one page" is a typical order, one which we ourselves heard many times as we worked in various organizations.

4. *Use of the "who does what" formula.* Most letters, memos, and reports tell the reader to believe something, to do something, or to believe *and* do something. The "who does what" formula is short for:

Who does what
Who did what
Who will do what
Who should do what
What did what
What might do what

This formula reminds you that you are discussing conditions and actions, and that you should make these clear to yourself *before* you write. Then, *as* you write, keep telling your reader *who does what* so he won't be confused. Suppose, for example, you are tempted to write this sentence:

> The cost of work which had been accomplished in the Assembly Section before the last inspection date would be difficult to determine due to faulty records for June.

Wordy, vague, and unemphatic, the sentence should be recast using the formula:

Who (what)	Does (did)	What
Assembly Section	lost	the records for June
I [the accountant]	cannot determine	the cost of work

And the revised sentence reads:

> Since the Assembly Section lost its records for June, I cannot determine the cost of work done before the last inspection date.

The *who does what* formula provides a simple method for making points clear. For instance, we used it in the first few lines of the last paragraph:

Who (what)	Does (did)	What
This formula	reminds	you
you	should make	these [clear]
[you]	keep telling	your reader
you	are tempted to write	this sentence

5. *A readable format.* "We are after total readability," wrote the chief engineer of a large company. "Readability means more than just using clear words, punctuation, and sentence structure. Our technical and business people should know how to use white space on the page, employ headings, use numbered lists, and so on."

As this comment implies, the *whole page* is a unit of communication in business writing. Readers need to be able to glance at a page and "place" themselves in the flow of the material. Here is how you help them do this:

a. Use as much white space as possible. Keep relatively wide margins. Where you can, break up paragraphs and indent. Of course, you should not use illogical breaks.

b. Use parallelism when you can. Many discussions can be easily broken down into parallel lists or outlines—for example,
the parts of a technical process or the explanation of operational costs in a business. Even brief numbered lists like this
one are helpful to your reader:

1. Use headings

2. Use numbered lists

You should also note our use of numbered headings and lists in this
chapter—and in other sections of the book, for that matter.

These five "emphases" apply to almost all kinds of business papers or reports. Bear them in mind as we explain the specific forms
that such communications ordinarily take. But before we deal with
these forms, it is necessary to go over briefly the strategy of using illustrations.

Using Illustrations

The other night we were putting together a new
outdoor grill, one of those cheap things you buy for $5.95, use for a
season, and then throw away. On a sheet of printed directions that
came with it, direction #4 said, "Place strap around the legs and
fasten with bolts." *Strap?* We hunted through the thingamajigs that
came in the cardboard box with the grill but found nothing that
looked like a strap. We got down on the floor and peered around for
anything that might have fallen out of the box, cursing Fate and the
manufacturer for omitting the one thing that held the grill together.
Just then, our son, a college freshman, wandered into the room,
watched us for a while, and then picked up a shiny thing from the
small pile of metal left in the box, and said: "Wrap this around where
the three legs meet." Here's what the thing looked like:

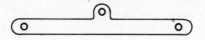

A *strap* indeed! Why didn't the manufacturer put a little drawing of
the "strap" on his direction sheet, so that we could tell what it was
and where it was supposed to go?

In many instances, a piece of business communication can greatly benefit from an *illustration* of some kind—a graph, table, schematic drawing, photograph, or cross section (to name only some of the possibilities). Every one of the writing jobs listed at the beginning of this chapter may require illustrations; many, like procedures manuals and budgets, will always require illustrative material. A picture or drawing can be worth more than just "a thousand words" in these cases; it can also prevent wasted time and unnecessary irritation. So where you can, help your readers with illustrations—give them something to look at that will explain more clearly and easily what you want them to know or to do. There are several basic types of illustrations that are simple to construct.

1. *Hand drawings.* The simplest of illustrations, the hand drawing, can be quickly made and inserted in the text. Here is an example, along with some brief instructions:

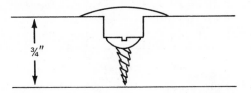

Countersink your screw one-third of the way through the wood and fill the hole with wood putty, rounding off the top of the putty.

2. *Tables.* A table uses rows and columns to explain data. Most tables can be typed or handwritten quite easily. Example:

Table III

Grade Distribution for Physics 100
(Number of Students)

GRADE	A	B	C	D	F
FALL SEMESTER	28	56	87	22	10
SPRING SEMESTER	31	61	77	18	8
TOTAL	59	117	164	40	18

3. *Graphs.* Graphs are of two basic kinds, *line* and *bar*. Here is a typical *line graph*, which shows sets of measurements plotted along a vertical side (y-axis) and a horizontal side (x-axis).

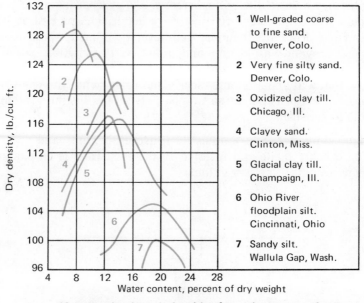

Moisture-density relationships for various types of soils as determined by standard Proctor compaction tests.

A *bar graph* consists of vertical or horizontal "bars," the lengths of which indicate certain quantities. Here is an example:

How the cost of living compares in 14 cities

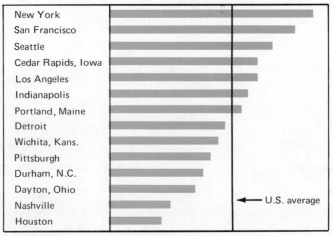

Data: U.S. Dept. of Labor, Bureau of Labor Statistics

How do you know when to use drawings, tables, or graphs? Much of the time, this question is answered by the nature of (a) the material, (b) your writer's stance. If your material deals with electrical circuits, you may use a schematic drawing:

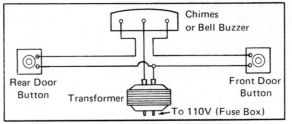

Two-way circuit above gives signal from either button.

If your material is geological, a structure map may be in order:

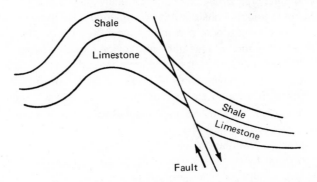

Using illustrations is a matter of common sense. If your reader is a layman, don't use a complicated technical illustration. But if you are writing for professionals working in your field, then they should have no trouble understanding such an illustration.

As much as possible, your illustrations should supplement and clarify your written material, like this:

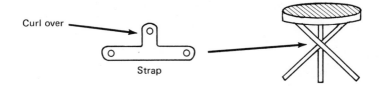

Wrap the strap around the joint where the three legs meet. Curl the top flap over and then fasten the strap to the legs with the 2-inch bolt provided, pushing the bolt through all three holes.

1. The three paragraphs below are the first and last two of a scientific report written by an internationally known botanist. From these paragraphs, can you describe the writer's stance? In particular, how limited is the writer's audience? Does the author use much technical language? Nontechnical language? How do you think he would defend his word choice?

> [1]Physiology is the study of vital, or "living," processes. From this definition it can be reasoned that the physiology of corn production is the study of vital processes underlying the growth and reproduction of corn plants. Production enters from the agricultural concern for maximizing growth and reproduction. What we need to understand are the vital processes involved, and then use this knowledge to secure increased yields.

> [2]There may be other economic benefits in the offing from basic physiological research, but I cannot identify them now. I am certain however that there are 3 basic levels of regulating plant growth—the environment, the genetic code, and the hormonal regulation of differentiation. Another generation of research will provide us with a better understanding of how to manipulate these controls. Already we are experienced in manipulating the environment by irrigating, draining, plowing, fertilizing, etc. There are sound empirical practices in breeding and hybridization which expand yearly as we learn more about the genetic apparatus. The controls to be revealed when we solve the hormone mystery can only be estimated, but will surely be considerable.

> [3]I'll end by going out on a limb. At the present rate of progress the corn belt should be averaging 150 bushels of corn per acre in the year 2000. The better farmers will be disappointed with less than 200 bushels.—J. B. Hanson, "The Physiology of Corn Production"

2. In New York City, officers of the First National City Bank believed that they had to make their messages clearer. Here is an example of how they rewrote a provision in their personal-loan policy:

Old	New
In the event of default in the payment of this or any other Obligation or the performance or observance of any term or covenant contained herein or in any note or other contract or agreement evidencing or relating to any Obligation or any Collateral on the Borrower's part to be performed or observed, or the undersigned Borrower shall die, or any of the	I'll be in default: 1. If I don't pay an installment on time; or 2. If any other creditor tries by legal process to take any money of mine in your possession.

undersigned become insolvent or make an assignment for the benefit of creditors, or a petition shall be filed by or against any of the undersigned under any provision of the Bankruptcy Act, or any money, securities or property of the undersigned now or hereafter on deposit with or in the possession or under the control of the Bank shall be attached or become subject to distraint proceedings or any order or process of any court.

Explain in detail how the officers used any of the "five emphases" of business writing to make their requirement more understandable.

3. A typical problem in business writing is that of giving clear, easy-to-read instructions or directions. The following directions are from an instruction sheet that each student at a certain college who registers his car receives from the Campus Police.

Prepare a *specific* critique of the instructions, showing how they violate each of the five emphases of business writing we have discussed. Then reorganize and rewrite the instructions.

Utilizing Permits and Stickers

This sticker must be properly displayed on the automobile for which it was issued, as indicated below (improper display may result in a monetary penalty).

1. On vehicles not equipped with a fixed rear window (e.g., convertibles, station wagons with retractable rear windows, or others), the sticker must be displayed in the lower left portion of the front windshield (driver's side).
2. On vehicles equipped with a fixed rear window (not retractable), the sticker must be displayed in the lower center portion of that window.
   THESE STICKERS ARE PRINTED ON THE GUMMED SIDE.
   THEREFORE, THEY MUST BE AFFIXED FROM THE INSIDE.

Permits are not transferable. When a permit holder changes cars, he must obtain a new permit, by making application to this Division *and surrendering the pieces of the old sticker.* (There is no charge.)

Permit holders who also are parking space renters should display the rental space sticker immediately adjacent to the registration sticker.

Only current stickers may be displayed on your vehicle.

The Letter

The *letter*, the jack-of-all-trades of business communication, performs a wide variety of duties. It can be a request for action, a set of instructions, an appraisal of a farm property, a cover letter for a scientific paper, an announcement, and so on.

A letter is ordinarily written in response to a specific situation or problem—you want a person to do something, to perform a job in a certain way, to give you an idea of what your farm is worth. Perhaps you wish to explain what your scientific paper covers and why you are sending it to a particular journal, or to announce to a group of businessmen that you are starting a new service that they might be interested in using.

Since letters can do so many different things, it is unwise to insist that you should use specific types of development or a particular rhetorical strategy when you write them. While it is true that a letter may define, compare and contrast, narrate an event, or illustrate a cause-and-effect relationship, in most cases you will not force a a strategy on the material in the letter. The *situation* to which you are responding determines the choice and development of the approach you take. For example, if you wish your reader to take a particular action on a problem, you might write a brief argument that contains both a thesis of fact, with a cause-and-effect relationship explained, and a thesis of action explaining exactly how you think the problem could be solved. (These theses of argument are explained on pp. 218–219.)

FORM OF THE LETTER

The *form* of the business letter is pretty well standardized now. In the example on the following page, note that the headings give complete information on addresses. Don't leave anything out of these addresses because information like street names and accurate zip codes is often vital for maintaining a correspondence and keeping people happy.

PSYCHOLOGY OF THE LETTER

Authorities on business writing have long agreed that successful letters require more than just good ideas and proper form, although these are certainly not to be sniffed at. A letter is usually a miniature piece of persuasion, with its own *ethical proof* and

```
                                          1001 Calhoun Avenue
                                          Columbus, Ohio 43215
                                          June 23, 1979


        Mr. Weston Sharpe
        Customer Services
        Imperial Manufacturing Company
        4207 Disston Avenue
        Westville, Kentucky 40881

        Subject: (optional)

        Dear Mr. Sharpe:

        _____
        _____
        _____
        _____

        _____
        _____
        _____
        _____

        _____
        _____
        _____
        _____
        _____


                                    Sincerely yours,


                                    Mrs. Verdeen Smith
```

you-attitude. You remember that these elements of persuasion, discussed in Chapter 10, help make your ideas more acceptable to your reader. Your ethical proof is the persuasive side of your character, as you present it to your reader. And your you-attitude is the impression that you give the reader that you are genuinely interested in him and his welfare, not just in yourself. You should, for example, think twice before writing an abrupt, unfriendly letter like the one below from a bank executive:

Dear _____:

Concerning your overdraft. That was not our fault, as you state. Our records show that we never received the $500 you say you deposited. Please remit $374.33 to cover the amount of your overdraft.

Instead, the writer should have used a little common-sense psychology, making himself look better and his customer feel better (*and* increasing his chances of retaining the customer):

Dear _____:

We are sorry that you were inconvenienced when your account was overdrawn recently by mistake. After receiving your letter, we checked immediately to see if we had failed to enter the $500 you mentioned. But we have no record here of having received your deposit. Since, as you say, the $500 was a check from your father, you might ask him to stop payment on his check until you discover what happened to it.

Since you have written no more checks on your account, your overdraft remains $374.33.

We are sorry this problem arose and hope that the matter can be cleared up soon.

The second version is an improvement for several reasons. The writer shows ethical proof by precisely reviewing the details of the transaction and by suggesting to the customer a clear and convenient course of action. The you-attitude is apparent throughout, especially when the writer clarifies the situation ("Since, as *you* say, the $500 was a check from your father"), and when he suggests how the customer can remedy the problem without embarrassment ("*you* might ask him to stop payment on his check until *you* discover what happened to it"). And nowhere in the letter is a harsh word uttered.

TWO SAMPLE LETTERS

When she got her spring grade report, Susan Langford was amazed to find that she had failed a course, one that she *knew* she had done well in. In order to take care of her problem, she defined it carefully, picked a precise writer's stance, organized her material, and wrote the letter on the following page.

In her letter, Susan carefully observes the five emphases of business writing listed at the beginning of this chapter. She takes a specific and clear stance, writing directly to a particular person, the one who can most quickly take care of her problem. Her point or thesis is clear: a mistake was made on her grade and she requests that the grade be changed. Her wording is accurate, and her organization is easy to follow, the three paragraphs forming a pattern that is logical and visually pleasant. The letter has a readable format and plenty of white space. Note especially her use of the "who does what" formula:

. . . report indicates that I failed I.S. 100. . . .
I took the course. . . .

I did four papers. . . .
I received B's. . . .
I should have received a "Pass."
I have my four papers. . . .

102 Sand Road
Green, Alabama 36110
June 10, 1979

Professor J. T. Barksdale
Chairman, Independent Studies
Magnolia Junior College
Arlington, Alabama 36109

Dear Professor Barksdale:

My spring grade report indicates that I failed I.S. 100, the Independent Study course I took on the pass-fail system last spring semester. I took the course from Mr. Winchell, who resigned at the end of the term to return to graduate school. I am writing to you because I presume that you can take care of my problem.

I did four papers for Mr. Winchell, three short and one long. I received B's for the three short papers and an A- on the long one. There were no tests or exams for the course. Given the grades on the papers, I should have received a "Pass."

It seems likely that someone at Magnolia made a clerical error. Would you please check on this for me and see if my grade can be changed to a "Pass"? I have my four papers which you can see for evidence. Thank you.

Sincerely yours,

Susan Langford

As we stated earlier, the "who does what" formula tells the reader what the situation is by making every action specific and clear. Susan does not write: "Written work was accomplished in the course." Instead, she gives the precise *action*: "I did four papers."

It is is also worth mentioning that Susan uses good psychology in her letter. Although she might justifiably be hurt and upset about receiving a "Fail" when she clearly deserved a "Pass," she does not let her feelings show or attack the administration of the college. The ethical proof and you-attitude implicit in the letter will make Professor Barksdale want to solve her problem as quickly as possible — and to solve it in her favor.

Our second sample letter is also a request for action to be taken, but the situation is different, and the standard format of the letter has been altered slightly.

November 8, 1978

Mr. Robert Marker
Assistant to Board of Directors
American Metal-Press Corporation
Winthrop, South Carolina 29730

Subject: Proposed Plan to Decrease Press Down-time

Problem:

The excessive amount of press down-time we have been experiencing at our Jefferson Street Plant needs immediate attention. I estimate that the down-time is costing the company about $24,000 a week, which cannot be considered a normal production cost. At the present time, we have no scheduled maintenance program for keeping the presses in proper working order. While studying production reports, I found that poor maintenance is the cause of most press down-time. The most troublesome areas are:

1. Gripper Settings
2. Damper Systems
3. Fountain Water-Acid Systems
4. Folder Problems

Solution:

I propose that a Saturday and Sunday maintenance program be established. On Saturday, two crews of four men could change dampers and set grippers on all the sheet-fed presses. On Sunday, another two crews would clean the fountain water-acid systems and make all the necessary adjustments on the web-press folder. The crews would alternate weekends to avoid conflicts concerning distribution of overtime.

Benefits of Program:

By having a maintenance program we will save many hours of press-time. With the repairs made on weekends, the presses would be able to start up on Monday mornings without any difficulty. This program would cut our production costs, allowing our company to increase its profits. The cost of the program and the savings that will be realized follow:

2 crews Saturday	$560
2 crews Sunday	$560
Total	$1,120
Present down-time loss	$24,000
Estimated Savings	$22,780

Sincerely,

Thomas Staff, Press Supervisor

We will leave most of the discussion of Staff's letter to the Practice that follows. But, in passing, we should observe something important about the wording of his letter, and also the wording of Susan's. Both letters use standard English. Neither one of the writers uses formal language or business jargon, or tries to put things in a fancy way. There is only one style in modern letter writing, the natural and informal style that makes its point without unnecessary words or rhetorical flourishes.

PRACTICE

1. The *five emphases* of business communication stress the use of: (1) a specific writer's stance; (2) clear word choice and sentence structure; (3) an easy-to-follow organization; (4) the "who does what" formula; and (5) a readable format. Using these emphases and our discussion of the psychology of letter writing, prepare notes for a critique of Staff's letter above. Be specific in your comments.

2. You own a new Glitter 8, a $7,000 car, which is still under warranty. In the past six months, you have had the following "new-car" problems: bad front-end alignment; leaks around the rear window; faulty engine tuning; a side window that won't close. (These are apparently "factory assembly" problems.) You have taken the car to Grump Motors, where you bought it, a total of seven times. The alignment is satisfactory now; the rear window still leaks, but not as badly as it did; the tuning, if anything, appears worse than before; the side window worked for a while, but now refuses to move. Every time you take the car to Grump Motors, somebody gets grease all over the upholstery. You know the shop manager personally. He is a capable, hardworking man, who seems to do the best job he can.

   Using the five emphases of business communication, write a persuasive letter to the Glitter Motor Corporation in Detroit requesting a specific solution to your problems.

3. Imagine that your school expenses are paid by the Warbucks Foundation. The Foundation, in effect, pays you $2,000 a year to go to school. There are no strings on this money, except that you must take a normal class load nine months of the year and maintain at least a B average each semester. You can have a part-time job if you wish.

At the end of the school year, you must write to Mr. Gawain Buck, Director of the Foundation, explaining to him (1) how you spent the $2,000, and (2) why you deserve a similar grant for the next year.

Write the letter. If you can, include pertinent tables or graphs that show Mr. Buck how you spent last year's money and what you intend to do with the money for next year.

The Job Application Letter

To get a job, you will often write a letter of application. But don't start off writing blindly to any company or employer that comes to mind. Make a plan — consider your ambitions, compile a list of your assets as a prospective employee, and try to find an employer you want to work for, one who needs a person with your qualifications. Your college or university has a placement office that can give you much up-to-date information on companies, schools, governmental agencies on all levels, and other organizations that are hiring; you can also find more information in the library and in professional magazines. Skim the available material and decide which organizations you want to apply to; narrow your list down to those you are genuinely interested in.

When you have decided on a reasonable list of your ambitions and professional assets, and have picked a group of prospective employers, you are ready to plan a letter of application. Such a letter ordinarily has two parts, the data sheet and the letter itself.

THE DATA SHEET

In the *data sheet* (also called the "résumé"), you give all the factual material about yourself and your history that can be easily listed: your age, health and marital status; education (including degrees and certificates); extracurricular activities; experience; and references. Some students like to put their grade-point averages on the sheet, but this information is optional.

In the data sheet, you should not only give a prospective employer specific detail about yourself, you should also save him reading time. So be brief, factual, and clear. Example:

DATA SHEET

John D. White

221 North Huff Drive
Urbana, Illinois 61801
Phone: (218) 367-2145

Personal Information:

>   Birthplace: Alliance, Illinois
>   Birth Date: September 8, 1956
>   Health: Excellent
>   Marital Status: Single

Education:

>   1970-1974: Mondale High School, Mondale, Illinois
>   1974-1976: attended Mondale Junior College, Mondale, Illinois
>   1976-1978: attended Winston College, Winston, Illinois; will
>   graduate May 25, 1978, with B.S. degree
>   Major: Business Administration
>   Minor: Economics

Extracurricular Activities:

>   1976-1978: member, Tau Phi Tau social fraternity (vice-
>   president, 1977-1978)
>   Winston College Marching Band
>   Men's Glee Club

Experience:

>   1971-1972: fry cook, McTavish Hamburger Unit 18
>   1972-1975: stock boy, Independent Grocery Company
>   1975-   : Assistant Manager, McTavish Hamburger Unit 11

References (by permission):

>   Dr. John R. Webster, Professor of Management, Winston College,
>   Winston, Illinois 61801
>   Dr. Lucille Carter, Associate Professor of Business Adminis-
>   tration, Winston College, Winston, Illinois 61801
>   Mr. Dilney Harder, District Supervisor, McTavish Hamburger
>   Company, 224 East Lake Avenue, Chicago, Illinois 60621

It is unwise to overload your data sheet with unnecessary information. Put yourself in an employer's place and ask: "What would I like to know about this person? What could he tell me that would make him a qualified candidate for a job?" A small point—do not abbreviate names, places, or titles any more than you can help; such practice makes you look careless and lazy.

Keep your data sheet clean, airy, with sufficient white space, and *perfectly typed.*

THE APPLICATION LETTER

Since your data sheet lists a great deal of specific information about you, the application letter tells the rest — what job you are seeking, why you want it, and what you have to offer the company. Again, put yourself in the employer's place: what do you have in the way of experience, training, or know-how that he might like to have in an employee?

The application letter is a selling device, and it should "sell" you — your abilities and your personality. But it should not sell too hard! We mention this because we have seen application letters which have had an effect opposite from what their authors intended. Consider this paragraph from an unsuccessful letter:

> The job description that your company has sent out fits me exactly; it calls for someone who can handle responsibility right away. My ability to take responsibility is something I have always been proud of. An example of this is my being president of the student body for last year. [And so on.]

The trouble with this approach is that the writer tries to force a favorable opinion of himself on the employer — he presents far too much of a "me-attitude." The successful application letter will sell you by (1) being *specific* about your good points, and (2) mentioning them *modestly* and *quietly.* For example, the writer of the unsuccessful letter could have expressed his skill in assuming responsibility by saying something like the following:

> Your company's job description states that you "wish to hire a person who can handle responsibility right away." I was president of the student body here at Collins College last year, and was responsible for appointing students to committees, delegating authority to the committee chairmen, and suggesting allocations for student funds to the student council. While I realize that these responsibilities may not be comparable to those in your company, the fact that I took them on may indicate to you that I am capable of assuming a good deal of responsibility in a job with your company.

Choosing the proper writer's stance will go far to help you achieve the right attitude and tone. You can use the same data sheet to apply for many different jobs, but each letter should be individually designed for the employer you are going to send it to. Employers are generally *not* alike; they have different needs for different kinds of employees. And as a matter of fact, the employer might be flattered that you have taken the time and trouble to create a letter just for him and his organization.

Observe how this letter (which was written to support the data sheet on p. 317) acts as a persuasive sales device for John White:

221 North Huff Drive
Urbana, Illinois 61801
April 1, 1979

Mr. Jarvis Chase
Chief, Personnel Division
Great Midwestern Grocery Company
Minneapolis, Minnesota 55456

Dear Mr. Chase:

Our Director of Student Employment here at Winston College told me that you are looking for a trainee for your store—management program.

I have seven years of part-time experience in food retailing work. My three years as a grocery stock boy and four years as an Assistant Manager for the McTavish Hamburger Company have allowed me to view food retailing and management from widely different perspectives. My ability to deal successfully with the kinds of problems I encountered in both jobs should prove beneficial in my future work.

My college training has also prepared me for a career in retailing and management. I have taken six courses in retailing and four in management, and have an average of 3.4 (B+) in them.

Considering my experience and training, I believe I could be of real service to your company and would be glad to enter your training program at whatever level you might place me.

I am available for an interview at your convenience. Please call or write if you have any questions about my qualifications. My data sheet is enclosed.

Sincerely,

John D. White

1. Analyze carefully the data sheet and the letter in John White's application to the Great Midwestern Grocery Company. What is his writer's stance? Make a detailed list of all the facts and statements in the data sheet and the letter to which you (if you were an executive of Great Midwestern) would react positively. Are there any facts and statements to which you might react negatively? Would *you* consider hiring John White?

2. Carol Weinstein saw this ad in a local paper:

MANAGEMENT TRAINEES
3 positions open. BA or MA in
Business Administration desirable.
Some experience very desirable.
Training will lead to management
appointment in health-care facilities.
Excellent opportunity. Send résumé
to Box 988 c/o the *Courier,* Champaign,
Ill. 61820. An Equal Opportunity
Employer.

She then wrote this letter:

March 4, 1979
405 Wardell Hall
Urbana, Illinois 61801

Box 988
c/o the *Champaign-Urbana Courier*
110 W. University Avenue
Champaign, Illinois 61820

Dear Sir or Madam:

I am answering the ad which was in the *Champaign-Urbana Courier* on Thursday, March 3, 1979. I am very interested in health-care administration, and would like to go into this field when I get my degree. Although I realize that your ad is for positions that are available now, I will not receive my degree until May 1980. However, I hope you will give me a chance to present my qualifications now, and that you will think them good enough to keep me in mind for possible positions in the next year or so.

In addition to working toward my Bachelor of Science degree in Business Administration, which gives me academic knowledge of business theory and practices, I also have practical experience working in an intermediate-care nursing home.

As you can see from the enclosed résumé, I have been the administrator's immediate assistant at Abbott Nursing Home since 1975. This has been mainly a part-time job. However, in the last four years I have worked in several areas of administration and management there. My duties have ranged from general secretarial functions to preparatory work for monthly audits.

Equally important, I have developed an ability to work with and relate well to older people. This is something I think a nursing-home administrator must be able to do in order to understand and solve the problems associated with running a good home. I am also taking several courses in social work which focus on the aged. These give me more exposure to the kinds of problems older people face in society.

My interest and experience in this field, combined with further training, make me feel I could be a competent administrator. As I said before, I realize you need applicants who are available now; but I hope you will keep me in mind for possible future openings. Thank you for your time.

Sincerely,

Carol L. Weinstein

Carol's letter received a very favorable reply from the employer. Why? Discuss in detail.

3. Assume that you need a job next summer. Pick out one specific job that is part-time or full-time. Do research on the job market and write a full job application (data sheet and letter) to a specific employer.

The Memo

How is the *memo* (short for *memorandum*) different from the letter? First, the memo is designed to be read inside your organizational unit—your company, school, governmental division, and so on. The outsider ordinarily does not see such memos, which communicate much of the day-to-day detail needed to run the unit. Second, the memo tends to be shorter and more informal than the letter. Because in most cases the writer knows the person (or persons) he is writing to, he communicates his message to them simply and quickly, but still courteously.

FORM OF THE MEMO

A typical memo *form* looks like this:

```
                                              DATE:

   TO:

   FROM:

   SUBJECT:


                    ――――――――――――――――――――――――――――
                    ――――――――――――――――――――――――――――
                    ――――――――――――  MESSAGE  ――――――――――――
                    ――――――――――――――――――――――――――――
                    ――――――――――――――――――――――――――――
                    ――――――――――――――――――――――――――――
                    ――――――――――――――――――――――――――――
```

TWO SAMPLE MEMOS

Joanne Larson will be showing a film on plant safety to eighty-three employees next week. Since the projection room will hold only fifty people comfortably, she writes this memo to the four chief supervisors of the plant:

DATE: March 17, 1978

TO: Stan Clark, Carl Fowler, Mark McFall, Jim Thomas

FROM: Joanne Larson

SUBJECT: Scheduling the safety film

As you know, we are showing the safety film, <u>Keep Your Eyes Open</u>, next week in the projection room, which holds only fifty people comfortably without overcrowding. I suggest we show the film to the forty-one people in the Assembly Section on Tuesday at 3:00 p.m., and to the remaining forty-two from the other sections on Thursday at the same time.

If there's any problem about this arrangement, please let me know.

Don Kildren of the Drafting Division has been asked to organize the flow of map copying so that fewer jam-ups occur in Photo Services. When Don has finished planning the reorganization, he writes his ten fellow draftsmen:

```
                                        DATE:  May 10, 1978


TO:  "the Inkmen"

FROM:  Don Kildren

SUBJECT:  Breaking up the jam in Photo Services


      Mr. Durkheim asked me to suggest a way to keep work from
      piling up for the two photocopy machines.  Apparently, no-
      body can get to them when we have a busy day copying maps.
      So, how is this for a suggested schedule?

         1. Mary, Anne, and Matt--Monday and Wednesday mornings
         2. Tom, Shirl, and Rich--Monday and Wednesday afternoons
         3. Liz, Nat, Paul, and I--Tuesday and Thursday mornings

      If you have an emergency need for photocopying, take the
      map down to Photo Services anyway--but please don't make a
      habit of it.

      Thanks.  If you have any ideas on the subject, let me know.
```

Both memos follow pretty well the five emphases of business writing and both effectively use ethical proof and the you-attitude. It seems likely that readers of both memos would be happy with what they are asked to do and how they are asked to do it.

Consider the memo as a little piece of "frozen talk." Write it as if you were speaking courteously to a friend who happens to work with you. Make it as short as possible without being abrupt.

PRACTICE

1. Here is the first draft of a memo from a college librarian to her student "stackers." Considering (a) the five emphases of business writing, (b) the proper form of the memo, and (c) the psychology of memos and letters, prepare an analysis of the memo for class discussion. Then rewrite it for greater clarity and brevity.

    Referring to my memo about a year ago concerning the method of stacking books in the stack area before the shelvers put them into the shelves in their proper places. At the time of my memo there were three shelvers but now we have only two because the third kept coming into the job drunk. This still occurred, so we fired him—as you remember the other two shelvers are still ok and are working as fast as they can getting the books properly on the shelves. But we need a better system of dividing the books in the stack area before the shelvers get to them because now they are just thrown on the floor in any order and the shelvers have to separate them in the various categories before they start to shelve. Something must be accomplished so that the separation is done before the shelvers get to them, so please see that before the books are put into the shelvers' area they are already divided into the main categories (fiction, nonfiction, biography) and this way the shelvers can simply pick them up and put them in their proper places. Another shelver will be hired as soon as money can be located or special allocating by the Library Board.

2. Here, in scratch form, is a budget breakdown prepared for Rho Rho Rho fraternity. A member of the fraternity drew it up to help him write a memo to the group's finance committee. Using the breakdown in the tables, the student has to (a) explain the meaning of the figures, and (b) make a short statement about the fraternity's financial situation. Prepare the student's memo for him.

BETA CHAPTER
RHO RHO RHO SOCIAL FRATERNITY
COMPARATIVE BUDGET REPORT
For the Semester Ending January 20, 1978

	Actual Results	Budget	Variance
CASH RECEIPTS:			
Room and board	$23,750	$25,000	($1,250)
Miscellaneous cash receipts (Parking revenue, cigarettes, pop, laundry)	1,780	1,600	180
Total cash receipts	$25,530	$26,600	($1,070)
CASH EXPENDITURES:			
Commissary (includes cook's salary)	$20,150	$19,500	($ 650)
Utilities	870	1,000	130
Repairs	1,395	500	(895)
Telephone	75	200	125
Entertainment	355	500	145
Communications (other than telephone)	125	100	(25)
Maintenance	715	1,000	285
Miscellaneous expenditures	950	1,000	50
Total cash expenditures	$24,635	$23,800	($ 835)
TOTAL CASH RECEIPTS:	$25,530	$26,600	($1,070)
− TOTAL CASH EXPENDITURES:	24,635	23,800	(835)
= EXCESS OF CASH RECEIPTS OVER CASH EXPENDITURES:	$ 895	$ 2,800	($1,905)
+ BEGINNING CASH BALANCE:	2,070	2,070	---------
= CASH BALANCE, 1/20/78:	$ 2,965	$ 4,870	($1,905)

Negative Messages

Since we occasionally act as consultants to firms that wish to improve their written communications, we are always interested in what their problems are. Lately, we have been hearing more of this kind of comment: "Right now we have so many *bad* things to tell people. Somebody's got to tell the vice-president we lost a contract; tell a customer the part for her ten-year-old washer is not available; tell a woman we can't hire her because the budget we thought we had we don't have; tell the paving inspector we are going to be six weeks late getting our entry to Vine Avenue finished. We've got an endless number of things like these going out."

The so-called *negative message*—one which the receiver would prefer not to read, and may be greatly disappointed or even enraged to read—has become one of the commonest problems in modern business communication. To solve that problem, authorities in business writing have suggested six techniques for shaping the typical negative message, which is usually a letter. As you consider these techniques, remember that such a letter is going to provide a shock, sometimes a big one, to its reader. In most forms, it is some kind of *turn-down*. It tells the reader that he won't get the job, the loan, the application for gas heat approved, the delivery of his new car on time. Although there is little you can do to avoid disappointing the reader, you should try to make your message as courteous as possible.

1. *Consider using a "buffer" at the beginning of the letter.* The *buffer* absorbs the shock of the turn-down; or, to describe it another way, provides a touch of human sympathy at the outset. These are typical buffers as they appear in letters:

> We have carefully read your application, and are impressed by your qualifications . . . . However . . . .
>
> Your proposal for a new water system has many obvious merits, among them . . . . Yet . . . .
>
> I have talked with all members of the committee about your situation, but . . . .

Authorities on business writing disagree about the use of a buffer. Some even argue against using it at all, believing that it tends to be an unthinking cliché. And sometimes it is. Yet we have often noticed the unhappiness of readers about a negative message that starts out too bluntly—they feel hurt, resentful, or put off. When they do, bluntness *is* a mistake. We believe that you should try (in your own way, using your own words) to provide a "shock absorber" in the negative message—assuming always that the message in question calls for one. It is true that some do not, and in those a buffer just gets in the way.

2. *Make your turn-down early.* Put it immediately after the beginning, whether the beginning contains a buffer or just a general introductory sentence or two. Here's an argument against a long buffer: it makes the reader wait for the turn-down, and waiting may make him quite angry. We once saw a businessman rip up a long letter and throw it on his office floor. What angered him was a two-paragraph buffer that made him think he was going to get something, when actually it was just the preparation for a turn-down.

3. *Make your turn-down clear.* Don't mince words, and don't be ambiguous. Your reader wants to know the worst, and he should know the worst in the clearest way possible. You should be as polite as you can, but don't be so diplomatic that the effect of your turn-down is lost on the reader. There is no getting around the fact that your message is essentially a negative one.

4. *Be factual.* After the turn-down, explain in reasonable detail why you cannot give the person what he wants. A reasonable and factual explanation will make him feel better because it indicates that you took the time to deal with his problem. Also, by giving him the facts you may well open the way to more negotiation of the problem.

5. If possible or practical, *leave hope for the future* at the end of the message.

> . . . Ms. Ryan, although the Recreation Committee did not accept your proposal at this time, why not submit it again in January? As you know, the company will have another $2,000 in the Recreation budget after the first of the year . . . .

Or:

> . . . We are sorry your router motor burned out. But, as a hobby model, it was not made for the sort of heavy work you tried to do. If you would try our Carpenter's Model, you will find that it can do that work easily; and we can guarantee the motor for heavy use.

Warning: Don't leave hope if there isn't any!

6. *Use a friendly tone throughout.* But don't be flippant, too casual, or humorous. Attempting to soften the impact of a negative message by a light-hearted tone and attitude can infuriate the receiver more than the turn-down itself.

PRACTICE

Discuss the effectiveness of this negative message:

LONGCHAMPS APARTMENTS

April 9, 1977

Mr. John Garst
505 N. First
Ross, Illinois 61880

Dear Mr. Garst:

I am very glad you have decided that Longchamps Apartments would be the ideal place for you to live. We are proud of the building and the reputation that it has earned over the years.

This year has been rather unusual because we are only midway through our renting season, and yet we are already full and have been forced to turn people away for the past two weeks. As a rule, we seldom have all twelve of our apartments available for renting since we always give priority to our present tenants and allow them the option of staying on before we even consider new ones. Many of them do stay — in fact, next year half of the apartments will be occupied by tenants who will be staying on, leaving only six apartments to be rented. In addition, the large number of students who are always interested in living at Longchamps contributes to our high occupancy rate so early in the season.

I wish you good luck in your search for housing for next year. I'm sure there are still many other apartments available. If you think you would possibly be interested in living here the following year, feel free to drop by our apartment any Saturday afternoon, when we would be happy to answer any questions you might have. Next spring, then, you should see us in mid-February to assure yourself of an apartment. You can stop by in person or write. As before, we can be reached by phone at 344-7996.

I hope you will keep us in mind. We are always ready to welcome students who will contribute to a graduate study atmosphere.

Very truly yours,

Jacqueline Tracy, Manager

Reports

A fair amount of useless information has been published about reports—their content, nature, and form, particularly their form. When they do a report, most successful writers don't use a special form; they simply take the situation they're writing about and adapt a form to fit it. A "report" can be written as a letter or memo. It can be composed mainly of figures, charts, and graphs, or it can have no illustrations at all. It can contain highly technical language, or it can be written in standard English that everyone would understand. Indeed, the unsuccessful way to write most reports is to take a formulaic organization—title page, letter of transmittal, table of contents, introduction, etc.—and try to jam the message into the formula.

By nature, the report is usually an argument. It asks people to *believe* or to *act*, and so can be either a *fact* or *action* argument, or both at the same time. (See Chapter 10 for information on arguments.) Accordingly, if you get your argument straight, maintain an appropriate stance, and follow the general rules of business writing, you will have no trouble writing reports. Some business organizations, of course, have developed their own formulas for report writing. If you work for one of them, you will probably follow the established formula—or write a report suggesting that the organization handle its reports differently.

Handbook

"I always choose the grammatical form unless it sounds affected," said the poet Marianne Moore. This is sensible advice for you as a writer, but first you must know what the grammatical form is. To find the correct form, or simply to polish your skills in grammar, usage, and mechanics, you should use this *Handbook*. We begin with the "small" building blocks of the language, the parts of speech. If, at any point, you need to look up unfamiliar terms, turn to the Glossary beginning on p. 391.

Grammatical Analysis

GA 1 LEARN THE PARTS OF SPEECH

The parts of speech are classified by the jobs they perform in a sentence. Memorize this table.

nouns }*name.*	(Nothing else *names.*)
pronouns	
verbs *state.*	(Nothing else *states.*)
adjectives }*modify.*	(Nothing else *modifies.*)
adverbs	
prepositions }*join.*	(Nothing else *joins.*)
conjunctions	

To explain how the parts of speech "perform their jobs" in a sentence, let's begin by considering some typical nouns and verbs.

Typical nouns:

The *draw* you made on the last poker hand was pure luck.
His was a great *run*.
The story started in a *place* called Shenandoah.

Typical verbs:

You will never *draw* another hand like that.
He had *run* that race before.
She could not *place* Jim, although she vaguely recognized him.

Draw, run, and *place* are nouns in the first group of sentences because they are *naming words*. But since they are acting as *stating words* in the second group, *draw, run,* and *place* are verbs there. (The verb phrases are *will draw, had run,* and *could place,* but we will ignore such phrases for the time being.)

In this half-mad sentence (perhaps uttered by a crazy sea captain who had dosed himself on too much rum and grammar), what parts of speech is *forward* acting as?

1	2	3	4	5

Forward the *forward* sail *forward* the *forward* *forwardly*!

1. *Forward* is a verb in the "command position," as in "*Do* a good job," or "*Pick* up my books." Military order: "*Forward*, march!"

2. *Forward* is an adjective, meaning "near the front," modifying *sail*.

3. *Forward* is a preposition, meaning "near to" and implying placement, as in "*by* the bridge," "*over* the hill," "*around* the house."

4. *Forward* is a noun, designating the front end of the ship.

5. *Forwardly* is an adverb (note the -*ly*), showing how something is done; it means "boldly and eagerly."

To explain further how the parts of speech work, let's expand the information given in the table at the beginning of this section.

1. Nouns are naming words. They fit in the slot in this sentence: "The _____ did it." Here are some examples:

> The *dog* did it.
> The *vandals* did it.
> The *Smiths* did it.
> The *running* did it.

Note that even though *running* appears to be a verb, it is acting as a noun, as the subject of the sentence. Therefore we call it a noun.

We can put two or more words together to make compound nouns: *truck driver, tenderfoot, like-mindedness, lady-in-waiting.*

2. Pronouns are noun substitutes. They are naming words that stand for nouns (*pro* means "for"). Examples:

> *We* did *that* for *you*.
> *This* is *what she* did for *her*.
> *What* is *it*?
> Are *they* coming to the party? *Some* are.

3. Verbs state. They can fit in the slot: "The thing(s) _____ it." (*Thing* here stands for any noun acting as a subject.) Examples:

> The thing *wanted* it.
> The things *were* happy.
> The thing *seems to be* a rat.
> The thing *will bake* a pie.
> The thing *should have been allowed to win* it.

As the last three examples indicate, words used as verbs can be combined to make verb phrases.

4. Adjectives modify (describe, qualify, or limit) nouns and pronouns. Examples:

> A *big* house, a *bigger* house, the *biggest* house
> The *sharp* stick, a *sharper* stick, the *sharpest* stick
> They were *young.*
> Truly *able* people are usually *happy.*
> It was *better.*
> *Middle-aged* executives make the *best* managers.

Note: When attached to nouns, words like *the, a, an, this, those, my, her, our,* and so on can be considered as adjectives (they describe, qualify, or limit): *the* market, *my* habit, *their* lives, *a* Pontiac, *that* diamond, *those* people, *one's* dormouse.

5. Adverbs modify a verb, adjective, or another adverb. They often end in -*ly*. Usually they tell *how, when, where,* or *how much.* Examples:

> The duck quacked *loudly.*
> It was a *very* old duck.
> Drive *slow(ly).*
> Put the chair *there.*
> I'll be home *early.*

6. Prepositions join nouns and pronouns to other elements in a sentence. The noun or pronoun is considered the *object of the preposition.* In "before the war," *before* is the preposition, and *war* the object of the preposition; in "in regard to it," *in* and *to* are prepositions, and *regard* and *it* are their objects.

Prepositions can also appear at the end of sentences:

> Which person did you give it *to*?
> I am giving the whole thing *up.*
> What did you do that *for*?

7. Conjunctions join. But unlike prepositions, they do not employ nouns or pronouns as objects.

a. Coordinating conjunctions connect word units of equal rank:

> You *and* I
> Tired *but* happy
> Cubs *or* White Sox
> Help us, *or* we will fail.
> I saw you, *so* I knew you were there.

b. Subordinating conjunctions connect subordinate clauses to main clauses (see the next section for more on clauses). Examples:

When the doorknob fell off, they were trapped in the room.

If it is raining, call a cab to get home.

The tests were postponed, *even though* all the students were ready to take them.

The angel lost his wings *because* he was careless.

PRACTICE

Identify the parts of speech of the italicized words in the following sentences.

1. *Many* colleges *suffer from* high *expenses and low* enrollments.
2. When *one sees* his life *pass before him, he is* not *necessarily ready for* death *or* the grave.
3. *The law* is *what* we *make it, in fact* as well as *action.*
4. *Running, jumping,* and *breathing* are *surely* all *verbs.* Is that *true*?
5. *All* women are *equal* to *men* (*say the feminists, who* are determined to shatter *many stereotypes* based *on* sex).
6. If *you believe this,* will *you* act *accordingly*?
7. It is *time to play* baseball *because spring* is *here.*
8. *Concerning your* raise *see* Mr. *Partin, the general assistant* manager.
9. "I *dreamed* I *was dreaming,* and of course I had to wake up from my *dream dream,* and that woke me out of my *dream* too." — Dwight Bolinger, *Aspects of Language*
10. *After dreaming, but* before being *entirely awake,* he *began* to snore fast *and loud.*

GA 2 LEARN TO IDENTIFY CLAUSES

A **clause** is a statement created by joining a noun-subject to its own verb. Without such joining, the clause cannot exist.

1. Main clauses make complete statements. A main clause can be a full sentence. In the following sentences, the subjects and verbs of the main clauses are italicized:

        S   V
Mrs. *Canaday will be* at home on Wednesday.

        S   V
Two *cars came* down the block to the two-story house.

```
   S    V
```
The *beer froze* on the back porch.

```
   S           S    V
```
Asthma and *pneumonia are* related conditions.

```
   S    V
```
Dogs bark.

2. Subordinate clauses are also created by joining noun-subjects to their own verbs. But these clauses differ in two ways from main clauses: (1) they do not make complete statements; and (2) they are almost without exception signaled by what we call here a *subordinating sign.* Here are some examples, with the subordinating signs capitalized:

```
          S       V
```
IF Mrs. *Canaday will be* at home on Wednesday . . . .

```
                S    V
```
. . . WHEN two *cars came* down the block.

```
            S    V
```
AFTER the *beer froze* on the back porch . . . .

```
                S     V
```
. . . EVEN THOUGH the *beer froze* on the back porch.

```
          S    V
```
WHAT *man has put* asunder . . . .

The spaced periods indicate that subordinate clauses cannot stand alone as complete sentences.

Many words can act as subordinating signs. They give readers a signal about what lies ahead in the grammar of the sentence. Here is a partial list (units of two or three words may function as one sign):

after	since	when
although	so that	whenever
as though	that	which
because	until	while
before	what	who
no matter what	whatever	whosoever

That as a subordinating sign may be omitted from its clause, but it should always be understood:

Car-makers agree [THAT] their products use too much gasoline.
The good [THAT] a person does never lasts.

Putting subordinating signs and main clauses together, we can write sentences like these (subordinating signs are capitalized):

Subordinate   Main

WHATEVER they decide to do, it should be of some help.

Main   Subordinate

The repairman said THAT the old icebox could be fixed.

Main   Subordinate   Main continued

Our singers, WHO had been practicing in the barn, moved into the church.

Main   Subordinate   Subordinate

The senator said THAT he would sue BECAUSE he had been slandered.

Main

THAT the major is honest is obvious.

Subordinate

(The subject of the main clause is "That the major is honest.")

PRACTICE

In each of the following sentences, insert a brace (⌒) over the main and subordinate clauses. Underline any subordinating signs, and insert any that are understood.

1. Annihilation is a risk we must not take.
2. A basic principle writers should follow is brevity.
3. "It is useless to go to bed to save the light, if the result is twins." —Chinese proverb.
4. Bacon was right when he said reading makes a full man.
5. The rhetoric teacher is an academic gravedigger who always has his shovel ready.
6. How one writes reflects how one feels.
7. If you are caught between despair and misery, the only way is up.
8. "When you are nine, you know that there are things that you don't know, but you know that when you know something you know it." —Robert Penn Warren, "Blackberry Winter"

Subordinate clauses act in three ways—as *nouns, adjectives,* or *adverbs.*

a. A **noun clause** substitutes for a noun or pronoun.

Noun: Work is a bore.
Clause: What we do is a bore.

Pronoun: I approve of him.
Clause: I approve of how he works.

Noun: His parents do not understand his politics.
Clause: His parents do not understand why he votes Democratic.

b. An **adjective clause** modifies a noun or pronoun.

A woman who has a good job should not be envious of housewives.

Americans who speak Japanese are rare.

The table, which had been recently painted, got wet in the rain.

Any drug that can cure cancer may have dangerous side effects.

She who raises children should not envy working women.

c. Some **adverb clauses** modify adjectives or other adverbs. A large number of adverb clauses answer questions such as *how, when, where, how much, why, to what extent.* In the years that we have been teaching grammar, however, it has become plain that these questions alone often do not help identify adverb clauses. In addition to the questions, we suggest a simple "negative formula": An adverb clause is any clause that is *not* nounal or adjectival. In other words, the adverb clause *does not* replace or modify a noun or pronoun.

She is sure that she will get the job. (Modifies an *adjective*.)
So that you can get home easily, I'll lend you my car. (Tells *why*.)
She came as soon as she got your note. (Tells *when*.)
They play tennis more than I do. (Tells *how much*.)
I knew you stole a cookie because you had a guilty expression. (Tells *why*.)

PRACTICE

Identify the italicized subordinate clauses as noun, adjective, or adverb.

1. They wondered *who he could be.*
2. The fact *that America is a great country* is beside the point.
3. Mr. Smith, *who is a medical technician*, can help us.
4. *If I were you*, I would ask him to call us.
5. She said *that more women would be having children in the next decade.*

6. *When we were in New York*, we stayed at the Biltmore.
7. I go *where I want to.*
8. He will do *what you tell him.*
9. *Whose fault it is* is a serious question.
10. Is this the book *which you had studied*?

GA 3 LEARN TO IDENTIFY PHRASES

A **phrase** is a grammatical unit "larger" than a single part of speech but "smaller" than a clause. A phrase must have at least two words in it. Unlike a clause, a phrase does not make a statement using a combination of noun-subject and its own verb. Here are five phrases that, taken together, form a complete sentence:

> The black horse   with the long mane   by the corral   will be ridden by an expert cowboy.

Phrases are classified as follows:

1. Noun phrases:

> *Puppy love* strikes *many sensible people* as *a pain* in the neck.

2. Prepositional phrases:

> *On the whole,* it is not a bad pain *in the neck.*

3. Verb phrases:

> Mr. Winchell *has been biting* into every peach in the store.
> The store owner *will consider* legal action.
> *Have* you *found* any whole peaches?

4. Verbal phrases (phrases made from verbs) are not main verbs or verb phrases; they cannot help make statements in clause or sentence form.

a.   Participial phrases act as adjectives:

> The wart *growing on my finger* was not painful.
> The child *hurt by shrapnel* did recover.
> *Relinquishing their rights,* they surrendered.
> *Born in San Antonio*, he grew up with a taste for hot weather.

b.   Infinitive phrases use the "to _____" form:

> *To act well* in this life is sometimes impossible.
> She wanted *to replace the astronaut.*
> That work is yet *to be done.*

c. **Gerund phrases** act as nouns:

Raising roses in this heat is impossible.
They considered *rearing children*, but later thought better of it.

The complexity of phrasal grammar lies partly in its nomenclature. You will often find, for instance, a phrase that is *labeled* one thing *performing a job* that is called by another name. Here are some typical phrases, along with the jobs they are performing:

Phrase	Name of Phrase	Job Performed (noun, adjective, adverb, verb)
To be a cop is dangerous.	infinitive	noun (*To be a cop* is the subject of the sentence.)
Her desire *to be a cop* is commendable.	infinitive	adjective (*To be a cop* modifies the noun *desire.*)
Their hurrying through the job was a mistake.	gerund	noun (*Their hurrying* is the subject of the sentence.)
They were people *of integrity*.	prepositional	adjective (*Of integrity* modifies the noun *people.*)
Locking the house, they ran to the car.	participial	adjective (*Locking the house* modifies *they.*)
The persons *locking the house* were the owners.	participial	adjective (*Locking the house* modifies *persons.*)
They protected the house by *locking it up*.	gerund	noun (*Locking it up* is the object of the preposition *by.*)
Before Sunday is soon enough.	prepositional	noun (*Before Sunday* is the subject of the sentence.)
If you must chew tobacco, do it *with style*.	prepositional	adverb (*With style* modifies the verb *do.*)
She was unhappy *to see him leave*.	infinitive	adverb (*To see him leave* modifies the adjective *unhappy.*)
The bad man is my uncle.	noun	noun
This job *is being done*.	verb	verb

PRACTICE

1. First identify the italicized phrases by name: *noun, prepositional, verb.* Then describe the job (*noun, adjective, adverb, verb*) that the phrase is performing. (The numeral following each sentence indicates the number of phrases contained in it.)

a. The fur *of the cat was sticking up*. (2) (Consider *up* as part of the verb.)
b. *By the chair* was where we found her, alternately purring and snarling. (1)
c. You *should sit* here *by me on the bench*. (3)
d. *Light bulbs can light our dark cellar*. (3)
e. *The comic strip* "Doonesbury" teaches *by indirection*. (2)
f. *Logan's Run* [a movie] *will be forgotten with considerable ease*. (3)

2. Identify the verbal phrases (*participial, infinitive,* and *gerund*) in the following sentences. Then state the job that each phrase is performing (*noun, adjective, adverb*).

a. *Riding a bicycle* is dangerous in this city. (1)
b. *Even double-locked*, her bike was stolen. (1)
c. She was eager *to get it back, calling the police* three times. (2)
d. *By warning the residents*, they prevented more injury. (1)
e. *Warning the residents* was a good idea. (1)
f. *To run away, leaving the area quickly*, was their only concern. (2)
g. Off went the residents, *leaving the area quickly*. (1)

Forms of Grammar

G 1 POSSESSIVE WITH GERUND

A *gerund* is a noun that ends in -ing:

Pitch*ing* is fun.
Learn*ing* is hard.
His ly*ing* is hard to take.

When the emphasis is on the activity, use the *possessive* form with the -ing noun.

Problem: She did not object to *me hugging* her.
Solution: She did not object to *my hugging* her.

Problem: The *officer commanding* me to pull over was a surprise.
Solution: The *officer's commanding* me to pull over was a surprise.

If the emphasis is not on the activity, you may write:

She did not object to *me* hugging her. (But she might have objected to any other person who hugged her.)
I prefer *John* pitching. (The emphasis is on John, rather than on his activity, pitching.)

PRACTICE

Correct the following sentences for faulty possessives, then explain your correction in a sentence or two. If you think that a sentence is correct as it stands, explain why.

1. Hal Johnson writing was the best I had ever read.
2. No one appreciates Elizabeth modeling more than I do.
3. He said that he wished you had stopped him joking about our mistakes so much.
4. The oxen in the zoo were disturbed by the lion roaring.
5. We heard them roaring.
6. Father objected to him dating Susie.
7. He insists on me chaperoning poor Susie on every date.
8. She hated him interfering with her private life.

G 2 VAGUE OR AMBIGUOUS PRONOUN REFERENCE

Make your pronoun references clear.

Problem: The dresser had glue blocks over the screw holes so that one had to remove the screws before removing the drawer supports. *This* required me to get help from my shop instructor. (What does *this* refer to?)

Solution: Since the dresser had glue blocks over the screw holes, I asked my shop instructor to help me remove the blocks without damaging the drawer supports.

Problem: Our dog knocked two lamps on the floor and broke several glasses on the lamp table. We found *them* smashed the next morning. (Does *them* refer to lamps, to glasses, or to lamps *and* glasses?)

Solution: Our dog knocked . . . We found the glasses smashed the next morning.

Problem: In discussing the language requirements, *it* made us feel that we had the wrong idea about the usefulness of a foreign language. (What does *it* refer to?)

Solution: As we were discussing the language requirements, we began to realize that we had the wrong idea about the usefulness of a foreign language.

G 3 WRONG FORM OF PRONOUN

To correct most errors in pronoun form, isolate (or set apart) the construction.

Problem: Would you call Jack and *he* on the phone?
Isolation: Would you call *he*? (*He* should be *him*.)
Solution: Would you call Jack and *him* on the phone?

Problem: Phyllis and *me* will walk to the library with you.
Isolation: *Me* will walk to the library with you. (*Me* should be *I*.)
Solution: Phyllis and *I* will walk to the library with you.

Problem: The movie program was specially designed for *we* college students.
Isolation: The movie program was specially designed for *we*. (*We* should be *us*.)
Solution: The movie program was specially designed for *us* college students.

Note: The following advice is the subject of debate by many language experts. But it is practical advice and firmly based on modern English usage.

Who vs. *whom.* Use *whom* when it is the object of a preposition: "for whom," "to whom," "beside whom." Use *who* with everything else.

I vs. *me; they* vs. *them;* etc. Where it sounds natural at the end of an expression use the *object* form *(me, her, him, them)*:

> It is *me.*
> That is *them* over there.
> This is *him* now.

PRACTICE

Find any vague or ambiguous pronoun references, or wrong pronoun forms, in the following sentences. Then correct each error.

1. In Oklahoma City they have the largest city (in area) in the country.
2. Margaret told Helen she was the wisest girl she ever knew.
3. It said in the manual that the car never needs an oil change.
4. Tell the Dean and he about the secret contract with the CIA.
5. Us faculty members knew about it all the time.
6. Mark and me were told from the beginning.
7. The money was supposed to have gone to we team members.
8. Carter is an airline pilot, and that is the profession his son wants to follow.
9. He can't see well. This is because he did not get glasses as a child.
10. Miles held on to the cat's paw, which bit him.
11. Mrs. Smith gave a talk on the antique business—in particular on the method of financing it and making a proper report to the IRS. It is a complicated affair.
12. Susie yelled at the owner of the new house on the corner that was watering his roses.

G 4 APPROPRIATE VERB TENSE

Tense refers to how the verb expresses *time.*

Present tense:	She *wishes* for money.
Past tense:	She *wished* for money.
Future tense:	She *will wish* for money.
Present perfect:	She *has wished* for money.
Past perfect:	She *had wished* for money.
Future perfect:	She *will have wished* for money.

Most questions of tense involve thinking through the logic of the time(s) you intend to put your statements in.

Problem:	Then the judge *recalled* that the prosecution *stated* its objections two weeks earlier.
Solution:	Then the judge *recalled* that the prosecution *had stated* its objections two weeks earlier. (The verbs logically belong in two different "times.")

Problem:	He *was* a handsome man before he *became* a vampire.
Solution:	He *had been* a handsome man before he *became* a vampire.

Note: The present tense is customarily used in literary criticism and reviews when describing action and psychological states in the literary work. But it is not used when making statements about the author or his background.

Problem:	Shakespeare *sees* Hamlet as a man who *believed* in the supernatural.
Solution:	Shakespeare *saw* Hamlet as a man who *believes* in the supernatural.

Problem:	In *The Catcher in the Rye*, Holden Caulfield *was* a tiresome adolescent. Perhaps the author, J. D. Salinger, *does* not *understand* his own creation.
Solution:	In *The Catcher in the Rye*, Holden Caulfield *is* a tiresome adolescent. Perhaps the author, J. D. Salinger, *did* not *understand* his own creation.

PRACTICE

Where necessary, change the tense of the verbs.

1. At first, Huck Finn believes that blacks are different; later he came to recognize that all human beings will share the same faults and virtues.
2. Here she was, staring angrily at me from the stage. So I say to her: "I can't hear you from the back row!"
3. Mrs. McMinn claimed that the Imperial Valley was the hottest place in California.
4. After Mr. McMinn went to California, his wife was concerned that he could be finding the heat unbearable, so she was writing him to rent an air conditioner.
5. Charles Dickens is a great writer; his *David Copperfield* is a story that every young person will be able to enjoy.
6. Mark Twain writes *Huckleberry Finn* on the top floor of his Hartford home, which he believes to be the best place to work.
7. Sandra remembers that the TV had blown a fuse on the night when we would have been watching a re-run of *Star Trek*.

G 5 FAULTY PRINCIPAL PART OF THE VERB

The so-called *principal parts* of the verb form this familiar pattern:

Present tense	Past tense	Past participle
ask	asked	asked
ring	rang	rung
bring	brought	brought

In its past tense and past participle, *ask* does not change much, adding only *-ed* (*ask, asked, asked*). *Ring* changes form twice, but *bring* changes only once. A verb like *ask* is called *regular*; verbs like *ring* and *bring* are said to be *irregular*. Through constant usage, most of us "know" most of these forms; but when we come to something like *lie* and *dive*, memory often fails. Should we write "I had *lain* there for an hour"? (One of us can never remember and so — when pushed — says, "I *had been* there for an hour.") Is it "The child *dived* in the pool"? Or *dove*?

The answers to such questions can be found in your standard desk dictionary under the present form of the verb (*lie* and *dive*). And there's your choice: memorize the forms; or avoid the verb; or look it up.

PRACTICE

In your dictionary, look up the principal parts of these verbs.

bid (command)	forget	seek	sit
bid (offer)	get	set	spring
burst	hang (execute)	shrink	swing
dive	lie	sink	weave

G 6 PROPER USE OF THE SUBJUNCTIVE

The subjunctive is a verb form used mainly in *contrary-to-fact* statements and after *wishes*. The verb form may be *were*, *be*, or the verb without the final *s*.

Contrary-to-fact statements:
I would not do that if I *were* you. (I am not you.)
If she *were* true to me she would not go out with other men. (She is not true to me.)
If this *be* patriotism, I am not a patriot. (This is not patriotism.)

After wishes:

I wish I *were* rich.

Let him *live.*

My father requested that his body *be* cremated.

I demand that Smith *be* reinstated. (A demand is a strong wish.)

PRACTICE

In the following sentences, correct the faulty forms of the subjunctive.

1. If he was to live a thousand years, he would not be able to support me adequately.
2. I wish this wasn't Tuesday.
3. I'd drop that gun if I was you.
4. If he was here, we would all leave.
5. Major Burns demands that he is given a transfer to another unit.
6. I would go to Monterey if I was given the opportunity.

G 7 PILING UP VERBS

The English verb system is complex and flexible, made so in part by the rich array of *auxiliaries* (or *helping verbs*): "*had been* kept," "*should have been* doing," "*will have* performed." Yet helping verbs can work against a writer if they are piled up in a sentence so that verb phrases are long and awkward:

> *Problem:* He *would have liked to have seen* the movie.
> *Solution:* He *wanted to see* the movie.

> *Problem:* We *did* not *desire to have become required* as participants by the coach.
> *Solution:* We *did* not *want* the coach *to make* us participate.

> *Problem:* They *had meant to have stopped* the murder.
> *Solution:* They *had meant to stop* the murder.

G 8 CONFUSION OF ADJECTIVES AND ADVERBS

Errors with adjectives and adverbs are sometimes created when you confuse the two. For instance, if you wanted to say that someone had body odor, it would be silly to write that he smelled *badly*, for *badly* would imply that his nose wasn't working properly. Follow these suggestions for distinguishing between adjectives and adverbs:

1. Know that adjectives modify nouns and that adverbs modify verbs, adjectives, and other adverbs. (See p. 333 for more discussion of adjectives and adverbs.)

2. Use your dictionary to check whether a word is an adjective or an adverb.

3. Substitute the word you are in doubt about into one of these patterns:

> Subject-verb-*adjective*-object:
> You injured a *well* person.
> You did a *good* job.

> Subject-verb-object-*adverb:*
> You did the job *well.*
> You did it *happily.*

> Subject-is-*adjective:*
> She is *good.*
> She is *happy.*

The substitution should tell you whether the word is an adjective or adverb.

G 9 DEGREES OF COMPARISON FOR ADJECTIVES AND ADVERBS

The degrees of comparison for adjectives and adverbs are *positive, comparative,* and *superlative;* for example:

Positive	*Comparative*	*Superlative*
cold	colder	coldest
big	bigger	biggest
good	better	best
much	more	most
easily	more easily	most easily
often	more often	most often

The shorter adjectives (and a small number of adverbs) form the degrees of comparison as *cold* does: cold, colder, coldest. A few are irregular: *bad, worse, worst.*

Many adjectives of two syllables and all of three or more syllables form the degrees of comparison with the use of *more* and *most:* beautiful, *more* beautiful, *most* beautiful. And most adverbs are formed the same way: curiously, *more* curiously, *most* curiously.

It is often claimed that certain adjectives — such as *unique, round,* and *dead* — have only one degree and logically cannot be compared.

Does *dead, deader, deadest* appear logical? When used figuratively or light-heartedly, it probably does. "That was the deadest party I ever went to" expresses the idea perfectly. But in most cases, *dead*, like *pregnant*, expresses an absolute condition—you either are or you aren't. Similarly, *unique* cannot be qualified in expressions like *more unique*—the word means "one of a kind," and you can't get "one-er" than "one." Yet you might reasonably write *almost unique*—almost "one of a kind."

G 10 MISUSE OF NOUN AS ADJECTIVE

Many nouns make poor adjectives: *liability* action, *validity* record, *believability* reasons, *plot* circumstances. The solution for most of these is to change the wording or the construction.

> *Problem:* I will now relate the *plot circumstances*.
> *Solution:* I will now relate the *circumstances of the plot*.

> *Problem:* His experiments have a poor *validity record*.
> *Solution:* His experiments *seldom work out*.

As you may have guessed, such problems are usually closely related to the use of jargon. See pp. 186–187 for more discussion of "nouny" writing.

PRACTICE

Correct these sentences for: (1) confusion of adjectives with adverbs, (2) the proper use of degrees of comparison, and (3) the misuse of nouns as adjectives.

1. The Maremont Corporation Harvey, Illinois research was conducted by three chemists.
2. The research was done as careful as any technician research in the lab, and it turned out to be the more useful of all the projects started there.
3. She looked deliciously and sweet in her new Levis. But she acted recklesser than she looked.
4. I run every day for endurance reasons. It is good exercise and makes me feel good.
5. Johanna's plane was built strong enough to carry an extra load of fuel easy.
6. "Hold tight to your religion beliefs," his elderly father had said.
7. Her position qualifications are most perfect for the supervisor job.
8. My high grade was the inevitably result of having a kindly teacher.
9. His ambition is the less good thing about him.

G 11 FAULTY VERB AGREEMENT

Verbs must ordinarily agree with their subjects:

> *Dogs are* canines.
> A *clue was* discovered.
> *Each* of the female bears *was* found with its cub.
> These *people were* innocent.

However, when in doubt let your meaning determine subject-verb agreement.

> *Problem:*   A *number* of these cures *was* (?) *were* (?) rejected.
> *Solution (1):*   A *number* of these cures *were* rejected. (Obviously, *number* designates more than one cure.)
> *Solution (2):*   *Several* of these cures *were* rejected.
> *Solution (3):*   A *few* of these cures *were* rejected.
> *Solution (4):*   The doctors rejected some of the cures.

Here are six typical errors in agreement:

1. With clumsy joiners (*as well as, along with, in addition to*, etc.).

> *Problem:*   My *baby, together with three other babies* in the maternity ward, *was* (?) *were* (?) saved by the nurse.
> *Solution (1):*   My *baby,* together with three other babies in the maternity ward, *was* saved by the nurse. (The general rule is that a singular subject, immediately followed by clumsy joiners or other interrupters, takes a singular verb.)
> *Solution (2):*   My *baby and* three other *babies* in the maternity ward *were* saved by the nurse. (Where you can, use *and* instead of clumsy joiners.)

2. With pronouns.

> *Problem:*   She is one of those *girls who is* (?) *are* (?) always well dressed.
> *Solution (1):*   She is one of those *girls who are* always well dressed. (Make the verb agree with the noun [*girls*] that the pronoun [*who*] stands for.)
> *Solution (2):*   She is the kind of *girl who is* always well dressed. (Put the whole thing in the singular.)

3. With "subject-is-noun" statements.

> *Problem:*   The main *issue is* (?) *are* (?) high prices.
> *Solution (1):*   The main *issue is* high prices. (Make the verb agree with the subject.)
> *Solution (2):*   The main *issue is that prices are too high.* (Change subject-*is*-noun to subject-*is*-clause.)

4. With collective nouns ("group" nouns).

>   *Problem:*   The *team is* (?) *are* (?) happy about their victory.
>   *Solution (1):*   The *team is* happy about its victory. (Consider the team as one group or unit.)
>   *Solution (2):*   The *members* of the team *are* happy about their victory. (Use a plural subject.)

>   *Problem:*   *A hundred feet* of electrical wire *is* (?) *are* (?) too much for this room.
>   *Solution (1):*   *A hundred feet* of electrical wire *is* too much for this room. (Consider *a hundred feet* as a unit.)
>   *Solution (2):*   We don't need a hundred feet of electrical wire for this room.

5. With "it-there" statements.

>   *Problem:*   There *is* (?) *are* (?) happy *cowboys* in Texas.
>   *Solution (1):*   There *are* happy *cowboys* in Texas. (Make the verb agree with the subject *cowboys*.)
>   *Solution (2):*   *Cowboys are* happy in Texas.

6. With "either-or" and "neither-nor" statements.

>   *Problem:*   *Either* the butler *or* the maid *was* (?) *were* (?) the murderer.
>   *Solution:*   *Either* the butler *or* the maid *was* the murderer. (In such constructions, pairs of singular subjects take singular verbs.)

>   *Problem:*   *Neither* the car *nor* the trucks *was* (?) *were* (?) stolen.
>   *Solution (1):*   *Neither* the car *nor* the trucks *were* stolen. (The verb should agree with the nearer of its subjects.)
>   *Solution (2):*   The car and the trucks *were* not stolen. (Revise the construction to avoid the "neither-nor" problem.)

PRACTICE

Correct these sentences. If you believe that a sentence is correct as it stands, state why.

1. There's lights on in my house.
2. Was any of his rabbits killed by the weasel?
3. Neither the puppy nor the kittens were responsible for making such a mess.
4. My biggest problem is C grades on themes.
5. I have heard that an army march on their stomachs.
6. There seem to be a great deal of noise coming from the next room.

7. The stadium is one of those structures that surprises you when you first see it.
8. His use of wallpaper, as well as his painting, make the living room quite pleasant.
9. My list of supplies were so long that Mr. Fenwick refused to buy them.
10. The advice of both counselors, which I heard from the next room, are that you go back to the dorm and talk to the resident advisor.
11. Their main complaint is loud stereos and people partying after midnight.
12. These are many of the kinds of reasoning that is mentioned in the Bill of Rights.

G 12 FAULTY PRONOUN AGREEMENT

Here is an example of faulty pronoun agreement: "Everyone was told to pick up *their* books and leave." Since *everyone* is singular, the pronoun *their* does not "agree" with it.

> *Problem:* I told *each girl* coming to the party to bring *their* own food.
>
> *Solution (1):* I told *each girl* coming to the party to bring *her* own food.
>
> *Solution (2):* I told *all the girls* coming to the party to bring *their* own food. (Instead of forcing the pronoun to agree with the expression appearing earlier in the sentence, try starting the sentence with a more logical word. *Each girl* really means *all the girls*.)

Observe the typical choices in the following agreement problem:

> *Problem:* If you want *an employee* to work hard for you, always give *them* plenty of praise for good work.
>
> *Solution (1):* If you want *an employee* to work hard for you, always give *him* . . . .
>
> *Solution (2):* If you want *employees* to work hard for you, always give *them* . . . .

Problems in pronoun agreement can often be avoided by going back to the beginning of the paragraph and deciding whether you want to be in the singular or the plural throughout your discussion. Decide early, for instance, whether you want to discuss *employees* in general, or the *employee* as an individual. Then simply be consistent in choosing pronouns.

PRACTICE

Correct the faulty pronoun agreement in these sentences.

1. Each person rented their own costume for the dance.
2. If someone tries to ride their bike through campus, they'll run over you every time.
3. The university is proud of their lawns and parks.
4. If anyone writes to Charlotte, have them tell her she left her skis here.
5. Each of the rules for the house can be considered practical only when they are enforced.
6. Everyone likes to have more freedom for themselves than they do for others.
7. After one retires, they like to have a hobby to keep them busy.
8. When a nursing student applies for her first job after graduation, they like to know how much money they are going to make.

G 13 THE GENERIC PRONOUN

There have been some recent attempts to create a "neutral" pronoun (for instance, *hir* or *shim*) that will take care of both sexes in ordinary statement-making. Unfortunately, none of the suggested substitutes for the generic *man*, *he*, and *him* has proved satisfactory; and none has been accepted in standard usage. The use of *he/she* and *him/her* is not standard at this time, probably because the constructions are so awkward. If you are referring to several people, you have several choices:

1. Use the standard generic pronouns, *man*, *one*, *he*, etc.

2. Use the plural *they* and *them*—this is possible, of course, only when referring to plural nouns.

3. Use *she* and *her* if the members of the group are primarily women.

However you manage this troublesome affair, try to be consistent.

Sentence Structure

S 1 UNNECESSARY SHIFTS

In avoiding unnecessary shifts in various sentence elements, follow the "rule of consistency," which is actually only a matter of common sense: In any rhetorical unit (particularly in the sentence), continue as you began.

1. If you began in the past tense, continue in it:

> *Problem:* Louise *stated* that the papers were filed a year ago, while her attorney *says* they were never filed.
>
> *Solution:* Louise *stated* . . . her attorney *said* . . . .

2. If you started with indirect discourse, stay with it:

> *Problem:* Mrs. McMinn said she was thirsty and would I get her some water from the cooler?
>
> *Solution:* Mrs. McMinn said she was thirsty and asked me to get her some water from the cooler.

3. If you started with one form of the pronoun, stick with it.

> *Problem:* *One* cannot understand when *you* are young that marriage is full of both pains and pleasures.
>
> *Solution:* When *you* are young, *you* cannot understand . . . .

Pronouns are slippery, shifty beasts:

> *Problem:* If traveling makes *one* sick, the airline provides paper bags for *you*.
>
> *Solution:* If traveling makes *one* sick, the airline provides paper bags for *him*.

This solution throws both pronouns into the third person and is, at least, grammatical. You could write ". . . makes *one* sick . . . paper bags for *one*." But this sounds like a British aristocrat at his most pompous. The best policy is to pick out your first pronoun (or noun) carefully and then continue in the same person:

> If traveling makes *you* sick . . . bags for *you*.
> If traveling makes *people* sick . . . bags for *them*.

Or simply avoid the slippery beast in the second clause:

> For anyone who gets sick, the airline provides a paper bag.

(See pp. 342–343 for more discussion of consistent pronoun use.)

Correct these sentences for consistency.

1. The airplane swooped close to the ground, and he blinked his landing lights twice.
2. As they were walking, Harley remarked that most of the elms were dying, but Sheridan explains that there is a new scientific method of saving them.
3. If the elms were all alive, and the method is easily available, we could protect thousands of them in this city alone.
4. The general ordered that the flags be lowered to half-mast on Tuesday and blow taps for the men who were lost.
5. The vice-president had to recognize Mrs. Carlin's ability, but this was not done gracefully by him.
6. A legislature does not like to tax its citizens, and they will usually try to get money some other way.
7. If you want to make a sailor happy, just give him plenty of shore leave.
8. First, mark down the pantsuits, and then you should put "50%-Off" tags on the women's blouses.
9. Macbeth has trouble with his conscience, but after a time he managed to kill it completely.
10. In a small town, one is never lonely; indeed, you usually feel that you know too many people.

S 2 OMISSIONS AND INCOMPLETE CONSTRUCTIONS

Omissions and incomplete constructions are often accidental; the writer leaves out a word on the page that his mind easily supplies for him — but not for the reader:

Don't leave out a word on ^*the* page.
Many have wondered what happened ^*to* Marilyn Monroe.

Other omissions are created by what might be called a "grammatical hiccup":

Wilma saw the bartender was watering the bourbon.

Obviously, the object of *saw* should not be *bartender* but the whole noun clause:

Wilma saw *that the bartender was watering the bourbon*.

Another example of a hiccup:

Problem: Since he's working here, he's been watering the stock.
Solution: Since he's *been* working here, he's been watering the stock.

Certain idioms seem to be particularly susceptible to incompleteness:

Problem: He was interested but undisturbed by her revelation.
Solution (1): He was interested *in* but undisturbed by her revelation.
Solution (2): He was interested in her revelation but undisturbed by it.

Problem: We would appreciate it if you would agree with and not protest our plans.
Solution: We would appreciate it if you would agree with and not protest *against* our plans.

PRACTICE

Supply the missing parts in these sentences.

1. Playing classical trumpet has and always will be a poorly paid profession.
2. Whenever I see the Statue of Liberty, I get impression power and glory.
3. They agree with Mrs. Kane's interpretation but object Mr. Kane's.
4. Winnie did a good job and earned a great deal money from the Ace Housebuilding Company.
5. The fat old dog was barking, and the puppies regarding him with wonder.
6. We promised the old dog would not bothering the neighbors any more.
7. I remember a dog had a bark like that.
8. He never has and undoubtedly never will speak confidently before an audience.

S 3 FAULTY COMPARISON

Comparisons should be logical and complete. Here is an example of a faulty comparison:

Walcott's beliefs were different from Clark.

The writer is comparing the wrong things — *beliefs* and *Clark.*

Solution (1): Walcott's beliefs were different from Clark's.
Solution (2): Walcott's beliefs were different from those expressed by Clark.

Problem:	We are as industrious, if not more industrious, than the East Germans. (This says that we are "as industrious . . . *than* the East Germans.")
Solution:	We are as industrious as the East Germans, if not more so.

Problem:	Our family's house cost more than Smith.
Solution (1):	Our family's house cost more than Smith's.
Solution (2):	Our family's house cost more than the Smiths' did.

Problem:	New York City is bigger than any city in the country. (This means that it is bigger than itself, since it is one of the cities "in the country.")
Solution (1):	New York is bigger than any *other* city in the country.
Solution (2):	New York is the biggest city in the country.

As these examples imply, faulty comparisons seem to be created when the writer does not think this question through: "*What (a)* am I comparing with *what (b)?*"

PRACTICE

Correct the faulty comparisons in these sentences. Rewrite as necessary.

1. Baseball talk makes Barb every bit as angry as those persons who talk endlessly of ballet and Bach.
2. My boyfriend says that his writing is easier to read than his teacher.
3. Fewer people went to the movies; more and more they bought their own TV sets instead of watching their neighbors.
4. In *Catch-22*, the plot is easier to follow than the other war novels.
5. This year's Chevrolet is smaller and more expensive.
6. The Swiss make more watches and other timepieces than England or France.
7. This fat goldfish is obviously more greedy than any fish in the tank.
8. Using contractions made Miss Wimm angrier even than when she caught anybody reading comic books in class.

S 4 SPLIT OR "SEPARATED" CONSTRUCTIONS

English grammar does its job in several ways. One of these can be described by the "rule of nearness": expressions that belong together are put near each other. Here are a few instances:

1. Objects are placed near their verbs:

Problem:	She *sent* to her congressman a *letter*.
Solution:	She *sent* a *letter* to her congressman.

Problem: *He* as it turned out when we found him *was* not lost at all.

Solution: As it turned out when we found him, *he was* not lost at all.

2. Adjective clauses are placed near the expression they modify:

Problem: Anders lost his *knife* on the seacoast *which his mother had bought for him.*

Solution: On the seacoast, Anders lost the *knife which his mother had bought for him.*

3. The sign of the infinitive (*to*) immediately precedes its verb:

Problem: They wanted *to* immediately and completely *pay back* the loan.

Solution: They wanted *to pay back* the loan immediately and completely.

Note: It is fashionable to say that good writers occasionally split infinitives. One excellent textbook (the first edition of which we used as freshmen back in the Middle Ages) says that "many times" infinitive splitting is "not only natural but also desirable." The authors use this example: "For her *to never complain* seems unreal." Is that better than "*never to complain*"?

It is interesting to note that for every infinitive split by an accomplished writer, there will be a hundred that he won't split. The rule of nearness is not made of granite, but it is not made of Jello either. If you glance over the problems in S 5, S 6, and S 7 on the following pages, you will discover that violating the rule can lead to some pretty comical sentences.

PRACTICE

In the following sentences, repair the split or "separation."

1. Mrs. McMinn told Mike when he went to the grocery store on the corner of First and Main to pick up some eggs.
2. Mike promised to quickly and faithfully carry out her request.
3. We may, if there is no objection, see a double-header this afternoon.
4. The second baseman, dismayed by the spikes of the two-hundred-pound runner bearing grimly down upon him, threw wildly to first.
5. We agreed as soon as the game was over and the noise of the crowd had abated that she would speak to me again.
6. The argument that beer makes one tipsy loses at a raucous major-league ball game all possible force.
7. When you watch people drink and sweat in 115-degree heat, it is impossible to even partly believe that any alcohol reaches the brain.

S 5 MISPLACED MODIFIERS

A *modifier* is a sentence element that describes, qualifies, or limits an expression. If a modifier is wrongly placed, the resulting construction may seem illogical. Examples:

> *Problem:* I departed for Europe on a freighter 3,000 miles away.
> *Solution (1):* I departed on a freighter for Europe—3,000 miles away.
> *Solution (2):* I got on a freighter bound for Europe, which was 3,000 miles away.

> *Problem:* He nearly tried to make all of his teachers happy.
> *Solution:* He tried to make nearly all of his teachers happy.

> *Problem:* We discovered the old well in the north corner of Marston's backyard, which was full of green, brackish water. (The *yard* was full of water?)
> *Solution:* The old well that we discovered in the north corner of Marston's backyard was full of green, brackish water.

PRACTICE

Correct the misplaced modifiers in these sentences. Because some of these errors cannot be satisfactorily corrected by moving the modifier to another position, you may have to rewrite some of the sentences.

1. Her stomach felt better after drinking the orange juice.
2. The fraternities voted for the Homecoming Queen as a body.
3. Men and women walked down the aisle to receive diplomas—not youngsters.
4. The final thrill came in eating the fish he caught with fried potatoes, sliced tomatoes, and a can of beer.
5. Look carefully at that old man with a beard about a block behind.
6. The Ratched Motel is fixing an early breakfast for campers who are leaving the area at 5:00 a.m. (Assume that the campers are leaving at 7:30.)
7. I'll investigate the crime when you finish with the body for possible clues.

S 6 SQUINTING MODIFIERS

The "squinting" *modifier* ambiguously points in two directions at once. Example:

Running away *occasionally* makes Sam feel better.

The reader wonders whether the writer means occasionally *running away* or occasionally *makes Sam feel better*. Such problems can be solved by tying the modifier firmly to what it modifies:

Occasionally, Sam runs away, after which he feels better.

PRACTICE

Correct these squinting constructions by rewriting the sentences.

1. The umpire claimed during the game that Detroit's manager spat in his direction.
2. The manager told us before we sportswriters left to apologize to him.
3. The lawyer who represents himself in most instances is his own "foolish client."
4. They promised after the end of the term to change her grade.
5. He wrote a treatise on mountaineering in the Gobi Desert.

S 7 DANGLING MODIFIERS

The typical *dangling modifier* is an introductory expression that is not "tied" logically to the main clause that follows:

Problem: Having eaten his lunch, the steamboat departed.

The "dangler" implies an action in the opening modifier, but supplies the wrong *actor* for it in the main clause. Such errors are easily corrected by creating a logical tie between both parts of the sentence. This correction can usually be made by changing the opening modifier or the main clause that follows. Sometimes it may be best to rewrite the sentence without the opener.

Solution (1): After lunch, the steamboat departed.
Solution (2): Having eaten his lunch, he boarded the departing steamboat.

Problem: Coming too fast to the stop sign, the brake was applied quickly. (The *brake* was coming too fast?)
Solution (1): Coming too fast to the stop sign, he applied the brake quickly.
Solution (2): He applied the brake quickly when he realized he was coming too fast to the stop sign.

Some danglers have no action stated (as such) in the opener, which is an elliptical expression:

Problem: Upon graduation, my family gave me a hundred dollars and a ticket to Hollywood. (The *family* graduated?)

Solution (1): When I graduated, my family gave me a hundred dollars and a ticket to Hollywood.

Solution (2): Upon graduation, I got a hundred dollars and a ticket to Hollywood from my family.

PRACTICE

Correct the dangling modifiers in these sentences:

1. Getting up from the typewriter when the water cooler exploded, my news story was completely forgotten.
2. Astonished at the intrusion, her hands fluttered wildly.
3. Inflated to an enormous size, I rode the rubber raft around the pool.
4. By stopping smoking, there was a belief that he could cure his asthma.
5. After snuggling warm on the couch all night, the dawn finally came.
6. Concentrating my orderly mind, the theme was written quickly.
7. After working all summer on the road gang, the tan that Melvin got was the envy of his friends.
8. When only a second grader, my mother was told that I was obviously near-sighted.

S 8 FAULTY PARALLELISM

Parallel elements in a sentence should be (a) roughly equal in importance, and (b) written in the same grammatical form. Examples:

Roger and *Tom* were terrible at ballroom dancing.
Ballroom dancing and *square dancing* are not activities for sissies.
Some small nations preferred to *watch, listen,* and *wait* in order to see what the larger nations might do.

Faulty parallelism fails to put parallel *ideas* in parallel *form:*

Problem: She *believes* in him, as well as *having* faith in him.
Solution: She *believes* in him and *has* faith in him.

Problem: That movie had too much *sex, violence,* and the *language was bad.*
Solution: That movie had too much *sex, violence,* and *profanity.*

Correct the faulty parallelism in the following sentences.

1. Her mother could always depend on Trish for going to class and to be making good grades.
2. When he owned that car, he never put in oil, checked the tires, and even the windshield was never washed.
3. In the race, a Porsche came in first, a Ferrari came in second, in addition to a Lotus having come in third.
4. Politicians are ruining this country, as well as its being destroyed by lenient judges.
5. Making the Dean's list and his captaincy of the football team made Strawbridge very popular.
6. The new seats in Howes Stadium are wide, comfortable, and of well-built quality.
7. Ask your roommate whether she wants to go to the party besides going to the picnic.

S 9 PROPER SUBORDINATION

Subordination allows you to shift the emphasis from one part of a sentence to another, thus making your prose smoother and more logical. An important reason for subordinating one clause to another is to show a logical relationship: "*Because we got cold, wet, and hungry,* we left the stadium at half-time." The following subordinate elements are in italics:

> Callie Marshall was unable to reach Denver, *even though she rode all night through the snow.*
> John Frye, *who was one of the most energetic small men we had ever known,* climbed Slew Mountain by himself.
> *Although he was small,* John Frye energetically climbed Slew Mountain by himself.

Note that a subordinate element can be put at the beginning, middle, or end of a sentence.

Use subordination to improve choppy or unemphatic sentences:

> *Problem:* His name was Bellmon. He was black. He was married in his sophomore year. He had two jobs that year.
> *Solution:* Bellmon, *the black married student,* had two jobs his sophomore year.

Problem: They were hungry, but there was a drought, and they lost their farms, so they decided to go to California.

Solution: They lost their farms *after the drought came. Later, driven by hunger,* they decided to go to California.

(Also see pp. 175–176, and 335–337.)

PRACTICE

Use subordination to improve these sentences.

1. He is poor, and he has an old Chevy pickup, but it uses too much oil, and it will eventually have to be sold.
2. The members of the first team could not understand the coach. The misunderstanding became an issue with the Athletic Council.
3. Friendship is of first importance. It helps to create harmony in human relationships.
4. He earned a great deal of money in business. He never worked hard. He paid little attention to conventions of manners and dress.
5. She wanted to major in computer science. She did not have many courses in science or math.
6. Accidents keep occurring on this busy corner. Two extra policemen have been stationed to warn motorists of the danger.
7. The manufacturer gave us a new air conditioner. This occurred before we could complain to the state Consumer's Protection Bureau. He wanted to improve his relationships with customers.

S 10 FAULTY SUBORDINATION

In subordinating one part of a sentence to another, the writer makes the sentence elements *unequal*. Unlike a main clause, a subordinated element can never stand alone. The relationship between main and subordinated elements is both grammatical and logical. In these two sentences, note the subordinated elements (in italics):

The old lady, *who had just put on her nightgown,* would not answer the doorbell.

The old lady, *who would not answer the doorbell,* had just put on her nightgown.

The subordination in the second sentence seems illogical. Here are other examples of faulty subordination.

Problem: Just last week I used that pay phone, *which was bombed this morning.*

Solution: This morning, someone bombed the pay phone *that I used last week.*

Problem: Barksdale is a former FBI agent *who was made president of the university today.*

Solution: Barksdale, *a former FBI agent,* was made president of the university today.

Problem: The Houndogs have lost 20 games in a row, *believing that they have no ability.*

Solution: *Since they believe they have no ability,* the Houndogs keep losing — 20 games in a row.

Problem: The old biplane burst into flames, *when the pilot dived out of the cockpit.*

Solution: *Just as the pilot dived out of the cockpit,* the old biplane burst into flames.

(Also see pp. 175 – 176, and 335 – 337.)

PRACTICE

Rewrite these examples of faulty subordination:

1. We are all hoping to move to a better neighborhood, believing that we now have enough money for a new house.
2. Although the grades for his themes stayed the same, most of the class did better on their themes.
3. My father was a poor man because he believed in democracy.
4. The agreement was not signed today, the workers believing it would be.
5. Cancer is related to cigarette smoking, although millions smoke.
6. Farwell, who knows how to act, has directed many plays successfully.
7. Because he had worked very hard for it, Mike was supported by most students for the Council.
8. I got my new teeth when I took Mrs. Farquhar to the theatre.

S 11 FAULTY COORDINATION

Coordinate elements in a sentence should be balanced against each other so that they seem "equal" in emphasis and logic. When "unequal" elements are joined, usually by a coordinating conjunction, an illogical (or faulty) coordination is the result. To correct the problem, subordinate one of the elements at the beginning, middle, or end of the sentence.

Problem: I had a lot of work to do, and I had a cup of coffee.

Solution: *Even though I had a lot of work to do,* I had a cup of coffee.

Problem: Liza was an excellent worker, and she got the best student job the college had.

Solution: Liza, *who was an excellent worker*, got the best student job the college had.

Problem: The new shingles have been nailed on the roof, and the men have not gone on lunch break.

Solution: The men have not gone to lunch, *although they have finished nailing the shingles on the roof.*

PRACTICE

Clarify the relationship between the coordinate elements in these sentences. When you can, subordinate an element at the beginning, middle, or end of the sentence.

1. Friends say that they go to Chicago as often as they used to, and it is a fairly safe city.
2. He was a handsome man and he had a short haircut.
3. There have been many students who have seen the play, and I think it is a good one.
4. The university had a poor debate team this year, and the debaters usually used incoherent arguments.
5. Tennessee is pretty, and we will visit many parts of the state on our vacation.
6. In botany, we learned about the permeability of cell walls, and surprising chemicals can pass through such walls.
7. Susan's husband has a Ph.D., and he shared the household duties with her, not without grumbling.

S 12 FAULTY COMPLEMENTS

Certain statements complete their idea with a linking verb (usually a form of *be*) and a noun element. This use of *complements* (or *completers*) supplies a logical equation:

Subject	"be" form (=)	Complement
Miss *Haversham*	*is* (=)	the *Woman* of the Year.
The *material* for the seminar	*will be* (=)	the first *topic* for the committee.

If the noun elements on either side of the sentence do not "equal" each other, you will get an illogical equation, as in these sentences:

Problem: The main problem of an accountant is his reputation. *(problem ≠ reputation)*

Solution (1): An accountant's main problem is that of keeping his reputation untarnished.

Solution (2): What is an accountant's main problem? It is how to maintain a good reputation.

Problem: One of the most important reasons for supporting the union is stable employment. *(One [reason] ≠ employment)*

Solution (1): Let's support the union so that we workers can have stable employment.

Solution (2): You should support the union—it helps you to keep your job.

In another kind of faulty complement, there is no noun element on the right side of the "equation":

Problem: Love is where you have a very strong liking for someone. *(Love ≠ where)*

Solution: Love is having a very strong liking for someone.

Problem: My greatest happiness is when I am alone. *(happiness ≠ when)*

Solution (1): I am most happy when I am alone.

Solution (2): My greatest happiness is in being alone.

PRACTICE

Change the faulty complements in these sentences. Rewrite as necessary.

1. Another good quality of our employees is their absentee record.
2. Democracy is where people vote for their leaders.
3. The feasibility of installing the carpet, we think, is a big problem.
4. Because the Dodgers lost their second baseman was the reason they lost the pennant.
5. My main wish is Dad will get to retire early.
6. My high salary was since I was needed by the company.
7. Marrying is when you take a woman for your lawful, wedded wife.
8. The main reason I passed the exam is good studying.
9. Another reason is because my teacher likes me.
10. Graduation is where you are finally finished forever with learning.

"The umpire called him out. Although he had already crossed the plate." The second statement is incomplete—a *sentence fragment*. Many fragments can be corrected by combining them with the previous sentence: "The umpire called him out, although he had already crossed the plate."

Problem: I refused the job. Because it was not interesting.
Solution: I refused the job because it was not interesting.

Problem: Virginia did not like the proposal. Even after her friends in the club had completely approved of it.
Solution: Virginia did not like the proposal, even after her friends in the club had completely approved of it.

Problem: James Earl Ray escaped from prison. A prison that was supposed to be escape-proof.
Solution: James Earl Ray escaped from a prison that was supposed to be escape-proof.

Note: In professional writing, the fragment is often used for emphasis or stylistic variation:

"Of course, there's not much in it [the movie *Bonnie and Clyde*] about the nameless, faceless dead men. *Or the orphans and widows and the never-healing scar of a man who never knew his father.*"—Mike Royko

Your instructor will probably object to fragments if (1) you don't know you are using them (unconscious use is a sign that you do not know what a sentence is), or (2) you overwork them. Be sure you know his opinions on the matter.

PRACTICE

Revise each of the following constructions so that the sentence fragment is removed.

1. Taxes should be lowered. Because citizens pay too much to the government already.
2. Furnace tape can be used to repair cloth. And many other household items.
3. What happened to the student revolutionaries? The ones who were so evident during the sixties?
4. Some Germans practiced civil disobedience during the Nazi regime. A very small number.
5. That was the final question. Which I did not know the answer to.

6. Earlier she could remember the answer. That had been emphasized in the text.
7. I do not believe in that idea of God. An angry old man with a long beard.

S 14 COMMA SPLICES

Here is a *comma splice:* "I am fond of you, he is fond of you too." The error is that of "splicing" two main clauses or sentences with a comma instead of separating them properly — usually with a period or semicolon. Sometimes a coordinating conjunction can be inserted between the two clauses. Or one main clause can be subordinated to the other.

Problem: The garden was full of beans, I ate most of them that summer.

Solution (1): The garden was full of beans; I ate most of them that summer.

Solution (2): The garden was full of beans, so I ate most of them that summer.

Solution (3): Since the garden was full of beans, I ate most of them that summer. (The first clause is subordinated to the second.)

Problem: I am in no way responsible for your good fortune, you earned everything you have.

Solution (1): I am in no way responsible for your good fortune. You earned everything you have.

Solution (2): I am in no way responsible for your good fortune because you earned everything you have. (The second clause is subordinated to the first.)

S 15 FUSED SENTENCES

"I stopped and opened my car door the pickup behind me hit it." This construction is called a *fused sentence.* It is actually made up of two sentences joined together without any punctuation or capitalization to indicate where the first sentence ends and the second begins. The problem can be solved in one of several ways.

Solution (1): I stopped and opened my car door. The pickup behind me hit it.

Solution (2): When I stopped and opened my car door, the pickup behind me hit it.

S 16 RUN-ON SENTENCES

The *run-on sentence* has a "stringy," unemphatic effect; it is usually created by a series of main clauses tied together with *or, and, but,* or *so:*

> Punishment is a good idea, and I believe that criminals should be punished, but they should not be put to death, for capital punishment is wrong.

Most sentences of this kind can be rewritten by using subordination and a change of emphasis:

> I believe that criminals should be punished. But since capital punishment is wrong, they should not be put to death.

Problem: Jim flew to New York, and his plane was late, so he was not able to get to the meeting on time, but his boss did not get angry with him.

Solution: When Jim flew to New York, his plane was late and he missed the meeting. His boss, however, did not get angry with him.

PRACTICE

These sentences are fused or run-on, or contain a comma splice. Identify the error, and correct the sentence. Rewrite where necessary.

1. George Orwell wrote a famous essay called "A Hanging," and in this essay he showed how cruel people could be, but in truth Orwell had never seen a hanging, for he told a friend that he had manufactured the whole story.
2. Reasonable debate in a college class is possible, we should encourage it.
3. Some scientists lie others lie part of the time, a few try always to tell the truth.
4. Suicide is available to every person not every thinking person should consider it seriously.
5. Romance shouts defiance at tradition, and tradition answers with a sneer, but the latter usually wins, for most people in the end become traditionalists in their own culture.
6. She walked the length of the street in front of the great Miami hotels, she saw rows of the living dead propped up in their chairs.
7. The young wisely ignore the old they think them to be prejudiced, this is not true they are merely tired of hearing the same old questions why don't you ask some new ones?

Punctuation

Punctuation marks show the "joints" or joining places in your sentences. In addition to signaling sentence structure or indicating how words phrases and sentences are put together these marks also tell the reader many small things for example that a string of words is a book title italics that something belongs to somebody apostrophe that a speech is coming comma and quotation marks

Did you have trouble reading that last sentence? No wonder—we didn't punctuate it. Now read it with the punctuation marks added (in *sixteen* places):

In addition to "signaling" sentence structure or indicating how words, phrases, and sentences are put together, these marks also tell the reader many small things—for example, that a string of words is a book title (italics); that something belongs to somebody (apostrophe); that a speech is coming (comma and quotation marks).

Now we will show you how to use the various punctuation marks.

P 1 USE A PERIOD WHEN . . .

a. You end a sentence:

Thomas Jefferson was both philosopher and politician.
I don't know when I'll be back from the movies.

b. You abbreviate:

M.A. degree   etc.   10:00 p.m.   Sept.   Calif.   Mr.

P 2 USE A QUESTION MARK WHEN . . .

You ask a question:

What did the senator do then?
What time is it?
How can I do better on the next test?

P 3 USE AN EXCLAMATION MARK WHEN . . .

You exclaim:

> Fight fiercely, Harvard!
> Never say die, say damn!
> That's the ugliest sports coat I ever saw!

Note: Don't exclaim very often or very loud.

P 4 USE A COMMA WHEN . . .

a. You join two main clauses with a coordinating conjunction (*and, or, but, so, for,*):

> The grass is bright green, *and* all the trees are beginning to bud.
> The river is flooding, *but* Dad won't be there to see it.
> It is extremely rainy here this season, *so* be sure to bring your raincoat when you come.

b. You join an opener, an interrupter, or a closer to a main clause:

> *Since Clarice was bored in the second grade,* her parents decided to let her skip a grade.
> We could not shake our pursuers, *although we tried to lose them several times that day.*
> That's what I want to do, *join the Army.*
> Our dachshund, *who was dozing near the fire,* suddenly began to bark loudly.
> You grabbed my foot, *not my hand!*

c. You use a parallel construction of three or more elements:

> *griffins, dragons, and elves*
> Were there *green, yellow,* or *orange* colors in the painting?
> This country must ban *arms, ammunition,* and *all other instruments of war.*
> *We lay on the ground, we stared at the stars,* and *we thought deep thoughts.*

d. You place "equal" descriptive words before a noun:

> new, nice-looking table

New and *nice-looking* describe *table,* a noun. They are "equal" because you can put *and* logically between them—"new *and* nice-looking." In the phrase "new coffee table," *new* and *coffee* are not equal: you wouldn't say "new *and* coffee table."

> *honest, wonderful* man (honest *and* wonderful man)
> *hot, dark* night (hot *and* dark night)
> But: *last spring* semester (not last *and* spring semester)

e. You employ direct address:

John, please wash the car.
Mrs. Rosenthal, would you sit over there?

f. You supply dates and places:

Chicago, Illinois
January 15, 1974
On May 14, 1916, in Houston, Texas
He died in Nashville, Tennessee, on October 14, 1943.

g. You identify speakers in dialogue:

James said, "Where can I find my umbrella?"
"It's in the hall closet," Mom said.
"If that's the way you're faithful," said Marie angrily, "we're through!"

h. You want to prevent misreading or ambiguity:

By speaking of the dead, Lincoln in his Gettysburg Address appealed to . . . .

If you write "By speaking of the dead Lincoln . . . ." your reader may be confused and have to re-read the sentence.

The deductions allowed, the taxpayer is able to . . . .

"The deductions allowed the taxpayer . . . ." may be confusing.

P 5 USE A SEMICOLON WHEN . . .

a. You want to join two main clauses without using a coordinating conjunction:

The snows of yesterday have all gone; they have melted away.
His technique on the guitar is sloppy; he doesn't seem to care whether he hits the right notes or not.

b. You want to join two main clauses with "long" conjunctions like *moreover, however, therefore, consequently*:

I caught you red-handed; *therefore*, you will go to jail.
Sam and Rena went to the church; *however*, they didn't get married.
The company cheated on its income tax; *consequently*, the Internal Revenue Service demanded back payment of tax.

Note: It is not necessary to discuss here the complicated theory of long conjunctions or "conjunctive adverbs" (*however, moreover, therefore, consequently*, etc.). Just remember that the short conjunction (*and, or, but, so*, etc.) between main clauses takes a comma, while the long conjunction takes a semicolon.

c. You need to clarify a parallel series:

Unclarified: At the meeting were Smithers the captain, Jones the first mate, and Watterson the bosun.

Clarified: At the meeting were Smithers, the captain; Jones, the first mate; and Watterson, the bosun.

Unclarified: My landlady tells my wife what kind of floor wax to use, the same as she uses, when to use it, the same time she does, where to set the refrigerator, the same place as hers, and, most helpful of all, when to get her husband up in the morning.

Clarified: My landlady tells my wife what kind of floor wax to use, the same as she uses; when to use it, the same time she does; where to set the refrigerator, the same place as hers; and, most helpful of all, when to get her husband up in the morning.

d. You wish to "strengthen" a comma. Note the difference between these two sentences:

The Prime Minister was right, *but* he should have been more careful in making his appeal.

In calling for devotion to duty, the Prime Minister was right; *but* he should have been more careful in making his appeal.

Because the second sentence already has a comma in it and is more complex than the first, the writer decided to strengthen the joint between the two clauses with a semicolon. In each of the following examples, the comma ordinarily used between rather long sentence units joined by a conjunction has been strengthened to a semicolon.

These rules may seem rather harsh; *but* if you will stop to consider them carefully, you will understand that they are for the good of everybody.

Unfortunately, we don't know very much about what goes on inside the brain; *and* many surgeons, indeed some of the best ones, will refuse to operate without careful diagnosis of this condition.

Before deciding which house to buy, look very carefully at all the listings that the Multiple Service carries; *but* don't ignore other sources like newspaper ads and notices on bulletin boards.

P 6 USE A COLON WHEN . . .

a. You introduce a list:

Please buy the following: butter, cheese, and bread.

It is often simpler to omit the colon and write: "Please buy butter, cheese, and bread."

b. You introduce quotations:

Toward the end of his life, Smith wrote to his son, making this plea: "Whatever you decide to do with the old property as a whole, never sell the north woods, for they meant everything to your mother."

c. You punctuate the salutation in a business letter:

Dear Dean Winkleboom:
Dear Sir:
Dear Mr. Ryan:
Dear Ms. Perez:

P 7 USE PARENTHESES WHEN . . .

You wish to set off a word or an expression firmly from the rest of the sentence.

The man I am referring to (Jenkins) is not necessary to our plans.
There are not enough women doctors and lawyers (this is what the girl said).
When it was over the ship, the winch (which was holding up the boom) suddenly collapsed.

Parentheses *always* come in pairs. See *Note* in P 8 below.

P 8 USE A DASH WHEN . . .

You need to show a strong break in thought:

He became president only four years later—the youngest man ever in the post.
I never want to get married—not under any circumstances.
Is there—listen to me—is there any hope for the survivors?

Note: Parentheses and dashes are quite helpful when you want to clarify a sentence that is loaded with too many commas. Observe how one writer, having already used commas around one interrupter, chooses to employ dashes around a second:

Edward Cole, an engineer who owned one of the first 300 Corvettes produced in 1953, remembers that on his first long ride in the rain—from suburban Detroit 150 miles to Kalamazoo—the water rising in the cockpit compelled him to take off his shoes and roll up his pants.—Coles Phinizy, "The Marque of Zora"

Of course, the writer could have used parentheses around either one of his interrupters. Don't rely too heavily on parentheses or dashes.

P 9 USE AN APOSTROPHE WHEN . . .

a. You use a possessive form:

the *trailer's* wheel (one trailer)
the *trailers'* wheels (more than one trailer)
Peter's arm
Persius' style

Note: Do not use the apostrophe with personal pronouns: "*his* car," "these are *hers*."

If you have trouble remembering whether the apostrophe goes inside or outside the *s*, simply think of this example. Take the word *dog*, add an apostrophe and the *s*: *dog's*. If the word already has an *s*, do the same—but drop the second *s*. And so *dogs* becomes *dogs's* becomes *dogs'*. Here are a few additional examples:

"The water supply of the town" becomes "the *town's* water supply."
"The water supply of the towns" becomes "the *towns'* water supply."

"The house belonging to Roger" becomes "*Roger's* house."
"The house belonging to the Rogers family" becomes "the *Rogers'* house."

b. You form plurals using numbers or letters:

Last semester, she got three *A's*, two *B's*, and a *C*.
There are four *3's* in the winning lottery number.
The *1950's* were a time of relative peace in the world.

c. You form a contraction:

It's the thing to do.
He'll be there.
I *can't* be at home today.

P 10 USE A HYPHEN WHEN . . .

a. You need a syllable break at the end of a line:

real-ization   *stereo-phonic*   *incor-porate*

(For more information on correct syllable breaks, see p. 384.)

b. You use a prefix before a syllable starting with *e*:

pre-empt   *de-emphasize*   *re-enforce*

c. You make a compound word:

self-analysis   *cease-fire* (noun)   *mother-in-law*

d. You make a compound modifier:

a *one-year* clause   a *big-time* actor   a *blue-eyed* rabbit

When in doubt about the use of a hyphen, particularly for prefixes and syllable breaks, check your dictionary.

P 11 USE QUOTATION MARKS WHEN . . .

a. You quote the exact spoken or written words of somebody else.

"No country on earth," shouted Senator Blanksley, "is richer than ours!"
It was John Donne who first said that "no man is an island."

b. You refer to titles of songs, paintings, and short literary works:

Faulkner wrote the short story "A Rose for Emily."
The song is called "Stardust."
Picasso's "Guernica" is one of the most famous paintings of the twentieth century.

There is always some confusion about where quotation marks are placed in relation to other punctuation marks. The "rules" for such placement are actually quite simple:

1. Commas and periods that end a sentence unit always go inside the quotation marks:

He remarked, "My house is haunted."
"My house," she said, "is not haunted."

2. Colons and semicolons, when they divide the quoted material from the rest of the text, always go outside the quotation marks:

The editorial gave three reasons why Maltby would be "by far the best candidate": his experience, honesty, and fiscal conservatism.
He remarked, "My house is haunted"; he didn't say anything else.

3. Question marks and exclamation marks go inside or outside the quotation marks according to how the quoted material is being used:

Did he say, "My house is haunted"? (The question mark is placed *outside* the quotation marks because the entire sentence is the question.)
He asked, "Is my house haunted?" (The question mark goes *inside* the quotation marks because the quotation, not the entire sentence, is the question.)
Were you frightened when the ghost said "Boo!"? (The exclamation mark is part of the quotation, while the question mark indicates that the entire sentence is a question.)

P 12 USE ITALICS (UNDERLINING) WHEN . . .

a. You refer to specific words or phrases:

> The word *fragrance* is euphonious.
> I do not understand what Marx meant by *democracy*.

b. You emphasize a word or phrase:

> Do the job *right.*
> I was referring to John *Adams*, not John Addison.

c. You refer to the titles of novels, stage productions, magazines, and newspapers:

> *Moby Dick* (novel)   *The Sound of Music* (movie)
> *Hamlet* (play)   *Sports Illustrated* (magazine)
> *La Traviata* (opera)   St. Louis *Post-Dispatch* (newspaper)

The relative length of works determines whether you use quotation marks or italics. Faulkner's short story, "A Rose for Emily," is put in quotation marks, but his novels (like *Sanctuary*) are italicized. Milton's "L'Allegro" is a short poem; his *Paradise Lost* is long—interminable.

PRACTICE

1. Punctuate the sentences below. Many of them can be punctuated in different ways—for example, students have suggested ten or so different solutions to *i*. For each sentence use the punctuation marks that seem to make it read most easily and clearly.

    a.   Read the chapter called Monopolies in Hansens book Economic Power.

    b.   Burns opinion is that the word rapport is French.

    c.   The boys lives are in danger so is yours.

    d.   The car was new shiny and very pretty but it cost eight thousand dollars.

    e.   Lindbergh flew his airplane a high wing monoplane across the Atlantic.

    f.   Before I come back you should have eaten your beans rice and honey.

    g.   At the end of the semester however one's work gets easier.

    h.   In the musical play Oklahoma there is a well known song called Oklahoma.

    i.   At the end of Act II I stabbed him John pulled out the blood red knife and we laid his body on the floor.

    j.   Its over taxed heart failing the racehorse dropped before the peoples eyes.

k.   Smith who had been there before looked around the house and moving swiftly we all searched the place.

l.   Jones father was a small time thug and politician in San Francisco in addition he was on drugs.

m.   In spite of the never ending rain however they pushed on and they finally came to the cave.

n.   Dickens wrote books for instance he wrote David Copperfield.

o.   Dean Woof said his secretary the Admissions Office called and wants to know what to do with the student program requests for pre registration.

p.   Steinbeck who wrote The Grapes of Wrath was a self made writer.

q.   The dogs forelegs were scratched bruised and broken its eyes were perfectly all right.

r.   You must return the child you must keep out of sight and you must above all not call the police.

2.   In the following passage, we have numbered each space where the author originally placed a punctuation mark inside a sentence. After you have punctuated the sentences, explain or defend in a brief phrase each punctuation mark you used.

[1]There are some students who can't remember how to spell a word even after they have looked it up in a dictionary. There are others who don't have much luck looking words up in a dictionary because they can't come close enough to guessing the spelling to have much chance of finding the words. Both kinds of students deserve a very limited amount of sympathy (1) especially from themselves. It is true that the English spelling system is the worst in the world (2) but it really wasn't invented out of pure malice (3) and the rules are the same for everybody. Resentment and alibis make the job of learning to spell enormously more difficult. The job does not require unusual intelligence (4) but it does require close attention and a long and patient effort. You may not think it is worth the effort (5) but on the whole the country does. Some kinds of ignorance can be concealed for years (6) but bad spelling can show up every time you write a sentence (7) and it can cost jobs and promotions as well as bad marks on English papers. Few people can afford not to learn to spell at least reasonably well.

[2]If you are a really poor speller (8) the first step is to find out what method of learning a new word works best for you. Some people do best by spelling a word out loud a number of times (9) others by writing it down repeatedly (10) and still others by tracing it with a pencil after it has been correctly written. Find out whether your eyes (11) your ears (12) or your muscles help you most in this particular job. As you try each method (13) be sure you give your full attention to what you are doing. It is a pure waste of time to use any of them while you are thinking about something else. Five minutes of *real* work on spelling is worth much more than an hour of semiconscious droning or purely mechanical copying.

³The next step is the critical one. Learn three new words a day every day for the next month (14) just everyday words that have been giving you trouble. Anybody bright enough to be in college can do this if he wants to. Most poor spellers give it up and find a new alibi before the first week is over. At first the results are slow and don't seem worth the effort (15) and if you figure that at this rate it would take you the rest of your life to learn a third of the words in your dictionary (16) the whole prospect seems pretty gloomy. But if you really work at the problem consistently and *alertly* for a month you will find that you have made real progress (17) and the ninety new words you know will be the smallest part of it. For one thing (18) you will find that you are seeing words more clearly (19) and new ones are easier to learn. For another (20) you'll have something to build on. You'll be ready to learn a good many words in groups instead of individually. This group method is so attractive that many people want to begin with it (21) but it seldom works well until a good foundation has been laid by the simple but unpopular one at a time (22) method.—L. M. Myers, *Guide to American English*

3. From a textbook, magazine, or other source, find a good short section of nonfiction prose. Copy out two paragraphs without the punctuation, and set your copied page aside for a few hours. Then go back over it and put in your own punctuation marks. How well does your punctuation agree with that of the original? Can you defend any of your variations?

RHETORIC OF PUNCTUATION

So far, we have been explaining the "mechanics" of punctuation. *Mechanics* refers to those more or less firm rules that govern how you punctuate most sentences. But in addition to using punctuation marks in a mechanical way, you can use them for effect, to help create certain patterns of emotion and logic in the reader's mind. This *rhetoric* of punctuation allows you to make choices on the basis of stylistic effectiveness and interest. In order to see how rhetorical punctuation works, consider the following scene. When Mr. Smith went to his garage to finish cleaning his Mercedes, he found a terrible and bloody scene inside the trunk, which he had left open the night before. To his ten-year-old son, he said:

> The cat dragged a dead rabbit into the Mercedes trunk last night / get a shovel / put the rabbit in the garbage / and clean up that mess out there.

These sentence structures, not to mention Mr. Smith's fatherly instructions, are clear as glass. But the structures can be punctuated differently, according to how you wish to create certain pauses, emphases, and effects:

> The cat dragged a dead rabbit into the Mercedes trunk last night. Get a shovel, put the rabbit in the garbage, and clean up that mess out there.

This is a calm father, even a dull one. He's obviously not very upset about the rabbit, for he plops down his commas and periods with bland regularity and precision. Here is another version:

> The cat dragged a dead rabbit into the Mercedes trunk last night—get a shovel. Put the rabbit in the garbage and clean up that mess out there!

In the first clause, this father has just seen the rabbit. He's a little sleepy, but by the time he gets out the first few words he's been pretty well awakened by the sight. It takes him a punctuational dash of time to think of the solution ("get a shovel"), after which he excitedly runs his words together in the following two main clauses and omits the comma before "and clean up."

Our third father is angry. He coldly bites off each sentence and stomps on it with a period:

> The cat dragged a dead rabbit into the Mercedes trunk last night. Get a shovel. Put the rabbit in the garbage. And clean up that mess out there.

The cat is going to catch it. So is the son, although he is as innocent as a lamb.

The fourth father is edging on hysteria: the rabbit is bloody, and it smells:

> The *cat* dragged a *dead rabbit* into the Mercedes *trunk* last night! Get a shovel, put the rabbit in the garbage—and *clean up* that *mess* out there!

Punctuation works best when it achieves both mechanical and rhetorical effects. When you separate clauses with commas or enclose a phrase between a pair of parentheses, you do so according to precise mechanical rules of grammar and sentence structure. But when you build on these rules to help write sentences that are particularly interesting or effective, you are using a punctuational rhetoric that varies according to the situation. Consider these situations:

Simple fact; two things happen:
> He looked at her, and she blushed.

Not-so-simple fact; cause and effect:
> He looked at her; she blushed.

The same, with a little drama added:
> He looked at her—she blushed.

Rapid cause-and-effect:
> He looked at her, she blushed. (The comma splice may be considered acceptable here because the clauses are so brief.)

A reported afterthought:
> He looked at her (and she blushed).

Deep, dark dramatic emphasis:
> *He looked at her* and she blushed.

At this point, let's remind ourselves that like all the other forms and devices of rhetoric, punctuation can get out of hand. You can get too flashy with it. You don't want your reader to take special notice of your.commas, periods, and dashes or to remark, "My, how clever this fellow is with the semicolon." Ideally, the main job of your punctuation marks should be to support your ideas and make easy the transmission of your thoughts to the reader. Sir Ernest Gowers, in his *Plain Words: Their ABC*, tells of a writer of a training manual for pilots who ended his comments with, "Pilots, whose minds are dull, do not usually live long." This writer's mispunctuation transmitted a thought he certainly did not intend and, as Sir Ernest commented, converted "a truism into an insult."

Good punctuation should separate with perfect clarity the parts of your sentences. In the long run of writing, such punctuation is the most effective kind there is.

PRACTICE

Here is Lincoln's Gettysburg Address—unpunctuated. If you were Lincoln, how would you punctuate it?

[1]Fourscore and seven years ago our fathers brought forth on this continent a new nation conceived in liberty and dedicated to the proposition that all men are created equal

[2]Now we are engaged in a great civil war testing whether that nation or any nation so conceived and so dedicated can long endure we are met on a great battlefield of that war we have come to dedicate a portion of that field as a final resting place for those who here gave their lives that that nation might live it is altogether fitting and proper that we should do this

[3]But in a larger sense we cannot dedicate we cannot consecrate we cannot hallow this ground the brave men living and dead who struggled here have consecrated it far above our poor power to add or detract the world will little note nor long remember what we say here but it can never forget what they did here it is for us the living rather to be dedicated here to the unfinished work which they who fought here have thus far so nobly advanced it is rather for us to be here dedicated to the great task remaining before us that from these honored dead we take increased devotion to that cause for which they gave the last full measure of devotion that we here highly resolve that these dead shall not have died in vain that this nation under God shall have a new birth of freedom and that government of the people by the people for the people shall not perish from the earth

Mechanics

M 1 ABBREVIATIONS

Although abbreviations are a useful form of shorthand in some kinds of writing, you should avoid them whenever possible. Write the full form: *university*, not *univ.* or *u.*; *August*, not *Aug.*; *New York*, not *N.Y.*

There are, however, certain abbreviations that have become the standard form: *a.m.* and *p.m.* to indicate time; *e.g.* (the abbreviation of the Latin phrase for "for example"); *Dr.* for *Doctor*, and so on. (Note that *Dr.* should be used only with the person's surname or full name— *Dr. Smith* or *Dr. John Smith.*)

When in doubt concerning an abbreviation, first take into account its context. Considering your subject and reader, would an abbreviation be proper? Then check your dictionary for the correct form and spelling. *Ect.*, for example, is a popular mistake for *etc.* (*et cetera*— "and so forth").

M 2 CAPITALIZATION

Capital letters are used to designate the following items:

a. The first word of a sentence:

Revision is important for the writer.
Encourage them to do better.

b. Proper nouns:

Spain   Atlanta, Georgia
Mary Ann   Korean War
Chrysler Corporation   House of Representatives

c. Proper adjectives:

Shakespearean sonnet   Freudian psychology
Colombian coffee   Buddhist temple

d. Titles of articles, poems, books, magazines, stage productions, etc.

"Ten Ways to Help Cut Inflation" (article)
"Dover Beach" (poem)

A Grammar of Modern English (book)
Good Housekeeping (magazine)
Waiting for Godot (play)

Capitalize all words in a title except *a*, *an*, and *the*, and except those coordinating conjunctions and prepositions that contain fewer than five letters. If these come first or last in the title, they must be capitalized:

A Farewell to Arms
To Have and Have Not
"A Place to Return To"

e.   The first word of a line in "regular" poetry:

Good friend, for Jesus' sake forbear
To dig the dust enclosed here;
Blest be the man that spares these stones,
And curst be he that moves my bones.

—William Shakespeare

M 3 MANUSCRIPT FORM

a.   Writing material:
Always use standard size paper, 8½ × 11 inches. Write on *one side* of the paper only. Use a ball-point pen with black, blue, or blue-black ink. If you type, use white typing paper that is thick enough so that writing on a second page does not show through the first.

b.   Spacing and margins:
Use double spaces between lines unless you are setting off long quotations. (For more on the format for long quotations, see p. 240.) When typing, allow about 1½ inches of space on the left side, and about one inch on all the others. When writing in longhand, use lined paper that has a vertical rule on the left-hand side.

c.   Indentation:
Indent the first line of each paragraph about one inch in handwritten papers, five spaces in typewritten ones.

d.   Titles:
Put your title on the first page of the paper, about two inches below the top. Leave about one inch between the title and the first line of the theme. Do not use quotation marks or underlining for the title. If your instructor wants you to use a title page, see the sample on p. 253.

e.   Numbering pages:
Whether or not you have a separate title page, number the page on which your theme begins with 1, and the rest of the pages in sequence.

f. Appearance:

The appearance of your final draft subtly influences the reader's impression of your efforts. A sloppy paper often indicates sloppy thinking; so always be neat. When proofreading, you can line through an error or insert a small revision if you do it carefully and then check the correction. When typing, do not strike over an error unless you first erase it—neatly. If your draft contains numerous corrections, redo it.

M 4 NUMBERS

There are several general rules for the use of numbers that you should be aware of.

a. Spell out in full the following numbers:

1. Those from *one* to *ninety-nine*: *two, seventeen, twenty-three,* etc.

2. Those used as adjectives: *first, second, seventeenth, twenty-third,* etc. (not *1st, 2nd, 17th, 23rd*).

   A street address, however, can be written with the endings *nd, rd, st, th*: East *75th* Street, 187 North *3rd* Street.

b. Use numerals for:

1. Numbers of more than two words:

   1979   2,170 $4,560,000

2. Dates, times, addresses:

   August 14, 1979   6:30 a.m.   1311 Locust Avenue
   December 25, 1859   10:00 p.m. (but 631 West 93rd Street
                          ten o'clock)

c. Hyphenate compound numbers:

1. From *twenty-one* to *ninety-nine*:

   thirty-seven
   fifty-eight
   seventy-two

2. Used as adjectival fractions:

   a *one-fourth* minority
   a *two-thirds'* vote

d. Do not begin a sentence with a numeral:

   Not: *107* people survived.
   But: *One hundred and seven people* survived.

When spelling out the number at the beginning of a sentence is awkward, revise the construction:

> *Not:* *Forty-five thousand, one hundred and eighty-six* voters are registered.
>
> *But:* The total number of registered voters is *45,186*.

M 5 SYLLABICATION

To keep an even margin on the right side of your paper, you will occasionally have to divide a word at the end of a line and run it over into the next. When you are in doubt about a word's syllabication, check your dictionary. Here are some general rules to keep in mind.

1. Never divide one-syllable words: *moist, hound, great, Tom, see.*

2. Divide a word with double consonants between the consonants: *wit-ty, refer-ral, com-mand.*

3. Never divide a word so that only one letter remains on a line. Try to get two—and preferably three—letters on a line:

> *Not:* e-bullient   intrica-cy
> *But:* ebul-lient   intri-cacy

For words that have prefixes and suffixes, divide where either joins the root: *cast-ing, pre-registration, manage-ment, dis-appear.*

DY Using the Dictionary

A good dictionary is important to you in many ways. But it is of special importance to you as a writer. It is a useful source for various kinds of information about words that you may need to know as you work toward improving your themes. At one time or another, you may wish to know such things as:

— the exact meaning of *ecology*
— the spelling of *capital (capitol?)*
— whether *overridden* should be hyphenated *(over-ridden?)*
— a synonym for *complete*
— the part of speech of *than* (is it a preposition or a conjunction?)
— when you may use *contact* as a verb
— whether you may write: *"Plus* I wanted more money for college."

Consider for a moment the last problem in the list. On p. 167, we discuss the employment of clear "word signals"—such as *before, but, also, since, then*—in opening positions in your sentences. There are so many possible signals that we could not mention them all, and you will have to depend on your dictionary for help when considering the use of certain signals. Should you, for instance, use *plus* as you might use *and* or *also* to signal the addition of a second or third reason for doing something? The major dictionaries will indicate that in standard written English *plus* can be used as a preposition, adjective, or noun, but not as a conjunction or adverb. Grammatically speaking, dictionaries allow these usages: "X *plus* Y," "on the *plus* side," or "a definite *plus*." But not: "*Plus* I wanted more money for college."

The following desk dictionaries have proved to be the most popular and reliable in regard to grammar, pronunciation, basic definitions, and usage. If you don't have one, you should buy one.

The American Heritage Dictionary of the English Language, 1973
Funk and Wagnalls Standard College Dictionary, 1968
The Random House Dictionary of the English Language, College Edition,
   1968
Webster's New Collegiate Dictionary, 1973
Webster's New World Dictionary of the American Language, Second College Edition, 1970

What does a typical dictionary entry tell you? Let's look at the entry for one of the most discussed words in modern English, *contact*. The source is *The American Heritage Dictionary*.

pronunciation of noun *noun*

con·tact (kŏn′tăkt′) *n.* **1. a.** The coming together or touching of two objects or surfaces. **b.** The fact or relation of touching. **2.** The state of being in communication. **3.** An acquaintance who might be of use; a connection. See Usage note below. **4.** *Electricity.* **a.** A connection between two conductors that permits a flow of current. **b.** A part or device that makes or breaks such a connection. **5.** *Medicine.* A person recently exposed to a contagious disease. **6.** *Plural. Informal.* Contact lenses. —*v.* (kŏn′tăkt, kən-tăkt′) **contacted, -tacting, -tacts.** —*tr.* **1.** To bring or put in contact. **2.** *Informal.* To get in touch with. See Usage note below. —*intr.* To be in or come into contact. —*adj.* (kŏn′tăkt′). **1.** Of, sustaining, or making contact. **2.** Caused or transmitted by touching: *a contact skin rash.* [Latin *contāctus,* from the past participle of *contingere,* to touch, border upon, attain to : *com-,* together + *tangere,* to touch (see **tag-** in Appendix*).] —**con·tac′tu·al** (kən-tăk′-chōō-əl) *adj.* —**con·tac′tu·al·ly** *adv.*
Usage: *Contact,* meaning to get in touch with, is widely used but still not appropriate to formal contexts, according to 66 per cent of the Usage Panel. *Contact* (noun), denoting a person as a source of assistance, is better established and is acceptable to 61 per cent of the Panel in formal usage.

[handwritten annotations: 6 meanings of contact *as a noun; pronunciation of* contact *as verb; parts of the verb; adjective meanings of* contact*; intransitive meanings of verb; comment on how* contact *should be used; verb; transitive meanings of verb; history of* contact*]*

Here you learn that *contact* may be used as a noun, verb, or adjective. You are given different pronunciations of the word and its various meanings. You also learn the major parts of the verb form of *contact* (note the boldface **contacted, -tacting, -tacts**). The usage note at the bottom of the entry tells you that two-thirds of the *Heritage Dictionary's* Usage Panel disapproves of the formal use of *contact* as a verb (meaning "to get in touch with"), an observation that may be helpful if you want to know whether to use that form of the word in a paper.

For most words, the standard desk dictionaries give similar information about grammar, pronunciation, and basic meanings. You'll find that dictionaries differ in regard to usage. As you've seen, the *Heritage* pretty much disapproves of *contact* in statements like "Contact your doctor before leaving work this afternoon." By contrast, the *Standard College Dictionary* remarks: "This informal usage, regarded with disfavor by some, is widely used." *Webster's New World* states that *contact* is "now widely used in this sense despite objections." *Webster's New Collegiate Dictionary* and *The Random House Dictionary* give definitions of *contact* in this sense but make no comment about its proper use.

Dictionaries also supply you with synonyms for many words. Suppose you are having difficulty choosing a word for a theme. You are writing about a certain pleasant emotion you've had recently. Words come into your mind—*happiness, joy, pleasure*—but none seems quite right. Remembering that dictionaries give synonyms, you look up *pleasure* in *The Random House Dictionary* and find at the end of the entry:

> —Syn. 1. happiness, gladness, delectation. PLEASURE, ENJOY-MENT, DELIGHT, JOY refer to the feeling of being pleased and happy. PLEASURE is the general term: *to take pleasure in beautiful scenery*. ENJOYMENT is a quiet sense of well-being and pleasurable satisfaction: *enjoyment at sitting in the shade on a warm day*. DELIGHT is a high degree of pleasure usually leading to active expression of it: *delight at receiving a hoped-for letter*. JOY is a feeling of delight so deep and lasting that a person radiates happiness and expresses it spontaneously: *joy at unexpected good news*. 4. luxury, voluptuousness. 7. preference, wish, inclination.

At least one of these words should work reasonably well in your sentence, and having used it you can get on with the rest of your writing.

Indeed, the dictionary is a special tool for "getting on with your writing." It not only supplies you with the kinds of knowledge that we have already mentioned, but it can also act as a small encyclopedia. Without leaving your room for the library, you can ascertain or verify many isolated facts: Who was *Pliny*? He was a Roman scholar who wrote the *Historia Naturalis*. He died in A.D. 79. What is *scrip*? It is paper money issued for temporary or emergency use. What is a *boycott*? Where did the word come from? It is an act of refusing to buy or use something; the word comes from the name of Charles Boycott, an English land agent in Ireland who was ostracized by his tenants for refusing to reduce rents. What is an *arroyo*? It is a deep, dry gulley or gulch cut out by floods or heavy rains.

As you can see, your desk dictionary is good for many things. Browse through it and enjoy.

PRACTICE

1. Read the introductory material in your desk dictionary. Since dictionaries vary somewhat, you should know exactly what pieces of information your dictionary has and how it is organized.

2. What do *liberal* and *conservative* mean? What is their etymology or history? (*Etymology* is discussed in the introduction to your dictionary.) Should you write, for example: "He has managed to avoid crashes for twenty-five years because he is a *liberal* [or *conservative*] pilot"?

What is the etymology of:

rape	rapture	Christian	tuxedo	noun
pencil	muscle	chivalrous	Dixie	agnostic

3. In writing themes, should you use, in their contexts, the italicized words below? In each case, give your reasons.

   a. My roommate, *yclept* Sandy, turned out to be a very friendly person.
   b. She *toted* her knapsack wherever she went, even carrying the *bloody* thing to basketball games.
   c. After *jazzing* up the engine a few times, Tinkham was satisfied with its *tune* and *killed* it.
   d. *Whither* the *paly* moon, I wondered, as I *jogged* back to the dorm in the *pitch* dark.

4. Consider this statement: "That word is not *fitting* in this context." In that statement, how many synonyms can you find for *fitting*? Give synonyms for the italicized words as they are used in these contexts:

   I have a *need* for a beer.
   We *command* you to release your prisoners.
   Why did the epidemic *happen*?

5. What is an *antonym*? After checking your dictionary, give antonyms for:

like (verb)	viciously	morose	light	raw
disinterested	creature	classy	sweetly	ignominious

6. Give the part of speech of the words below. If the word is a *noun*, state whether it is singular or plural; if a *verb*, give its tense.

criteria	rung (verb)	bade	slow	data
than	when	but	quickly	dived

7. Look up the following words to see whether they are written with a hyphen, as two words, or as one word.

drawback	drawingroom	coffeecake	Jacobsladder
gunrunning	doublejointed	touchback	dragonshead

8. Who or what is?

Hapsburg	pimpernel	upbraid (verb)	pillory (noun)
Biarritz	ringworm	lug (noun)	Lancastrian

Polishing and Proofreading

Writers create in different ways. Some work hard on their thesis statements; others concentrate on outlines; a few scribble draft after draft, searching for ideas they sense are inside them somewhere. It has been argued that it matters little where you begin in the writing process — as long as at the end of your first satisfactory draft everything ties together. A *satisfactory* draft is not usually a final draft; it is not perfect in grammar, punctuation, and other compositional matters. It is one that has a firm thesis and outline and that specifically satisfies the main details of the assignment.

POLISHING

After you have finished a satisfactory first draft, a good deal of polishing will probably have to be done on the manuscript. You can insert sentences and phrases, delete words here and there, repunctuate, correct misspellings, and generally improve the entire theme. It's a good idea to leave wide margins and plenty of line space on the first-draft manuscript for corrections. If you handwrite on lined paper, skip every other line; if you type, triple space. Here is a part of a satisfactory first draft, with the writer's corrections:

<pre>
                                        my father, mother, and I
    I was four, ᴧabout that age, when our farmhouse burned. We were
              or
                    cannot remember
in the barn doing something--I have no idea what--when I happened to
                 clouds of yellowish billowing away from the house.
look out the big front door and saw a great deal of smoke.ᴧ It seemed

to come from every where, even from the sides of the house and the

basement windows. I yelled to my father, who came to the barn door.
                       quietly as if in surprise   'll
He looked at the house, and said quitely and surprisedly: "Well, Iᴧ

be damned, the house is burning down."
                                         my parents
    We all ran for the house to save what we could. They ordered me
                                         they could,
to stay out, while they dashed in to save what little we had. Mainly
                                         and some bedclothes.
this was clothing and sheets, and a few pieces of furnitureᴧ I carried
   bedclothes
what I could away from the flying sparks, crying and blubbering and
                          h
tripping over the seets and quilts. I said over and over to myself
             my
through ᴧtears: "I'll be damned, the house is burning down."
</pre>

The writer's polishing of these paragraphs is of several kinds. He inserts words he omitted, corrects punctuation and spelling, and makes the sentencing smoother. More importantly, he tries to explain matters more clearly and precisely. *We* becomes *My mother, father, and I,* and *a great deal of smoke* becomes *clouds of yellowish smoke billowing away from the house.* The reader will probably be grateful for the writer's changes, since they improve the original considerably.

PROOFREADING

After you have polished your draft, let it cool off for a while—overnight, longer if possible. You want it to look unfamiliar, so that problems or errors will stand out as you read it. (Don't read the theme over and over; you'll just unconsciously memorize it, flaws and all.) Make whatever changes are necessary and copy your work into the final draft.

Let the final draft cool for another period. Now proofread the theme before handing it in. Proofreading is a small but important art. It consists mainly of trying to fool your brain into picking up errors that it either hasn't caught before or has inadvertently memorized. Persons who read proof in publishers' houses usually do the job in pairs. One reads the original manuscript to the other, who has the freshly printed version before him. In this way, each word and punctuation mark are orally checked by two persons. (Despite this system, errors still appear in a great deal of published material.)

A variation on the oral method works quite well for the student writer. Take your cooled-off final draft to a secluded spot and read it aloud *slowly* to yourself, pronouncing each word exactly as you wrote it. Read each paragraph *out of its normal order.* For example, if you have a seven-paragraph theme, read the paragraphs in a sequence like this: 3, 2, 7, 4, 1, 6, 5. In doing this, you can make the whole theme appear odd and unfamiliar, and your ear will pick up errors of several kinds—in logic, for example, as well as in spelling. A faulty generalization may well stand out as you read it aloud, and you can then insert a word or phrase to qualify it. ("Fraternities are dens of iniquity" becomes "Most fraternities at People's College are dens of iniquity.") Some words misspelled sound so odd when pronounced as written that you may catch the mistake (*eariler,* for example, instead of *earlier*).

Even if you take all of these precautions, prepare yourself to accept the fact that errors are going to slip through. But accurate proofreading will cut down their number considerably.

Glossary

GL

This Glossary presents a list, alphabetically arranged, of troublesome words and constructions, along with certain terms that you may find useful in your writing. As we considered each problem of usage, we asked ourselves: "What would the careful writer think about this? What are his choices, and how would he respond to the issue?" We have consulted many authorities (too many to list here), and confess that where they disagreed, we consulted our own experience.

Good writing is what a good writer writes. So if you find that something here contradicts your own experience and the evidence of your reading, feel free to question our advice. The rules of English usage are not carved in stone.

a, an. Use *a* before words that begin with a consonant sound: *a* pole, *a* unit (the sound is *yew*-nit), *a* history. Use *an* before words starting with a vowel sound or a silent *h*: *an* alley, *an* hour, *an* ellipse.

above, below. If you are "pointing" to something graphic on the page, like a chart or an illustration, *above* and *below* are useful: "The table *below* shows you how much money is spent on billiards in Marin County." If you are referring to ideas, it is wise to use a different expression: "The facts I have just mentioned," rather than "The above facts."

absolute construction. A phrase that is linked to a sentence by logic but not by any specific grammatical "tie." It may look like a modifier but isn't one:

The play did very well, *considering the circumstances.*
My money having vanished, I decided to leave the hotel.
The last quarter of the game, *everything taken into account*, was better than we hoped.

accept, except. The verb *accept* means "to receive with approval" or "to answer in the affirmative"; the verb *except* means "to omit or exclude." The preposition *except* means, roughly, "but" or "other than": "All the women *except* Mary came from Denver."

accidentally. Commonly misspelled as *accidently*. In the correct spelling of this adverb, *-ly* is added to the adjective *accidental*.

adjective. One of two basic modifiers, the other being the adverb. Adjectives modify nouns or noun elements:

small person (*Small* modifies the noun *person*.)
the woman (*The* modifies the noun *woman*.)
coach *of the year* (*Of the year* modifies the noun *coach*.)
the milk pitcher *that broke* (The adjective clause, *that broke*, modifies the noun *pitcher*.)
Flying at top speed, the squadron overtook the enemy planes. (The participial phrase, *flying at top speed*, modifies the noun *squadron*.)

adverb. One of the two basic modifiers, the other being the adjective. Adverbs modify verbs, adjectives, or other adverbs. Most adverbs end in *-ly*, but a few, like *now*, *very*, and *there*, do not. And not all words ending in *-ly* (the adjectives *slovenly* and *heavenly*, for example) are adverbs. Here are a few typical adverbial constructions:

They spoke *bitterly*. (*Bitterly* modifies the verb *spoke*.)
It was a *bitterly* cold night. (*Bitterly* modifies the adjective *cold*.)
They spoke *very* bitterly. (*Very* modifies the adverb *bitterly*.)
They spoke *in the heat of anger*. (The prepositional phrase is acting adverbially.)
When he beat the rug, the dust made him sneeze. (The subordinate clause is acting adverbially.)

Also see *flat adverb*.

affect, effect. As a verb, *affect* means "to bring about a change" or "to influence." As a verb, *effect* means "to do or to accomplish something." Example: "He was *affected* by her attempt to *effect* a change in policy."

As a noun, *affect* is a psychological term referring to emotion or feeling. *Effect* as a noun means "result."

agenda. A Latin word; the singular in Latin is *agendum*. In modern standard English, you can use *agenda* for the singular and *agendas* for the plural. An *agenda* is a list of things that are to be accomplished or covered at a meeting.

aggravate. For many years, *aggravate* has carried two meanings— "to make worse" and "to irritate or annoy." Both meanings are acceptable in standard English, although many good writers consider the second too casual in careful writing. Certainly, *irritate* or *annoy* will express the second meaning well enough.

agreement. The "matching up" of elements in gender, number, case, or person.

1. Subjects and verbs must agree:

She is a trumpet player.
They are the boys from Syracuse.

2. Certain adjectives (those that can change form) agree with their nouns:

Those mice are cowards.
This mouse is a hero.

3. A pronoun agrees with its antecedent:

The *quarterback* broke *his* arm.
Everyone did *his* job. (Some writers prefer *his or her job*, a construction which is not standard now, although it may be in the future.)
Mrs. Tompkins had *her* way.
Women should vote for *their* candidates.

all ready, already. The first expression, used adjectivally, means "prepared": "We are *all ready* to go." *Already* is an adverb, as in "She has *already* gone ahead."

allusion. This word is best discussed with a closely related word, *reference.* A reference is a direct remark about something: "She *referred* to his failure to pay for lunch as a sign that he was cheap." An *allusion* is indirect or oblique: "She said that he was a regular *Shylock.*" Allusions are understood only if their original is known; in this instance, if you know that Shylock is a Shakespearean character who is close with his money.

alot. An incorrect form for *a lot.*

alright. A nonstandard spelling; use *all right.*

alumnus, alumna. These words refer to graduates of educational institutions. The first is a male graduate, the second a female. The plural of *alumnus* is *alumni;* of *alumna, alumnae.* You will probably be better off simply using the term *graduate* in most instances.

among, between. Generally, *between* is used when two things are involved ("They were caught *between* the two thieves."); and *among* with three or more things ("They fell *among* thieves."). Informal usage, however, allows expressions like "The difference *between* the three baseballs is not great," and "He stood midway *between* the three policemen."

Note that since *between* is a preposition, its object always takes the object form: "between you and *me*" (not "you and *I*").

and/or. An expression that almost nobody will say a kind word for, but that some writers will use from time to time. It has an odor of legalese or of business jargon, and the careful writer tends to avoid it:

> *Not this:* You may be fined *and/or* jailed.
> *But this:* You may be fined or jailed, or both.

anymore. Should be *any more*: "Alice doesn't live here any more."

appositive. A noun that identifies and explains the noun it is set beside:

> Mr. Smith, our *instructor*, was quite old.
> Our son *John* is a rascal.
> I talked to Sheila, the *director*.

apt, likely, liable. Good writers often use *apt* or *likely* when a meaning of probability is intended: "If you run in front of a car, you are *apt (likely)* to get hit." Used as an adjective, *apt* means "able" or "capable": "She was an *apt* student of burglary."

Liable ordinarily is restricted to matters of responsibility or legal obligation: "*liable* to imprisonment"; "*liable* for military service." Note that *liable* implies a consequence that is not usually considered pleasant.

article. *A, an,* and *the* are frequently called *articles*. In this book, however, we treat them as adjectives because they modify nouns: *a* tree, *an* omen, *the* part.

as. Properly used, *as* is a sign of subordination that implies a *time* relation: "I saw you *as* you were coming down the street." Used to indicate a causal relation, *as* is weak and ambiguous: "*As* you are going to stay in the dorm over vacation, would you keep my stereo in your room?" *Since* or *because* is better in statements that imply or show cause.

author (verb). The careful writer does not use *author* as a verb: "Smith *authored* the new rules for the parking garage." Just say that he *wrote* them.

auxiliary verb. A "helping word" — like *have, had, do, might* — used with the main verb in a verb phrase. The auxiliary allows you to express tense, person, number, mood, and voice:

had written	*will be* writing	*might have been* written
do write	*was* written	*has* written

Modal auxiliaries are important because they supply you with a stock of options to express shades of meaning:

must do	*should* do	*would* do	*might* do	*could* do

Notice the difference between *had* and *must*, for example. *Had* may indicate tense (time) only, while *must* indicates not only time (the future) but also obligation.

    Shall and *will* should probably be considered as "dead" modals. A clear distinction between the two no longer exists (if it ever did), and most writers appear to use them merely as signs of tense.

backlash. A vivid and rather useful metaphorical word, *backlash* ("a violent or sudden reaction") has been worked rather hard in recent years. Try substituting *reaction*, or consider rewriting to avoid the word: "The people are growing hostile to the governor's plans for an increase in taxes."

bad, badly. With a linking verb, use *bad* (an adjective) in these situations:

> It smells *bad.*
> I feel *bad.*
> It is *bad.*
> It seems *bad.*

Use *badly* (an adverb) in situations where the verb is a nonlinking one:

> They do it *badly.*
> Standish needs the money *badly.*
> She sang the aria *badly.*
> I feel *badly*—my fingers don't work as they should. (Better, perhaps, would be: My fingers are numb.)

bi-, semi-. As in *biannual, semimonthly,* etc. Authorities agree that the uses of these prefixes have become confused. *Bimonthly,* for instance, can mean "every two months," "twice a month," or "every two weeks." *Semi-* poses less of a problem—it roughly means "half" ("half-monthly" or "twice a month"). To avoid the confusion surrounding both prefixes, just say, for example, "every two months" or "twice a year."

bug. As a verb meaning "annoy" or "bother," *bug* is an effervescent little word, but too slangy for most situations.

bummer. Slang for *letdown, disappointment,* or *unpleasant occurrence.* Do not use it.

c., ca. Abbreviations for the Latin *circa,* these mean "about." Used with approximate dates or figures: "c. 1670."

can, may. *Can* refers to ability; *may* to permission or possibility. "I *can* do it" means "I am *able* to do it." "I *may* do it" can mean "I have *permission* to do it," or "It is *possible* that I will do it." *Can* and *may* are modal auxiliaries. See *auxiliary verb.*

cannot barely, cannot hardly, cannot help but. These are double negatives, and are considered nonstandard. Here are suggested substitutions:

> *Not this:* I *cannot hardly* believe that.
> *But this:* I can hardly believe that.
> *Or:* I cannot believe that.

> *Not this:* I *cannot help but* wonder about the issue.
> *But this:* I cannot help wondering about the issue.

caret. A proofreader's symbol (∧), it is used to indicate an insertion in the written copy:

> *that*
> I wish ∧ you were here.

case. The customary objection to the word *case* is that it is redundant in many expressions.

> *Not this:* In some *cases,* the streets were iced over.
> *But this:* Some streets were iced over.

> *Not this:* Except in the *case* of Dr. Denny, the surgeons were exonerated.
> *But this:* All the surgeons but Dr. Denny were exonerated.

Note that no satisfactory alternative has ever been found for "In case of fire, break glass."

casualism. We borrow the term from Theodore M. Bernstein, who remarks in his book *The Careful Writer* that some modern acceptable writing is relaxed and familiar—in a word, *casual.* To call an expression a *casualism* is not necessarily to condemn it because there are gradations of the casual. To use Bernstein's examples, contractions such as *don't* and *can't* and colloquial terms like *face the music* and *skulduggery* may be acceptable casualisms, while *falsies* may not be. Whether a casualism is acceptable depends upon your subject and writer's stance.

center around. Both a logical and geometrical impossibility. The *center* and the *around* of something are in different places. Write *center on*, which suggests a tight grouping; or *cluster about*, which suggests a looser grouping.

clause. See pp. 334–337.

cliché. A cliché is an expression that has grown hackneyed or trite from excessive use. A surprising number of clichés are metaphorical: *slick as ice, knee high to a grasshopper.* Generally, avoid them—unless you can twist them to your advantage:

> Slick as the ice in her martini-on-the-rocks.
> Knee-high to a rabbit and twice as bouncy.

collective noun. A word whose form is singular but whose meaning can be singular or plural: *team, group, crowd, family, couple.* (See p. 350 for advice on using singular or plural verbs with this form.)

colloquial, colloquialism. Technically *colloquial* refers merely to "the language of speech," and a *colloquialism* is an expression typical of speech. Since speech is often more informal than writing, teachers and editors have developed the habit of referring to excessively informal usages in writing as being colloquial (that is, inappropriate). This unfortunate development implies that the language of speech is necessarily inferior to the written language. In many instances, such judgment is obviously untrue: "I didn't do it" (colloquial) is obviously better than a stiffly written version like "This event was not performed by me." From Shakespeare to Hemingway and E. B. White, one finds that the colloquial is, when rightly used, lively and precise. It is objectionable only when it is inappropriate or excessively casual. See *casualism.*

comma splice. See p. 367.

compare to, compare with. *Compare to* is most often used when you want to show how two things are similar (particularly in a figurative sense), as in Shakespeare's "Shall I *compare* thee *to* a summer's day?"

Compare with is the best way to introduce a literal comparison involving both similarities and differences: "I intend to *compare* the freshman course in speech *with* the composition course in English."

comparison of adjectives and adverbs. Adjectives and adverbs change form to indicate three "degrees":

Positive	Comparative	Superlative
low	lower	lowest
good	better	best
honest	more honest	most honest
easily	more easily	most easily

complement. A grammatical term meaning "something that completes." Complements are used to complete ideas (or parts of ideas presented earlier in a sentence).

1. Direct objects as complements:

You did see *her*.
You did give her a *present*.

2. Subject complements:

She is *happy*.
She is a happy *woman*.

3. Object complements:

They made him *king*.
They appointed her *director*.
I dyed the shirt *green*.

compliment, complement. As a verb, *complement* means "to complete or finish something." As a noun, it means "something that completes or rounds out another thing."

They are a perfect pair; their personalities *complement* each other.
The *complement* of 60 degrees is 30 degrees.

Compliment, as a verb, means "to say something good," usually about a person. As a noun, it refers to the act of congratulating.

I *compliment* you on your good performance.
I gave her a *compliment*.

compound words. Words made up of two or more words that work together as a unit: *sister-in-law, crapshooter* (or *crap shooter*), *overdrive*. There are no firm rules for determining whether such words should be written separately, together, or with hyphens. When you are unsure of a particular word, check your dictionary.

comprise. Historically, *comprise* comes from an old French word that meant "comprehend" or "include." The word, in careful usage, still maintains this meaning. The whole *comprises* ("includes") its parts. You may write: "The College of Liberal Arts *comprises* four departments," not "The College of Liberal Arts *is comprised of* four departments." An alternative is to use *com-*

pose: "Four departments *compose* (or *make up*) the College of Liberal Arts"; or "The College of Liberal Arts *is composed of* four departments."

conjugation. A listing of the forms of a verb, showing tense, person, number, voice, and mood:

Verb: To see
Principal Parts: see, saw, seen

Active Voice   Passive Voice

INDICATIVE MOOD

Present Tense

I, you, we, or they *see*   I *am seen,* he, she, or it *is seen*
he, she, or it *sees*   You, we, or they *are seen*

Note: In the rest of the table, pronouns are limited to one for each verb form.

Past Tense

I *saw*   I *was seen*
                                 you *were seen*

Future Tense

I *will* (or *shall*) see   I *will* (or *shall*) *be seen*

Present Perfect Tense

I *have seen*   I *have been seen*
he *has seen*   he *has been seen*

Past Perfect Tense

I *had seen*   I *had been seen*

Future Perfect Tense

I *will* (or *shall*) *have seen*   I *will* (or *shall*) *have been seen*

SUBJUNCTIVE MOOD

Present Tense

that I *see*   that I *be seen*

that I *saw*   that I were *seen*

Present Perfect Tense

that I *have seen*   that I *have been seen*

Past Perfect Tense
(Same as Indicative Mood)

IMPERATIVE MOOD

Present Tense

see   be *seen*

conjunction. The *conjunction* is a "joiner," a word that is used to connect words, phrases, clauses, or complete sentences. *Coordinating conjunctions* join words and word elements of equal grammatical rank: *and, but, or, nor, so.*

Subordinating *conjunctions* act as "signs" of subordination. They typically appear just before the subject of the subordinate clause:

When you are near, ...
Even though the spider plant needs water, ...

Subordinating conjunctions sometimes are formed by two words: *as if, even though,* etc. To see how the subordinating conjunction works in the sentence, see pp. 333–334.

conjunctive adverb. A rather clumsy term that grammarians have seized upon to describe what is essentially a sentence modifier:

Accordingly, Mrs. McMinn will not come to work today.
However, work on the project will continue as usual.
The mud is a foot deep across the canal; *therefore,* we will leave all the heavy equipment in the shed today. (Note the punctuation of the conjunctive adverb when it occurs between two main clauses.)

A partial list of conjunctive adverbs: *also, besides, consequently, furthermore, however, instead, likewise, moreover, still, then, therefore, thus.*

connotation, denotation. *Denotation* refers to the literal, explicit meaning of a word, *connotation* to the associations and suggestions of a word. The former madam of a bawdy house was able to employ both rhetorical devices in her book title: *A House Is Not a*

Home. For more discussion of denotation and connotation, see pp. 146–147.

consensus. A *consensus* is an agreement reached by most (but not necessarily all) of the people involved. "The consensus of the student editors was to run the editorial unchanged." *Consensus of opinion* is redundant, since the notion expressed by *of opinion* is built into the idea of *consensus.*

contact (verb). People have been debating the uses of this word for many years: "*Contact* Mrs. O'Leary when you get to Chicago." For those who dislike such uses, here is the typical reaction: "Really, I don't know the lady well enough to *contact* her—I will *call* her, *write* her, or *go to see* her." Since *contact* carries the idea of touching ("the coming together or touching of two objects or surfaces," runs a typical dictionary definition), the careful writer may well avoid it when touching is not meant. Many educated people consider the use of *contact* instead of *call* or *write* to be improper. (See *shibboleths of usage.*)

contractions. *Contractions* (*isn't, won't, weren't,* etc.) are acceptable in standard English. They tend to be somewhat colloquial and casual, and are perhaps not suitable for very formal occasions. Yet it is impossible either to embrace or denounce contractions in any blanket fashion. Their use depends on your stance and subject—not to mention the tone and rhythm of words in the surrounding passage. It is usually true that too many contractions will make your prose seem excessively casual and familiar, and that avoiding them entirely may make you seem stuffy and Victorian. Hit a happy medium, and listen to the *sounds* of your writing.

correlatives. These are conjunctions that are used in pairs: *either . . . or; neither . . . nor; not only . . . but also; whether . . . or; both . . . and.*

Generally, use the expression *whether . . . or not* only when you wish to give equal stress to both ideas: "We will vote on this issue *whether* you like it *or not.*" Otherwise, omit the *or not,* which is unnecessary here: "*Whether* Smith will be chosen is up to the committee."

could of, should of, would of. Nonstandard verb forms that incorrectly use the preposition *of* rather than the auxiliary verb *have.*

crisis. A badly overworked word. A *crisis* is a crucial point or condition, a major turning point in human affairs. A strong word for strong situations, save it for a time when the wolves are at the door. Otherwise, when you yell "Crisis!" people may merely yawn and turn away.

criterion. An overworked, voguish, and rather pedantic word. Try *standard, rule, test, judgment.* If you must use *criterion,* employ the proper form — singular: *criterion;* plural: *criteria.*

dangling modifier. See pp. 359–360.

data. As used in most situations, *data* is a pompous word for *information, evidence, facts, figures,* or *statistics.* It is, in addition, one of those Latin words that usage has treated unkindly. Originally, *datum* was the singular; *data,* the plural. (Now *datum* is seldom used, except in certain technical specialties.) In modern English *data* can be both singular and plural, but usually does not sound right as either.

decimate. An overworked expression that does not mean "to wipe out" or "annihilate." It originally meant "to take a tenth part" of something; now it means "to kill or destroy a large part." Think twice before using the word.

deprecate, depreciate. *Depreciate* is the opposite of *appreciate,* so when you depreciate a thing you lessen it or belittle it. *Deprecate* (literally, "to pray against") means "to disapprove of or protest a thing." The distinction between the two words is narrowing, but it should still be observed.

desire (verb). Unless you are talking about love or passion, better use *wish, want,* or some other expression. To say "He desired a large plate of ice cream" creates a strange mental picture indeed.

dialect. "Any one of the mutually comprehensible geographic or social varieties of which a natural language consists." The definition is borrowed from the linguist Joseph Friend. A neutral term, *dialect* refers to a special grouping of linguistic features — words, forms, idioms, grammatical structures, pronunciations, etc. It is not bad to speak a dialect; everyone does.

different from, different than. *Different from* is preferred in modern English: "My belief is *different from* hers." But when the expression is followed by a clause or "condensed clause," *different than* works well enough: "Don't do this job *differently than* you used to." This is neater than "Don't do this job *differently from* the way you used to."

disinterested, uninterested. *Disinterested* means "impartial"; *uninterested* means "lacking interest." To be disinterested is to be consciously neutral about an issue; to be uninterested is to be bored or lack interest in it. *Disinterested* sounds stronger and fresher. Perhaps that is why many of us have a sneaking affection for the word, and use it when we shouldn't.

double possessive. A strange construction really, because you make the possessive twice, once with an *of* and again with an *'s*, with or without the apostrophe: "a dog *of* Martha's," "a ship *of theirs*," "a photograph *of* Ms. Smith's." Note that the double possessive can have an effect on meaning: "A photograph of Mrs. *Smith's*" is different from "A photograph of Mrs. *Smith*." With pronouns, however, the double possessive is always natural: "that old gang *of mine*," never "that old gang *of me*."

due to. Authorities have long objected to this expression when used in this fashion: "*Due to* hard work, she succeeded." The reason usually given is that *due* is adjectival; so one should write: "Her success was *due* to hard work." If you do not find this explanation convincing, consider other options, such as, "She succeeded because she worked hard," or "Owing to hard work, she succeeded."

due to the fact that. A cumbersome and redundant expression — replace with *because*.

e.g. Abbreviation for *exempli gratia* (Latin), it means "for example." Use with a comma or colon after. If at all possible, however, use the English phrase.

Do not confuse *e.g.* with *i.e.*, the abbreviation of the Latin phrase meaning "that is."

elliptical construction. Such constructions have missing (but understood) parts: "We are getting tired of them, and they [*are getting tired*] of us." "[*You*] Stop doing that." "His purpose was evil and his mind [*was*] disordered." Elliptical constructions are normal in English usage.

end result. If you have a series of results, and you wish to mention the last of them, *end result* (or *final result, last result*) is not a bad choice. But in most instances, all you need is *result*, and tacking *end* to the word does not help.

enormity. Refers to something that is greatly wicked or outrageous, not to something huge or enormous in size.

enthuse.   This verb is nonstandard and, therefore, not recommended. Instead of "She was enthused about going to college," write

> She was very *happy* about . . . .
> She was *enthusiastic* about . . . .
> She was *pleased* with . . . .

etc.   Abbreviation for *et cetera* (which implies "and other things of the same kind"). *And etc.* is redundant.

exists.   Often a sign of deadwood: "a feeling like that which *exists* in the heart." This probably means: "a feeling in the heart."

expedite.   Jargon. Sometimes used with modifiers, as in "to expedite more quickly." Since the word means "to do something faster," the modifiers are unnecessary, as are most uses of the word.

expertise.   A noun borrowed from the French and much in vogue. As *The Harper Dictionary of Contemporary Usage* remarks: "It says nothing that *expertness* does not."

expletive.   A grammarian's term for the "filler phrases" that begin sentences like these:

> *There is* a new house going up on Bleeker Street.
> *It's* too bad we must live in this neighborhood.

facet.   Literally, a polished "cut" face on a gemstone, such as a diamond. Used figuratively, it is badly overworked for *phase* or *aspect*. Do not use unless desperate.

factor.   Jargon for *cause, event, fact, idea, occurrence*, the word contributes to wordiness and vagueness: "His good looks were a great *factor* in his success."

farther, further.   *Farther* usually is reserved for physical distance ("She threw the ball *farther* than anyone else"), *further* for all other uses ("That explanation couldn't be *further* from the truth").

fewer, less.   Use *fewer* for items that you can count: "If you have *fewer* spoons after a friend leaves your house, he should no longer be your friend." Use *less* for degree or amount: "I have *less* money (*fewer* dollars)."

firstly.   Write *first* (and *second, third, fourth*, etc.). *Firstly* used to be thought adverbially urbane. But *first* is a legitimate flat adverb, and the *-ly* can be awkward: *fourthly, fifthly, eleventhly, twelfthly.*

flat adverb.   An adverb without the *-ly:* "Drive slow." Often used in somewhat poetic contexts: "They played the song *low* and *sweet.*"

flaunt, flout.   *Flaunt* means "to show off something or act ostentatiously" ("Not only was the embezzler unashamed of his crimes, he actually *flaunted* them."). *Flout* means "to show disregard or contempt for" ("If he continues to *flout* the rules, he should go elsewhere."). When using either, make sure you know the difference in meanings.

former, latter.   Avoid, where possible. When you use them, you make your reader hunt back through the sentence or paragraph looking for the first thing, and then the second one; after which he has to find the place where you interrupted him with *former* or *latter.* Using either is seldom worth the trouble.

fulsome.   Can mean "offensive," "insincere," "odious," or "repulsive." It does not mean "abundant." The expression *fulsome praise,* besides being a cliché, is often misused.

fun.   Never use it as an adjective: "*fun* time," "*fun* person," "*fun* course."

fused sentence.   See p. 367.

gender.   In grammar, *gender* refers to the classifying of nouns and pronouns as masculine, feminine, or neuter.

gerund.   A verbal noun that ends in *-ing:* "*Losing* worried him." "He liked *winning.*"

gobbledygook.   Congressman Maury Maverick's term for jargon and nonsense, particularly of the bureaucratic kind. It employs expressions like *function, maximum, inoperative, in terms of, expertise,* and so on.

good, well.   *Good* is ordinarily an adjective: "a *good* child," "She is *good.*" Do not use it in this fashion: "She shoveled coal *good.*" Rather, use the adverb *well:* "She shoveled it *well.*" *Good* and *well* have a complex relationship; check your dictionary if you are unsure of a particular usage.

his/her, his or her.   The use of such pronouns to refer to both males and females in a group ("Each student should get his or her grades next week.") is usually awkward, especially when repeated several times in a short span. As William Watt remarked, these "awkward straddlers . . . suggest legal documents or towels and cocktail glasses for newlyweds." (See p. 352 for more advice on this vexing problem.)

hopefully. Few clichés irritate more people today than this "floating adverb" tied to the front of a sentence: "*Hopefully*, the new rule will help us do a better job." Two suggestions:

a. Tie the word to what it modifies:

She said *hopefully* that the new rule will help . . . . (This means she *said* it hopefully, that is, in a hopeful tone.)

b. Identify the person(s) being hopeful:

She hoped that the new rule . . . .
They hoped that the new rule . . . .
McTavish hoped that the new rule . . . .

identify with. A vague cliché. Say what you mean; be specific.

Not this: She *identified with* the antifeminist movement.
But this: She believed that ERA should not be adopted.

if and when. Redundant. In most statements, use either *if* or *when*.

image. It can mean "a likeness," "a reflection," "a personification" ("she is the *image* of grace"), or "a mental picture." It is also a literary device (see p. 277). Although recently it has come to mean "reputation" or "public impression," the careful writer will avoid these vague usages:

They were worried about the company's *image*.
The child had a poor *self-image*.

impact. Use it sparingly, and only when a great force or collision is implied. To call every result or effect an *impact* is, as Theodore Bernstein remarks, to employ "a flamethrower to light a cigarette."

implement (verb). Jargon.

Not this: The library will *implement* greater use of desks in the reading room.
But this: The library will use more desks in the reading room.

imply, infer. The speaker or writer *implies* ("Wilkens *implied* that he was going to quit."); the hearer or reader *infers* ("I *inferred* from his remark that he was going to quit."). When you put forth an idea, you may also put forth *implications*; when you guess or interpret the ideas of others, you draw *inferences*.

infinitive.   A verbal using this form: "*to* win," "*to* do," "*to* be," "*to* illuminate."

inter-, intra-.   *Inter-* (as in "*inter*-company trade") means "between units or groups." *Intra-* (as in "*intra*-company memos") means "within or inside of."

irony.   See *sarcasm*.

irregardless.   Never use; always write *regardless*.

jargon.   Although for some time it has meant "the special language of a group or trade," *jargon* has long implied something closer to gibberish. Its primary definition in *The American Heritage Dictionary* is "nonsensical, incoherent, or meaningless utterance." Such expressions as *conceptualize, maximization, parameters,* and *implementation* are examples of recent jargon.

kid(s).   Slang for child (children).

like, as.   *Like* used as a preposition: "*Like* the Bears, the Cardinals are slowly improving." Observe that *like* takes the object form of the pronoun: "like me," "like *them*," "like *her*."

When *as* is used as a conjunction, the preposition *like* should not be substituted for it:

Not this: The tree is blooming, *like* it should in the spring.
But this: The tree is blooming, *as* it should in the spring.

This sentence shows a typical distinction made between *like* and *as*:

He speaks *as* his father does, but he looks *like* his mother. (That is, he looks *like her*.)

linking verb.   This type of verb ties, relates, or "links" the subject to a *complement* (a "completer") in the sentence. The test for a linking verb is to answer this question: "Can I substitute a form of *seem* for it?"

We *are* [*seem*] happy.
That *was* [*seemed*] a perfect day.
It *tasted* [*seemed*] good.

literally.   *Literally* means "verbatim, word for word; prosaic." It can also mean "nonfigurative." If you say, "The facts he read in the newspaper *literally* floored him," you mean that he fell down after he read them.

The word is not an intensifier and does not mean "very" or "very much." If you write "Sam's blood *literally* turned to ice water," in the next paragraph you had better mention that Sam died shortly after.

mad.   Don't use for *angry, irritated,* or *annoyed. Mad* means "insane," or apparently so.

massive.   Journalese for *big.* Use (only when necessary) for physical objects. Also consider using these words: *solid, bulky, heavy, huge, large.*

maximum, minimum.   Both words are jargon, and ordinarily unnecessary. Instead of writing "*Maximum* effort will be put forth by the students," write "The students will work as hard as they can."

medium, media.   Vogue words. Note that *media* is the plural of *medium.* Do not use these nouns as adjectives: "*media* study," "*media* analysis." It will clear the mind if you try to substitute the real things for *media: newspapers, magazines, television,* and *radio.* Given the logic of classification, you will seldom refer to all of these at once—to claim that "the media" are responsible for something or other is probably a false generalization.

misplaced modifier.   See p. 358.

modifier.   The only modifiers available in English are adjectives and adverbs. A modifier describes, qualifies, or limits another word or word group.

mood.   Refers to the attitudes one has about the meaning expressed by a verb:

Indicative mood (the verb expresses *fact* or *reality*):
I *see* that you *are* here.

Imperative mood (the verb expresses a *command* or *request*):
Let me in!
Do your work immediately.

Subjunctive mood (the verb expresses a *wish* or *possibility*):
I wish that you *were* here.
If she *were* here, we would do the work.
Let the work *begin.*

Ms., ms.   As a title of courtesy before a woman's name, *Ms.* has created considerable controversy. Some women dislike it intensely.

One well-known American novelist, for instance, remarks that she will not accept mail addressing her as *Ms.*

Ordinarily, however, it seems safe to use *Ms.* when you don't know whether the woman addressed is single or married. We ask our own female students what they want to be called in class, and they vote about four to one in favor of *Mrs.* or *Miss.* It doesn't matter to us, of course—if it matters to the woman involved, we will accept her wishes.

Without the capital *m, ms.* is the standard abbreviation for *manuscript.*

nice. An overworked, vague casualism. Use a more vivid and specific word.

none. Because this pronoun means "no one," it is technically singular and takes a singular verb. But usage allows the plural "none are," if the pronoun stands for more than one thing.

nonstandard English. See *standard English.*

noun. A part of speech that names something: *woman, building, sweetness, Angela, Houston, covey.*

nowhere near. Slang for *not nearly, far from.*

off of. In "He got *off of* the couch," the preposition *of* is unnecessary: "He got *off* the couch." Sometimes the construction should be changed:

Not this: He fell *off of* the top of the car.
But this: He fell *from* the top of the car.

OK. *OK* (or *okay*) has been in the language for about 140 years, but it remains too slangy for all uses except the most casual.

on account of. Use *because:* "He stole the bread *because* he was hungry."

one . . . his. "*One* must do what *he* has to do" is normal and idiomatic. It is a bit stiff and old-fashioned to write "*One* must do what *one* has to do," but such constructions may be acceptable in certain contexts. For the problem of gender implied by *he,* see p. 352.

only. When you can, put *only* next to the word or element that it modifies:

She likes *only* men wearing beards. (She does not like clean-shaven ones.)

Only she likes men wearing beards. (She is the sole member of the group who likes them.)

The rule is not very firm, however; and you don't have to worry much about *only* unless a reader might mistake your meaning:

She likes men wearing *only* beards. (And nothing else?)

opt.   A vogue word for *choose* or *select.* Avoid it.

oral, verbal.   Make a distinction between the two words. *Oral* refers only to speech; *verbal* refers to speech, writing, or both. In legal matters, a *verbal* agreement is unwritten.

out of.   Retain the *of* in certain idioms meaning "away from":

She walked *out of* my life.
They stumbled *out of* the burning building.

Otherwise, avoid using *of*:

He ran *out* the door in a hurry.

overall.   A vogue word for the idea expressed by *main(ly)*, *general(ly)*, or *usual(ly)*.

Not this: Their *overall* attitude was poor.
But this: *Usually*, they had a poor attitude.
Or: Their *general* attitude was poor.

parallelism.   A grammatical balancing of similar elements:

She and I are both here.
To be right and *to be righteous* are not the same thing.
Believe *what we say* and *watch what we do.*

See also pp. 170–174, 360.

participle.   A verbal that serves as an adjective or as a part of a verb phrase; it ends usually in *-ing, -ed, -t, -en*:

Adjective	*Verb Phrase*
The *abandoned* house	They *had abandoned* it.
The *burned* (or *burnt*) toast	It *was burned* (or *burnt*).
The *running* elephant	It *is running.*
The *sunken* living room	The boat *had sunk.*

passive voice.   In the passive voice the subject of the sentence receives the action:

Mrs. Blount was astonished by his appearance.
Something must be done.

The passive construction consists of a form of *be* and a past participle: *were made, will be accomplished, are riveted.* See pp. 188–190 for more discussion of how the passive voice functions.

pejorative.   When referring to words, *pejorative* implies a negative connotation. One might write: "I do not use *communist* in a pejorative sense, but rather as a name for a philosophy of government."

person.   A grammatical term that refers to the form of verb and pronoun indicating whether someone is speaking, spoken to, or spoken about:

> *First person:*   *I see* Fritz.
> *Second person:*   Do *you see* Fritz?
> *Third person:*   *She sees* Fritz.

personnel.   Avoid this jargon, if possible. Say *people*, or when necessary, state specifically who is involved:

> *Not this:*   Why aren't the cleaning *personnel* working on the second floor this week?
> *But this:*   Why aren't the *janitors* working on the second floor this week?

phrase.   See pp. 338–339.

phenomenon.   Can be applied to any fact or occurrence that is observable. But in most instances, you can replace it with more exact or specific wording.

> *Not this:*   It was a strange natural *phenomenon*.
> *But this:*   It was the largest flood in twenty years.

And note that the plural of *phenomenon* is *phenomena*.

predominant, predominate.   *Predominant* is an adjective; *predominate* is a verb.

preposition.   A part of speech that links nouns to other parts of the sentence:

> He was mentioned *in* the terms *of* the will.
> No one would dare go *over* the hill.
> I found some old letters *among* the pages *of* the book.

Although some purists object to ending a sentence with a preposition, the construction can be idiomatic and useful:

What did you hang the picture *on*?
That is the kind of behavior I will not put *up with*.

prior to.   Jargon; do not use. Say *before*.

pronoun.   A part of speech that "replaces" or stands for a noun:

This is the method that *she* employed to do *it*.
Each of *us* helps *himself*.

quotation.   Use *quote* as a verb, *quotation* as a noun. *Quote* as a noun ("Where are your *quotes* in this paper?") is a casualism.

raise, rise (verbs).   *Raise* means "to elevate, lift up, or increase." *Rise* means "to get up." *Raise* used to be condemned in the expression "raising children" or "raising a family," but this is considered acceptable usage nowadays.

real (adverb).   Should not be used as an adverb to mean "very." This is poor usage: "They did a *real* good job raising the ship from the ocean floor."

reason is because.   One of the most condemned expressions in written English, yet (oddly enough) it is at certain times useful. There are two objections to it: (1) It is wordy: "The *reason* they are deserting the Army *is because* they never get leave." This can be shortened simply to: "They are deserting the Army *because* they never get leave." (2) It is ungrammatical. "Because they never get leave" is technically an adverb clause, yet it is being used (in *reason . . . is because*) as a noun clause. The grammatical clause here would be: "that they never get leave."

Both objections carry some weight. But professional writers still occasionally use the expression because — at least, this is our guess — it employs two clear "signals" at the beginning of a statement about causation: *reason* and *because*. In a long or complex sentence, such signals can help a reader: "The *reason* the Meville Land Company did not move its cattle quickly from the area was, first, *because* it had no head rider to take charge and, second, *because* the company was demoralized by the several legal actions recently taken against it."

reference.   See *allusion*.

relative pronoun.   A substitute for a noun that acts as a sign or signal for a subordinate clause:

I have a husband *who* never picks up a hammer.
A house *that* never needs painting would be wonderful to own.

résumé. A résumé is a short account of one's experience and qualifications. It is usually written as a part of a job application. Note the accent marks. Without the accent marks, *resume* is a verb that means "to begin again."

run-on sentence. See p. 368.

sarcasm, irony. *Sarcasm* is a bitter and cutting expression of contempt. If, when your roommate knocks over your study lamp, you say, "*That* was a bright thing to do," your remark is sarcasm. The meaning is clear, and your roommate is perfectly aware that you are attacking him. By contrast, *irony* is more indirect and subtle, and the reader or listener may not get its underlying meaning at the time or later. When Ambrose Bierce defined *bride* as "a woman with a fine prospect of happiness behind her." he was being ironical.

sensual, sensuous. *Sensual* refers to the gratification of the physical appetites, particularly the sexual. Typical synonyms are *carnal*, *voluptuous*, and *licentious*. *Sensuous* means "appealing to the senses." Clearly, something can be sensuous without being sensual.

sentence. A unit of expression that ordinarily presents at least one complete thought. In writing, it starts with a capital letter and ends with a period. For further discussion of the sentence, see Chapters 8 and 9, and the various entries under "Sentence Structure," pp. 353 – 368.

shall, will. There used to be a distinction made between these two verb auxiliaries or helpers, but authorities do not accept it now. To many writers, *shall* appears more dignified (or expresses a greater degree of determination), but such opinions are more a matter of tone and style than of grammar.

shibboleths of usage. In the Bible, we learn that the Gileadites used the word *shibboleth* to distinguish the fleeing Ephraimites, who could not pronounce *sh*. *Shibboleth* has become a word symbolizing the idea of a password, or the "test" of a militant group or party.

Each generation has its own shibboleths of usage. For various reasons, these are used to divide writers of "good" English from writers of "bad." Some shibboleths last a long time. *Ain't* is an old one; *contact* is more recent, and *hopefully* (as in "Hopefully, it won't rain") more recent still. *Hopefully* so irritated novelist

Jean Stafford that she placed this sign on the back door of her house: "The word 'hopefully' must not be misused on these premises. Violators will be humiliated."

situation. Avoid if it creates padding, as in the jargon of sports announcers: "Now we have a passing *situation.*"

slang. The mainly oral vocabulary — often employing quite popular words — found in a culture or subculture. Examples: *uptight, slap-happy, screw up, turkey* (referring to a person), *fatso, What's the diff (difference)?, smooch.* As the last two examples show, slang tends to go out of date quickly. Avoid it in your writing, except when using dialogue.

split infinitive. You "split" the infinitive by putting a word (or words) between the sign of the infinitive *(to)* and the main verb: "to *quickly* run," "to *sharply* define," "to *clearly and without ambiguity* state." The split infinitive is often awkward. Do not use the construction unless your "splitting" improves the meaning and rhythm of the sentence. See p. 357.

standard English. The language that educated people generally accept as proper and suitable. Nonstandard English is often a deviation "downward" from standard — it is perhaps too casual, slangy, vulgar, or otherwise inappropriate. By contrast, some nonstandard English is too formal or pedantic. See our discussion in Chapter 7. Also see *casualism; colloquial, colloquialism; dialect; jargon; shibboleths of usage; slang; vogue words.*

structure. A vogue word, often employed as a loose synonym for *organize* or *organization. The Harper Dictionary of Contemporary Usage* says: "*Structure* is very popular with people who use words like *crunch, thrust,* and *seminal.* Such people are best avoided." Perhaps the word is most usefully employed to describe physical objects like buildings.

> *Not this:* His ideas were *unstructured.*
> *But this:* His ideas were *disorganized.*

that, which, who. Much of the time these words take care of themselves, and no particular notice of them need be taken. Generally, you can rely on the old rule: *Which* refers to things, *who* to persons, and *that* to persons or things.

thru. Should be spelled *through.*

type. As in "that *type* auto," "this *type* of shotgun." With or without the *of, type* is overworked and often unnecessary. "*Soft-drink-*

type refreshment" says no more than "soft drinks." "*Essay-type exam*" is redundant for "essay exam." If you think you need the idea that *type* expresses, try *kind, class,* or *sort* first; and include the *of*: "this *kind of* quarterback."

unique.   Means "one of a kind," and so something cannot be "more unique" or "most unique." *Unique* does not mean *unusual, remarkable,* or *excellent.*

utilize, utilization.   Jargon for *use.* Never use either word.

verb.   A *verb* is a word which *states:*

> They *returned.*
> These *are* the questions.
> I *will be* home when you *arrive.*
> The old stump *had been decaying* for years.

Transitive verbs pass the action over from the subject to an object; *intransitive verbs* do not pass any action to an object.

> *Transitive:*   The farmer *plowed* his field.
> *Intransitive:*   He *plowed* happily.

As the examples imply, most verbs can be either transitive or intransitive, depending on whether the object is present in the sentence. Some verbs are by nature transitive (*ignore*) or intransitive (*snore*). *Ignore* always takes an object—one always ignores *something*—a person, a slight, a distraction. By contrast, one never "snores" anything, at least not in normal idiom. See also *auxiliary verb* and *linking verb.*

verbal.   See *oral.*

verbal.   A *verbal* is a word that is derived from a verb but that cannot act as the main verb in a sentence. A verbal can take complements, objects, modifiers, and in some instances subjects. There are three kinds of verbals: *participles, infinitives,* and *gerunds.*

vogue words.   These are words and phrases that seem to appear everywhere at once in magazines, newspapers, public speeches, and on television and radio. Like new clothing styles, they are a matter of fashion; and so they are picked up (and dropped) by the public with alarming rapidity. Examples: *détente, structure* (verb), *crunch, meaningful, thrust, Back to Basics*—several of these are going out of style even as we write. *Relevant,* perhaps the most popular vogue word of a few years back, is now completely unfashionable.

whether. See *correlatives.*

who, whom. With prepositions, always use *whom*: "to *whom*," "with *whom*," "for *whom*," "after *whom*." Use *who* with everything else.

will. See *shall, will.*

Entry for the word *contact*. © 1969, 1970, 1971, 1973, 1975, 1976, 1978, Houghton Mifflin Company. Reprinted by permission from *The American Heritage Dictionary of the English Language.*

"Death of the Afternoon." Reprinted by permission from *Time,* The Weekly Newsmagazine; Copyright Time Inc. 1965.

Gerald M. Durrell. Excerpt from *The Overloaded Ark;* copyright 1953 by Gerald M. Durrell. Reprinted by permission of The Viking Press, Inc. and Faber and Faber Ltd.

Entry for *Family* from *Encyclopedia Americana.* Reprinted with permission of the Encyclopedia Americana, copyright 1978, The Americana Corporation.

Excerpt from "Examining Sex Discrimination." From the *Wall Street Journal* (April 1974). Reprinted by permission of the *Wall Street Journal,* © Dow Jones & Company, Inc. (1974). All Rights Reserved.

Excerpt from "Family: New Breed v. the Old." Reprinted by permission from *Time,* The Weekly Newsmagazine; Copyright Time Inc. 1977.

Excerpt from "The Fine Print Translated." Reprinted as it appears in *Time* magazine, September 22, 1975, p. 74. Copyright © 1975 by Citibank, N.A. Reprinted by permission.

Charles Foley. Excerpt from "The Leap from Golden Gate Bridge: Who Jumps? And Why?" from the *Washington Post* (June 1, 1975). Copyright © 1975 by The Washington Post. Reprinted by permission of The Washington Post.

"For Every Right There Is an Obligation." Reprinted from *Newsweek* (February 21, 1966) by permission of Warner & Swasey Company.

Robert Frost. "Nothing Gold Can Stay" from *The Poetry of Robert Frost* edited by Edward Connery Lathem. Copyright 1923, © 1969 by Holt, Rinehart and Winston. Copyright 1951 by Robert Frost. Reprinted by permission of Holt, Rinehart and Winston, Publishers.

Bil Gilbert. Excerpt from "Gospel of False Prophets" by Bil Gilbert reprinted from *Sports Illustrated,* April 24, 1972. © 1972 Time Inc. All Rights Reserved.

Bernard Gladstone. Illustration of circuit for a doorbell from *The New York Times Complete Manual of Home Repair* by Bernard Gladstone. © 1968 by The New York Times Company. Reprinted by permission.

Paul Goodman. Excerpt from "The New Aristocrats," from *Like a Conquered Province.* © 1967 Paul Goodman. Reprinted by permission of Sally Goodman.

J. B. Hanson. Excerpt from "The Physiology of Corn Production," in *Proceedings,* 23rd Annual Corn and Sorghum Research Conference, eds. J. Sutherland and R. Falasca, American Seed Trade Association, Washington, D.C., 1969.

Sydney J. Harris. Excerpt from "Gun Lobby Arguments Are Absurd," from *Strictly Personal.* Copyright 1975 Field Enterprises, Inc. Courtesy of Field Newspaper Syndicate.

Richard Holben. Excerpt from "The Wire That Won the West," from *Americana* magazine. © 1974 by American Heritage Publishing Co., Inc. Reprinted by permission from *Americana,* March 1974.

John S. Knight. "Tragedy Spotlights Contrasts of Two Americans" reprinted from the *Chicago Daily News* (January 1973). Copyright © 1973 by Knight Newspaper Syndicate. Reprinted by permission of John S. Knight.

Irving Kristol. Excerpt from "Is the American Worker 'Alienated'?" from the *Wall Street Journal* (January 18, 1973). Reprinted with permission of the author and The Wall Street Journal. © 1973 Dow Jones & Company, Inc. All Rights Reserved.

Alfred Lansing. Excerpt from *Endurance,* copyright © 1959 by Alfred Lansing. Reprinted by permission of Curtis Brown, Ltd.

D. H. Lawrence. Excerpts from *Women in Love.* Copyright 1920, 1922 by David Herbert Lawrence; copyright renewed 1948, 1950 by Frieda Lawrence. Reprinted by permission of The Viking Press, Inc.

Richard J. Marince. "On Meddling with Idioms" from *English Journal,* February 1968. Copyright © 1968 by the National Council of Teachers of English. Reprinted by permission of the publisher and the author.

Karl Menninger. Excerpt from "Verdict Guilty — Now What?" from *The Crime of Punishment.* © 1966, 1968 by Karl Menninger M.D. Reprinted by permission of The Viking Press, Inc.

Graph of "moisture-density relationships." From *Foundation Engineering* by Ralph Peck, Walter Hanson, and Thomas Thornburn. Copyright 1953 by John Wiley and Sons; reprinted by permission.

Jay Molishever. Excerpt from "Changing Expectations of Marriage," from *Glamour* magazine (October 1974). Copyright © 1974 by The Conde Nast Publications Inc. Reprinted by permission of the author.

Morris Neiburger. Excerpt from "Where Is Science Taking Us?" Copyright © 1965 by Saturday Review Co. First appeared in *Saturday Review* (July 3, 1965); used with permission.

Excerpt from the entry for *pleasure*. From *The Random House Dictionary of the English Language*, College Edition, copyright © 1968 by Random House, Inc.

George Plimpton. Excerpt from speech reprinted in the *New York Times* (June 30, 1977). © 1977 by The New York Times Company. Reprinted by permission.

J. H. Plumb. Excerpt from "The Private Grief of Public Persons." Copyright © 1967 by Saturday Review Co. First appeared in *Saturday Review* (January 21, 1967); used with permission.

Fletcher Pratt. Excerpt from *A Short History of the Civil War*. Copyright 1952 by Pocket Books, Inc. Cardinal Edition.

Bruce Price. Excerpt from "An Inquiry into Modifier Noun Proliferation," from *Book World* (April 1970). Copyright © 1970 by Postrib Corporation. Reprinted by permission of The Washington Post.

Excerpt from *Readers' Guide to Periodical Literature*. Copyright © 1976, 1977 by The H. W. Wilson Company. Material reproduced by permission of the publisher.

Edwin Arlington Robinson. "How Annandale Went Out," from *The Town Down the River*, is reprinted with the permission of Charles Scribner's Sons. Copyright 1910 Charles Scribner's Sons.

Robert Rosefsky. Excerpt from article in the *Chicago Daily News* (February 17, 1975). Copyright 1975 Field Enterprises, Inc. Courtesy of Field Newspaper Syndicate.

Robert Sherrill. Excerpt from "It Isn't True That Nobody Starves in America," from *New York Times Magazine*, June 4, 1967. © 1967 by The New York Times Company. Reprinted by permission.

Excerpt from "Skyscrapers: Builders and Their Tools." Reprinted from the October 1930 issue of *Fortune* magazine by special permission. Copyright 1930 Time Inc.

J. Clayton Stewart. Excerpt from "Growing Cold by Degrees," from *Sports Illustrated*, March 10, 1973. © 1973 Time Inc.

Mary Lou Thibeault. Excerpt from "The Hazards of Equality," from *Vital Speeches of the Day* (July 1974). Copyright © 1974 by The City News Publishing Company. Reprinted by permission of The City News Publishing Company.

James Thurber. Excerpt from "The Gathering of the Klan." Copyright 1952 by James Thurber. From *The Thurber Album*, published by Simon and Schuster. Reprinted by permission of Mrs. James Thurber.

A. M. Tibbetts. Excerpt from "Stephen Crane's 'The Bride Comes to Yellow Sky,'" from *English Journal*, April 1965. Copyright © 1965 by the National Council of Teachers of English. Reprinted by permission.

John Tobias. "Reflections on a Gift of Watermelon Pickle Received from a Friend Called Felicity," from *New Mexico Quarterly* (Spring 1961). Copyright © 1961 by University of New Mexico Press. Reprinted by permission of John Tobias.

Bill Veeck and Ed Linn. Excerpt from "Racing Has Its Dirty Side," from *Sports Illustrated* (June 1972). Copyright © 1972 by Scott Meredith Literary Agency. Reprinted by permission of the author and the author's agents, Scott Meredith Literary Agency, Inc., 845 Third Avenue, New York, New York 10022.

Judith Viorst. Excerpt from "A Dieter's Lament," from *Redbook* magazine (March 1971). Copyright © 1971 by Judith Viorst. Reprinted by permission of Robert Lescher Literary Agency.

Roger Warner. Excerpt from "Riding Freights." Copyright 1975 Smithsonian Institution, from *Smithsonian* magazine, December 1975.

Excerpt from "Why Mexican Jumping Beans Jump," from *The Watchtower* (September 1973). Copyright © 1973. Reprinted by permission of Bible and Tract Society.

William H. Whyte. Excerpts from "The Language of Business" reprinted from the November 1950 issue of *Fortune* magazine by special permission. © 1950 Time Inc.

Index

A

a, an, 391
abbreviations
  proper form of, 381
  use of periods with, 369
above, below, 391
absolute construction, 391
accept, except, 391
accidentally, 392
action arguments, organization of, 218, 219, 221–223
active voice, 188–191, 399–400
ad hominem fallacy, 212, 216
adjective clauses, 337
  placement of, 357
adjectives, 331, 333, 392
  confused with adverbs, 346–347
  degrees of comparison for, 347–348
  nouns misused as, 348
  proper, 381
adverb clauses, 337
adverbs, 331, 333, 392
  confused with adjectives, 346–347
  conjunctive, 400
  degrees of comparison for, 347–348
  flat, 405
affect, effect, 392
agenda, 392
aggravate, 392
agreement
  pronoun-antecedent, 351
  subject-verb, 349–350
all ready, already, 393
allusion, 278, 393
almanacs, list of, 268
alot, a lot, 393
alright, all right, 393
alumnus, alumni, 393
among, between, 393–394
analogy, 105
  false, 215
  figurative, 68, 69
  literal, 67–68, 68–70
  as a rhetorical strategy, 38, 67–70
and/or, 394
anymore, any more, 394
apostrophe, uses of, 374
appositive, 175, 394
apt, likely, liable, 394
argument, formal

fallacies in, 211–216
human approach in, 198–201
literary paper as, 289
logical organization of, 206–210
types of, 218–225
use of evidence in, 202–205
article, 394
as, 394, 407
association, sign of, in cause and effect, 54
atlases, list of, 268
author (verb), 394
author entries, in card catalog, 232
authoritative evidence in argument, 203–206
auxiliary verbs, 394–395, 396

B

backlash, 395
bad, badly, 395
begging the question, 212
bi-, semi-, 395
bibliographies, list of, 269
bibliography
  format for, 248–250
  sample, 264
bibliography cards, 236–237
biographical dictionaries, list of, 268
"block" method of comparison-contrast, 82, 83
books, documentation of
  in bibliographies, 248–249
  in footnotes, 244–246
bug, 395
bummer, 396
business letters, 310–321
  negative messages in, 325–326
business writing
  five emphases of, 301–304
  illustrations in, 304–307
  letters, 310–321, 325–326
  memos, 321–323
  reports, 328

C

c., ca., 396
can, may, 396

cannot, improper uses of, 396
capitalization, 381–382
card catalog, 230, 232–233, 235
caret, 396
case, 396
casualism, 396
  see also contractions; jargon; slang
causal fallacy, 214–215
causation
  signs of, 54–55
  see also cause and effect
cause and effect, as a rhetorical
    strategy, 38, 53–61
center around, 397
characterization, 278
character, literary, 278, 284, 286
classification
  in logical definitions, 47–48
  papers, suggestions for, 77–78
  as a rhetorical strategy, 38, 73–78
  ruling principle in, 74–76
clauses, 334–337
  adjective, 337
  adverb, 412
  main, 334–335
  punctuation of, 367, 370, 371–372
  subordinate, 333–334, 335–337,
    361–363
clichés, 158, 397
climax, in narrative plots, 278, 284
closers, sentence, 164, 165, 166–167,
    168
collective nouns, 397
colloquial, colloquialism, 397
colon, uses of, 372–373
comma splices, 367
comma, uses of, 370–371
compare, proper use of, 397
comparison
  of adjectives and adverbs, 347–348,
    397–398
  faulty, 355–356
comparison-contrast
  "block" method of, 82, 83
  planning to write, 80
  "point-by-point" method of, 82,
    85–86
  as a rhetorical strategy, 39, 80–86
  "similarities-differences" method of,
    82, 83–85
complements, 364–365, 398
compliment, complement, 398
compound words, 398
  use of hyphen with, 374–375
comprise, compose, 398, 399
conclusions, 107–110
  in action arguments, 222
  in fact arguments, 219
  in refutation arguments, 225
conflict, as a literary element,
    278–279, 284

conjugation of verbs, 399–400
conjunctions, 331, 333–334, 400
  correlative, 401
  punctuation with, 370, 371, 372
conjunctive adverb, 400
connotation, 146–148, 400–401
consensus, 401
contact (verb), 401
contractions
  punctuation of, 374
  in standard English, 401
  see also casualism
coordinating conjunctions, 333–334
coordination, 363–364
correlatives, 401
could of, would of, should of, 401
"creative repetition," 111–112
crisis, 401–402
criterion, 402

D

dangling modifiers, 359–360
data, 402
data sheet, 316–318
dates, punctuation of, 371
decimate, 402
deductive logic, 207–209
definition
  by analogy, 105
  by classification, 47–48
  common errors in, 49–50
  by example, 48
  faulty, 224
  by negation, 47
  by operation, 49
  as a rhetorical strategy, 38, 45–51
  suggestions for writing, 50–51
  by synonym, 48
denotation, 146–148, 400–401
deprecate, depreciate, 402
description, as a rhetorical technique,
    131–135
desire (verb), 402
details, use of, 126–129, 131–139
dialect, 402
dialogue
  punctuation of, 371
  use of in narrative, 136–138
  use of slang in, 414
diction, see words
dictionaries, use of, 385–387
different from, different than, 402
direct address, punctuation of, 371
disinterested, uninterested, 403
"distance," rhetorical, 10–12
documentation
  in bibliographies, 248–250
  in footnotes, 244–248
double possessive, 403

dramatic monologue, 281–282
due to, 403
due to the fact that, 403

E

e.g., 403
either-or fallacy, 213
ellipses, 240–241
elliptical constructions, 403
Encyclopedia Americana, 231
encyclopedias
   list of, 268
   use of in research, 230–231
end result, 403
English, standard, 153, 414
enormity, 403
enthuse, 404
enthymeme, 208
etc., 404
ethical proof
   in arguments, 198–201
   in business letters, 310–311, 312,
      313
evidence
   in fact arguments, 219–221
   faulty use of, 224
   to support argument, 202–206
exaggeration, unnecessary, 158
exclamation mark, use of, 370
exists, 404
expedite, 404
experience, personal, as a rhetorical
      strategy, 38, 40–41
expertise, 404
expletives, 190, 404
exposition, in plot structure, 278

F

facet, 404
fact arguments, organization of, 218,
      219–221
factor, 404
facts
   in creating good content, 117–121
   general, 119–120
   in logical argument, 207
   particular, 119–120
factual evidence in argument,
      202–203
factual writing, 117–121
fallacies
   basic causes of, 211
   types of, 211–216
false dilemma, 213
familiar idea, use of in themes,
      104–105

farther, further, 404
fewer, less, 404
figurative analogy, 68, 69
figures of speech, 68, 149–151
firstly, 404
first person, use of to create
      "distance," 10, 11
flat adverb, 405
flaunt, flout, 405
formal writing, 155
   in business communication, 315
former, latter, 405
footnotes
   proper forms for, 244–248
   sequence of, 247–248
   use of in the first draft, 243
fragments, sentence, 366
fulsome, 405
fun, 405
fused sentences, 367

G

gender, 405
generalizations, 119–120, 129
   in induction and deduction, 207–211
   loose, 123–124, 214
   qualified, 124–125
genre, literary, 287
gerund phrases, 339
gerunds, 405
   use of possessive with, 341
gobbledygook, 405
good, well, 405
government sources, documentation
      of, 247
graded order of ideas, 105–107
   use of in fact arguments, 219, 220
graphs, use of in business writing,
      306–307

H

his/her, 405
"hook," use of in introductions,
      107–108
hopefully, 406
hyphens, uses of, 374–375, 383

I

ideas, organization of, 103–106
identify with, 406
idioms, 155
if and when, 406
ignoring the question, 215–216
illustrations, in business writing,
      304–307

image, 406
imagery, 279, 287
impact, 406
imperative mood, 400, 408
implement (verb), 406
imply, infer, 406
indicative mood, 399, 408
inductive logic, 207–209
inductive paragraphs, 101–102, 103
inferences, as bases for factual
    statements, 120–121
infinitive phrases, 338
infinitives, 407
  placement of, 357
  split, 357, 414
insertions, in quotations, 240
inter-, intra-, 407
interrupters, sentence, 164, 165, 166,
    168
interviews, documentation of
  in bibliographies, 250
  in footnotes, 247
intransitive verbs, 415
introductions, 107–110
  in action arguments, 221
  in fact arguments, 219
  in refutation arguments, 225
inversion, use of in sentences,
    178–179
irony, 278, 285, 413
italics, uses of, 376

J

jargon, 159–160, 407
  in business writing, 302, 315

K

kid(s), 407

L

letters
  business, 310–321
  job application, 316–319
  negative message in, 325–327
liable, 394
Library of Congress Subject Headings,
    232
library research, 229–238
like, as, 407
likely, 394
linking verbs, 364, 407
literal analogy, 67–68, 68–70
literally, 407–408
literary devices, 278–279

literary papers
  analyzing assignments for, 286–288
  definition of, 275
  what to avoid in writing, 289–290
  writer's stance in, 288–289
literary works
  analyzing, 278–283, 288
  questions to ask about, 284–286
logic
  deductive, 207–209
  inductive, 207–209
logical definition, 47–48

M

mad, 408
main clause, *see* clauses, main
major premise, 207, 208, 209
manuscript form, 382–383
  for the research paper, 243–244
massive, 408
maximum, minimum, 408
medium, media, 408
memos, 321–324
metaphor, 68, 149–151
microfilm, in libraries, 235
minor premise, 207, 208, 209
misplaced modifiers, 358
mixed outline, 28, 29–30
Modern Language Association (MLA),
    244
modifiers, 408
  dangling, 359–360
  misplaced, 358
  squinting, 358–359
  see also adjectives; adverbs
mood, of verbs, 399–400, 408
Ms., ms., 408–409

N

narrative
  as a literary form, 279, 280–282
  as a rhetorical technique, 131,
    135–139
negation, definition by, 47
negative messages, in business
    writing, 325–326
newspaper indexes, list of, 269
newspapers, documentation of
  in bibliographies, 250
  in footnotes, 246–247
nice, 409
none, no one, 409
non-narrative literature, 282–284
nonstandard English, 414
note cards, use of in research,
    236–238, 243–244

note-taking, in research, 229, 236–238
noun clauses, 337
noun phrases, 338, 339
nouniness, *see* nouns, improper use of
nouns, 331, 332, 409
  appositive, 175, 394
  collective, 350
  improper use of, 186–187
  misuse of as adjective, 348
  proper, 381
nowhere near, 409
numbers, rules for use of, 383–384

O

off of, 409
OK, 409
on account of, 409
one . . . his, 409
only, 409–410
openers, sentence, 164, 165, 166, 168
opt, 410
oral, verbal, 410
outlines
  consistency in, 30–31, 34–35
  mixed form, 28, 29–30
  paragraph form, 28, 30
  for research papers, 243, 251, 254
  sentence form, 28, 29, 33
  theses and, 32–33, 34
  topic form, 28–29
out of, 410
overall, 410

P

pamphlet indexes, list of, 269
pamphlets, documentation of in
    footnotes, 247
paragraph outline, 28, 30
paragraphs
  concluding, 107, 108–109, 110
  "creative repetition" in, 111–112
  fragmentary, 98–99
  graded order of ideas in, 105–106
  introductory, 107–110
  promise pattern in, 91–93, 96–99
  supporting details in, 99, 104–105
  suspense, 101–102
  time and *space* as organizing
      patterns in, 97–98
  transitional, 102–103
  transitions within, 110–111
parallelism, 170–172, 410
  faulty, 173–174, 360
  use of commas with, 370
paraphrasing, in note-taking, 238–239
parentheses, use of, 373
participial phrases, 338, 339

participles, 410
parts of speech, 331–334
  see also individual parts of speech
passive voice, 188–190, 399–400,
    410–411
pathetic fallacy, 134–135
pejorative, 411
periodical indexes
  list of, 269
  use of in research, 233–235
periodicals, documentation of
  in bibliographies, 250
  in footnotes, 246
periodic sentences, 179
period, uses of, 369
person, 411
personal experience, as a rhetorical
    strategy, 38, 39, 40–41
personification, 149
personnel, 411
persuasion
  in business letters, 310–311
  see also argument
phenomenon, 411
phrases, as grammatical units,
    338–339
plagiarism, 239, 241
plot, in narratives, 279, 280, 284
plurals, use of apostrophe with, 374
poetry
  analyzing, 279–283
  capitalization in, 382
"point-by-point" method of
    comparison-contrast, 82, 85–86
point of view
  in literary works, 279, 285–286, 287
  in writing description, 133–134
possessive
  double, 403
  use of apostrophe with, 374
  use of with gerunds, 341
post hoc fallacy, 54
predominant, predominate, 411
premises
  faulty, 223–224
  in syllogisms, 207, 208, 209
prepositional phrases, 338, 339
"preposition piling," 186–187
prepositions, 186–187, 331, 333,
    411–412
  capitalization of in titles, 382
prior to, 412
process
  artificial, 61, 63
  natural, 61, 64
  as a rhetorical strategy, 40–41,
      61–64
promise pattern, 91–93, 96–99, 108
  in business writing, 302
pronouns, 331, 332, 412
  agreement of, 351

errors in form of, 342–343, 353
  generic, 352
  references, avoiding ambiguous, 342
  relative, 412
proofreading, 390
  of research paper, 252
punctuation, 369–376
  of bibliography entries, 248
  of footnotes, 244
  rhetorical uses of, 378–380
  of sentence units, 165, 168
  of subordinate clauses, 175
  see also individual punctuation
    marks

Q

qualifying devices in sentences,
    179–180
question marks, use of, 369
quotation, 412
quotation marks, uses of, 375
quotations
  form of in research papers, 240–241
  use of colon with, 373
  use of in research, 238

R

raise, rise, 412
reader, analysis of, 4, 5, 6, 8–9, 9–12
*Readers' Guide to Periodical
    Literature,* 233–234
real, 412
reason is because, 412
redundancy, 158
reference, 393
reference works
  documentation of in bibliographies,
    250
  documentation of in footnotes, 246
  general, 268–269
  specific, 269–273
  uses of in research, 230–232, 236
refutation arguments, organization of,
    218, 223–225
relative pronoun, 412
reports, business, 328
research paper
  bibliography format, 248–250
  checklist for first draft, 251–252
  footnote format, 243–248
  note-taking, 236–238
  outline, 243
  reference works, list of, 268–272
  sample paper, 253–265
  selection of topic, 229–235
  thesis of, 242
  use of paraphrase and quotation in,
    240–241

  use of resource material, 230–235
  writer's stance in, 242
résumé, 413
  see also data sheet
rhetoric, 12–13
rhetorical question, 212
rhetorical strategies
  analogy, 67–70
  cause and effect, 53–58
  classification, 73–78
  comparison-contrast, 80–86
  definition, 45–51
  personal experience, 40–41
  process, 61–64
  writer's stance and, 12–13, 39
role, writer's, 4, 5, 6–7, 9, 10, 12
"rule of nearness" in sentences, 356
"ruling principle" in classification,
    74–76
run-on sentences, 368

S

sampling, faulty, 214
sarcasm, 413
satire, 279
Sears List of Subject Headings, 232
sensual, sensuous, 413
sentence(s)
  closers, 164, 165, 166–167, 168
  balancing devices in, 179–180
  bases, 164–167, 168–169
  fragments, 366
  free units in, 166–167, 168
  fused, 367
  interrupters, 164, 165, 166, 168
  inversion, 178–179
  openers, 164, 165, 166, 168
  parallelism in, 170–174, 360
  periodic, 179
  qualifying devices in, 179
  revision of, 184–191
  run-on, 368
  signals, 167, 168
  structure, effect of meaning on,
    180–181
  subordination in, 175–176, 361–363
  unnecessary shifts within, 353
sentence base rule, 168–169, 186
sentence outline, 28, 29, 33
shall, will, 413
shelf list, use of in research, 233
shibboleths of usage, 413–414
"similarities-differences" method of
    comparison-contrast, 82, 83
simile, 149
situation, 414
slang, 414
sonnet, Italian, 281–282
specificity in word choice, 143–144
split infinitive, 357, 414

stance, *see* writer's stance
standard English, 153, 414
statistical fallacy, 213–214
stereotyping as a fallacy, 213
structure, 414
structure, of literary works, 279, 284
subject card, use of in research, 232
subject-verb relationships, 185,
    349–350
  in clauses, 334, 335
subjunctive mood, 345–346, 399–400,
    408
subordinate clauses, *see* clauses
subordinating conjunctions, 333–334
  as signs of subordination, 335–336,
    400
subordination, 175–176, 335–337,
    361–363
suspense paragraph, 101–102
syllabication, 384
syllogisms, 207, 208, 209
symbol, literary, 279, 284
synonyms
  definition by, 48
  use of dictionary to find, 386–387

T

tables, in business writing, 305
tense, verb, *see* verbs, tense of
that, which, who, 414
theme, of a literary work, 279, 281,
    284–285, 287–288
thesis, 18
  of action, 218–219, 310
  development of from assignment,
    20–24
  of fact, 218–219, 310
  outline and, 34
  promise pattern and, 91, 93
  refinement of, 24–26
  in research papers, 242
  writer's stance and, 4, 7–8, 10
thesis statement, *see* thesis
thru, 414
time-sequence, in cause-and-effect,
    54, 57, 58
titles
  capitalization of, 381–382
  punctuation of, 373
topic outline, 28–29
topic, selection of
  for research paper, 229–236
  see also writer's stance
topic sentences, 92
transitional paragraphs, 101–102
transitions, 110–111
transitive verb, 415
type, 414–415

U

unique, 415
utilize, 415

V

value judgments, 120
verbal phrases, 338–339
verbals, 415
verb phrases, 338
verbs, 331, 332, 415
  agreement with subject, 349–350
  auxiliary, 346, 394–395
  conjugation of, 399–400
  intransitive, 415
  linking, 364, 407
  piling up, 346
  principal parts of, 345
  tense of, 343–344, 345
    shifts in, 353
  subjunctive form of, 345–346
  transitive, 415
vogue words, 415

W

whether . . . or, 401
"who does what" formula, in business
    writing, 302–303, 312–313
who, whom, 416
will, 413
wordiness, 157–158
words
  accurate, 140–142
  in business writing, 302
  compound, 374–375, 398
  connotation of, 146–147, 400–401
  denotation of, 146–147, 400–401
  division of, *see* syllabication
  idiomatic, 155
  ineffective, types of, 157–158
  jargon, 159–160
  specific, 143–144
  suitable, 142, 153
writer's stance, 4–10, 18
  for business writing, 302
  for literary papers, 288–289
  for research papers, 242
  rhetorical "distance" and, 10–12
  rhetorical strategies and, 12–13, 39
  suitable wording and, 142, 160

Y

"you attitude"
  in argument, 198
  in business letters, 310–311, 313

Final

1. (ad hominem) fallacy   pg. 212

2. confusing groups of words. pg.391-416

3. allusion

          105   215   68-69   38,67-70   67-70
4. analogy - false, figinative, rhetorical, literal

5. types of argument 218-225

6. cliche's   158; 397

7. cause and effect 38, 53-61

                                       207-209
8. deductive and inductive reasoning

9. Vocabulary - + vocabulary of declaration

   pg. 287   of Independence

10.

Key to the Handbook

GA
Grammatical Analysis
331–340

GA	1	Parts of speech	331
GA	2	Clauses	334
GA	3	Phrases	338

G
Forms of Grammar
341–353

possessive	G	1	Possessive with gerund	341

pronouns	G	2	Pronoun reference	342
	G	3	Pronoun form	342

verbs	G	4	Verb tense	343
	G	5	Principal parts	345
	G	6	Subjunctive mood	345
	G	7	Piling up verbs	346

modifiers	G	8	Adjectives vs. adverbs	346
	G	9	Degrees of comparison	347
	G	10	Noun as adjective	348

agreement	G	11	Verb agreement	349
	G	12	Pronoun agreement	351
	G	13	Generic pronoun	352

S
Sentence Structure
353–368

	S	1	Unnecessary shift	353
	S	2	Omission	354
	S	3	Faulty comparison	355
	S	4	Split construction	356
	S	5	Misplaced modifier	358
	S	6	Squinting modifier	358
	S	7	Dangling modifier	359
	S	8	Faulty parallelism	360
	S	9	Proper subordination	361
	S	10	Faulty subordination	362